W9-BFH-349

Standard Book
of
Letter Writing

Books by Lillian Eichler Watson

The Book of Etiquette
Standard Book of Etiquette
Customs of Mankind
Art of Conversation
Stillborn
Well-bred English
Manners for Wee Moderns
Light from Many Lamps

And in collaboration with Walter A. Lowen

How to Get a Job and Win Success in Advertising

Lillian Eichler Watson's

Standard Book

of

Letter Writing

and Correct Social Forms

REVISED AND ENLARGED
EDITION

PRENTICE-HALL, INC.
Englewood Cliffs, N. J.

Acknowledgment

The author wishes to thank the following for permission to use material in this book:

John B. Opdycke: *Take a Letter, Please!*

Thomas Y. Crowell Company: Curtis Gentry, *Fifty Famous Letters of History.*

Doubleday and Company, Inc.: Captain Robert E. Lee, *Recollections and Letters of General Robert E. Lee.*

Simon and Schuster, Inc.: M. Lincoln Schuster, *A Treasury of the World's Great Letters.*

Latham Ovens: "Letter to a Soldier."

Pantheon Books Inc.: G. Selden-Goth, *Felix Mendelssohn-Bartholdy Letters.*

Charles Scribner's Sons: Elliot Merrick, *Northern Nurse.*

R. H. Morris Associates: "How to Pre-judge the Effectiveness of Your Letter."

Table of Contents

BOOK IV

YOUR BUSINESS AND CLUB CORRESPONDENCE

For good wishes
For message of sympathy, condolence
For hospitality received
For a personal favor or some special help
For favorable mention or review
Thanks to an immediate superior or an em-
    ployer
Letters of congratulation, good wishes
    On a new venture or connection
    On a promotion or advancement
    On an honor or distinction
    On a speech, article, book
    On accomplishment of son or daughter
    On a business anniversary
    On an important personal occasion
    On retirement
Letters of condolence, sympathy
A wife's social letters to her husband's business
    associates

BOOK VIII

SPECIAL, DIFFICULT, AND UNUSUAL LETTERS

1. Special, Difficult, and Unusual Letters   633

    Letter of complaint to a neighbor
    Neighbor's letter of apology
    Letter of request to teacher, school principal
    Letter of complaint to a manufacturer
    Letter of request to a manufacturer
    Requesting a loan; acknowledging the request
    Requesting a contribution
    Refusing request for a contribution
    Refusing use of name for fund raising
    Inviting participation in a project or activity
    Refusing to participate in a project or activity

Preface

This is a new edition of *The Standard Book of Letter Writing,* revised to include much that is timely and useful.

In addition to complete information on all phases of business, social and personal correspondence, *The Standard Book of Letter Writing* now provides a wealth of ideas and suggestions for those special, unusual and often difficult letters we are all called upon to write nowadays. New sections have been added on travel correspondence, club correspondence, and the frequently puzzling social letters of business.

Would you like to appear on a television program? Here are sample letters that may help you get your opportunity.

Have you received an unusual or unexpected promotion, and would you like to express your appreciation to your employer in writing? Here are suggestions to help you produce an impressive letter.

Do you have an idea you would like to submit to an editor or producer, or a new product you would like to suggest to a manufacturer? Here are the kinds of letters that get attention.

Have you a letter of request, complaint, explanation, refusal, or perhaps a letter of apology to write? Here are suggestions you are sure to find helpful and stimulating.

Today the need to write with skill and facility is greater than it has ever been. More than half the business of the world is conducted by means of correspondence. Much of the time-consuming details of social life are taken care of by letters. People travel more today than ever before in history, and letters provide the link with family and friends. Letters are convenient and useful ambassadors of good will that represent us whenever we ourselves cannot be present. The busier and more complex life becomes, the greater grows the need to write good letters, to write them with ease and skill, and to write them with enjoyment.

The Standard Book of Letter Writing has been the national best seller in its field, and a recommendation of the Book-of-the-Month Club, for many years. Now revised and enlarged, it takes its place beside the dictionary and thesaurus as an essential desk book, the standard and dependable guide to good letter writing and correct social forms.

LILLIAN EICHLER WATSON

Book I

The Basic Rules
of
Successful Letter Writing

I

Letter Writing as a Social Asset

There's an old familiar saying that you must have heard many times: "To have a friend, you must be a friend."

It's equally true that to receive interesting letters, you must *write* interesting letters. If you write only when absolutely necessary, when duty or responsibility demand, you are missing out on what can be one of the greatest personal enjoyments of life.

But apart from the pleasure and satisfaction that a wide correspondence with friends can mean to you, letter writing is an important social asset. The ability to write good letters can be as useful to you socially as the ability to talk well or entertain successfully. In some ways letter writing can be even more useful to you, for it helps facilitate all social activities—often saves you much time, trouble and inconvenience.

The letter you write is your personal representative. It takes your place when circumstances make it impossible for you to be there in person. It goes to the hospital to cheer a sick friend. It goes to your hostess to thank her for entertaining you. It conveys your best wishes, congratulations, condolences—when you are not able to do so in person.

WHAT THE ABILITY TO WRITE
GOOD LETTERS CAN MEAN TO YOU

No other form of written language is used more frequently than the letter, for it's the most convenient and effective substitute there is for direct conversation.

Letters can be one of the most powerful and far-reaching influences in your life, if you let them be. They can do amazing

3

things—can help you in more ways than you may realize. In fact, few accomplishments can serve you so well, in so many varied ways, all through life, as the ability to write good letters.

We are not here concerned with the great *practical* value of letter writing, which is discussed in a later chapter. Everybody knows and realizes the tremendous importance of letter writing as a business asset. Everybody knows that good convincing letters win more jobs and influence more people than dull, stereotyped, rubber-stamp letters.

But what is not so well-known and well-realized is the importance of letter writing as a personal asset. Letters can add in every way, and in very great measure, to the enjoyment of life. They can bridge any distance . . . bring friends closer in intimacy and understanding . . . enrich social relationships . . . increase personal popularity . . . win affection . . . inspire love . . . provide a most satisfying means of self-expression!

The value of regular correspondence in fostering and maintaining friendships is especially significant, for it adds much to the fullness and graciousness of life . . . especially in later years. It must be evident, however, that unless you make a deliberate, conscious effort to build up such a correspondence, you will not have it to enjoy when you want it.

A LETTER IS LIKE A
VISIT ON PAPER

If you "hate to write letters," it's simply because you have not yet discovered the fun it can be to write and receive letters that are *good talk* on paper. Do you hate to visit your friends and talk with them face to face? Then why hate to write a letter which is—or should be—a pleasant "visit" on paper?

Many people actually disregard letters from family and friends, deliberately neglecting to answer them. Others put off answering until the person who wrote has every reason to feel slighted and hurt. To leave a letter unanswered is like saying, "I can't be bothered writing! I don't think you're worth the time and effort it takes to write a letter."

Surely you wouldn't dream of saying that directly to anyone!

Then don't imply it by leaving letters unanswered, or by putting off your answer for too long a time. Courtesy demands that every letter you receive be answered . . . and answered promptly.

This is especially true of family letters. It is not only a discourtesy but an unkindness to ignore letters from relatives who are concerned about your welfare, or the welfare of members of your immediate family. Few things can give a greater lift to the spirit, a greater boost to morale, than a cheerful, newsy letter . . . an intimate visit on paper with someone near and dear.

The late General Smedley D. Butler said, "Give our fighting men bullets and biscuits and a letter from home and they'll lick the world!"

He rated letters from home right up at the top with ammunition and food . . . the three most vital elements for a fighting man's well-being and morale.

How eagerly, in all times and all places, have people waited for mail from home! How wistfully have they repeated, over and over again, that old familiar question: "Any mail for me?"

"I wonder what letter was ever received with such thankfulness!" wrote Thomas Carlyle's wife, thanking him for a letter that arrived on her birthday.

"I long for a letter from you!" wrote Princess Alice of England—happily married to Prince Louis of Hesse and living with him in Darmstadt—but lonely for her mother, Queen Victoria, as any child might be lonely for a parent.

"Your letter and mother's have come at last! I was so glad to get them I cried," wrote Anne Sullivan Macy to Helen Keller, her beloved pupil and lifelong friend.

HOW LETTERS CAN ENRICH LIFE— CREATE MORE ENDURING FRIENDSHIPS

There's a lot of truth in the old saying, "Out of sight, out of mind!" But letters keep your influence and personality alive— keep you in the hearts and minds of those far removed from you. Through an appreciation and understanding of the best uses of letter writing, you can not only maintain your friendships uninterrupted over long periods of separation, but you can lay the foundations for much real pleasure and enjoyment in future years. Letter writing brings its own great rewards; and not the least of these are more enduring friendships and far less likelihood of ever being lonely or bored.

History tells us of many beautiful and inspiring friendships built on letters alone. A hundred years ago, Elizabeth Barrett, a lonely invalid, published a volume of poems which brought a friendly letter of praise from Robert Browning. Miss Barrett, in her own words, "pounced upon the opportunity of corresponding with the poet" . . . and the whole world knows the result of that correspondence.

George Bernard Shaw and Ellen Terry carried on a fascinating correspondence for more than twenty-five years—a delightful romance on paper that enriched the lives of both.

Charles Lamb, Horace Walpole, Madame de Sévigné, Madame de Staël, John Keats, Robert L. Stevenson are only a few of the notable letter writers of the past.

Perhaps you have read some of the interesting letters in M. Lincoln Schuster's anthology, *The World's Great Letters.** They make fascinating reading because they reveal so much that is not commonly known about the great personalities and great events of the past. Of course, letters as *literature* do not fit in with our modern fast-moving scheme of life. Few people write long, leisurely, news-filled letters nowadays. Few people have the time for such letters.

But though the tone and pace of letters may have changed, their importance in establishing and maintaining pleasant human relationships has not. All of us, even the busiest of us, must make time to write the letters that help to enrich life and add to its enjoyment.

THE BUSIEST PEOPLE MAKE
THE BEST LETTER WRITERS

So don't ever say, "I haven't the time to write!" Everyone has exactly twenty-four hours a day—no more, no less. The time is

---

* M. Lincoln Schuster, *A Treasury of the World's Great Letters* (New York: Simon & Schuster, Inc., 1940).

there; it's up to you to use some part of it for writing interesting letters *if you want to receive interesting letters in return.*

After all, it's the busiest people who usually make the best letter writers! They have so much more to write about.

Washington, Hamilton, Emerson, Mark Twain—all were conscientious letter writers who took time from their busy careers to correspond regularly with family and friends.

Lincoln was often too busy to eat or sleep, but never too busy to write the letters he wanted to write. Some of the most human and touching letters in existence are from his pen, written when he was most oppressed and most obsessed by the state of the Union.

But by far one of the most brilliant and prodigious correspondents of all time was Benjamin Franklin. Scientist, statesman, philosopher, editor, printer, inventor—Franklin had so many busy careers, you would think he had no time at all for personal correspondence. Yet he wrote regularly to friends on both sides of the Atlantic. He thoroughly *enjoyed* letter writing. He looked upon it as a pleasant relaxation and as an enrichment of life rather than a dull, time-consuming duty.

The busiest woman in Labrador, one bitter cold Christmas not very long ago, was an Australian nurse by the name of Kate Austen. But Nurse Austen was not too busy to acknowledge with a long, friendly letter every gift of food or clothing received for distribution to the natives in that bleak and barren outpost of the north. Among the gifts was a box of knitted things for children, made and sent by a woman in Toronto. Nurse Austen, busy, harassed, and not too well that winter, could have written just an ordinary routine note of thanks, cold and informal. But that was not her way. She sat down and wrote a *real* letter telling all about the village, and the names of the children who were wearing the knitted gloves and caps, and what they said when they got them, and how they looked when they wore them. She wanted the woman who had made and sent all those lovely knitted things "to see how much happiness and warmth she had created."

Here is the answer Nurse Austen received.* It illustrates perfectly what I said at the very beginning of this chapter: that to *receive* interesting letters, you must *write* interesting letters!

Dear Miss Austen,
  Your letter made me happy. I did not expect such a full return. I am eighty years old, and I am blind. There is little I can do except knit, and that is why I make so many caps and sweaters and scarves. Of course I cannot write this, so my daughter-in-law is doing it for me. She also sewed the seams and made the buttonholes for the knitted things.
  I know something of the work you are doing. At the age of nineteen I married a man who was going to China to be a missionary. For forty years, with an occasional year at home in America, we worked in China, and during that time our two sons and a daughter were born to us, of whom only one son survives. After forty years, my husband's health began to fail. We returned to the States where he took charge of a settlement house in Brooklyn, New York. A surprising number of the problems we faced there were similar to problems we had met in China. When my husband died, I came to Toronto to live with my son and daughter-in-law. They are very good to me, and I pride myself that I am little trouble to them, though it is hard for a blind old lady to be sure of anything.
  What I most wanted to say, my dear, is this. For sixty years I have been making up missionary packages of such clothing or food or medicine or books as I could collect. In various parts of the world and to various parts of the world I have sent them. Sometimes I have received a printed slip of acknowledgement from the headquarters depot or mission board, sometimes nothing. Occasionally I have been informed that my contribution was destined for Syria or Armenia or the upper Yangtze. But never before in all that time have I had a personal letter picturing the village and telling me

---

* Elliott Merrick, *Northern Nurse* (New York: Charles Scribner's Sons, 1942), p. 179.

who is wearing the clothing and what they said. I did not suppose that ever in my lifetime I should receive a letter like that. May God bless you.

Sincerely yours,
Laura N. Russell

WRITE THE LETTERS THAT
DON'T NEED TO BE WRITTEN

Comparatively few of us ever discover the joy of writing the letters *we do not need to write.* How long has it been since you sat down to write a letter for no other purpose than to give someone pleasure? Why not form the habit of writing little notes now and then to those you like, and whose friendship you value? Try to make opportunities to write, instead of waiting for some logical reason or excuse to come up.

For example, you might write a friendly little note of encouragement to someone just entering college . . . or someone just starting out in business. You might write a few words of cheer to an invalid . . . a shut-in . . . or someone you know is lonely, worried or unhappy. Or you might try a letter of congratulation to someone who has just had a promotion, wishing him or her success in the new job. Such notes are always received with gratitude, and often remembered a lifetime.

You can endear yourself so easily, to so many people, by writing these letters-that-don't-need-to-be-written! Try it for a few weeks and see what happens. You may be surprised by the fascinating letters you receive in return.

SEND PERSONAL LETTERS INSTEAD
OF GREETING CARDS WHENEVER YOU CAN

A good time to write personal notes to your friends is on birthdays and holidays, instead of sending the customary greeting cards. A personal message is more gracious, and means so much more than a printed sentiment. Even the old traditional "Happy New Year!" has more meaning—sounds more eloquent and sincere—when it's in your own handwriting.

One Christmas—among hundreds of printed and engraved

cards, with their pleasant but impersonal greetings—I received an exciting little handwritten note. It was from a friend who lived thousands of miles away and from whom I had not heard in some time. That unexpected letter was like a warm handclasp across the miles. It meant far more to me than all the expensive and elaborate cards I received that day. In fact, it meant so much to me that I kept it . . . and still have it.

> I am thinking of all the wonderful times we used to have together during the Christmas holidays [my friend wrote], and I am wondering how you and your family are. I can just imagine how your children have grown, and what a joy they must be to you now! I wish I could see them—but I guess it will be quite a long time before we get to New York.
> Tom is doing very nicely; and it would be wonderful living here if we weren't so far from all the friends we like best.
> Both of us wish you and your family the gayest, merriest Christmas ever, and everything in the New Year that your hearts desire. Be sure to write and let us know what interesting things you have been doing, and how you have all been. My thoughts are with you often!
>   Always affectionately yours,

It's not an unusual letter. There isn't anything especially interesting about it—except to me. But compare it with this typical "ready-made" Christmas greeting:

> I have so many things to say,
> I'll say them in the shortest way;
> I'll say them all in this one rhyme:
> I wish you joy at Christmas-time!

Surely any written message, however short, is far more complimentary, and has far more meaning to the person who receives it, than such doggerel!

But perhaps you are thinking, "*I* don't send such silly verse to anyone! I send simple, dignified greetings. And I *must* send greeting cards—they save time! I couldn't possibly write personal notes to all my friends at Christmas."

That's true, of course, if you have a great many friends and acquaintances. It would be too big a job to write letters to all of them; and a needless waste of time and energy when greeting cards are so universally used (and fortunately are not *all* as bad as the one quoted!).

But among those many friends, aren't there a few who would deeply appreciate a personal message? Isn't it worth a little extra effort for the intense satisfaction that an unexpected "visit on paper" can mean to them . . . and to you?

IF YOU "DON'T KNOW WHAT TO SAY" IN A LETTER

If you complain that you never know what to say in a letter, it's only because you still think of writing as somehow different from talking. It isn't! Talking is an expression of thoughts and ideas in spoken words. Writing is, or should be, those same words on paper.

The only person who can truthfully say he has nothing interesting to write about is the person who sits alone in an empty room twenty-four hours a day—seeing no one, doing nothing— just sitting and staring. And even he could write an interesting letter telling his impressions of complete solitude!

So don't ever say that you don't know what to write in a letter! It's an admission that you are leading a dull and empty life. Write about the things you see, and hear and do—and plan to do! Write to share good news or relate an interesting experience. Write to express your thoughts and ideas on whatever subjects are mutually interesting to you and your correspondent.

Has he been ill? *Ask how he's feeling!* Has he been worried about his job? *Ask how he's getting along!* Is he interested in gardening? *Tell him about some recent experience—successful or otherwise—that you have had with flowers!* Does he like to read? *Tell him about the interesting book you've just read, and why you think he may enjoy it!*

In other words, write about the very same things you'd talk about if you were together.

During the war, on the impulse of the moment I wrote to a woman—a stranger to me—who was doing what I thought was a particularly outstanding and unselfish piece of work. I didn't wonder what to say in my letter. I just wrote what I sincerely thought: that she was doing a swell job and deserved a lot of credit for it. Her answer was so stimulating that I wrote again . . . and she wrote again . . . and out of that correspondence has grown a firm and delightful friendship.

I am not suggesting that you make a habit of writing to strangers! That can have definite nuisance value—especially if the purpose is a selfish one and the letter is clearly written for personal gain.

I am suggesting only that you apply the best uses of correspondence to your personal life . . . that you make time for the letters that don't need to be written as well as those that do . . . and above all, that you make whatever *extra effort* is required to produce letters that are something more than just run-of-the-mill: letters that are interesting, individual and provocative.

2

Personality in Letter Writing

You may not have thought of it just this way, but the letter you write is part of *you*, an expression of your personality. Therefore to write letters that are mere patterns of form is to present a *colorless* personality.

Letters, by their very nature, are too individual to be standardized. A letter may be absolutely perfect according to the standards of good taste and good form; but unless it also expresses something of the writer's personality, it is not a good letter.

In other words, don't be satisfied to write letters that are just *correct* and nothing more. Try to write letters that are *correct for you* . . . letters that are warm and alive with reflections of your own personality.

And if this sounds like a platitude, stop for a moment and think back over your recent correspondence. What was the most interesting letter you received? Was it a letter anyone could have written? Or was it a letter that instantly "came alive" as you read it—that brought the personality of the sender right into the room with you, as though you were face to face, *listening* instead of *reading?*

The fault with too many letters, today as in the past—the reason so many letters are dull and lifeless, and often fail to accomplish the purpose for which they are written, is simply this: *They sound exactly like the letters everyone else writes.* They are neither exciting to receive nor stimulating to read.

MAKE YOUR LETTERS SOUND
THE WAY YOU DO

By all the approved standards of today, the most natural letters are the best letters.

Therefore the very first thing you should strive for in letter writing is a natural, spontaneous sincerity. The first and most important rule is *"Be yourself!"*

Just bear in mind that letter writing is a substitute for conversation, and that a good letter is primarily good talk on paper. The exchange of letters should be like the exchange of conversation: lively, stimulating and enjoyable.

The whole secret is to write in an easy, natural way—without self-consciousness—like one friendly human being talking to another. Make your letters sound as much as possible like your conversation. Make your letters sound the way *you* sound . . . and they'll take on your personality.

So few people write naturally and without constraint that letters so written are bound to be outstanding. The trouble is that most of us try to compose letters instead of just writing as we speak. We try to sound literary and impressive instead of just sounding like ourselves.

There is no reason why you should write to your friends any differently than you speak to them—except, of course, in a strictly formal communication. To talk one way and write another is an affectation that betrays itself in the forced and insincere language of your letters.

The ideal is to write *without awareness of writing*—to let the words flow from your pen as they flow from your lips. The person who receives your letter should be almost able to see and hear you while reading it. That's the final test. That's what tells whether or not your letter has *personality.*

VISUALIZE THE PERSON TO
WHOM YOU ARE WRITING

Before you start a letter, always try to visualize the person to whom you are writing. It will help you express yourself in an easier and more natural style.

Here's the way to do it: Look at the fresh, untouched sheet of paper on the desk before you. Try to picture on that blank sheet the face of the person to whom you are writing. Think intently of that person for a few moments, until you see him clearly in your mind's eye. Think of his interests, his likes and dislikes, his activities, his hobbies. Imagine yourself seated in a room with that person, talking of things that are mutually interesting. What information would you volunteer? What questions would you ask? Or what questions would *he* ask, and how would you answer them? Map out in your mind what you would be most likely to say to that person if you were with him . . . and say
· it. Say it out loud, and listen to the sound of it.

Then write your letter! Write it exactly as though you were talking it . . . using the words that come readily and easily to your mind. Let your personality animate your letter as it does your speech . . . so that your very words conjure an image of you on the page . . . and even your voice and gestures are brought to mind.

JUST WRITE AS YOU SPEAK—
THAT'S THE WHOLE SECRET

You'll find that writing letters is easier, and a lot more fun, when you get on to the knack of writing as you speak. There's really no great trick to it. Just keep thinking of what you want to say, not the way to say it. Remember that the important thing is the message, not the words. If you keep thinking of what you want to say, the words will take care of themselves. The *first* way of saying it that comes to your mind is usually the best way for you. It's your way; it gives *your personality* to the letter. The more you keep thinking about *how* to say it, the more stilted and involved its expression is likely to become.

This is not an original idea. William Cobbett, a vigorous and terse writer of the early nineteenth century—and William Hazlitt, a contemporary—are two of many who advised a style of writing "as natural as effortless conversation." The advice applies to letter writing as it does to all other forms of writing; and is as sound and workable today as it was then. Here are Cobbett's words—a source of inspiration to some of our best-known modern writers:

> Sit down to write what you have thought, and not to think what you shall write! Use the first words that occur to you, and never attempt to alter a thought; for that which has come of itself into your mind is likely to pass into that of another more readily and with more effect than anything which you can, by reflection, invent.

Many people become "tongue-tied" when they sit down to write a letter. They find it difficult to express themselves in a simple, natural way—because, for some reason, they think they must write "better" than they speak. Usually, though, they succeed only in writing less interestingly. Their sentences creak with the mechanics of construction; and their letters sound labored and forced . . . and what is worse, insincere.

As you know, people always talk best when they don't stop to think about it. And the same is true of letter writing. The best letters are lively, smooth-flowing "talk," put down on paper without too much thought to the actual mechanics of writing. It's the letter written with *least difficulty*—the letter written without the distressing "labor pains" of construction—that sounds most natural and sincere.

Your aim, therefore, should be to write with ease. And that is best accomplished by writing as you speak: by using the identical words and phrases—even the very slang and the familiar patter —of your ordinary everyday speech.

USE YOUR CUSTOMARY
WORDS AND PATTER

If you were talking directly to someone, you wouldn't be very likely to say, "I *encountered* two friends in the park this morning." Then why write it that way in a letter? *Be natural!* Write it the way you'd say it: "I *met* two friends." And if you are sick, why not say so—plainly and without frills? Why write that you are "indisposed" or "confined to bed"?

The more closely your letter follows your own characteristic patter, the more engagingly it reflects the color and warmth of your personality.

So don't grope for flowery words that just make you sound affected! Don't try to write any differently than you speak!

For example, if you would ordinarily say to a friend: "Guess what? The most wonderful thing has happened! We're going to California to live!" . . . don't get tangled up in pompous rhetoric when you sit down to write! It will sound delightfully vivid and alive if you write it just that way in your letter. It will sound like *you*. But even with the same interesting news to tell, your letter is dull—it's commonplace—if you use such forced and unnatural phraseology as the following:

> It has occurred to me that you might be interested to know that we are considering a change of locale. We are planning to take up our residence in California in the near future.

That's not an exaggeration! Many people who speak with force and vigor become so word-conscious when they sit down to write that their letters sound just like that.

There is nothing actually wrong about the following letter of thanks. It's typical of the usual letter of this kind, written by the average person:

> Thanks for a most delightful evening. The dinner was superb and we enjoyed it very much. We look forward to reciprocating in the near future.

But it is not the purpose of this book to teach you the "average" or "typical" way of writing letters! That destroys the very quality we believe most desirable: an easy, natural sincerity. Surely if you met your hostess in the street, you wouldn't thank her in such careful, studied words! You would be yourself. You would let your personality shine through. You would sound cordial and enthusiastic. You would let her see that you really enjoyed and appreciated her hospitality.

Well, the letter you write can sound every bit as cordial and sincere as your spoken words of thanks. *Just use the same words.* If the following is approximately what you would say to your hostess in person, write it exactly that way in your letters:

> We had real fun at your house last night, Jane! And the dinner was tops, as usual. Jim is still raving about that luscious dessert. (I wish *I* could make it!) Thanks a million for a really swell evening. It will be our turn next—soon, I hope.

That's *you* talking! That's not "fine English"—nor studied form—nor cut-and-dried, run-of-the-mill phraseology! It's just YOU: *your* words, *your* patter, *your* personality. And that's why it has a freshness and charm that are lacking in the first letter.

Naturally, you must consider the person to whom you are writing. You do not speak to a dignified public official, a visiting celebrity, nor the principal of your daughter's school on the same intimate, carefree basis that you speak to an old friend. Nor do you *write* to everyone on the same basis.

Ask yourself, "For whom am I writing?"—then make your letter fit that person.

Ask yourself, "What would I say in conversation with that person?"—then say those same things, in the same way, in your letter.

By all means let yourself go when thanking a favorite uncle for a lovely hand-carved figure he sent from halfway round the world—even to the point of calling him a "silly old extravagant darling," if that's the bantering way you usually talk to him. But don't suddenly go coy in a letter to someone you wouldn't dream of addressing in person with anything but the greatest dignity and reserve.

Keep your correspondent in mind. Read your letter through his eyes. Does it ring true? Does it sound natural and sincere? Is that what you would say in conversation with him?

You wouldn't write a long letter to a boy at prep school, telling him about the difficulties you have had growing peonies in your garden. A sister, an old friend, or a maiden aunt who loves flowers might be interested in the state of your garden to the extent of reading a whole letter about it. But a boy away at school would be plain bored! He'd much rather know what his friends back home are doing . . . how the neighbor's new pup is getting along . . . what exciting things have happened in town since he went away.

If you want your letter to be pounced upon and eagerly read from start to finish—*consider the person to whom you are writing.*

SOME EASY WAYS TO MAKE YOUR
LETTERS SOUND CONVERSATIONAL

Here are some simple little tricks you can use to make your letters sound conversational . . . and to give them more life and sparkle.

You have probably noticed that in conversation with people you rarely say "I am," or "you have" or "they are." Such careful enunciation of each word sounds stilted and formal. You almost always contract the two words into one. "I'm going to the park" is the way you'd say it. Or "You've been away so long!" Or "They're coming for the week end." Try writing it that way; you'll find it adds a more amiable and informal touch to your letters.

Another good idea is to put occasional "asides" in your letters, the way you do in conversation. They provide an interesting change of pace. For example, if you were talking to someone, you might say: "I went to see Mary's new house yesterday. Remember she told us about it last Christmas? It's a beauty!" Merely by changing the pitch of your voice, you can easily change from one subject to another in conversation. And here's how you can do the same thing in a letter:

> I went to see Mary's new house yesterday. (Remember she told us about it last Christmas?) It's a beauty! It's exactly the kind of house Bill and I would like to have some day (if we ever have a house of our own!).

Conversation is always livelier and more colorful when it's sprinkled with such reminders and "asides." And they go a long way toward making your *letters* more interesting and readable, too.

Still another good trick is to address the person by name occasionally, just as you do in conversation. "Bob, it's so beautiful here!" is more intimate and personal than the flat statement, "This is a beautiful place." And "I'd love to see you soon, Eileen," is not only more conversational, but more flattering than "I hope to have the pleasure of seeing you before long." There's nothing a person enjoys more in a letter than the frequent repetition of his own name!

You know that you can always hold a person's interest in conversation by telling a story or relating an incident that has some bearing on the subject under discussion. The same principle applies to letter writing. Any letter is more enjoyable if it contains at least one interesting personal anecdote. For example, you might be writing about a mutual friend who is planning a first air flight, and is excited by the prospect. In telling about it in your letter, you might say:

> That reminds me of the first flight *I* made, years ago! It was on the *Bermuda Clipper;* and although I've made hundreds of flights since, I'll never forget the thrill of that first one. Imagine! About an hour out of Bermuda we passed a ship that had left port the day before! But I think the most interesting part of all was when we flew into a sudden storm. To avoid it, we began to climb, and climb . . . until we were actually flying *above* the storm! There we were in brilliant sunshine; and below us were the black clouds, and the rain. We could look down and see where the rain began! It gave me a sort of *uncanny* feeling. . . ."

Surely such personal anecdotes make for more fascinating reading than the mere blunt statement of fact! Compare the above paragraph with this: "Bill is flying to California next week. He's very excited about it." Don't let it go at that! Add something out of your own experience—som.thing only *you* can write—something that makes your letter *individual*.

When you are talking with people, you give emphasis to important words and ideas by the inflections of your voice. In letter writing you can achieve the same effect by *underlining* the important words and ideas. For example, read this paragraph:

> I'm so disappointed I could cry. I had another letter from Bob and now he says it looks as though he can not be back in time for your wedding. He says he's frightfully sorry, but there's just nothing he can do about it. Oh, Anne—isn't it awful!

Now see how underlining gives emphasis where needed, and makes the paragraph come to life:

> I'm so disappointed I could <u>cry</u>. I had another letter from Bob and <u>now</u> he says it looks as though he can <u>not</u> be back in time for your wedding. He says he's frightfully sorry, but there's just <u>nothing he can do about it</u>. Oh, Anne—isn't it <u>awful</u>!

An occasional word of slang, or a favorite phrase or colloquialism, adds spice to your letters—as it does to your conversation. But don't overdo it! Such phrases as "It's raining cats and dogs!" . . . "Was my face red!" . . . "I'm pleased as Punch!" . . . "Thanks a million!"—if you used them in your speech—add a pleasantly characteristic tang to your letters. *But only if used once!* A "pet" phrase used over and over again in a letter soon becomes boring—and even irritating.

Above all, avoid those stuffy, stereotyped, rubber-stamp, bewhiskered words and phrases that belong to the past! No letter can possibly sound conversational if it's full of such overworked phrases as "in regard to" . . . "on the other hand" . . . "in accordance with" . . . "as a matter of fact" . . . "along the lines of" . . . "at my earliest convenience." It's true that such antiquated phraseology is more likely to be found in business letters than in social and personal correspondence. But there are still too many pompous, old-fashioned words and phrases in general use; and your letters will have more sparkle and personality if you avoid them.*

KEEP YOUR LANGUAGE SIMPLE—
SHORT WORDS ARE THE BEST

One of the most important factors in producing interesting letters—letters with a pleasant, conversational tone to them—is the use of simple, understandable language. You don't ordinarily use elaborate, five-syllable words in your conversation; nor should you strive to use them in your letters. Plain, familiar words are the best. Short, rugged words—the simple, homespun words of everyday speech—are usually more vivid and expressive than the bookish, important-sounding words many people like to use in their letters.

So keep your language simple! Keep it clear, concise and understandable. *Write as you speak.* Don't use formal, high-sounding words that you wouldn't think of using in conversation. Remember that the finest English in the world is *simple* English.

do	is a better word than	*accomplish*
write	is a better word than	*correspond*
try	is a better word than	*endeavor*
help	is a better word than	*assist*
often	is a better word than	*frequently*
so	is a better word than	*consequently*
about	is a better word than	*approximately*
but	is a better word than	*however*
sent	is a better word than	*forwarded*
read	is a better word than	*peruse*
live	is a better word than	*reside*
keep	is a better word than	*retain*
find	is a better word than	*locate*
go	is a better word than	*attend*
bought	is a better word than	*purchased*
talk	is a better word than	*converse*

* For a list of stereotyped words and phrases to avoid, see pages 449 to 451.

The use of bookish words and flowery expressions merely tends to clutter up your ideas. So try to be as brief and direct as you can when writing letters. Say what you have to say in good, crisp words—words that clearly express your meaning.

And whenever you can, use a single vigorous word instead of an elaborate, complicated phrase. Why use two or three words when *one* will do? Frozen forms of expression become a habit; you use them because they "sound right"; but try short, concise words—such as you use in your speech—and see how your sentences take on new life and movement!

for	is better than	*for the purpose of*
if	is better than	*in case of*
to	is better than	*in order to*
please	is better than	*will you be good enough to*
when	is better than	*on that occasion*
now	is better than	*at the present time*
soon	is better than	*in the near future*
like	is better than	*along the lines of*
so	is better than	*for this reason*
stop	is better than	*put an end to*
about	is better than	*with regard to*
since	is better than	*inasmuch as*
by	is better than	*in accordance with*

Writing *simply* does not mean writing *obviously*, without beauty or style. Your simple words should have meaning, substance and life. They should be colorful and expressive . . . words that have force and vigor . . . *words that say something.*

Use lots of verbs, for verbs are the busy little motors that give movement and action to your writing. A simple sentence in which somebody *does* something, or *goes* somewhere, is more forceful and effective than a long, involved sentence with a lot of adverbs, participles and infinitives. And keep your verbs *short!* Keep them rugged and expressive. Make them say what you have to say crisply and to the point. Verbs like come, go, run, walk, do, fly, jump, send, meet, buy, cry, coax, break, give force and action to your sentences. They are better than such limp, elongated verbs as encounter, accomplish, persuade, purchase, transfer, present, inhabit.

HOW TO WRITE WITH GREATER

EASE AND CLARITY

Before you sit down to write a letter, be sure you know exactly what you want to say. For when a thought is sharp and clear in your own mind, you can explain it more easily to others. It's only when you, yourself, are confused or in doubt that the expression of your ideas becomes vague and obscure.

In writing a letter, always be sure that you present your thoughts or ideas in logical order. Keep in mind what you want to say . . . develop it along lines of clear, simple reasoning . . . and let each idea suggest the one that follows. Don't jump around from one thing to another. Always complete what you have to say before going on to something else; and be sure to use a new paragraph for every new thought or idea.

Often the last sentence of a paragraph will suggest the first sentence of the next one. For example, if you are writing about a trip you plan to make, and the last sentence of the paragraph reads: "We are leaving at the end of this month, after Robert returns to school"—that gives you a perfect lead for the next paragraph: "We are quite pleased with Robert's first report from Andover. He is apparently doing very well in all his subjects" . . . and so on.

If you get "lost" in the middle of a letter and don't know how to continue, put down your pen—read what you have written so far—then get up and walk around the room. Think what you would say next if the person were right there in the room with you. Think what would logically come next in a conversation. *Say it* . . . as though it *were* a conversation! Then go back and write it in your letter.

Try to avoid long, rambling sentences and long involved paragraphs. A letter composed of short sentences and short paragraphs is not only more inviting to the eye, but reads more easily and delivers your message or idea with greater speed. If a reader is obliged to wade through long sentences, and a lot of competing ideas all jumbled up in a single paragraph—perhaps going back once or twice to "pick up the threads"—he is likely to miss what you mean entirely.

Two or three short sentences are always better than one long one. A sentence gets tangled up and obscure when you start filling it with ideas. The reader must be given a "breathing space" —a chance to understand and digest one thing before going on to another. The simpler a sentence is the more quickly and easily the reader will get its meaning. Here, for example, is a long, involved sentence which the average person would have to read at least twice to understand:

> Married to a former war correspondent who is now writing fiction, she is living with him and his family in New York and studying voice and dancing—prior to going to Hollywood in the Spring for a screen test.

See what a tremendous increase in force and clarity there is when this long sentence becomes three short ones:

> She is married to a former war correspondent who is now writing fiction. They are currently living with his family in New York. She is studying voice and dancing, and will go to Hollywood in the Spring for a screen test.

Another way to give your letters sharpness and clarity is to use concrete, specific words whenever possible. For example, when you say "I am going abroad next month," the word "abroad" is vague and indefinite. The sentence instantly takes on more life and vitality when you say, "I am going to England next month." "She has a child" isn't nearly as expressive as "She has a two-year-old son." "He sent me flowers for my birthday" isn't as interesting as the specific "He sent me yellow tea roses for my birthday."

PEOPLE JUDGE YOU BY YOUR LETTERS

Any letter worth writing at all is worth writing well. For letters tell more about you than you think! They are as revealing as your clothes and speech—often even more revealing than your manners.

Every letter you write creates either a *good* or *bad* impression on the person who receives it. Yet so many of us write letters quickly, carelessly—without regard for what they may tell about our character and personality.

Surely it is better to be represented favorably by your letters than to have them betray you as careless or rude, as tactless or unkind.

So be as well-groomed in your letters as you are in your dress— as well-mannered as you are in your personal contacts! Don't ever say anything in a letter you wouldn't say to a person's face. Don't spread rumors, or repeat unkind gossip, or write anything that is confidential and shouldn't be revealed . . . for such letter-writing conduct is in bad taste.

If you can't be proud of the letter you have written—if you wouldn't be willing to have strangers judge you by its appearance and its contents—*don't mail it*. Even if it's a letter to a relative or close friend who will understand—*don't mail it!* There's no guarantee your letter won't be seen by outsiders; you can't be sure your thoughtlessly or carelessly written letter won't show up some day to cause you embarrassment and regret.

All people, even your intimate friends, judge you by your letters. So be careful—be critical! Don't let any letter go out under your name unless you feel that it does you justice, that it's a credit to you in every way . . . and that you'd be perfectly willing to be judged by it. Don't let any letter go out under your name unless you feel it will create a *good impression* on the person who receives it. It's far better not to send any letter at all than to send one that stamps you a thoughtless or ill-bred person.

Remember—*your letter represents you*. Be sure it represents you to best advantage!

AVOID CARELESS REMARKS
THAT MAY BE MISUNDERSTOOD

There is this important difference between conversation and letter writing: What is spoken is done with and gone. It may or may not be remembered. A careless or thoughtless remark can be retracted, explained, or made to seem unimportant by the friendliness of a gesture or a smile.

But not so with a careless or thoughtless "remark" in a letter! It's there in black and white, and there it remains, repeating itself with each reading. It may have been meant as a jest. It may not have been meant at all the way it sounds. But you aren't there to explain it! You can't tuck yourself into the envelope and go along with your letter to prevent misunderstanding.

You must be *even more careful* what you write in a letter than what you say to a person directly. For in conversation there are always voice, gesture, expression to help you . . . to make your meaning clear. But when you write, there are just your words and nothing more. What may sound gay and bantering in speech may cause deep hurt in a letter. What is meant to be amusing may give offense.

So *think before you write!* Don't say anything that can be misunderstood, that can be construed as curt or unkind . . . as unfriendly or rude.

Never mail a letter without reading it over from beginning to end. It's a good idea to read it aloud and listen to the sound of it. Listen through the ears of the person who is to receive it. Make sure that he will not get any implications or shades of meaning that you do not intend. If there's even one word or phrase that can be misinterpreted, it's better to rewrite the letter. For remember, *Litera scripta manet* [The written letter remains].

DON'T WRITE ANYTHING
YOU MAY LATER REGRET

Often it's a great emotional relief to sit down and write someone a letter when you are worried, angry or annoyed. But watch out! That's exactly when you are most likely to write something you may be sorry about later—something you'd wish very much you *hadn't* said.

Make it a practice never to send out a letter written in anger, or in a mood of depression or despair. Write it, by all means! Pour out your heart on paper. It's a wonderful way to get rid of the "blues" . . . to rid your system of the poisons of worry, bitterness or fear. *But don't mail it.* Even if you want to very much, *don't mail it.* Put it aside for a while; then take it out and read it over in a day or so when your anger has cooled or you see the bright side of things again. You may thank your lucky stars you didn't mail it!

History is full of famous letters, written in the white heat of anger but never mailed. One of the most interesting of these is the letter written by Benjamin Franklin to an old friend in England—William Strahan. For many years there had been a warm and intimate transatlantic correspondence between the two men. But on the eve of the American Revolution, when Strahan became a member of Parliament and voted for the measures which led to Lexington and Bunker Hill, Franklin was so overcome with bitterness that he sat down and wrote this letter:

Phila., July 5, 1775

Mr. Strahan,

You are a Member of Parliament, and one of that Majority which has doomed my Country to Destruction. You have begun to burn our Towns and murder our People. Look upon your hands!—They are stained with the Blood of your Relations!—You and I were long Friends:—You are now my Enemy,—and

I am,
Yours,
B. Franklin

Franklin undoubtedly felt a lot better after writing that fiery letter. He had said exactly what he wanted to say, put it down on paper. *But he never mailed it.* Perhaps if he had, it would have ended forever the long friendship between him and Strahan. Instead he wrote a less embittered letter a few days later, received a cordial answer in return . . . and his friendship with Strahan continued on a firmer footing and deeper understanding than ever.

Perhaps the most famous of all historic letters, written but not mailed, is the one Lincoln wrote to General Meade in July, 1863. It was a letter written in furious anger and disappointment. Lee and his army were trapped between the swollen, raging torrents of the Potomac—made impassable by the rains—and the victorious Union army behind them. The war could have been ended then and there; Lincoln ordered Meade to attack at once. But Meade hesitated . . . made excuses . . . delayed . . . until finally the swollen waters receded and Lee and his army escaped across the river. Angry because his orders had not been obeyed, disappointed because the war was now prolonged, Lincoln wrote the following letter to Meade:

My dear General,

I do not believe you appreciate the magnitude of the misfortune involved in Lee's escape. He was within our easy grasp, and to have closed upon him would, in connection with our other late successes, have ended the war. As it is, the war will be prolonged indefinitely.

If you could not safely attack Lee last Monday, how can you possibly do so south of the river, when you can take with you very few—no more than two-thirds of the force you then had in hand? It would be unreasonable to expect and I do not expect that you can now effect much. Your golden opportunity is gone, and I am distressed immeasurably because of it.

The letter was found among Lincoln's papers after his death. It was never mailed because Lincoln no doubt realized such a rebuke could only cause further hard feeling, and perhaps even impair the progress of the war. But writing it unquestionably helped to relieve his outraged feelings.

SOME PHRASES THAT
GIVE OFFENSE

If you occasionally start your letters with that old familiar apology: "I meant to write sooner but I was busy" . . . make a solemn vow right now that you'll never do so again! It is one of the most *uncomplimentary* ways possible to open a letter. It's like calling on a friend who eagerly opens the door to welcome you . . . then instantly offending that person by saying, "I had a lot of far more important things than you to think about, but at last I got around to visiting you."

Naturally you wouldn't dream of saying that to anyone. Yet it's exactly what you are saying when you write in a letter: "I've been so busy, I just couldn't find time to write before this!" See how much more gracious and flattering it sounds when you phrase it this way: "I've thought of you so many, many times during these busy weeks!"

Even so outstanding a letter writer as Mark Twain was sometimes guilty of an unintentional discourtesy in his letters. "I have only time to write a line!" he wrote his sister on one occasion. She could not have been especially flattered on receipt of that letter! How very much better was the opening sentence of Mark Twain's letter to his good friend, Dr. Brown, of Edinburgh: "It was a perfect delight to see your well-known handwriting again!"

Try to compliment the reader in the first sentence, if you can possibly do so. It gets your letter off to a good start. You might say, for example, "You write such wonderful letters, it's always a real treat to get one from you!" Or you might say, "I think it's simply *marvelous*, the way you find time to do so many important things and find time to write me nice long letters, too!"

It's certainly no compliment to say, "I just have time to scribble a few words before the children come home from school." Nor is it a compliment to say, "I thought I'd write because I know you'll be disappointed if I don't . . . or "I promised to write, so I'm going to." You can see by these few examples how the tone of your opening sentence can determine the effect or impression of the entire letter on the person who receives it. So be sure to give that opening sentence some real thought! It's well worth the effort.

There is frequently an implied discourtesy in the *closing* of a letter, too. "In haste" means you are busy, or bored, or annoyed, or impatient . . . that you want to end the letter, get it over and done with. Try to avoid such offensive phrases as, "I must close, as I have some sewing to do" . . . "That's all for now; I'm in a big rush" . . . "There's nothing else to write so I guess I'll close."

How much more gracious and friendly it sounds to end your letter with a last thought—not of yourself—but of the person to whom you are writing! For example, "Next time I write, Jean, I'll have that recipe I promised to get for you." Or, "I'll write next week, Bob—from Boston—and I promise to remember everything interesting or amusing that happens at the meeting so I can tell you all about it in my letter."

THE LETTER EVERYONE
LOVES TO RECEIVE

"What makes a letter alive?" asks John B. Opdycke. "What makes a letter breathe and pulsate? What makes us read a letter again and again . . . marks it off from the average, impresses and moves and stirs its readers . . . ? The answer is *personality*." *

To make your letter sparkling and alive—to give it personality —you must put yourself in the place of the person who is to receive it. What would he like to know? What interesting news can you give him? What would he most enjoy hearing about?

Nobody likes people who continually talk about themselves, either in conversation or in a letter. The most *welcome* letter— the letter that is received with joy and read with satisfaction— is the letter written from the *reader's* point of view, with the reader's interests and problems in mind. It's the letter with an amiable *"you"* attitude, rather than a self-centered *"I"* attitude, that everyone loves to receive.

So try to acquire the knack of putting yourself in the reader's place, of trying to see things from the reader's point of view! Failure to recognize and fully appreciate this human element in letter writing . . . failure to see things from the other person's point of view . . . is the cause of most of the dull, tactless, uninteresting and *unwelcome* letters that get into the mail.

* From *Take a Letter, Please!* by John Baker Opdycke, published by Funk & Wagnalls Company, New York City.

It's always best to write your letters when you feel especially friendly and kindly disposed toward the person to whom you are writing. And start off with a compliment or word of praise, if you can! It will win attention and influence your reader as nothing else can! But be sure you *mean* what you say—that your compliment is honest and sincere—otherwise it won't ring true.

People like to feel important, and they resent very much any implication that they are *not* important. Bear that in mind when writing letters! Don't boast about your accomplishments. Don't try to impress the reader with *your* knowledge, *your* importance. The one sure way to a person's heart is to let him know you consider him rather superior, that you recognize and respect his knowledge and judgment. In other words, *make your reader feel important.*

And watch the tone of your letter! No one ever really enjoys a letter that is filled with "peeves" and complaints—a letter that is gloomy and pessimistic. Remember that in letters, as in personal contact, people respond most eagerly to enthusiasm and good cheer.

So try not to pour all your worries and troubles into your letters! Don't write of ill-health . . . of servant problems . . . of domestic difficulties . . . of business reverses. Don't write bad news in a letter, if you can help it. Don't write of disagreeable or unpleasant things . . . of shocking or disturbing things . . . that is, of course, if you want your letter to be read with enjoyment.

The letter everyone loves to receive is natural and spontaneous. It's good "talk" written down. It's cheerful in tone, and gay in spirit. It contains news but no gossip. It contains personal anecdotes, but no private confidences to cause embarrassment if read by an outsider. It is sometimes long and chatty, but never runs on glibly from page to page in a tiresome narration of meaningless details.

The letter everyone loves to receive is *friendly*. It's like a smile . . . a handclasp . . . a warm and cheery "Hello!" The letter everyone loves to receive is alive and sparkling with the writer's *personality*.

3

The Physical Characteristics
of Your Letter

What you write in your letter—its message, the tone and spirit of its contents, the news you tell and the friendliness and cheer you radiate—*these are of first importance.*

But almost equally important is the *appearance* of your letter. It should not only be interesting to read, but attractive and inviting to the eye.

For the appearance of your letter reveals character and personality as surely as the clothes you wear and the language you use. A letter full of blots and erasures, written on shoddy paper with a violent shade of ink, and with no regard for margins, punctuation or sequence of pages, is as offensive in its way as bad table manners. It's no pleasure . . . and certainly no compliment! . . . to receive such a letter.

And yet, evident as this must be to almost everyone, people in general are surprisingly *careless* about the appearance of their letters. Most people pay little or no attention to those few simple, but extremely important fundamentals, dictated by good manners and good taste.

After all, no one but a complete boor would dream of making a social call in tennis shoes—a business call in dungarees! People *dress up* when they go to make a call, in order to make the best possible impression. And for that very same reason you should "dress up" your letters!

Remember—the letter you write is your personal representative. *Be sure it represents you to best advantage.* Be sure that every letter you send out makes as good an impression as you would in a face-to-face visit. That means a neat, clean letter . . .

33

a pleasant-looking and prepossessing letter. It means a letter that in no way repels or offends by its physical characteristics.

So be as individual as you like in the contents of your letter; be as original as the limits of your imagination permit! But in regard to those fundamentals of good taste which govern the *appearance* of your letter—be guided by the rules! There are just a few of them; but they are as essential to good letters as table manners are essential to good social behavior. You are often judged more by the appearance of your letter—and more harshly judged!—than by its contents. By following the suggestions in this chapter, you can be sure your letters will always make a good appearance . . . and therefore a good impression.

THE CORRECT STATIONERY FOR
SOCIAL AND PERSONAL CORRESPONDENCE

The first thing to consider is the choice of stationery. Always use the best texture and quality of paper you can afford—not only because it makes a better impression, but because it's more practical. It's easier to write on good paper, easier to produce a neat, attractive-looking letter. Paper of inferior quality generally absorbs ink and gives a rough, feathery edge to the writing. Then, too, paper of good quality stands up better under the rough treatment it may receive on its way through the mail; it isn't likely to arrive in a battered or untidy condition. That's important if your letter is going a long way. So be sure the stationery you select (1) *takes ink well*, (2) *travels well.*

For your *social* correspondence, such as invitations, acknowledgments, formal notes of thanks and condolence, plain white unruled paper of standard size and shape is always best. It should be a double sheet; and it may fold once into its envelope, or go in without folding, as preferred. The envelope should, of course, match exactly. Stationery that is mismated is never acceptable.

For *informal* correspondence—such as friendly letters, family letters, informal notes of thanks or congratulation and the like— there is a much wider scope for personal choice. The only limitations are those of good taste. In stationery, as in everything else, there are new styles almost every season, and you may indulge your fancy as you like. There are no inflexible rules; just be sure to avoid extremes of size, shape, color or style. Any extreme that makes your letter conspicuously different from others is in poor taste—like loud and flashy clothing.

The use of vivid, highly colored stationery is an example. Avoid the use of such striking shades as red, green and purple, which instantly call attention to themselves. If you like color in your stationery, choose a delicate, subdued shade such as ivory, tan or gray. Even a very light shade of blue or pink is permissible, if your taste runs that way. But avoid the loud, gaudy shades. And remember, white is always acceptable, always in good form, for every type of correspondence.

Giddy borders and decorations on letter paper are for the very young only (or for the immature in taste). Keep *your* stationery simple and dignified. Envelope linings of contrasting color may be used provided they are not too vivid and conspicuous.

Folded sheets are still the most widely used, and are best for the general run of personal correspondence. However, if you like long letters, if your handwriting is bold and large, or if you use a typewriter for your personal correspondence, you may find single sheets more convenient. Both types are equally correct for informal letters; but remember that for *formal* purposes, only the conventional double sheet may be used.

Don't use ruled stationery for your letters. Ruled paper is only for children learning how to write! If you can't keep your lines straight, use one of those handy dark-lined guides which are usually furnished with stationery. You just slip it under the page and let it guide you while you are writing. Of course anyone who really *wants* to write in a straight line can! It just takes a little time and some sincere effort.

Try to use stationery that fits the letter. For example, if you are writing a long, chatty letter with all the accumulated news of the past month, use fairly large sheets of paper. But if you are writing a short message, perhaps just a few words, use smaller-size stationery. It's not advisable to use correspondence cards or tiny sheets that fit into very small envelopes. Undersize letters are discouraged by the postal authorities because they present difficulty in handling and are easily lost or misplaced. A letter is assured quicker and safer delivery if it's more nearly regular size.

It's not considered good form to use *postal cards* for personal or social correspondence. This does not refer to the picture post cards on which travelers send greetings back home (a good old custom, dear to our hearts!). It refers to the stamped postal cards issued by the government and intended primarily for business use. It is certainly not the best of taste to air one's private affairs on the back of a card for everyone to see and read.

The use of office or hotel stationery for personal correspondence is not recommended, except in an emergency. The use of a sheet of paper from a child's school tablet, and any stray envelope that happens to be around, is *never* recommended under any circumstances! If you don't have suitable stationery available, put off writing the letter until you can get some . . . or if the message can't wait, telephone.

Many people like to have their personal stationery engraved with their name and address. Others like to have an attractive engraved monogram on their letter paper. Either is correct . . . but never use *both* on the same stationery. That's ostentatious— like wearing too much jewelry. If you use a monogram, be sure it's a *simple* one. An elaborate, highly colored monogram shows as poor taste as the choice of loud paper.

Don't use a crest, unless such distinction rightfully belongs to your family. The use of a crest that doesn't belong to you is not far removed in principle from the use of a "phony" title.

If you are planning engraved writing paper—or engraved invitations or announcements of any kind—it's best to consult a reputable stationer. He can show you samples of paper and engraving, and help you make a correct and satisfactory choice.

SHORT NOTES SHOULD
BE HANDWRITTEN

Although the typewriter is being used more and more generally for personal correspondence, there can be no denying the fact that a handwritten note is more intimate and personal . . . and somehow, more sincere. Therefore it is best to write short notes, especially notes of thanks, congratulation, sympathy and so forth, by hand.

But be sure to write *plainly!* Nobody likes to puzzle over words, trying to figure them out. A poor handwriting—an illegible hard-to-read handwriting—is usually just *careless, indifferent writing.*

You can greatly improve your penmanship if you want to. It may take a little time, and it may take a lot of practice; but it's certainly worth it! Try copying a style of writing you admire. Copy the words over and over again, until they look the way you want them to. You may be surprised at the great difference in your writing in a very short time, if you make a real effort to improve it and make it more legible. Experiment with types of pens, too. Often the type of point used makes a difference in the smoothness and legibility of your writing.

Remember—no letter can present a pleasing, attractive appearance if it's poorly written. So don't scribble! Don't scrawl! Write with deliberation and care, taking time to complete every word—to dot every *i* and cross every *t*. Only in that way can you improve your penmanship to the point where clear and legible writing becomes habitual with you.

Don't use very brightly colored ink to write your letters. Black is the best; though dark blue and dark green are also acceptable. Violet, bright green and red are not good taste.

I once received a letter written in *gold ink.* It was obviously meant to create an impression . . . and it did. A *bad* impression! Even before reading a word of the letter, I had formed an unfavorable opinion of the person who wrote it. For looking at that gaudy gold ink, I couldn't help thinking, "What an affectation! What abominably bad taste!"

You know, of course, that only pen and ink will do for your handwritten correspondence. Never write in pencil unless you are ill, or are in a moving vehicle like a train or plane. Writing a letter in pencil is a rudeness to the person who receives your letter, unless circumstances make it unavoidable (in which case you should be sure to explain).

Blots, erasures, lines drawn through words and sentences crossed out—all add up to an untidy and unprepossessing letter. It's much better to rewrite an untidy letter than to let it go out and show you to bad advantage.

I think the classic example of rudeness is to be found in a letter written by Guy de Maupassant to a young and charming woman —an ardent admirer of his literary abilities. At the close of a very untidy letter, he added this postscript:

> Pardon the erasures in my letter. I cannot write without them and have no time to recopy.

De Maupassant may have been a very great short-story writer; but he apparently didn't know even the first principles of courtesy in letter writing!

USE OF THE TYPEWRITER

The use of the typewriter is so convenient, and such a great timesaver, that any prejudice against its use for social correspondence which may have existed in the past is now completely gone.

Social leaders who once frowned upon the use of the typewriter for anything but business letters now employ secretaries to type their club and social correspondence. And many of them use a typewriter themselves for their personal and family letters.

There are probably more personal letters written on the typewriter today than are written by hand. And the use of the typewriter for social correspondence has also increased enormously. In fact, it's now good form to type practically every kind of letter—the only important exceptions being *formal* invitations, acknowledgments and the like. Also, as mentioned before, short notes of thanks, congratulation and sympathy are best written in long hand, as they seem more personal and sincere when they are in your own handwriting.

So type all your personal correspondence and your informal social notes, if you want to! Just be sure you *know how* to type—

that your letters are clean and neat and well-spaced, without errors or erasures—as pleasing to the eye as though you had carefully written them by hand. In fact, they should be even more pleasing to the eye . . . for typing adds a special neatness and precise legibility of its own.

Of course that neatness and legibility depend to a great extent upon the condition of your typewriter; so be sure it's in *good* condition. Change the ribbon as soon as the impressions begin to look light and faded. And keep the type faces sharp and clean.

All typewritten letters *must be signed by hand,* with pen and ink. A typed signature is discourteous.

THE SPACING AND ARRANGEMENT
OF A LETTER

Whether your letter is typed or written by hand, it should "sit nicely" on the page. That means it should be well-spaced and well-balanced, with reasonably wide and straight margins.

When writing with pen and ink, leave adequate space *between* the lines as well as generous margins at the sides. A well-spaced letter is more inviting to the eye and easier to read.

If your letter is to be typewritten, give some thought beforehand to the approximate length of it, so you can plan its spacing. A letter that is typed grotesquely off-center on a page does not make a good impression. The final appearance of your letter, handwritten or typed, should be of a picture set neatly in a frame.

Don't use folded stationery for typing letters; it's neither convenient nor practical. Special paper for typing personal correspondence is available wherever stationery is sold. It comes in single sheets, of course; and is about 7½ x 10 inches in size. That's slightly smaller than commercial letterheads which are 8½ x 11 inches. For a long letter that fills the page, there should be a margin of at least an inch and a half at the top, bottom and left-hand side—and approximately the same margin on the right-hand side. For short notes, the margins are proportionately wider—so that the letter looks well-spaced on the page.

It is not advisable to type on both sides of a sheet of paper.

If you cannot get your letter on one sheet, use a second sheet to complete it.

SEQUENCE OF PAGES AND
FOLDING THE LETTER

Obviously the proper sequence of pages and the correct folding of a letter are extremely minor and unimportant details in the art of letter writing. But even these minor details must be included for those who specifically want the information and would be disappointed not to find it here. Moreover, even such comparatively unimportant details as sequence and folding help add up to a well-constructed and well-integrated letter . . . enjoyable to receive and to read.

The sequence of pages depends upon the length of the letter. Social notes—like informal invitations, notes of thanks, condolence, and so forth—should be short enough to go on the first page. Personal letters that carry over to a second page of a folded sheet should be written on pages *one* and *three*. A long letter should follow the natural page order, and not skip around from *one* to *three,* from *two* to *four.* Skipping around in a letter confuses the reader, and can be very irritating. Even when you write in the natural order of pages, it's a good idea to *number* them as it makes reading easier. Writing sideways or crosswise in a letter is bad taste and should be avoided.

Most letter paper folds once into its envelope, although large-size sheets for typewriter use may require two folds. Take the little time necessary to fold your letter *neatly,* with the *edges even.* A carelessly folded letter implies indifference toward the person to whom the letter is sent.

A double sheet is folded evenly from the lower to the top edge, and inserted in the envelope fold first.

A single sheet is also folded evenly from the lower to the top edge, and is also inserted in the envelope fold first.

A sheet too large to go into the envelope with a single fold should be folded in three equal sections, and placed in the envelope with the closed end first.

AVOID MISUSED WORDS AND
MISTAKES IN SPELLING

Just as people appraise and judge you by your speech, they instinctively judge you by your letters. Careless mistakes in spelling, punctuation, the use of words and so on, can make a bad impression. In business correspondence especially, errors in spelling and the use of words can reflect unfavorably, perhaps unfairly, on your abilities; and can place you at a disadvantage.

We suggest, therefore, that you get into the habit of consulting a dictionary whenever you are in doubt about a word. Be sure you are using it properly and spelling it correctly. And after you have looked up a word and checked on its exact meaning and how to spell and pronounce it, make a point of using it frequently in your conversation and in your letters, until it becomes an easy and familiar part of your vocabulary.

Many words sound the same but have quite different meanings. We have listed a few one often sees misused in letters. However these few merely demonstrate the possibility of error in the use and spelling of words, and the importance of keeping a dictionary handy and referring to it when in doubt.

altar means a place of worship
alter means to change

ascent means a slope or rise
assent means to agree

canvas means a kind of cloth
canvass means to solicit

councilor means a member of a council
counselor means a lawyer

formally means in a formal manner
formerly means before

hole means an opening or excavation
whole means complete, entire

ingenious means clever or inventive
ingenuous means noble, generous, frank

isle means a little island
aisle means a passageway or row

lie means to recline or prevaricate
lye means a caustic alkaline solution

strait means narrow or restricted
straight means not curved or crooked

stationary means fixed, immovable
stationery means paper for writing

vale means a valley
veil means a covering

write means to put down in legible characters
right means correct

yoke means a bond or crosspiece
yolk means the yellow of an egg

PLURAL FORMS

Often the plurals of nouns present difficulty. Most nouns form the plural simply by adding *s* to the singular, as for example: *book, books; house, houses; trunk, trunks.*

Nouns ending in *s* or *ss, sh, ch, x* or *z* generally form the plural by adding *es*, as for example: *dress, dresses; fox, foxes; brush, brushes; church, churches.*

Nouns ending in *y* preceded by a consonant form the plural by changing *y* to *i* and adding *es*. For example: *sky, skies; lady, ladies; army, armies.* But nouns ending in *y* preceded by a vowel take only the addition of *s* for the plural: *key, keys; delay, delays; attorney, attorneys; alloy, alloys.*

Nouns ending in *o* preceded by a vowel take *s* for the plural: *folio, folios; rodeo, rodeos.* As a rule nouns ending in *o* preceded by a consonant add *es* to form the plural: *cargo, cargoes; hero, heroes; tomato, tomatoes.* However there are a number of exceptions to this rule, as indicated by the following list. These words, though ending in *o* and preceded by a consonant, add *s* only to form the plural. There are a number of other less familiar words in this same category; when in doubt, refer to your dictionary.

albinos	kimonos
armadillos	lassos
avocados	magnetos
banjos	mementos
cantos	pianos
dynamos	solos
embryos	tobaccos
Eskimos	zeros
halos	

Nouns ending in *f* and *fe* usually form the plural by changing *f* to *v* and adding *es*. For example: *calf, calves; half, halves; knife, knives; scarf, scarves.*

Some words are the same for both singular and plural, such as *chassis, sheep, deer, fowl*. The collective plural of *fish* is the same as the singular; however it is permissible to use *fishes* when one is denoting various specific species.

The plurals of compounds and combined words are variously formed; and here again it is advisable to check your dictionary when in doubt. In general, however, in forming the plurals of compound terms, the most significant or most descriptive word takes the plural form. Frequently the important word is first, as in the following correct plural forms:

aides-de-camp	commanders in chief
ambassadors at large	sergeants major
attorneys at law	surgeons general
bills of fare	courts martial
daughters-in-law	rights-of-way
consuls general	postmasters general

Sometimes the important word is in the middle, giving us such plural forms as these:

assistant surgeons general
assistant attorneys general
deputy chiefs of staff

Often the significant word is last, and the plural forms are correctly indicated as follows:

assistant attorneys	judge advocates
assistant commissioners	lieutenant colonels
assistant directors	major generals
brigadier generals	maid servants
deputy judges	trade-unions
deputy sheriffs	

When both parts of a compound term are of equal significance, both take the plural form. For example:

women artists	coats of arms
men buyers	men employees

When no one word is especially significant in itself, the last word takes the plural form—like the following:

hand-me-downs
pick-me-ups
forget-me-nots
will-o'-the-wisps

In a combination of a preposition hyphened with a noun, the plural is formed on the noun: *goings-on, hangers-on, fillers-in, passers-by*. But when neither part of the combination is a noun, the plural is formed on the last word: *lay-offs, sell-outs, tie-ins, write-ups, also-rans*.

The plural of abbreviations, figures, sizes, symbols and so on is formed by the addition of an apostrophe and *s*, as for example: *ABC's; Do's and Don't's; 1950's; size 12's.*

COMMON MISTAKES IN GRAMMAR
AND ENGLISH USAGE

Obviously we cannot cover even the broad, general principles of grammar in a book on letter writing. But we urge you to watch your grammar as well as your spelling, and to make a conscientious effort to avoid errors. Both a grammar and dictionary are essential desk books for all who wish to do any kind of writing.

Following is a list of errors in grammar and English usage

frequently made in correspondence. Some of these are conspicuous errors which you would probably never make. But there are many others, not nearly so obvious; and we urge you to check and make sure whenever there is any doubt in your mind as to what is correct.

Wrong	*Right*
I do not believe it was *her*.	I do not believe it was *she*.
I'll come *irregardless* of the weather.	I'll come *regardless* of the weather.
She was *kind* of surprised.	She was *somewhat* surprised.
He meant it for you and *I*.	He meant it for you and *me*.
They *learned* the baby to talk.	They *taught* the baby to talk.
The mountains are *healthy*.	The mountains are *healthful*.
I *left* her alone.	I *let* her alone.
I'll *bring* him the letters.	I'll *take* him the letters.
Who do you *want* to see?	*Whom* do you *wish* to see?
Will you *loan* me your book?	Will you *lend* me your book?
Mary *don't* like candy.	Mary *doesn't* like candy.
They don't want *none*.	They don't want *any*.
Just between you and *I*.	Just between you and *me*.
Everyone's entitled to *their* opinion.	Everyone's entitled to *his* opinion.
Neither Bob nor Bill *have* come.	Neither Bob nor Bill *has* come.
I appreciate *you* trying to help me.	I appreciate *your* trying to help me.
There have been *less* accidents this year.	There have been *fewer* accidents this year.
I will *likely* remain there.	I will *probably* remain there.
I'll be there *up* to six o'clock.	I'll be there *until* six o'clock.
He is *very* interested in art.	He is *very much* interested in art.
Set it on my desk.	*Put* (or *place*) it on my desk.
He *done* it all by himself.	He *did* it all by himself.
We sat *besides* him.	We sat *beside* him.
No one came *beside* me.	No one came *besides* me.
Where are they *going to*?	Where are they *going*?

Wrong	*Right*
I'll *advise* you of my plans.	I'll *inform* you of my plans.
He came *around* two o'clock.	He came *about* two o'clock.
I *anticipate* a busy week.	I *expect* a busy week.
He has not *as yet* heard about it.	He has not *yet* heard about it.
It is different *than* mine.	It is different *from* mine.
I *expect* he is home now.	I *suppose* he is home now.
I was surprised at *him* doing it.	I was surprised at *his* doing it.
He'll be married *inside of* a month.	He'll be married *within* a month.
There's no chance of *me* going.	There's no chance of *my* going.
She did it *over again*.	She did it *over*.
I wish it were all *over with*.	I wish it were all *over*.
Is he the *party* you mean?	Is he the *person* you mean?
Keep me *posted* as to developments.	Keep me *informed* as to developments.
The house is in good *shape*.	The house is in good *condition*.
Would you *sooner* come here?	Would you *rather* come here?
These kind are the best.	*This* kind is the best.
Please try *and* come.	Please try *to* come.
I'll go *providing* you will.	I'll go *provided* you will.
He's *got* to leave the city.	He *must* leave the city.
She likes *those* kind of clothes.	She likes *that* kind of clothes.
If I *was* you.	If I *were* you.
For *who* is he painting it?	For *whom* is he painting it?
Divide it *between* all of them.	Divide it *among* all of them.
Please *except* my thanks.	Please *accept* my thanks.
They *affected* an entrance.	They *effected* an entrance.
He climbed the fence *easy*.	He climbed the fence *easily*.
Why is he so *mad*?	Why is he so *angry*?
I'm *anxious* to go abroad.	I'm *eager* to go abroad.
The *two twins* were here.	The *twins* were here.
I *would* like to go.	I *should* like to go.

Wrong	*Right*
He *makes* a lot of money.	He *earns* a lot of money.
He behaved very *bad*.	He behaved very *badly*.
They never go *nowhere*.	They never go *anywhere*.
I shouldn't *of* done it.	I shouldn't *have* done it.
He has not *as yet* heard about it.	He has not *yet* heard about it.
You can *count* on my co-operation.	You can *depend* on my co-operation.
It is worth $500 or *better*.	It is worth $500 or *more*.
That is his lowest *figure*.	That is his lowest *price*.
He's in the furniture *line*.	He's in the furniture *business*.
It's one thing *that* has impressed me.	It's one thing *which* has impressed me.
I didn't mean to *infer* that!	I didn't mean to *imply* that!
It's a field *where* ideas count.	It's a field *in which* ideas count.
I've had *pretty* nearly a year of experience.	I've had *very* nearly a year of experience.
The cost was *under* $100.	The cost was *less than* $100.

CAPITALIZATION IN LETTER WRITING

Following are the general rules of capitalization as applied to letter writing:

1. Capitalize the first word of the salutation (Dear Mary; My dear Mary).
2. Capitalize the first word of the complimentary close (Yours truly; Very cordially yours; Always affectionately yours).
3. Capitalize the names of people (John Smith), and of places (Pike's Peak, Wall Street, the Missouri River).
4. Capitalize the title, rank or position of an individual when it accompanies the name (Mr. John Smith; Governor Frank Blair; Vice-President Warren King); but not when it merely designates the person's rank or position in a general sense (He is the president of a large organization).

5. Capitalize the names of the months and the days of the week (I will expect you on Wednesday, June 10).

6. Capitalize the names of the seasons when they refer to some specific function or event (Spring Reunion); but not when they are used in a general sense (We are planning to visit you next summer).

7. Capitalize the names of regions or localities (North Pole, Torrid Zone, the Orient). Capitalize points of the compass when they designate a section of the country (She lives in the Northwest) but not when they indicate merely a direction (You travel south to go from New York to Philadelphia).

8. Capitalize common nouns that are part of a proper name (Boulder *Dam*, Panama *Canal*); but not when used alone (We saw the dam, but we missed the canal).

9. Capitalize the names of colleges or universities (University of Pennsylvania); but not the general use of the word as a common noun (Many universities have received large endowments).

10. Capitalize the names of various fields of learning when used to designate a specific course of study (She majored in Comparative Religions); or when they are derivatives of proper nouns (He said he would take courses in Spanish and French before going abroad). Do not capitalize the names of various fields of learning when used in a general rather than a specific sense (His preparation included research in history, sociology and religion).

11. Capitalize the principal words in a title (I am interested in your lecture on "The Origins of Fear and Tension").

12. Capitalize the names of business firms, government bureaus, committees, leagues, groups, political parties, commissions (Republican Party, British Embassy, Board of Health, United Nations). Capitalize also the names of members or adherents of organized groups or bodies (Shriner, Communist, Boy Scout).

13. Capitalize the names of holidays (Thanksgiving).

THE USE OF PUNCTUATION

Punctuation is a device for making things easier to read and interpret. It gives the emphasis and expression to *writing* that pauses, gestures and the raising and lowering of the voice give to *speech*.

The use of punctuation can make your letter *look* more interesting . . . can make it *read* more excitingly. If you were to look at the script of a popular radio show, as broadcast, you would see that it's broken up into short sentences, with lots of dots and dashes and exclamation points. A well-written script looks nearly as interesting on paper as it sounds on the air.

I don't say that your letter should look like a radio script! But it should look interesting and inviting to the eye . . . it should look readable, *exciting*. And the way to achieve that effect . . . the way to avoid an unbroken, forbidding look that bores the reader before he even begins to read! . . . is by the proper use of punctuation.

If you want to see the difference that punctuation can make, look first at this "anemic" paragraph:

> I have just heard the good news. Congratulations. I think it's wonderful, simply wonderful, that you have at last received the recognition you deserve. Tell me how does it feel to be president of the company where you were once an office boy. I can just imagine how happy and proud Edith is. The best of luck to you Jim in your new job.

Now look at it, and see how punctuation has given it new life and sparkle, new *meaning!*

> I have just heard the good news. Congratulations! I think it's wonderful—simply wonderful—that you have at last received the recognition you deserve! Tell me: how does it feel to be president of the company where you were once an office boy? I can just imagine how happy and proud Edith is. . . . The best of luck to you, Jim, in your new job!

The PERIOD (.) *is used:*

1. At the end of all sentences.
2. After every abbreviation, such as *Dr., Mr., N.Y., Sept.*

The COMMA (,) *is used:*

1. To set off appositives. (The president, a friend of ours, met us in the library.)
2. To set off a geographical name that explains the one preceding it. (Tomorrow we are going to Bar Harbor, Maine.)
3. To set off parenthetical expressions. (It is important, therefore, that we contact the man at once.)
4. To separate a series of names or nouns. (We bought apples, oranges, plums and grapes.)
5. To separate clauses of a compound sentence when they are connected by a simple conjunction. (I outlined my difficulties, and he told me how I could solve them.)
6. To separate a series of words that equally modify a common noun. (He is a good, noble, honest and trustworthy man.)
7. To separate words or phrases included by way of explanation. (That man, judging from his record, is not to be trusted.)
8. To separate a prepositional phrase placed before the subject. (To be exact, it will take two weeks to complete it.)
9. To separate the various parts of an address or date. (250 Park Avenue, New York, 17, N.Y.) (April 3, 1960.)
10. Following a salutation, if preferred to the colon. (Dear Mary,)
11. Following a complimentary close. (Very truly yours,)

The COLON (:) *is used:*

1. Following a salutation, if preferred to the comma. (Dear Mary:)
2. To introduce a list. (He brought the following items back with him: sugar, spices, flour, nuts.)

3. To give emphasis to an idea: (There can be only one reason for this tragic accident: carelessness.)
4. As a form of introduction to a series of statements. (At the meeting today we discussed the following subjects:)

The SEMICOLON (;) *is used:*

1. To wield several facts into a single event. (I went to the park; I saw him sitting on a bench; I went to him and asked his name; he was so startled he jumped up and dropped the paper he had been reading.)
2. Between clauses of a compound sentence that are not connected by a conjunction. (Advertising increases sales; it also cuts down unit costs.)
3. Between clauses of a compound sentence that are connected by a conjunctive adverb such as *then, moreover, thus, consequently, also, therefore.* (The inventor is not in this country; therefore we cannot proceed with the experiments.)
4. Before such words as *namely, that is, as, thus* when they introduce examples or illustrations. (Three things are especially important in letter writing; namely, simple words, concise expression and a conversational tone.)
5. Between two thoughts in one sentence that are closely connected in meaning. (He is a writer; he is very famous.)

The DASH (—) *is used:*

1. To set off interpolated words. (He said—and I have no reason to doubt him—that his business is better now than it has ever been.)
2. To indicate an abrupt change of thought in the middle of a sentence. (We asked him what he meant, and he said—well, what do you think?)
3. To indicate the repetition or expansion of a preceding thought. (There are several answers to your question—answers that prove my point conclusively.)
4. To make parenthetical expressions stand out clearly. (Mr. John Blake—the man in the case—has disappeared and cannot be located.)

The HYPHEN (-) *is used:*

1. To tie words together for the purpose of creating quick and colorful expressions. (He had a big-bad-wolf expression.) (It was a heads-I-win-tails-you-lose proposition.) (Nobody liked his high-wide-and-handsome manner.)

PARENTHESES (( )) *are used:*

1. To set off interpolated matter. Example: The new editor, Mr. Curtis (formerly of the Rockland *News*) took charge today.
2. To explain a previous remark. Example: A delicate shade of tan or gray paper may be used (instead of white).
3. To set off numerals in a sentence. Example: The purpose of the law is (1) . . . (2) . . .

QUOTATION MARKS (" ") *are used:*

1. To set off the actual words written or spoken by someone else. (She said, "I will go with you tomorrow.")
2. To set off slang words or phrases for which the writer does not care to take responsibility. (We told him to "cut it out.") (The use of crests which do not rightfully belong to the family is not far removed in principle from the use of "phony" titles.)
3. To set off titles of chapters, articles, lectures, books. (I sent him a copy of my lecture "What Men Live By.") (He borrowed my copy of "Strange Sacrifice.")
4. A quotation within a quotation is enclosed within single marks. ("Please tell him 'Mrs. Brown is not at home' and let me know what he answers.")

DOTS (. . .) are used the way dashes are, to separate thoughts or ideas, to indicate an unfinished quotation, or merely to give special emphasis to a statement or idea.

4

The Parts of a Letter

Every well-constructed letter is made up of five essential parts. They comprise the structure, or framework, of your letter. You don't need to follow exactly all details within each part; but you *must* follow the general form if you want to produce a correct and acceptable letter. All letters—social, personal and business*—should conform to this basic outline:

1. THE HEADING
   which is your address and the date

2. THE SALUTATION
   which is your complimentary greeting

3. THE BODY OF THE LETTER
   which is your message

4. THE CLOSE
   which is your complimentary "good-by'

5. THE SIGNATURE
   which should be in pen and ink, and *legible!*

In addition to these five basic parts there is also the *super-scription*—which is not, strictly speaking, a part of the letter. The superscription is the outside address, written on the envelope . . . and it must be very carefully and correctly written, if the letter is not to go astray!

But let us discuss individually and in detail each of the five parts which go to make up a well-written, well-integrated letter.

* For specific information on the form, structure and content of business letters, see Book IV, beginning on page 427.

THE HEADING

The very first thing you write in a letter is the heading, which is simply your address and the date. Of course, if the stationery used has a printed or engraved address already inscribed, the heading consists of the date only.

Place the heading at least one inch from the top edge of the sheet. Start writing approximately in the center, so that the heading ends three-quarters of an inch or so from the right margin. Here is the way the heading should look at the top of your letter:

250 Park Avenue
New York 17, N.Y.
July 6, 19—

You can indent the lines if you like. But a straight edge is considered more modern and better form. Notice that there are no commas at the ends of the lines; and no period after the date. The names of cities—even long names like Philadelphia, San Francisco, Minneapolis, Cincinnati—should be written out completely. But the names of states may be abbreviated if you like . . . especially if the abbreviations are well-known and familiar like N.Y., N.J., Mass., Cal. and so forth. In general it's best *not* to abbreviate the names of places.

Don't ever write a letter without a heading. It's curt . . . like pushing open a door without knocking. And it's best to write the *complete* heading, even though your letter is going to an intimate friend who knows your address. It's a courtesy—a custom—and if you omit it, the person who receives your letter has the right to assume (1) that you don't know any better or (2) that you know better but are indifferent and just don't care about it.

Of course, in any communication requiring acknowledgment —such as a letter of thanks or condolence—it's not only a rudeness but a distinct inconvenience to omit the address. For in that case the person may be required to look up your address; and with dozens of other letters to be acknowledged, that can be a nuisance—and even a hardship.

The date, too, is important and should never be omitted. It goes immediately below the address—never above it, or on the same line with it. Don't abbreviate the month—like Dec., Jan., Feb., Apr. Write it out; it looks much better. And you don't need an *st* or *rd* or *th* after the day of the month—like April 1st, 3rd, 10th. The correct form is: April 1, 19—; April 3, 19—; April 10, 19—. Always put a comma between the day of the month and the year, to separate the numerals and prevent confusion.

THE SALUTATION

The salutation of a letter is the complimentary greeting to the person to whom the letter is written. It's like saying, *"Hello."*

You write the salutation at the left side of the sheet, generally about half an inch below the heading—unless the letter is a short one and must be centered on the page. The point at which you start the salutation will be your left-hand margin; the rest of the letter will be in a straight line with it. Therefore the salutation should be at whatever point you wish the margin to be, anywhere from one to several inches from the edge of the paper.

Long use and familiar custom have made "Dear John" or "Dear Mary" the popular form of salutation in letters. But that doesn't mean you cannot say "Dearest" or "Darling" or "My own precious Anne" in an intimate letter to someone you love. Just bear in mind that in routine everyday correspondence, standard forms of salutation are best . . . and any sharp deviation from the customary and familiar should be avoided.

"My dear" is considered more formal than "Dear"—so if you are writing a friendly, informal letter to someone, the salutation should be "Dear Frank" or "Dear Mr. Smith." But if you are writing a formal note—or if you are writing to someone you don't know very well, perhaps a new acquaintance, the salutation should be "My dear Mr. Smith."

Some forms of address are looked upon as bad taste and should be avoided. For example, never use "Dear Friend" or "My dear Friend," as your salutation. Equally undesirable are "Madame," "Dear Miss" and "Friend Jack." The use of the name alone as a salutation is rude and incorrect. So never start a letter like this:

Mr. Frank Smith:

This is to inform you that the tickets which you sent me . . . and so on.

Conform to standard familiar styles of salutation—except in intimate family letters, or in love letters, where you use your own private endearments.

THE BODY OF THE LETTER

The body of a letter is naturally the most important part of it. It's what you write in the letter . . . what you say . . . your message.

And that's strictly *your* department! No one can tell you what to say in your letters. The most we can do is make suggestions; and that's what all the remaining chapters of this book are about. But the tone and spirit of your letters . . . their charm and personality . . . their power and influence on those who read them . . . all depend on you.

Obviously one of the first requisites of a good letter is to have something to say. You aren't very likely to produce an interesting letter if there is neither the reason nor the inclination to write. So first of all, know *why* you are writing—and then be sure your letter accomplishes its purpose.

You may write to cheer a sick friend . . . to share good news with a distant relative . . . to express sympathy, thanks or regret . . . to accept an invitation or explain why you cannot accept it. But whatever the purpose of your letter, *keep that purpose clearly in mind as you write.* Say what you have to say— simply and to the point, leading naturally from one subject to another as though you were talking.

Get your letter off to a good start with something interesting in the very first sentence. Avoid the obvious, "I received your letter and am answering it." Of course you're answering it; you both know that! Then why waste the all-important opening sentence on something so inane and unnecessary?*

Avoid particularly starting your letter with any word that ends in "ing." Don't, for example, ever begin a letter like this:

> Having heard that you are in New York, I am writ-
> ing . . .

or

> Learning of your illness, I hasten to write and . . .

Such leads almost always make a letter sound stereotyped and dull.

Before you start to write, organize your thoughts and decide what you want to say. Then plunge right in and say it! Naturally what you say depends on why the letter is being written. If it's to greet an old friend, sit down and write "Welcome to New York!" just as cordially and spontaneously as you would say it in person. If it's to cheer someone who is sick, don't try to camouflage the purpose of your letter with a lot of unrelated opening remarks. Start off with the same sort of cheerful nonsense you might indulge in if you visited the patient's bedside: "What's the

---

* For examples of interesting opening sentences taken from letters of famous people, see page 347.

idea of being sick? Don't you realize how your friends all miss you?" Then go on to the next thought that logically presents itself, exactly what you would say if you were right there at the bedside, chatting with your friend. "Honestly, John—we just can't get along without you. So hurry and get well! You know there's a golf tournament at the end of this month, and you just can't miss that!"

If it's a letter of thanks, be sure it's written promptly and for the purpose—expressing cordial and sincere thanks—not rambling on page after page about the house your neighbor is building and the prize your daughter won at school.

If it's a letter inviting someone to dinner, go straight to the point—instead of jumping from one unrelated subject to another, then suddenly remembering the purpose of the letter and adding a postscript! Don't think that is an exaggeration. Such letters are written and mailed every day of the week, and they certainly do not show up the writers to good advantage!

I once received a long and rather incoherent letter that discussed everything from the weather to the political situation. While I was busy trying to figure out the purpose of the letter, I received a telephone call from the woman who had written it. She had meant to invite me to a party, but had forgotten to mention it in her letter. Could I come? I got out of it gracefully, knowing she was as scatterbrained a hostess as she was a letter writer.

In writing the body of your letter, start a new paragraph every time you change to a new subject. Begin each sentence with a capital and end it with a period. Watch your spelling. Watch your grammar. Keep your letter cheerful, concise and correct. Keep it *conversational*.

The length of your letter is not important. It may be just a short note, or it may be a long, chatty letter, full of news—like a leisurely visit with a friend. Just be sure that your short letter doesn't sound abrupt; that your long letter doesn't ramble on and on until the reader becomes confused and bored. It's a wonderful quality in letter writing to know what you want to say—to say it—and *to stop*.

THE PARTS OF A LETTER

HEADING

SALUTATION:

BODY

COMPLIMENTARY CLOSE,

SIGNATURE

THE COMPLIMENTARY CLOSE

The close of a letter is the "good-by"—the complimentary greeting before you sign your name and slip the letter into its envelope.

You write this closing phrase two or three spaces below the body of the letter, beginning about in the center of the page. Only the first word should be capitalized; and there should be a comma at the end.

The wording varies according to the type of letter, and according to the degree of friendship and intimacy with the person addressed. You wouldn't write "Devotedly yours," or "With deepest affection," to someone who is little more than a casual acquaintance. Nor would you write a cold and impersonal "Very truly yours," to an old and well-loved friend. Your closing phrase should be neither flowery nor curt, but friendly to the degree that you are friendly with your correspondent.

Business letters, letters to professional people, and formal notes generally close with "Yours truly," or "Very truly yours;" though "Cordially" and "Sincerely" are also frequently used.

For informal social notes and the general run of friendly correspondence, you might use any of the following, or your own variations of them:

Very cordially yours,   Sincerely yours,
Yours most cordially,   Always heartily yours,
Always sincerely,   Faithfully yours,

It isn't necessary to conform always to the familiar "Sincerely" and "Cordially" in your informal correspondence. If you wish to use something a little newer and fresher, try such phrases as "Yours with kindest remembrances,"—"Yours in friendly affection,"—"Warmly yours,"—"Cheerfully yours,"—perhaps even, if the letter contains pleasant news, "Happily yours."

Letters to intimate friends or relatives might close with any of the following forms, or your own variations of them:

Yours affectionately,   Lovingly yours,
Always affectionately,   Your loving sister,
In fond affection,   Lovingly, your sister,
Fondly,   With loving thoughts,
As ever, fondly,   Most affectionately,

As for love letters, the wording is whatever the degree of affection inspires, from a simple "Fondly yours," to a fervent "Yours with the utmost devotion."

Though it is best to conform to conventional closings in business and social letters, you may be as original and imaginative as you like in your personal and family correspondence. Here you may use your own pet expressions, your favorite phrases of endearment. You may even eliminate formal openings and closings entirely, if that is your preference. In letters to his young son away at school, Alexander Hamilton liked to close with some such affectionate phrase as, "Good-by, dearest boy—my thoughts are ever with you;" or "A good night to you, my darling son!"

Mark Twain frequently signed his letters, "Yrs Affy, Sam." His family loved the quaint, familiar phrase, and his friends considered it a compliment when he signed his letters to them in such a way.

To an old comrade he loved but rarely saw, Lincoln signed himself, "Your friend forever, A. Lincoln."

To people he especially liked, William H. Page closed his letters with, "Always heartily yours."

So if you wish to start your letter, "I've been thinking of you all day, Kate darling!"—and if you wish to close your letter, "Good-by, my dearest one!"—by all means write it just that way. Traditional openings and closings are expected in formal correspondence; but in letters to your intimate friends, no rules need inhibit your natural, spontaneous expressions of greeting and farewell.

The position of the word "yours" in a formal complimentary closing may be either at the beginning or the end of the phrase, as you prefer. There's not the slightest shade of difference in meaning between "Yours sincerely," and "Sincerely yours." Strictly speaking, the use of an adverb ending in *ly* (like truly, cordially, lovingly) calls for the use of the accompanying pro- noun "yours" to complete the phrase. Therefore, it's always better to include it in your very formal correspondence. But in your friendly and informal correspondence, you may omit the pronoun if you like—closing with a simple "Sincerely," or "Cor- dially."

It is not advisable to use the word "yours" alone—except, perhaps, at the close of a love letter where the word takes on special meaning and eloquence. But "Yours, John Smith" at the close of a business or social letter sounds hurried and abrupt, and is not especially complimentary.

Always be sure that the salutation and the close of your letter conform. For example, a letter that begins with "Tom, my beloved," should certainly close with the same warmth of feel- ing—not with a cold and formal "Very truly yours." A letter that expresses no warmth of feeling all the way through should not end with a sudden protestation of love or affection, like an afterthought tacked on at the end. "With loads of love," is just such an overworked appendage, gushy and insincere.

"Warmly yours," is bad form and should be avoided. "Hastily yours," and "Yours in haste," are rude and unflattering.

The phrase, "Respectfully yours," should be used only by a tradesman to a customer, or by an employee to an employer. It is frequently used when writing to church dignitaries or to high public officials; but "Faithfully yours," is considered a more acceptable form for that purpose.

"Gratefully yours," should be used only when a benefit has been received. You might use it, for example, in a letter to a surgeon who has successfully operated on someone dear to you . . . or a lawyer who has won a difficult case . . . or a teacher who has given special attention to your child.

"Fraternally yours," is often used between members of the same society, but the phrase is stodgy and old-fashioned. "Faithfully yours," or "Cordially yours," sounds more sincere, and certainly more up-to-date.

"Believe me, Sincerely yours," is an old English form still used by many people to express formality in the closing of a note. But it is a timeworn and cumbersome phrase and should be avoided, along with such other stilted expressions as "I beg to remain,"—"I have the honor to remain,"—"I remain, Your Humble servant,"—"I am, Yours obediently." It is surprising to find that some comparatively recent books on the subject still accept these clumsy, antiquated forms; but they have no place in modern letter writing and are not recommended.

Less offensive ornaments of expression are "With best wishes," and "With kindest regards. Use them occasionally, if you like; but guard against using one pet expression over and over again in your letters. And bear in mind that the trend today is for simple, natural expression in all correspondence.

THE SIGNATURE

The signature of a letter is written below the complimentary close and somewhat to the right, so that it ends just about in line with the right-hand margin of the letter. There are three basic rules to observe:

1. Always sign by hand, in ink.
2. Write *legibly*, so there can be no doubt as to the exact spelling of your name.
3. Sign your name without any accompanying title.

Your name is your own, of course, to sign as you choose. If "Chuck" is the name by which you are most fondly and familiarly known to your correspondent—then "Chuck" it should be in your letter! Signing a sedate "Edgar" or "Thomas" to someone who always calls you "Chuck" destroys the friendly tone of your letter.

But for your less intimate correspondence, you will want to know these few simple rules of good form:

A gentleman does not write "Mr." before his name when signing a letter. He signs all formal social correspondence—and all business letters, unless the business associate is also a personal friend*—with his full name but no title: "Thomas Matthew Benton." Informal social notes and letters to friends are signed simply "Thomas" or "Tom."

A married woman does not sign letters with "Mrs." preceding the name. In social correspondence, she uses her given name alone (Elizabeth) . . . or the nickname by which she is affectionately known to her friends (Betty) . . . or her full name (Elizabeth Kingsley Benton), depending upon the degree of intimacy between her and her correspondent. Under no circumstances does she sign a letter "Mrs. Thomas M. Benton." However, in a business letter or a letter to a complete stranger, she may wish to indicate how the reply to her should be addressed. In that case she adds her married name, *in parentheses*, either directly below the signature or over toward the left—in line with the left-hand margin. For example:

> Yours very truly,
> Elizabeth Kingsley Benton
> (Mrs. Thomas Matthew Benton)

> or

> Yours very truly
> Elizabeth K. Benton

(Mrs. Thomas M. Benton)

In a letter to a tradesman or servant, a married woman may not wish to use her first name. In that case she signs "E. K. Benton" (for Elizabeth Kingsley Benton) . . . and in the lower left-hand corner of her letter, in parentheses, she writes her married name.

An unmarried woman signs her social correspondence "Anita"

* For detailed information on business signatures, see page 438.

or "Anita Benton." In business letters she may use the form "(Miss) Anita Benton."

A widow signs her social correspondence exactly as she did before her husband's death. Her business letters may also be signed as before, with "Mrs. Thomas M. Benton" in parentheses below the signature. Or if she prefers, she may just put "Mrs." in parentheses before her own name:

> Yours very truly,
> (Mrs.) Elizabeth Kingsley Benton

A divorced woman, unless she legally resumes her maiden name, signs her social letters as before . . . with her own first name and surname, and her former husband's surname: "Elizabeth Kingsley Benton." In business correspondence, instead of her former husband's name in parentheses below the signature, she uses her own—as follows:

> Yours very truly,
> Elizabeth Kingsley Benton
> (Mrs. Elizabeth K. Benton)

A doctor signs his letters, "Thomas Matthew Benton" or "Thomas Matthew Benton, M.D."—*never* "Dr. Thomas Matthew Benton."

A minister signs his letters "John Francis Pratt" or "John Francis Pratt, D.D."—*never* Rev. John Francis Pratt.

Whether a man is a college professor, a justice of the Supreme Court, or President of the United States, he signs his letters without any title or "handle" attached to his name. Of course in a business letter, a letter to an editor or colleague, or a letter of a professional or scientific nature, a man's title, position, affiliations and so forth may be required—to give substance and authority to his communication. In that case, the essential data are written *below the name*, not as a part of it. For example, a physicist who writes a paper on atomic energy and sends it to the editor of a scientific journal for publication, would sign his covering letter:

Edward T. Hill, Ph.D.
Professor, Department of Physics
University of Maine

If the letter is written on University of Maine stationery, as it is very likely to be, that part of the data need not be included under the signature.

A degree following the name is not in the same category as a title, and is entirely acceptable. But it should be used only when the nature of the communication calls for it: when it has some definite bearing on the subject of the letter and denotes authority to discuss that subject. Naturally one doesn't tack a degree to one's name when writing a letter of sympathy or acknowledging a dinner invitation!

In a letter to a stranger, a degree following the name is often helpful in indicating how the reply should be addressed. For example, earned degrees such as Ph.D., M.D., D.D. and D.D.S. entitle the person to be addressed as "Doctor" (Dr.). But holders of honorary degrees such as LL.D. and Litt.D. are *not* ordinarily addressed as "Doctor." A bachelor of arts or science (B.A. or B.S.) or a master of arts or science (M.A. or M.S.) is addressed simply as "Mr."

In all correspondence—business or social—it is important to avoid confusion due to incomplete or misleading signatures. While there are no hard and fast rules against the use of initials or abbreviations (such as "T. M. Jones" or "Mac"), it is always advisable to write out the full name if there is any possibility of being mistaken for someone else.

The use of "Junior" and similar terms helps to prevent confusion when two or more people in the same family have the same name. "Jr." should be used only by a son whose signature is identical to the signature of his father . . . as, for example, "John D. Rockefeller, Jr." But if a man is named for a grandfather or an uncle, he is "James Carter, 2nd"—*not* "James

Carter, Jr." If he, his father and grandfather *all* have the same name, he is "James Carter, 3rd."

As a rule, the "Jr." is dropped on the death of the father, and the son becomes simply "James Carter." But it is often desirable to retain the "Jr." for business reasons. This is especially true if a man has achieved prominence in some field, and is known to many people by name and by reputation. In that case the "Jr." must be regarded as a permanent part of his signature, and he should continue to use it indefinitely in correspondence—even though the need to distinguish son from father has ceased to exist.

No special problem of signature is involved when a daughter's name is identically the same as her mother's. In intimate correspondence, the contents of the letter naturally tell whether it's "Jane Keith" the daughter, or "Jane Keith" the mother writing. And in all other correspondence, the daughter uses "Miss" in parentheses before her name—the mother uses "Mrs. Henry Keith" in parentheses below *her* name—to differentiate between them and avoid confusion. There is no term similar to "Jr." that a woman can use; and since "Jr." is as masculine as "Mr.," it should certainly never be borrowed for that purpose! "Mary Blake, Jr." must be regarded as contradictory and incorrect, even though we see it occasionally in the letters of prominent people.

And now, just one thing more before we leave the subject of signatures: When you sign your name, *your letter is completed.* It is, or should be, ready to slip into its envelope and send on its way. To add postscripts after signing your name is like standing at the open door after saying good-by and remembering a number of things you wanted to say but didn't. Try to put everything you want to say in your letter before signing your name, for postscripts are unsightly and unnecessary. But if you *must* add something you forgot to say, do so without the use of the "P.S." Just add another paragraph to your letter, below the signature, making it as brief as possible.*

---

* In business letters, postscripts are often deliberately added to give emphasis to some important point. But that's another matter! See page 463 in the special section on business letters.

HOW TO ADDRESS
THE ENVELOPE

The day when you could address a letter to "Mary Pickford, Hollywood" or "Will Rogers, U.S.A." and expect it to be delivered is gone. For reasons of economy and efficiency, the Post Office Department has forbidden the searching of directories and telephone books for correct addresses. The complete address should always be given: full name, street address, city or town, zone number, state. The zone system was developed to speed up and facilitate mail service, and it is helpful to all who must handle the mail in the post office and on the delivery route. Therefore the zone number should always be used, when available.

If a letter is typewritten, the address on the envelope should also be typewritten. If a letter is written by hand, the address on the envelope should be carefully and legibly handwritten. In either case, a clear and complete address should be given, otherwise your letter may be lost or delayed.

Begin writing the address slightly below the middle of the envelope, far enough to the left to permit the name to be written without crowding. Give all the necessary data, and *be sure you are right*. If there is even the slightest doubt in your mind as to the name of the street, the number of the house, or the spelling of the town, look it up.

Try to arrange the writing on the envelope so that it looks balanced and inviting to the eye. Avoid crowding the name and address too high against the top of the envelope, or too low against the bottom edge. When completed, the block of writing or typing should tend toward the right side of the envelope, slightly below the middle, with some white space to the right and below.

In writing the name and address, you may use either a straight margin (one line directly below the other), or you may indent each line in "step" fashion. Postal authorities prefer the slanting arrangement as it is easier to read. Here is how a properly addressed envelope should look:

Mrs. Thomas Matthew Benton

250 Park Avenue

New York 17, N.Y.

Punctuation is not generally used on an envelope, except when it helps to prevent confusion or misdirection. For example, commas at the end of each line are not necessary and are now rarely used. But a dash between a house number and a street number is always advisable (341–85th Street); and commas separating the zone number from the name of the city and state make for greater legibility and easier reading (New York 23, N.Y.). So use whatever punctuation helps the postman read the name and address correctly—but omit punctuation that serves no useful purpose.

The name of the person to whom you are writing should be given in full on the envelope, whenever possible. If it's a very long name—like Roger Delvin Keyes de Bruf—you would naturally find it more practical to use middle initials, addressing the envelope: "Mr. Roger D. K. de Bruf." But Mrs. John Price Hunt should be addressed as such—not as "Mrs. Hunt" or "Mrs. J. P. Hunt."

If you are writing to a new acquaintance, or to a stranger, give particular attention to the spelling of the name. Some people deeply resent a mistake in the spelling of their name—look upon it almost as a personal affront. So check and make sure! *Spell it right.* Don't address Mr. Wolfe as "Mr. Wolf"—or Mrs. Rumpel as "Mrs. Rumple." That's not the way to win friends and influence people!

If there is something unusual about the spelling of a name—like "Alys" for Alice, or "Ffrida" for Freda—try to remember that fact, and write it so on the envelope. But don't use nicknames like "Sid" or "Gert" in an outside address—unless, of course, the nickname is inseparably associated with the person's identity and he is widely known by it, socially and professionally (like Bing Crosby).

A married woman is ordinarily addressed in social correspondence by her husband's name: "Mrs. Thomas Matthew Benton."

A widow remains "Mrs. Thomas Benton." She is not addressed socially as Mrs. Elizabeth Benton—unless, due to business or professional activities, that is the name by which she is best known to her associates and friends.

A divorced woman continues to be addressed in correspondence by her former husband's name; unless she has indicated, in her own correspondence, that she prefers to be addressed as "Mrs. Elizabeth Kingsley Benton" or "Mrs. Kingsley Benton" (*Kingsley* having been her maiden name). The way she indicates this preference is to write it in parentheses in the lower left corner of her letters.

Always bear in mind that the way a woman writes her name in parentheses below her signature, or in the lower left corner of her letter, is the way she wants to be addressed. But if you receive a letter from a woman who is a stranger to you, and she signs herself "Mary Brown" without any other name in parentheses below it, you can assume she is unmarried and address her on the envelope as "Miss."

A woman is never addressed by her husband's title—as, for example, "Mrs. Dr. Thomas M. Benton" or "Mrs. Professor Edward T. Hill."

A woman doctor who practices her profession has the choice of using either her maiden name or her married name in her career, as does any other professional woman. If she uses her husband's name, she is Dr. Margaret Johnson Symonds professionally; and, as a rule, Mrs. Frank Symonds socially. However she may also use Dr. Margaret Johnson Symonds socially, if she wishes, on her cards and stationery, and for invitations and other social correspondence.

A delicate situation arises when a woman who is a doctor, and her husband who is a layman, are both addressed on one envelope. In the past the form "Mr. and Mrs. Frank Symonds" was always recommended for social use; and that form may still be used if, under the circumstances and in one's best judgment, it is the most desirable procedure. But if Dr. Margaret Johnson Symonds is a woman of great prominence and distinction in her profession, surely it would be more gracious to address her by her title. In that case the form to use would be: "Mr. Frank Symonds and Dr. Margaret J. Symonds." Though this is a departure from older usage, it is becoming common practice today, when there are so many distinguished women doctors.

A husband and wife who are *both* doctors may be addressed socially *either* as "Dr. and Mrs. Charles F. Schiller" *or* as "Drs. Charles and Katherine Schiller."

A married woman who has a professional name but no professional title, like a writer or singer, is addressed by whatever name she is known to her correspondent. In her work, of course, it would be impractical to use any name but the one under which she functions and by which she is known. But in social life, she is customarily addressed by her married name.

A man is always addressed as "Mr.," unless he has some other title—*in which case that title should be used.**

"Esq." following a man's name is for "Esquire" which originally, in British use, was a lesser title, usually applied to the younger members of a noble house. Later it lost this significance and came to be used mainly for addressing professional men, especially those in arts, letters and the law. "Esq." is not generally used in this country; but if it is used, it should be only as an equivalent of and a substitute for "Mr." ("John Smith, Esq."—*not* "Mr. John Smith, Esq.") It may be used on the envelope and the inside address; but never in the salutation.

---

* A list giving correct forms of address for public officials, church dignitaries, army and navy officers, etc. will be found on page 667.

The use of "Jr." following a man's name does not eliminate the need for "Mr." preceding it. "Mr." and "Jr." do not mean the same thing (like "Mr." and "Esq.")—therefore the use of both is not a duplication. In other words, you would not address your letter to "John Barrow, Jr." but to "Mr. John Barrow, Jr."

Always be sure to write the proper title before a man's name, as it is highly uncomplimentary to address him without it. But do *not* use both title and degree at the same time. For example, a doctor is addressed *either* "Dr. Thomas M. Benton" *or* "Thomas M. Benton, M.D." The title is usually abbreviated; but in very formal social communications, such as engraved invitations and announcements, it is often spelled out (Doctor Thomas M. Benton).

When addressing a letter or gift to a small boy, up to the age of 12, use the form "Master Robert Whitney." He is just "Robert Whitney" from 13 to 18—then he is "Mr. Robert Whitney."

A girl is "Miss" right from the cradle, and is so addressed until she becomes "Mrs." One does not use a period after "Miss" as it is not an abbreviation.

A letter to a servant was formerly addressed (very rudely, I think!) by name alone—as, for example, "Bertha Miller" or "Carl Lindstrom." But today most people prefer to address servants more graciously as "Miss Bertha Miller," "Mr. Carl Lindstrom."

Two or more men are usually addressed as "Messrs.," which is an abbreviation of "Messieurs" and means "Misters." Thus unmarried brothers living at the same address and invited to the same function, or perhaps thanked jointly for a gift sent by both of them, might be addressed as "Messrs. John and Stephen Howell."

A father and son, however, should not be lumped together as "Messrs." in social correspondence. They should be addressed individually, with separate invitations or notes of thanks sent to each. Or if they are addressed jointly, it should be as follows—with the name of the father at the top:

Mr. Courtney Howell
Mr. Stephen Howell
10 Hilltop Drive
Ellsworth, Maine

Sisters living together may be addressed individually or jointly, depending upon the occasion and the circumstances. For example, when sisters are invited to an important dinner or reception, *separate* invitations are more desirable for they imply a greater personal compliment to each. But it would be silly to send two identical announcements of a birth or marriage . . . or even two similar notes of thanks for a joint gift, or for hospitality received . . . to sisters living at the same address. One announcement, one letter of thanks, to both is the usual procedure. The envelope may be addressed simply to "Misses Mary and Joan Howell." Or, if you prefer, the full name of each may be written out—one below the other on the envelope, with the name of the older sister at the top.

Holiday greetings, such as Easter or Christmas cards, may be sent to "Mr. and Mrs. Frank North and family." But the phrase "and family" should never be used when addressing invitations . . . for it's no compliment to be tacked on unceremoniously, like an afterthought! Invitations should be addressed specifically to all members of a family who are invited. That doesn't necessarily mean *separate* invitations for every member of the family. Today even formal invitations may be addressed to "Mr. and Mrs. Frank North," with "Miss Barabara North" written below the names of her parents. If the Norths have two daughters, the names of both may be added. Or *two* invitations may be sent: one to "Mr. and Mrs. Frank North"—another to "Misses Barbara and Sandra North." If there is also a small son in the family, either a separate invitation is sent to him or the words "Master Robert North" are written below the other names on the envelope.

The name of the city should not be abbreviated in addressing the envelope. Do not write "Frisco" for "San Francisco" or "Philly" for Philadelphia"—however familiar the abbreviated form may be in its own locality. "L.A." may be dear to the hearts of those who live in Los Angeles and fondly refer to their city in that fashion, but it's a nuisance to the postal authorities who may have to stop and figure out what the addresser means.

However the name of a *state* may be abbreviated, especially if it is a long name like "Massachusetts" or "Pennsylvania," or if the abbreviation is well-known and familiar like "N.Y." or "N.J." Following are the standard abbreviations:

Alabama (Ala.)

Alaska (Alas.)

Arizona (Ariz.)

Arkansas (Ark.)

California (Cal.)

Colorado (Colo.)

Connecticut (Conn.)

Delaware (Del.)

District of Columbia (D.C.)

Florida (Fla.)

Georgia (Ga.)

Idaho (Ida.)

Illinois (Ill.)

Indiana (Ind.)

Iowa (Ia.)

Kansas (Kan.)

Kentucky (Ky.)

Louisiana (La.)

Maine (Me.)

Maryland (Md.)

Massachusetts (Mass.)

Michigan (Mich.)

Minnesota (Minn.)

Mississippi (Miss.)

Missouri (Mo.)

Montana (Mont.)

Nebraska (Neb.)

Nevada (Nev.)

New Hampshire (N.H.)

New Jersey (N.J.)

New Mexico (N. Mex.)

New York (N.Y.)

North Carolina (N.C.)

North Dakota (N.D.)

Ohio (O.)

Oklahoma (Okla.)

Oregon (Ore. or Oreg.)

Pennsylvania (Pa.)

Rhode Island (R.I.)

South Carolina (S.C.)

South Dakota (S.D.)

Tennessee (Tenn.)

Texas (Tex.)

Utah (Ut.)

Vermont (Vt.)

Virginia (Va.)

Washington (Wash.)

West Virginia (W. Va.)

Wisconsin (Wis.)

Wyoming (Wyo.)

Canal Zone (C.Z.)

Philippine Islands (P.I.)

Puerto Rico (P.R.)

Territory of Hawaii (T.H.)

Virgin Islands (V.I.)

If you are not using stationery with your name and address already printed or engraved on the envelope, be sure to include this important information. It makes it possible for your letter to be returned to you if for some reason it cannot be delivered. Give your *complete* name and address; and though the writing may be small, it should be legible. Postal authorities like to see the sender's name and address on the face of the envelope, in the upper left corner. But in social correspondence one generally puts the return address on the back of the envelope.

The stamp is placed in the upper right corner of the envelope. There should be a narrow edge of envelope showing at the top and to the right of the stamp. Take an extra second or two to apply it properly, for your letter will make a better impression on arrival if it is in a neatly stamped, neatly addressed envelope.

If there is any special instruction you want to add, such as "Personal" or "Please Forward," put it in the lower left corner of the envelope. But don't write any messages on the envelope. Save that afterthought for your next letter; or if it is too urgent to put off, open up the envelope, take out your letter, and add what you forgot to say. An envelope with a message scribbled on it is in bad taste and does not represent you to best advantage.

Book II

Your Social Correspondence

I

The General Rules of
Social Correspondence

A large part of everyone's correspondence is made up of what might be called the "letters of etiquette." These are the little notes of congratulation and condolence . . . the thank-you's . . . the bread-and-butter letters . . . the invitations and announcements . . . the acceptances and regrets.

It is with these so-called "duty" letters—these many and varied communications of social life—that most people are concerned. For here *correct form* counts more than it does in any other kind of correspondence. Here problems frequently present themselves; it's possible to make glaring errors; and one is likely to be judged more sternly than by ordinary correspondence.

So naturally, it's in writing these "letters of etiquette" that people want most to feel sure of themselves, to know what forms are acceptable according to the best current standards. A friendly letter may be gay and lighthearted as the writer's own personality, as original and different as one pleases. A business letter may be keyed to the special problem at hand, may go so far as to ignore form and precedent entirely to secure the results desired. But a social communication *must be correct*. Whether it's a brief note inviting friends to dinner, or an engraved invitation to an elaborate wedding reception, it must conform to the general rules.

This is simpler than may appear on the surface. Actually, there need never be any problem concerning social correspondence; for the forms are more or less fixed, and are easy to follow. Though these forms may be varied within the limits of good taste, and according to your own particular needs or preferences, it's better to follow them closely than try to be different just for the sake of being different. So confine your originality and unusual ideas to intimate, informal letters to friends. But in social correspondence, be guided by the fixed forms in general use today . . . and by the few simple, basic rules that follow.

ALL SOCIAL CORRESPONDENCE
HAS A SPECIFIC PURPOSE

The first thing to bear in mind is that all social communications are for a definite, specific purpose. The important thing is to keep that purpose in mind . . . to let nothing else obtrude . . . to convey your message graciously and to the point.

In a friendly letter, of course, you can ramble to your heart's content; the more ground you cover, the more interesting your letter is likely to be! But in a social communication, written for a specific purpose, stay with the subject and don't permit yourself to wander from it.

For example, if it's a letter of thanks, don't write about Aunt Tilly's tulips.

If it's a letter of condolence, don't write even briefly about some unrelated subject.

If it's an invitation, give only the essential facts: the time, the place, the occasion.

Many people make the mistake of combining business and social matters in one letter. That's something you should never do, however much you may be tempted to save time and trouble. *Always keep the specific purpose of the letter in mind, and stay with it.* If you are writing to thank your hostess for a wonderful week end at her country house, don't make that the opportunity to inquire about the Child Aid Society she has organized, to send a check, and to inquire how else you can help. Your note of thanks should be a simple, gracious note of thanks—that and nothing more. Your check and your inquiries about the Child Aid Society should be sent as a separate communication.

NEVER INJECT A BUSINESS MATTER
INTO A SOCIAL NOTE—LIKE THIS:

Dear Mrs. Compton:

Thanks for a perfect week end! I enjoyed every minute of it.

By the way, I'd like to inquire about the Child Aid Society in which you are so interested. Can you use any old clothes or toys for the children? I'm enclosing a check for $10.00 to help in the work you are doing.

Again, many thanks for your hospitality!

Sincerely yours,
Martha Winters

ALWAYS SEND TWO SEPARATE
COMMUNICATIONS—LIKE THIS:

Dear Mrs. Compton:

I want to thank you for the wonderful week end at Fair Acres. It was just about the most delightful week end I've ever had.

I particularly enjoyed the beach picnic on Saturday. I must say you're a *perfect* hostess to have planned so many pleasant things for your guests!

Thanks again for a week end I'll long remember!

Sincerely yours,
Martha Winters

Dear Mrs. Compton:

I'm very much interested in the Child Aid Society you organized, and would like to know more about it.

Is there any way I can help in the work you are doing? Are you interested in old clothes or toys for the children? I'm sure I can round up a lot of useful things among my friends, if you want them.

In the meantime, I'm enclosing a check for $10.00—
my donation to the fund.

Sincerely yours,
Martha Winters

THE DIFFERENCE BETWEEN
FORMAL AND INFORMAL CORRESPONDENCE

All social correspondence falls into two general classifications:
formal and *informal*.

Informal communications are simply handwritten notes, in
the *first* person . . . like any little note you might write to an
acquaintance or friend. They include the many brief notes of
congratulation, appreciation, condolence and so forth that we
are all called upon to write. They also include notes of invitation,
acceptance and regret for simple, informal social affairs like
bridge parties, small dinners and luncheons.

A formal invitation implies a large or elaborate social function
. . . like a church wedding, a ceremonious dinner, an important
reception or dance. Formal invitations are usually, but not
necessarily, engraved. They are not written in the first person
("I would like you to come to dinner next Wednesday . . .)
but in the *third* person ("Mr. and Mrs. Frank B. Hawes cordially
invite you to dinner . . .). They are not written like ordinary
letters, but are arranged in a decorative, irregularly indented
form on the page.

EXAMPLE OF INFORMAL SOCIAL NOTE

Dear Mrs. Harris:

Will you come to luncheon on Wednesday, April
twenty-seventh at one o'clock? My niece, Doris Fernell,
is visiting us, and you have so often mentioned you
would like to meet her.

I do hope you will be able to come!

Cordially yours,
Elizabeth K. Benton

EXAMPLE OF FORMAL SOCIAL
COMMUNICATION

Dr. and Mrs. Thomas Matthew Benton
request the pleasure of your company
at a dinner dance for their niece
Miss Doris Fernell
Wednesday, the fourth of May
at eight o'clock
Hotel Pierre

Naturally the type of invitation you send out depends entirely on the type of affair. You wouldn't send formal engraved invitations for a simple little dinner party attended by just a few friends. Nor would you send informal handwritten notes to a long list of people invited to an elaborate church or hotel wedding. Good taste requires that the invitation *suit the occasion.*

In the past it was permissible to use visiting cards for invitations, when one didn't wish to be formal or informal but somewhere midway between the two. The procedure was to write the occasion and the date in the lower left corner of the card, as follows:

Dinner at eight
May the fifth

The card was then slipped into an envelope and mailed, without further comment. Though one still occasionally sees this type of invitation, it is no longer generally used; and is, in fact, poor taste and should be avoided.

WHAT YOU SHOULD KNOW ABOUT INFORMAL CORRESPONDENCE

1. Don't be fooled by the word "informal." The stationery you used for your notes of invitation, acceptance, regret— for your messages of condolence or congratulation—should

be *important-looking*. Don't use tinted or decorated note paper; that's for your intimate, personal correspondence only. Don't use business or club stationery; that's definitely bad taste. Use only good quality plain white note paper of standard size. Double sheets are more impressive than single sheets for social use; and it's considered better form to get all the message on one page than to carry it over.

2. Informal social notes are usually brief, and should be hand-written. Some people prefer to type all their correspondence, including social notes; and although it's not actually incorrect to do so, it's more *gracious* to write a note of sympathy or thanks by hand. Invitations, of course, should not be typed; a handwritten invitation is much more personal and friendly.

3. Make it a point never to put off writing your necessary social correspondence. A message of sympathy or appreciation, long delayed, loses much of its effectiveness. So attend to your little "duty" notes promptly! *Don't put off till tomorrow what you can write today.*

4. Be sure that any note of invitation you send out is explicit and *complete*. Don't leave anything to the imagination. Give the occasion, the place, the date, the time. For example don't say "I'd like you and Tom to come to dinner next Wednesday." Say "I'd like you and Tom to come to dinner on Wednesday, June tenth."

5. Evening invitations, whether formal or informal, must include both husband and wife—unless, of course, it's a "stag." An informal invitation is addressed to the wife alone, for herself and her husband. The envelope is addressed to "Mrs. Thomas M. Benton"—but the invitation makes specific mention of the husband. For example:

Dear Betty:

We are planning a little dinner to celebrate our tenth anniversary, and of course we want you and Tom to come. It's next Friday, June eighth, at seven o'clock.

I do hope you can make it, as Jim and I are looking forward with great pleasure to seeing you both.

Affectionately yours,
Rosalind

6. An informal note of invitation like the one above is answered the same way—by means of a brief, handwritten note. It's written by the wife, for her husband and herself; and though the envelope is addressed to the hostess alone, the names of *both* host and hostess should be mentioned in the acknowledgment. For example:

Dear Rosalind:

Tom and I are delighted to accept your invitation to dinner on Friday, June eighth, at seven o'clock. Thanks for asking us.

We are greatly complimented that you and Jim should have asked us to share in such a very *special* celebration as your tenth anniversary!

Cordially yours,
Betty

7. Bear in mind that an invitation is a compliment and deserves a prompt and gracious reply. Always try to answer an informal note of invitation within twenty-four hours if you can—but certainly within three days at the most. Your hostess may want to make other arrangements if you can not accept. Always answer by note if you are invited by note. There are times, of course, when it may be necessary to telephone your acceptance or regret. But a note in your own handwriting is more courteous . . . and therefore more desirable.

8. Your response to an invitation should be a *definite* acceptance or regret. Don't keep your hostess in doubt with such vague comments as:

"I hope I can come."
"I'll try my best to come."
"I'll come if I'm in town."
"I'll come if the baby is well."

State definitely that you are coming or that you are *not* coming, so your hostess can make her plans accordingly. She may want to invite someone else if you can't come.

9. When you write a note accepting an invitation, be sure to express pleasure at having been invited. It's the gracious thing to do. If you cannot accept the invitation, express your disappointment and regret . . . and give the reason for not accepting. Don't just say, "I'm sorry I can't come to your luncheon next Tuesday" . . . but "I'm sorry I can't come to your luncheon next Tuesday because that's the day Bob gets home from school." Make your note cordial and appreciative, but *stay with the subject*: discuss the matter of the luncheon invitation only. Don't be tempted to write about the fine marks your son got at school, or the way you had his room redecorated as a surprise.

10. In accepting an invitation, always repeat essential data such as the day of the week, the date, the hour and so forth. For example, don't just write "I'll be delighted to attend your luncheon . . ." but "I'll be delighted to attend your luncheon on Thursday, May tenth, at one o'clock." This enables the hostess to correct any mistake in date or time that either you or she may have made.

WHAT YOU SHOULD KNOW ABOUT
FORMAL CORRESPONDENCE

1. Formal correspondence may seem difficult and forbidding to the uninitiated; but actually it should present no real problems. For its very phraseology is standard and fixed, and entails less composition than the simplest little informal note. As a rule, formal invitations and announcements—issued only for elaborate and important affairs—are *engraved* on

double sheets of fine quality white paper, in keeping with the dignity of the occasion. They may also be *handwritten*, in which case the wording, spacing and arrangement should follow the engraved forms exactly. Formal communications should *not* be printed; they should either be engraved in the traditional way, or written carefully by hand.

2. The style of lettering used in an engraved invitation is entirely a matter of personal choice. Script, gothic and shaded roman are the most popular choices; but this and other details of engraved forms are best decided in conjunction with your stationer or engraver. Either *plain* or *paneled* double sheets may be used; and though a family crest or coat of arms may be embossed without color at the top of the sheet, remember that here—as in *all* correspondence—simplicity is the keynote of good taste. The engraved form is decorative enough in itself without the use of monograms or other personal devices.

3. There are two distinct types of formal invitation. Both are correct, and either may be used . . . depending upon your own personal preference. The first is engraved *in full*, with the generalized phrase "request the pleasure of your company" instead of the specific name of the guest. Here is a typical example of such an invitation:

Dr. and Mrs. Thomas Matthew Benton
request the pleasure of your company
on the Twenty-fifth Anniversary of their marriage
on Thursday, the tenth of June
from four until seven o'clock
The Park Lane
New York

The second has a *blank space* in which the name of the individual guest is written by hand. This fill-in type of invitation is somewhat more personal, and therefore many people prefer it:

Dr. and Mrs. Thomas Matthew Benton
request the pleasure of

Mr. and Mrs. Frank North's

company at a dance
on Friday, the twelfth of October
at ten o'clock
The Sherry-Netherland

4. No abbreviations, no nicknames, no informal phraseology
   of any kind are used in an engraved communication. Names
   should be spelled out in full, without the use of initials. The
   date, the time, even the year when it is given, are all spelled
   out instead of being written numerically. House numbers
   should be spelled out when short, but may be written
   numerically when long. Thus you would use "Ten Park
   Avenue" but "428 Ocean Drive." Telephone numbers are
   never used on engraved invitations.

5. The phrase "request the *honor of your presence*" is used for
   wedding invitations, and especially church weddings. "Request the *pleasure of your company*" is used for dinners,
   dances and similar functions. "Honour" and "favour" are
   British forms of spelling to which many still cling; but we
   prefer the American style of spelling, without the *u*, and
   recommend its use.

6. Formal invitations to dinners, dances, luncheons should be
   sent out three weeks in advance. This gives the hostess time
   to fill in, in case of regrets. Wedding invitations are generally
   mailed a month in advance. *Announcements* are sent out the
   day of the event or after it, not before.

7. A formal invitation should always include husband and
   wife; neither should be invited without the other unless it's
   a stag, or an afternoon function for ladies only (such as a
   luncheon or tea). If a daughter is included in the invitation,
   her name is written on the envelope below that of her
   parents. If two or more daughters are included, their names
   may either appear on the envelope below their parents'

names; or they may be addressed separately—with individual invitations to each, or one invitation addressed jointly to "The Misses Howell" or "Misses Mary and Joan Howell." A young son may be included by adding his name to the envelope; but an adult male member of a family is invited by separate invitation. Brothers may be invited as "Messrs. John and Stephen Howell."

8. Surely it should not be necessary to have to ask for a reply to an invitation! But in these hurried and careless times, it is often advisable to do so. If a reply is requested, one of the following forms should be used. Its proper position is in the lower left corner of the invitation, engraved in a somewhat smaller-size lettering than the rest of the message—or written in by hand if it is a handwritten communication:

> Please reply
> An answer is requested
> The favor of a reply is requested
> Please address reply to (address)
> Please send response to (address)
> Kindly reply to (address)

One of the most commonly used forms is "R.s.v.p." This is the abbreviation for *"Réspondez s'il vous plaît"* which is French for "Reply if you please." The abbreviation frequently appears in capitals (R.S.V.P.), but to be strictly correct only the first letter should be a capital and the other letters should be small (R.s.v.p.). While this form of request for a reply is very popular and widely used, our own preference is for a simple English phrase like "Please reply."

9. The acceptance or regret of a formal invitation should be in *your own handwriting.* Don't use a printed form, to be filled in as the occasion requires. Such ready-made response to an invitation is in poor taste. Nor do we recommend the practice of sending a visiting card with "Accepts" or "Regrets" written in the corner—once good form, but now looked upon as a rudeness. Your reply should be written out carefully, in exactly the same phraseology as the invitation

. . . and in the same irregularly indented form. It should be written on the first page of a double sheet of good quality plain white note paper, approximating as closely as possible the appearance of the invitation. Here, for example, is how the invitation of Dr. and Mrs. Benton on page 88 should be acknowledged.

> Mr. and Mrs. Frank North
> accept with pleasure
> Dr. and Mrs. Thomas M. Benton's
> invitation to a dance
> on Friday, the twelfth of October
> at ten o'clock
> The Sherry-Netherland

This would be in your own handwriting, of course—but placed and arranged as above, following the form of the engraved invitation. And no matter how well you know your hostess, or how eagerly you would prefer writing a cordial, friendly little note in reply . . . resist the temptation! For good social usage requires that a formal communication always be answered *in kind*.

10. Notice that the acknowledgment above is from both Mr. and Mrs. North—not Mrs. North alone. And notice also that the acknowledgment is made to *both* Dr. and Mrs. Benton. However, the envelope in which the acknowledgment is mailed should be addressed to Mrs. Benton only. When an invitation includes another member of the family, the acknowledgment should also include that person's name. For example, if the Norths' daughter, Sandra, was also invited to the Bentons' dance, the acknowledgment would read:

> Mr. and Mrs. Frank North
> Miss Sandra North
> accept with pleasure
> and so forth

11. If a husband and wife are invited to a formal dinner or reception, and the husband is unable to attend, the wife should send regrets for both. The reason for the regret is not always given in a formal acknowledgment; but it is more courteous to do so. For example, if Mr. North is out of town, Mrs. North might write as follows to Mrs. Benton . . . who could then invite her alone, or not, as she sees fit:

> Owing to Mr. North's
> absence from town on business
> Mrs. Frank North
> regrets she is unable to accept
> Dr. and Mrs. Thomas M. Benton's
> kind invitation
> for Friday, the twelfth of October

12. Occasionally an invitation must be recalled due to illness, a death in the family, or perhaps a broken engagement. Such recalls must go out as quickly as possible; and as there is no time to have them engraved, they should be carefully handwritten in formal phraseology—but in this case, not necessarily formal spacing. The reason for the recall of the invitation may or may not be given, at the discretion of the persons most involved; but of course it's always more courteous to make an explanation. For example:

> Dr. and Mrs. Thomas Matthew
> Benton regret that, owing to the
> sudden illness of their son, they
> are obliged to recall their invitations for Friday, the twelfth of
> October.

2

Dinner Invitations and Acknowledgments

Engraved third-person invitations are a last lingering reminder of the extreme formality that once existed in social life. Comparatively few of us have occasion to issue such invitations today, except for certain special functions like weddings. In fact, there is considerably less formality in social life today than ever before in the past. Invitations are now frequently made by telephone, and even more casually when friends chance to meet. But as long as there are still occasions that call for formal announcements or invitations—and still the need to reply to such communications properly—you should be familiar with the forms that good usage has established and tradition preserved.

One occasion that still calls for a strictly formal invitation is the elaborate, ceremonious dinner. This may be a dinner to honor a famous or special guest, to introduce a debutante daughter to society, or perhaps to celebrate a wedding anniversary. If the dinner is given at a club or hotel, the invitations are usually engraved. If given at home, the invitations may still be engraved; but frequently they are written by hand, especially when the dinner is a small one. But bear in mind that when formal invitations are written by hand, they do not deviate from the traditional form: they follow the wording and spacing of the engraved form exactly.

Now obviously, the type of invitation you send out does not determine the kind of dinner party you give. It's the other way around: the *type of dinner* determines the invitation. If you are planning a simple little dinner for a few friends—and you habitually call those friends on the telephone and say, "How about coming for dinner next Thursday"—that's the way to keep on doing it! But if you are planning a formal dinner, you must plan on formal invitations as well. Such invitations must be mailed two or three weeks in advance; and if you have them engraved, that takes another week or two—so you can see you need to make your plans well ahead of time. And be very sure you give the correct information to the engraver, for mistakes in spelling, in date, place, hour, etc. cannot be corrected once the form is run off.

ENGRAVED INVITATION

TO A FORMAL DINNER

Dr. and Mrs. Thomas Matthew Benton

request the pleasure of your company

at dinner

on Thursday, September the twentieth

at eight o'clock

250 Park Avenue

ENGRAVED FILL-IN TYPE

OF DINNER INVITATION

Dr. and Mrs. Thomas Matthew Benton

request the pleasure of

Mr. and Mrs. Roger B. Clark's

company at dinner

on Thursday, September the twentieth

at eight o'clock

250 Park Avenue

HANDWRITTEN INVITATION
TO A FORMAL DINNER

Dr. and Mrs. Thomas Matthew Benton
request the pleasure of
Mr. and Mrs. Robert B. Clark's
company at dinner
on Thursday, September the twentieth
at eight o'clock.

Handwritten invitations, as a rule, do not include the address
. . . as most note paper used for social correspondence already
has the address at the top. But cards or note paper to be engraved
do *not* have the address at the top, and it must therefore be
included in the body of the invitation.

Don't use "Mr. & Mrs." in social correspondence. Make it a
point to spell out the word "and" between "Mr. and Mrs." in all
social correspondence. The symbol & is for business correspondence only.

ALWAYS RESPOND PROMPTLY
TO A DINNER INVITATION

A dinner invitation is one of the highest forms of social courtesy. It's a compliment to you and should be treated as such,
being acknowledged promptly and with a definite acceptance
or regret.

A formal invitation should be acknowledged within twenty-
four hours, if possible. That gives the hostess time to make other
arrangements if you send regrets. Don't reply with an informal
note, as that suggests you are unfamiliar with good social usage.
Follow the exact wording of the invitation, writing on the first
page of your note paper only, and centering the message at-
tractively so that it not only *reads* but *looks* formal. Here, for
example, is the way an acceptance of the invitation above should
look:

30 Sutton Place

*Mr. and Mrs. Roger B. Clark
accept with pleasure
Dr. and Mrs. Thomas M. Benton's
kind invitation for dinner
on Thursday, September twentieth
at eight o'clock*

There is a growing tendency nowadays to write formal acknowledgments without indented margins, following only the wording and not the arrangement of the invitation. There's no real objection to writing your acknowledgment this way, if you find the style more to your taste and liking. But the very best social usage still calls for decorative spacing; and though the following *may* be used, the form shown above is still preferred:

Mr. and Mrs. Roger B. Clark accept
with pleasure Dr. and Mrs. Thomas
M. Benton's kind invitation for
dinner on Thursday, September the
twentieth, at eight o'clock

If you cannot accept a dinner invitation, it's always courteous to give the reason why in your response. Formerly an acknowledgment was all that was required—no explanation. But that is now looked upon as rude and ungracious according to today's standards. The following are typical "regrets" to a formal dinner invitation—written by hand, of course, on your best white note paper:

> Mr. and Mrs. Robert B. Clark
> regret that a previous engagement
> prevents their accepting
> Dr. and Mrs. Thomas M. Benton's
> kind invitation for dinner
> on Thursday, September the twentieth

> Mr. and Mrs. Robert B. Clark
> regret exceedingly that they
> are unable to accept
> Dr. and Mrs. Thomas M. Benton's
> kind invitation for dinner
> on Thursday, September the twentieth
> owing to illness in the family

An acceptance always requires the repetition of both the date and the hour to prevent the possibility of a misunderstanding. But a regret requires the repetition of the date only.

DINNER IN HONOR OF A SPECIAL GUEST OR GUESTS

Invitation

> Dr. and Mrs. Thomas Matthew Benton
> request the pleasure of
> Mr. and Mrs. Roger B. Clark's
> company at dinner
> on Thursday, September the twentieth
> at eight o'clock
> to meet Mr. John T. Alden

> 250 Park Avenue

Acceptance

Mr. and Mrs. Roger B. Clark
accept with pleasure
Dr. and Mrs. Thomas M. Benton's
kind invitation for dinner
on Thursday, September the twentieth
at eight o'clock
to meet Mr. John T. Alden

Regret

Mr. and Mrs. Roger B. Clark
regret that a previous engagement
prevents their accepting
Dr. and Mrs. Thomas M. Benton's
kind invitation for dinner
on Thursday, September the twentieth
to meet Mr. John T. Alden

Frequently, when the guests of honor are persons of particular importance or prominence, their names are placed at the top of the invitation. The words *"To meet"* may be used as shown; or the entire phrase, *"To meet General and Mrs. Wayne R. Pratt"* may be used as the first line.

Invitation

To meet
General and Mrs. Wayne R. Pratt
Dr. and Mrs. Thomas Matthew Benton
request the pleasure of your company
at dinner
at the Ritz-Carlton
on Thursday, September the twentieth
at half past seven o'clock

Acceptance

To meet
General and Mrs. Wayne R. Pratt
Mr. and Mrs. Roger B. Clark
accept with pleasure
Dr. and Mrs. Thomas M. Benton's
kind invitation for dinner
at the Ritz-Carlton
on Thursday, September the twentieth
at half past seven o'clock

Regret

Mr. and Mrs. Roger B. Clark
regret that owing to illness
they are unable to accept
Dr. and Mrs. Thomas M. Benton's
kind invitation for dinner
on Thursday, September the twentieth
to meet General and Mrs. Wayne R. Pratt

DINNER TO CELEBRATE
A SPECIAL OCCASION

When a dinner is given to celebrate some special occasion—like a wedding anniversary or a daughter's debut—that purpose is usually stated in the invitation.

Invitation

Mr. and Mrs. Paul Preston
request the pleasure of your company
at dinner
on the Twenty-fifth Anniversary of their marriage
Wednesday, the fifth of June
at seven o'clock
20 Lake Drive

Acceptance

Mr. and Mrs. Robert G. Scully
accept with pleasure
Mr. and Mrs. Paul Preston's
invitation for dinner
on the Twenty-fifth Anniversary of their marriage
Wednesday, the fifth of June
at seven o'clock

Regret

Mr. and Mrs. Robert G. Scully
regret exceedingly that they
are unable to accept
Mr. and Mrs. Paul Preston's
invitation for dinner
on the Twenty-fifth Anniversary of their marriage
Wednesday, the fifth of June
owing to serious illness in the family

DINNER FOR A DEBUTANTE DAUGHTER

Invitation

Dr. and Mrs. Thomas Matthew Benton
request the pleasure of your company
at dinner
in honor of their daughter
Miss Anita Benton
on Saturday, the fifteenth of November
at eight o'clock
The Waldorf-Astoria

Please send reply to
250 Park Avenue

Acceptance

Mr. and Mr. Carl Whitney
accept with pleasure
Dr. and Mrs. Thomas M. Benton's
invitation for dinner
in honor of their daughter
Miss Anita Benton
on Saturday, the fifteenth of November
at eight o'clock
The Waldorf-Astoria

Regret

Mr. and Mrs. Carl Whitney
regret that they are unable to accept
Dr. and Mrs. Thomas M. Benton's
invitation for dinner
in honor of their daughter
Miss Anita Benton
on Saturday, the fifteenth of November
as they will be abroad at that time

DINNER FOLLOWED BY
CONCERT OR OPERA

Formal dinner invitations sometimes include an invitation to
a play, opera, concert or lecture later on in the evening. As only
a comparatively few guests can be invited to share such an evening, the invitations are almost always written by hand. Nowadays, of course, the trend is toward much simpler and less pre-
tentious entertaining of small groups than this. Most of us would
be more inclined to have an informal little dinner, either at home
or at a restaurant or hotel, before going on to the theater or
opera; and we would write simple little notes to our guests, or

even invite them by telephone. But for those who still cling to the old social traditions, and who like to entertain even small groups of friends occasionally with old-fashioned formality, we include these examples of correct invitations for "dinner and afterward."

Invitation

Dr. and Mrs. Thomas Matthew Benton
request the pleasure of
Mr. and Mrs. Peter Kenway's
company at dinner
on Wednesday, April the eighteenth
at seven o'clock
and at the Leonard Bernstein recital afterward

or

Dr. and Mrs. Thomas Matthew Benton
request the pleasure of
Mr. and Mrs. Peter Kenway's
company for dinner and the opera
on Wednesday, April the eighteenth
at seven o'clock

Please reply to
250 Park Avenue

Acceptance

Mr. and Mrs. Peter Kenway
accept with pleasure
Dr. and Mrs. Thomas M. Benton's
kind invitation for dinner
on Wednesday, April the eighteenth
at seven o'clock
and for the Leonard Bernstein recital afterward

Mr. and Mrs. Peter Kenway
accept with pleasure
Dr. and Mrs. Thomas M. Benton's
invitation for dinner and the opera
on Wednesday, April the eighteenth
at seven o'clock

Regret

Mr. and Mrs. Peter Kenway
regret exceedingly that a previous engagement
prevents their accepting
Dr. and Mrs. Thomas M. Benton's
kind invitation for dinner
on Wednesday, April the eighteenth
and for the Leonard Bernstein recital afterward

Mr. and Mrs. Peter Kenway
regret that they are
unable to accept
Dr. and Mrs. Thomas M. Benton's
invitation for dinner and the opera
on Wednesday, April the eighteenth
owing to a previous engagement

DINNER BY SONS AND DAUGHTERS
IN HONOR OF PARENTS

When a group of children, married and unmarried, give a
formal dinner in honor of their parents' silver or golden wedding
anniversary, an invitation like the following is the most practical.
It is issued in the names of all the sons and daughters, with a
reply requested in the name of one person in the group selected
to handle this part of the arrangements:

In honor of the
Fiftieth Wedding Anniversary of
Mr. and Mrs. James Gray
their sons and daughters
request the pleasure of

Mr. and Mrs. Thomas M. Benton's

company at dinner
on Friday, the sixth of June
at eight o'clock
The Hampshire House

Kindly send reply to
Miss Joyce Gray
Tuxedo Park, New York

A person receiving the invitation above is required to make
formal acknowledgment to all the sons and daughters; but the
envelope is addressed only to "Miss Joyce Gray," as requested.
The acceptance or regret should be carefully written by hand,
on good quality white note paper, and mailed within twenty-
four hours after receipt of the invitation:

Acceptance

Mr. and Mrs. Thomas M. Benton
accept with great pleasure
the invitation of
the sons and daughters of
Mr. and Mrs. James Gray
for dinner
in honor of their parents'
Fiftieth Wedding Anniversary
on Friday, the sixth of June
at eight o'clock
at the Hampshire House

If you prefer to write your acknowledgment without the indented margins, you may do so—as previously mentioned. But remember that to be socially correct, *the wording must follow the wording of the invitation.*

Regret

Mr. and Mrs. Thomas M. Benton
regret extremely that
they are unable to accept
the invitation of
the sons and daughters of
Mr. and Mrs. James Gray
for dinner
in honor of their parents'
Fiftieth Wedding Anniversary
on Friday, the sixth of June
owing to a previous engagement

Those who are especially courteous and social-minded, send congratulations on the day of the dinner; and later write a note to the guests of honor (in this case, the parents)—explaining why they were unable to be present and how sorry they were to have missed it.

HOW TO POSTPONE OR CANCEL
FORMAL DINNER INVITATIONS

It frequently happens that a dinner party must be canceled or postponed, sometimes almost at the very last minute, due to illness or other circumstances. If there is time, the hostess writes a formal note . . . assuming, of course, that this was to have been a formal dinner and engraved invitations were sent out. If there isn't time for a note, the hostess (or someone representing her) should telephone or telegraph all guests at once.

The following examples show how formal dinner invitations are usually recalled or postponed. Because of the nature of the communication, these notes—though in the third person—are not, as a rule, written with indented spacing. It is considered somewhat better taste, in this particular instance, to eliminate the decorative arrangement—and write the notes as follows:

Dr. and Mrs. Thomas Matthew Benton
regret that, owing to the severe illness
of their son, the dinner arranged for
next Friday must be postponed.

Mr. and Mrs. Frank B. Hawes wish to
announce that the dinner planned for
next Tuesday, in honor of their niece,
is temporarily postponed due to illness in the family.

Mr. and Mrs. Paul Preston regret that
damages done to their house by a
recent fire make it necessary to postpone the dinner arranged for April third
until May fifth at the same time.

Mr. and Mrs. Carl Whitney wish to
announce that the dinner planned for
next Saturday has been postponed until
the following Saturday, October the
tenth, owing to the fact that Mr.
Whitney has been unexpectedly called
out of town.

Mr. and Mrs. James Carter, Jr. regret
that they are obliged to recall their
invitations for Thursday, the second
of November, because of the death of
their nephew, Mr. Henry Pierce Lowe.

Owing to injuries sustained in a recent
automobile accident, Mr. and Mrs. Curtis
Henning regret that they must cancel
their dinner planned for Wednesday,
October the eighth.

Mr. and Mrs. Peter Kenway regret that
they are obliged to recall their invitations for next Thursday, due to
unavoidable circumstances.

The last of the above is the least courteous, for it offers no
explanation. Bear in mind that these are *formal* notes, correct
only when engraved invitations have been sent. For canceling
or postponing a simple, informal dinner, you would write a
personal note of explanation, or you would telephone.

HOW TO BREAK A FORMAL
DINNER ENGAGEMENT

Sometimes it's the *guest* and not the hostess who is obliged to
make a last-minute change of plans due to illness or other circumstances. It goes without saying, of course, that a dinner
engagement should never be broken unless there is a very good
reason for it. And if there is such a reason, it calls for *prompt
action*—either by letter or telephone. The hostess must be informed fully and at once of the circumstances which prevent the
guest from being present as planned.

Dear Mrs. Benton:

Mr. Carter has been called to Philadelphia on account of the sudden illness of his sister. We are very
anxious about her, and I am sure you will understand
why it is impossible for either of us to attend your dinner party next Tuesday.

We are both extremely sorry to break our engagement at this late date; and hope you and Dr. Benton will forgive us.

Sincerely yours,

Florence Carter

Dear Mrs. Whitney:

I have just learned that my sister, who lives in Rochester, has been seriously injured in an automobile accident. Mr. Hunt and I are leaving at once to be with her.

I'm sure we cannot be back in time for your dinner on Thursday, and hope you will understand and forgive us under the circumstances.

With many regrets,

Sincerely yours,

Alice T. Hunt

INVITING A FRIEND TO FILL
AN EMPTY PLACE AT DINNER

When a hostess finds herself short one dinner guest, due to the fact that someone was unable to come at the last minute, the usual thing is to call on a friend to fill in the gap. If time is short, she telephones; otherwise she writes a note frankly explaining the situation and asking the friend to fill in as a special favor. It's not an easy letter to write. No one likes to play "second fiddle"—to be invited only because someone else was unable to come. But it's much better to put it on this frank basis than to invite someone only a day or two ahead of time *without* an explanation. That sort of last-minute invitation fools no one, and is much more likely to injure sensitive feelings than a straightforward note like the following:

Dear Frank:

If you have no other plans for this Thursday night, the twelfth, will you join my dinner party? One of my guests has just telephoned that he can't come because of illness.

So you see, Frank, I'm putting it to you very honestly! I need another guest—and Jim and I can think of no one we'd rather have than you. Will you overlook the informality of this rather hurried invitation and make us both very happy by accepting?

Sincerely yours,
Laura Winston

There is usually no time to respond by letter to such an invitation. It's more likely to be acknowledged by telephone. But if there *is* time to write, the letter should be especially friendly and cordial. The invitation should either be accepted graciously . . . or a very good reason for not accepting it should be given.

Dear Laura:

I guess I should be sorry for that chap who is ill . . . but I'm not at all! I'm very glad of the opportunity to enjoy another of your delightful dinners.

So you and Jim can count me in, and thanks for asking me!

Yours sincerely,
Frank Lennon

Dear Laura:

I wish I could accept your invitation for Thursday night! I know I'd enjoy it as I have always enjoyed your charming dinner parties. But unfortunately I am leaving on a business trip tomorrow, and will be far from New York by Thursday.

My very best to you and Jim, and thanks for thinking of me!

Sincerely yours,
Frank Lennon

INFORMAL DINNER INVITATIONS
—AND HOW TO ANSWER THEM

The invitations and acknowledgments we have been discussing up to this point are for elaborately formal and "special occasion" dinners only. But the average person today entertains *informally*, and has far more occasion to write simple little notes of invitation than to send out engraved social forms.

However, though informal notes provide much greater latitude than formal third-person invitations . . . they, too, follow a fairly fixed pattern. They are usually written in two brief paragraphs; and however the words may vary, the message always remains essentially this: "Will you come to dinner on a certain date, at a certain time?"

A note inviting people to dinner is always written by the hostess for her husband and herself. It is addressed to "Mrs." only, not to "Mr. and Mrs."—but the note should include mention of the husband, otherwise it is a discourtesy to him. For example:

> Dear Mrs. Jennings:
>
> Will you and Mr. Jennings have dinner with us on Tuesday, the fifth of May, at seven o'clock?
>
> It's a long time since we have had the pleasure of seeing you, and we do hope you can come.
>
> > Sincerely yours,
> > Elizabeth K. Benton

The person who receives such a note should answer it promptly, and with a *definite* acceptance or regret. It should not be a vague or conditional response, such as: "I'd like to come if I can; it depends on whether or not Paul gets back from Baltimore in time." That leaves the hostess "up a tree," so to speak. The answer should be a specific, "Yes, we'll be delighted to come!"—or "So sorry! We can't come because . . ."

The acceptance of any invitation, of course, should be an implied "Thank you"—graciously and unmistakably expressed. The words may say it any way you like; but the tone or spirit of your note must clearly convey the impression that you are pleased to have been invited . . . that you are glad to accept . . . and that you are looking forward to the occasion with eagerness.

Dear Mrs. Benton:

Mr. Jennings and I will be delighted to dine with you on Tuesday, the fifth of May, at seven o'clock. How very nice of you to ask us!

We are both looking forward with great pleasure to seeing you and Dr. Benton again.

Very sincerely yours,
Susan Jennings

If it's necessary to decline a dinner invitation, the note should be very carefully written to avoid giving offense. The reason for not being able to accept should be given; and it's always courteous to say how sorry you are, and to suggest how very hard you tried to overcome the obstacle that stood in the way. The tone of the letter should be one of sincere regret:

Dear Mrs. Benton:

I've been putting off this note until the last possible moment, hoping and hoping Mr. Jennings would get back from Baltimore in time for your dinner party. But now I must regretfully write that he'll still be out of town on Tuesday, the fifth; and we therefore cannot accept your kind invitation for dinner on that day.

It was sweet of you to ask us; and I know Mr. Jennings will be as sorry as I am to miss an evening with you and Dr. Benton. We know how delightful such evenings at your house usually are!

Sincerely yours,
Susan Jennings

The easiest way out of an invitation you do not care to accept is to plead a previous engagement. That is always an acceptable excuse. But be sure your note, however brief, sounds as though you are really sorry:

Dear Mrs. Benton:

I just can't tell you how sorry Mr. Jennings and I are that we cannot dine with you on Tuesday, the fifth of May. Unfortunately we already have an engage ment for that evening.

Thank you for asking us, and we hope you will give us the opportunity to say "yes" some other time.

Sincerely yours,
Susan Jennings

Obviously the above invitations and acknowledgments are not intended for intimate friends. They are the kind of notes you would write to people you know *casually,* not closely . . . people you invite *occasionally,* for purely social reasons, not *frequently* because you love them and enjoy being with them.

But bear in mind that even to an intimate friend, an invitation should be an *invitation*—not a minor detail lost in a long account of local news, family gossip and other idle writing! An invitation seems much more important to the person who receives it when it's sent as a special and separate communication . . . instead of just part of a chatty letter.

Here, for example, is how you might invite a close friend to dinner . . . *correctly,* yet *cordially:*

Dear Ruth:

Tom and I are having some very special friends here for dinner on Thursday, October second. Naturally the party wouldn't be complete without you and Bill!

We hope you can come, as we are planning to show the movies we made in Nassau, and we know you and Bill are thinking of going there this winter.

Dinner is at seven, as usual. We'll be looking for you two charming people at that time, so don't disappoint us!

Affectionately yours,
Betty

Not even close friendship permits of laxity in the matter of response to a dinner invitation. A note like the above should be acknowledged promptly, and in kind. Although many people now prefer the convenience of telephoning a response, it's always better form to *answer by note when invited by note*. This applies to invitations from personal friends as well as those you know less intimately.

Dear Betty:

How could we even *think* of turning down the prospect of another delightful evening with you and Tom? Of course we'll be there on Thursday, October second —promptly at seven!

Bill and I are both excited about seeing those Nassau pictures. We think that's where we're going for our vacation this winter; so it will be wonderful seeing your pictures and getting a "preview" of the island.

Thanks for asking us, Betty. . . . We're certainly looking forward to next Tuesday!

Affectionately yours,
Ruth

There's an old familiar saying: "You never need to explain to a friend." But that doesn't apply to dinner invitations! If you refuse an invitation, you must explain why—even to a friend. Especially to a friend!

Dear Betty:

What a shame! We won't be able to come to your dinner party on Thursday because that's the day we're having the Gilmores *here* for dinner.

You remember I told you about Mr. Gilmore last week. He's one of Bill's most important clients. If it were anyone else, I'd alter my plans—even at the very last moment—rather than miss an evening with you and Tom! But I just can't do that with the Gilmores, **Betty. I'm sure you understand.**

Bill and I would certainly like to see those Nassau pictures, as we think that's where we're going this winter. Will you give us a private showing some time? Just say when and we'll be there!

Have a good time on Tuesday. I certainly wish we could be with you!

Affectionately,
Ruth

INVITING FRIENDS TO
DINNER AND THE THEATER

Notes of invitation are often quite brief, these busy days, and no one thinks anything of it. An invitation for dinner and the theater is frequently just a hurried line or two from one friend to another. But that doesn't necessarily mean the note is curt or abrupt. It's just written fast, as so many things must be now.

Dear Ann:

We have four seats for the opening of the O'Neill play this Friday, the tenth. Will you and John join us here for dinner at seven sharp; and then go on with us later to the play? We'll be looking for you Friday night, so don't disappoint us!

Fondly,
Doris

Acceptance

Dear Doris:

Delighted! We'll be there Friday at seven, and go with you afterward to the theater. How wonderful of you and Frank to ask us!

With affection,
Ann

Regret

Dear Doris:

I think you'd better ask some other couple for Friday. John's in Washington and won't be back for another week. Wait till he hears what a wonderful evening he missed with you and Frank! Thanks for asking us, Doris. I'm certainly sorry we can't say "yes"!

Affectionately yours,   -

Ann

WHEN A DAUGHTER ACTS
AS HOSTESS

In a motherless home, a young daughter is often required to act as hostess for her father. She does not send out dinner invitations in her own name, but always includes mention of her father and makes it clear that she is acting for him, at his request.

Dear Mrs. Everett:

Father wishes me to ask if you and Mr. Everett can dine with us on Monday, March the fifth, at seven o'clock.

We hope you can come, and look forward to seeing you.

Sincerely yours,

Marcia Curtis

The acknowledgment must go to the *daughter*, not the father. The response to any invitation must go to the person who writes it.

Acceptance

Dear Miss Curtis:

Mr. Everett and I are delighted to accept your father's invitation for dinner on Monday, March the fifth, at seven o'clock.

We send our affectionate greetings to both of you!

Sincerely yours,

Janet P. Everett

Regret

Dear Miss Curtis:

I regret that a previous engagement prevents us from accepting your father's kind invitation for dinner on Monday, March the fifth.

Please tell him that Mr. Everett and I thank him for asking us, and we are very sorry indeed that we cannot come.

Sincerely yours,
Janet P. Everett

NOTE TO RECALL AN INFORMAL
DINNER INVITATION

Dear Mrs. Jennings:

I have just learned that my son, who is at school in Massachusetts, was injured in a basketball game. Although the injury is not serious, Dr. Benton and I feel we must go to him at once; and we are leaving tomorrow morning.

Under the circumstances, we must recall our dinner invitations for Tuesday, the fifth of May . . . and plan on a later date for our party.

I'm sure that you and Mr. Jennings will understand our anxiety, and will forgive this last-minute change in plans.

Sincerely yours,
Elizabeth K. Benton

NOTE TO BREAK AN INFORMAL
DINNER ENGAGEMENT

Dear Mrs. Benton:

I'm so very sorry to have to write you this letter! After accepting your kind invitation for dinner on Tuesday, May the fifth, I now find that we cannot be there after all.

Mr. Jennings has just been called to Chicago on business; and although he tried very hard to postpone the trip until after the fifth, he was unable to do so.

We had been looking forward with great pleasure to seeing you and Dr. Benton; and we both feel very badly about this unexpected development. We hope you understand, and that you will not be inconvenienced.

Sincerely yours,
Susan Jennings

NOTE TO AN INTIMATE FRIEND
RECALLING A DINNER INVITATION

Ruth, dear:

The dinner for Thursday, October the second, is off! Anita has the measles—of all things!—and it looks as though I'll have to suspend all plans for entertaining for the time being.

Anita isn't very ill; but she demands a great deal of attention and I'm with her most of the time. Then, too, of course, the measles are contagious—so this is certainly no time to have friends at the house!

I'm sure you and Bill will understand, Ruth—and that you will forgive this last-minute change in plans. I'll write you as soon as the Benton household is back to normal again; and we'll plan another date for dinner.

My love to you both!

Betty

NOTE TO AN INTIMATE FRIEND
BREAKING A DINNER ENGAGEMENT

Dear Betty:

I'm so disappointed, I could *cry!* You know how I've been looking forward to your dinner next Thursday; and now, at almost the last moment, I find we can't make it after all.

As usual, Bill's been called out of town just when it's most inconvenient for us. He tried to postpone the trip for a few days, but couldn't do it. So here I am all alone again, Betty . . . with Bill on his way to Chicago . . . and both of us sorry as can be to break a dinner engagement with you at the last moment. I can't say I'd blame you if you stopped inviting us completely!

But you know it isn't our fault, darling. There's nothing we'd rather do than spend an evening with you and Tom. And we especially hate to miss those Nassau pictures! Will you let us come some evening and see them after Tom gets back?

Affectionately yours,
Ruth

A hostess who receives a note like the above should decide whether or not she wants her friend to come by herself. If she would rather not have an odd woman guest at the table, it's best not to answer the note at all; it doesn't actually require an acknowledgment. But if she wants her friend to come even without her husband, she telephones or writes at once, depending upon how much time remains. If there's no time for further correspondence, she calls and says in effect: "Never mind if Bill's out of town! Come to my dinner party anyway! I'm counting on you. . . ." Otherwise she writes a note somewhat along the lines of the following:

Dear Ruth:

Too bad Bill had to go out of town again so soon! He's practically commuting between New York and Chicago these days, isn't he?

But why don't you come to my dinner anyway, Ruth? I know it won't be nearly as much fun for you without Bill; but I think I can promise you a good time. The Norths and the Prestons will be here, and I know you always enjoy being with them. The Norths practically pass your house on the way home, and I'm sure they'll be glad to drop you off.

So come on, Ruth—and see those Nassau pictures I've been bragging about! Then we'll show them again some evening after Bill gets back, and he can see them too.

Remember—it's Thursday, October the second, at seven o'clock. Tom and I are looking forward to seeing you, so don't disappoint us!

Yours affectionately,
Betty

3

Luncheon and Supper Invitations and Acknowledgments

Luncheons and suppers are, by their very nature, gay and light-hearted—the informal, and often impromptu, gathering of friends for a good time. They represent a less serious type of entertaining than dinners; and are for the most part quite simple and unpretentious in character.

Invitations for such functions are informal, too. More often than not they are just telephoned; or they are given casually, without previous plan, when friends chance to meet. Any written invitations are in the form of friendly little notes. Formal third-person invitations are rarely used for either a luncheon or supper; and then, only when it's a large, elaborate affair planned for some special purpose or to honor some special guest.

For example, a large and ceremonious luncheon is sometimes given, at home or at a hotel, to announce an engagement . . . to celebrate a wedding anniversary . . . to present a debutante daughter . . . or for some similar purpose. Such socially important luncheons warrant the dignity and formality of engraved invitations. They are sent out two or three weeks in advance, and closely follow the phraseology of a dinner invitation:

Dr. and Mrs. Thomas Matthew Benton
request the pleasure of

Mr. and Mrs. Frank North's

company at luncheon
in honor of their daughter
Miss Anita Benton
on Saturday, May the third
at one o'clock
250 Park Avenue
Please respond

The person who receives such an invitation should answer at
once with a definite acceptance or regret, following the same
formal wording as the invitation.

Another type of luncheon for which formal invitations are
sometimes issued is the luncheon preceding an important sport-
ing event such as a tennis match or football game. As only half
a dozen people at the most are ordinarily invited to such a
luncheon, invitations are rarely, if ever, engraved. They are carefully written by hand, following the decorative spacing and
arrangement of engraved formal invitations.

Mr. and Mrs. Robert G. Scully
request the pleasure of your company
at luncheon
Saturday, the eighteenth of August
at one o'clock
at the Pickwick Club
before the tennis finals at Lynn Field

Please send reply to
10 Lake Drive

The above invitation includes the tennis match following
luncheon, the host and hostess assuming responsibility for the

tickets. Therefore an acceptance or regret should be written and mailed at once, so that other disposition can be made of the tickets if you are unable to accept the invitation. (Do not *telephone* your reply to a formal invitation unless you have been out of town and return too late to write . . . in which case you should explain the circumstances to the hostess.)

As a rule, luncheons are not given jointly by a husband and wife, except for special occasions like the above. Most men cannot attend social functions in the middle of the day; and luncheons are therefore generally planned for women alone, and invitations are issued in the name of the hostess alone. The name of the host never appears unless he is to be present at the luncheon and other men are to be invited as guests.

When a luncheon is given for a group of women—even a large, formal luncheon at a club or hotel—the invitations may be in the form of personal notes written by the hostess to her guests. But some women prefer formality even in their invitations, as they feel it gives more social significance to the occasion. Following is the standard form for an elaborate luncheon. It may be engraved for a large number of guests; but should be hand-written if only six or eight guests are invited.

Mrs. Thomas Matthew Benton
requests the pleasure of
your company at luncheon
on Friday, November the seventh
at one o'clock
250 Park Avenue

Please respond

Acceptance

Mrs. Wayne R. Pratt
accepts with pleasure
Mrs. Thomas M. Benton's
invitation for luncheon
on Friday, November the seventh
at one o'clock

Regret

Mrs. Wayne R. Pratt
regrets that a previous engagement
prevents her from accepting
Mrs. Thomas M. Benton's
invitation for luncheon
on Friday, November the seventh

It is not socially correct to write a personal note of explanation when declining a formal invitation. The regret should be as formal as the invitation itself, in the same wording and spacing. However, it is a courteous and friendly gesture to write a personal note to the hostess a week or so following the luncheon, to say how sorry you were to have missed it. This note would not be *instead* of the formal response, but in *addition to it*. It's one of those "letters-that-don't-need-to-be-written" which we discussed in an earlier chapter . . . letters that people do not expect, and are therefore especially delighted to receive.

When a luncheon is given to present a celebrity, a new bride, or an out-of-town guest to a group of friends, that fact should be clearly specified in the invitation. If it's a personal note, as it's very likely to be, it should be brief and to the point:

Dear Mrs. Pratt:

Miss Marta Lang, the portrait painter, is visiting me this week and I am inviting a few friends to meet her. I am giving a luncheon on Thursday, September the third, at one o'clock; and I do hope you can come.

Miss Lang is a most charming and fascinating person, and I know you'll enjoy her company as much as she will enjoy yours. So please write and say you'll be here!

Cordially yours,
Elizabeth K. Benton

If it's a formal invitation instead of a personal note, the phrase "To meet Miss Marta Lang" is used as the *first* or *last* line of the invitation:

To meet Miss Marta Lang
Mrs. Thomas Matthew Benton
requests the pleasure of

Mrs. Wayne L. Pratt's

company at luncheon
on Thursday, September the third
at one o'clock
250 Park Avenue

Please respond

or

Mrs. Thomas Matthew Benton
requests the pleasure of
your company at luncheon
on Thursday, September the third
at one o'clock
to meet Miss Marta Lang

250 Park Avenue

Whether an invitation specifically calls for a response or not, send an acceptance or regret promptly. It's difficult and inconvenient for a hostess not to know how many guests to expect. The reply to a personal note is, of course, a personal note:

Dear Mrs. Benton:

I'm delighted by your invitation to luncheon on Thursday, September the third, at one o'clock—to meet Miss Marta Lang.

I know Miss Lang's work and have long admired it;
and I welcome this opportunity to make her personal
acquaintance. Thank you for asking me!

Very sincerely yours,
Eleanor Pratt

The reply to a formal invitation can be only a formal acceptance or regret. A personal note or a telephone message may accomplish the same purpose, but does not do it properly from a
social standpoint.

Acceptance

Mrs. Wayne R. Pratt
accepts with pleasure
Mrs. Thomas M. Benton's
invitation to luncheon
on Thursday, September the third
at one o'clock
to meet Miss Marta Lang

Regret

Mrs. Wayne R. Pratt
regrets that she is unable to accept
Mrs. Thomas M. Benton's
kind invitation to luncheon
on Thursday, September the third
at one o'clock
to meet Miss Marta Lang
owing to a previous engagement

Sometimes a large and elaborate luncheon is given by two or
more women. The invitations are usually engraved, and the
names of all the women appear on it. For example:

Mrs. Carl Whitney
Mrs. Robert G. Scully
Mrs. Thomas Matthew Benton
request the pleasure of
your company at luncheon
on Wednesday, April the second
at half past one o'clock
The Savoy Plaza

Please reply to
Mrs. Thomas M. Benton
250 Park Avenue

Your reply to the above invitation should list *all* the names of the hostesses, exactly as in the invitation. But the envelope should be addressed only to the person whose name and address are indicated in the lower left corner. If no name and address are given, the envelope should be addressed to *all* the hostesses and sent to the hotel, as it can be assumed that arrangements have been made to receive them there.

INVITATIONS FOR SIMPLE INFORMAL LUNCHEONS

Up to this point we have been discussing formal, ceremonious luncheons . . . elaborate social affairs that are sometimes given by husband and wife jointly, but are for the most part planned *by* women, *for* women . . . and usually for some very special occasion.

But far more familiar to most of us are the gay, informal luncheons that are planned for no other purpose than to enjoy the company of a few congenial, well-chosen friends. For most such luncheons, a telephone call is more likely than not to be the only invitation. But there are many who prefer writing personal notes of invitation, looking upon it as a somewhat more gracious custom.

The typical informal luncheon invitation is a brief note giving the time, the place and usually—but not necessarily—the reason for the luncheon.

> Dear Ruth:
>
> Will you come to luncheon on Friday, May the fifth, at one o'clock?
>
> My niece, Doris Fernell, is visiting us, and I think you will enjoy meeting her. She is a charming, witty girl, and very good company!
>
> Laura Winston and Susan Jennings will be here, and perhaps we can play a little bridge after luncheon. Do say you'll come!
>
> > Affectionately yours,
> > Betty

Acceptance

> Dear Betty:
>
> How very nice to receive your invitation for luncheon on Friday, May the fifth! I'll be there promptly at one.
>
> I'm looking forward to meeting your niece; she sounds fascinating. But most of all, Betty, I'm looking forward to seeing *you!* It's been a long time since I had that pleasure.
>
> > As ever,
> > Ruth

Regret

> Dear Betty:
>
> I can't think of anything I'd enjoy more than coming to your luncheon on Friday, May the fifth, and meeting your charming niece.
>
> But darling, I *can't!* Friday's the day my sister is flying to Paris, and I promised to see her off. I'm due at the airport at one-thirty. She'll be expecting me, and I cannot disappoint her.

But thanks so much for asking me, Betty. I'm certainly sorry to miss your luncheon, and to miss meeting Miss Fernell.

> Fondly,
> Ruth

The response to a luncheon invitation should, of course, be a definite acceptance or regret. But occasionally a hostess, familiar with a friend's plans and eager to have that friend attend her luncheon, writes as follows:

> I know you are planning to be in Chicago on the tenth; but if you can possibly get back in time, will you come to my luncheon in honor of Kay Bolton, the writer?

In that case, the person who receives the invitation may answer in kind, giving neither a definite acceptance nor regret, but promising to come if she can:

> I'll try my best to be back by the tenth, as I'd like very much to come to your luncheon and meet Kay Bolton. But please don't count on it, as I wouldn't like to disappoint you.

If she returns in time—even if it's the very morning of the luncheon—she should telephone and say, in effect: "Well, I made it! I'm home and I'm coming to lunch* today!"

If she does *not* get home in time, she should telephone or write immediately upon her return to say she was looking forward to the luncheon and was very sorry to have missed it.

INVITING SOMEONE YOU
DO NOT KNOW

An ordinary note of invitation to someone you know well is comparatively easy to write. But not all invitations are to intimate friends. Sometimes it's necessary to invite people you do not

---

* The word "luncheon" is used in writing, and especially in invitations. The word "lunch" is more familiarly used in conversation. "Luncheon" has a somewhat more social implication, but it is rarely if ever *spoken*.

know well . . . perhaps do not know at all. Such letters are considerably more difficult to write.

The most important thing to bear in mind when inviting a stranger to luncheon (or to any other social affair) is that you must *explain the reason* for the invitation. Be sure it's a real reason, a *legitimate* reason, otherwise your invitation may seem offensive and in poor taste. It's important also to make your luncheon sound as though it will be interesting and enjoyable. Most people have busy social lives of their own, and do not like to accept invitations from strangers unless they know *why*, and can be reasonably sure they'll enjoy themselves if they accept.

> Dear Mrs. Johnson:
>
> If you have no other plans for Wednesday, April the sixth, will you come to a little informal luncheon here at my home?
>
> My Richard and your Larry have been roommates at Andover for so long that it's about time their mothers got to know each other—don't you think so?
>
> I have asked two friends whom I think you will like; and perhaps we can play some bridge in the afternoon.
>
> Luncheon is at one, and I'll expect you at that time unless I hear from you to the contrary.
>
> > Cordially yours,
> > Elizabeth K. Benton

If you receive a luncheon invitation like the above, and plan to accept it, you may reply or not as you prefer. An acknowledgment is not actually required, as your appearance on the day of the luncheon is expected if you do not send regrets within a day or two. However, a note like the following paves the way for a more friendly and cordial relationship:

> Dear Mrs. Benton:
>
> I'll be delighted to come to your luncheon on Wednesday, April the sixth, at one o'clock.

Larry has often spoken to me of Richard, and has told me how very much he enjoys having him for a roommate. Although I have never met Richard, I feel as though I know him from hearing so much about him.

I assure you it will be a very great pleasure indeed to meet Richard's mother! Thank you so much for asking me.

Sincerely yours,
Mildred Johnson

If you receive an invitation from someone you don't know, and you cannot accept it, be sure that your reply is very carefully and very tactfully worded. For it would be most unkind to give the impression that you do not *want* to accept an invitation so graciously extended.

Dear Mrs. Benton:

I have heard so much about Richard from Larry that I almost feel as though I know him. I would certainly enjoy meeting his mother!

But unfortunately I expect guests myself on Wednesday, the sixth of April; and therefore cannot accept your invitation for luncheon on that day.

It was thoughtful of you to invite me, and I am extremely sorry I cannot accept. I do hope you will ask me again some time!

Sincerely yours,
Mildred Johnson

However disappointed the hostess may be to receive a note like the above, she cannot feel hurt or resentful. For it is a gracious and friendly note, expressing sincere regret, and it gives a real excuse for not coming. In other words, it does not slam the door shut . . . as *this* note does:

Dear Mrs. Benton:

I'm sorry I cannot accept your invitation for luncheon on Wednesday, April sixth, as I have other plans for that day.

Sincerely yours,
Mildred Johnson

Surely a cold, curt note like that leaves no further possibility of friendly overtures! It stamps the writer as rude and ill-mannered . . . and totally lacking in the social graces.

SUPPER INVITATIONS

Supper parties are the most *informal* of all types of entertaining. Guests are generally intimate friends or members of the family; and invitations are almost always telephoned.

"How about you and Ted coming to supper next Tuesday night?" is the way supper guests are most likely to be invited. Or "We're having a buffet supper Sunday night. Can you and Bill come?"

A written note of invitation should be on about the same general level. If you customarily say to a friend, "How about supper Tuesday night?"—don't suddenly become stilted in your letter and write, "May we have the pleasure of entertaining you at supper next Tuesday evening?" Formal language doesn't go with simple supper party informality. *Write it as you would say it.*

Dear Ann:

We're having a buffet supper Sunday night, June the fourth—and of course we want you and Bob!

Come at six, if you can. We'll have supper early and play some bridge afterwards. The Clarks and the Prestons will be here, and I know you always enjoy their company.

We'll be expecting you on the fourth, so don't disappoint us!

With love,
Marjorie

No response to the above is necessary unless you like to be especially courteous and considerate. In that case, you write a note (always provided there is time, of course!) telling your hostess you'll be there. Ordinarily your presence at the supper party is all the acknowledgment necessary. But if you *cannot* attend the party, you must reply—and promptly.

Dear Marjorie:

I'm so sorry we can't come to your buffet supper Sunday night! Bob's mother is ill, and we're going to Philadelphia this week end to see her.

Thanks for asking us, Marjorie. We certainly hate to miss any of your parties . . . they're always such fun!

Affectionately,
Ann

Guests do not ordinarily expect to meet strangers at an intimate supper party. Therefore if you are inviting someone outside your usual circle of friends and acquaintances, it's a good idea to explain about the details beforehand in your note of invitation:

Dear Margaret:

Do you remember Helen Foster, the girl who used to wear such funny hats at high school? Well, guess what! She's Ellen Fontaine now—the well-known fashion designer!

I told her about the work you are doing, and she is extremely interested. She wants to know more about your fashion-chart idea. I'm giving a buffet supper for her here at my apartment on Tuesday, May the tenth, and I'd like you to come. Then you can tell her about your work directly.

Supper is at seven o'clock. Ann and Bob will be here, and the Carters are coming in later. Do try and make it, Margaret! I think I can promise you an interesting evening.

Yours affectionately,
Eileen

Dear Eileen:

Imagine the famous Ellen Fontaine turning out to be that madcap Helen Foster we knew at high school! I can hardly believe it.

It will be very interesting to meet her again after all these years. And I just can't tell you how delighted I am at the chance to discuss my fashion charts with her!

I'm looking forward to Tuesday, May tenth, with great pleasure. Thanks for asking me, Eileen—I'm sure it will be a fascinating evening!

Affectionately yours,
Margaret

An invitation to share an evening with strangers is not always appealing to those who receive it. Consequently it should be made to *sound* interesting and worth while. In other words, the invitation should "sell" the idea of accepting the invitation—should give a real reason for accepting it, and for looking forward to the occasion with pleasure and anticipation.

Dear Susan:

I know you are interested in old china and glassware, so I'm sure you'll be interested in the Bartons! They are coming here to supper next Sunday night, October the twelfth, and we'd like you and Walter to come, too.

The Bartons are that very charming couple we met in Montreal last summer. They have a wonderful collection of old china and glassware; and I understand that Mrs. Barton is quite an authority on English china. I'm sure you and Walter will thoroughly enjoy an evening in their company.

We're planning supper at six; that will give us a nice long evening to talk. If I don't hear from you before then, I'll be expecting you on the twelfth!

Affectionately yours,
Laura

It is not easy to turn down an invitation so cordially and personally extended. The hostess who invites congenial people and plans an evening for their special enjoyment—and who goes to the trouble of writing notes to "sell" the evening to her guests—*should not be turned down unless absolutely necessary.* When an evening is so obviously planned for certain people, those people should make every effort to accept—even though it may mean a change in previous plans for the evening. If such plans cannot be changed, and the invitation cannot therefore be accepted, the hostess should be notified immediately. It is then up to her either to proceed according to plan, or to postpone the supper until the people she wants can be there.

Dear Laura:

We would *love* to come to your supper on Sunday, the twelfth, and meet the Bartons. But that's the night Walter's brother is arriving from England, and he is expecting us to meet him at the airport and drive him home.

If it were anything else, Laura, we'd just change our plans and come. You know that, I'm sure. But we haven't seen Paul in nearly a year, and Walter is practically counting the hours to his arrival! We couldn't possibly disappoint him when we know he'll be expecting to see us as he steps off the plane. He is scheduled to arrive at six-fifteen; and as we are driving him out to Westchester, we couldn't get to your party until much too late.

We're *most* sorry to miss the opportunity of meeting the Bartons! Walter and I would have enjoyed so very much talking with them about old English china. But perhaps we'll have that pleasure at some future time.

You were sweet to ask us, Laura, and we appreciate it. Our very best to you and Jim!

With love,
Susan

Occasionally a supper of more elaborate and ceremonious proportions than the usual intimate type for friends, is given for some special purpose. For example, instead of the elaborate formality of a dinner *preceding* the theater or opera (for a group of people who are to be entertained for one reason or another)—a supper is given *following* it. This is not, as a rule, the popular buffet supper, but a more impressive "sit down" affair. Nevertheless, invitations are still in the form of friendly, informal notes.

Dear Mrs. North:

We have eight tickets for the opening of the new Moss Hart show on Wednesday, September third. We are asking a group of friends to join us at the theater, and come back with us later for a little supper party at the house. Dr. Benton and I hope that you and Mr. North have no previous engagement, and can join us for the evening.

We are meeting in the lobby of the Globe Theater at eight-fifteen. Please let us know if you *cannot* come; otherwise we will expect to see you there.

Cordially yours,
Elizabeth K. Benton

Acceptance

Even when an invitation specifically says to answer only if you cannot come, it is more gracious to send a note of acceptance.

Dear Mrs. Benton:

How very kind of you and Dr. Benton to include us in your theater and supper party for Wednesday, September third! We'll be delighted to come, and will be in the lobby of the Globe Theater at eight-fifteen.

It sounds like a wonderful evening, and we are looking forward to it with great pleasure. Thank you for asking us!

Cordially yours,
Alice North

Regret

Dear Mrs. Benton:

It is with the greatest reluctance that I must write and tell you we cannot accept your most generous invitation for Wednesday, September third, for the Moss Hart opening and your supper party afterwards.

We are expecting friends from Canada; and as they will be here for that one evening only, we cannot leave them on their own.

Thank you very much for asking us. Mr. North and I sincerely regret missing such a marvelous party as yours promises to be!

Sincerely yours,
Alice North

4

Party Invitations and Acknowledgments

The invitations you send out for your simple informal partie at home may be as original and "different" as you wish. It is not necessary to conform to any special wording or style. Birthday invitations may be in the form of amusing jingles. Shower invitations may be in the form of tiny, umbrella-shaped cards, if that appeals to your fancy. Invitations for holiday parties—such as Easter, Christmas, New Year—may be whatever is cleverly in keeping with the occasion.

But there are certain generalities of good taste that apply to *all* invitations. And there are certain basic "unwritten laws" of good hospitality that everyone should know about.

In the first place, no matter how informal the party may be, invitations should be sent out—or telephoned—at least one week in advance. Obviously this doesn't apply to unplanned, impromptu parties for which no regular invitations are issued. It applies to the parties you plan ahead of time . . . and to which guests should be invited far enough in advance to make it *convenient for them to accept*. In these busy days it's definitely bad form to telephone or write even intimate friends just a day or two ahead of a party; for few people can accept such last-minute invitations without a hurried, last-minute change of plans— often at considerable inconvenience to others as well as themselves.

So if you like your friends and want to keep them, invite them as informally as you like . . . but *invite them well ahead of time*. And once you have arranged a party and invited your guests, don't make any sudden last-minute change in plans unless absolutely necessary. To inconvenience half a dozen or more people for your own convenience is basically bad manners; and something not even a close friend soon forgets.

The second "unwritten law" of hospitality is to *choose your guests carefully*. Always try to invite people who are congenial and have something in common, and can therefore be reasonably expected to enjoy one another's company. Don't, for example, invite experts and beginners to the same bridge party. Don't invite two people you know dislike each other, or who are for one reason or another uncomfortable or unhappy in each other's company.

The keynote of good manners is *consideration for others*. That also is the keynote of good hospitality.

Don't invite a busy doctor on an evening when he has late office hours. Find out when he does *not* have regular hours, and plan your party for that evening.

Don't invite people who never drink to a cocktail party, nor people who do not enjoy cards to a card party.

Even the most simple, informal party should be planned for the enjoyment of the guests. If the people you invite are the kind who enjoy good conversation, and would rather sit around and talk than do anything else—don't try to foist charades or home movies on them! They'll have a much better time just talking.

So if you want to be sure that your invitations are always received with pleasure and appreciation: (1) Plan your parties to suit the people you expect to invite. (2) Invite only those you know to be congenial. (3) Get your invitations out early! Give your guests the pleasure of looking forward to your party, instead of the inconvenience of scrambling about at the last minute trying to "make it."

CARD PARTY INVITATIONS

If you have friends who like to play bridge, canasta, or gin rummy, one of the simplest and most enjoyable ways to entertain them is by means of a card party. Invitations are either by telephone or by informal note. Many hostesses prefer to telephone their bridge invitations, as this provides an immediate acceptance or regret from each guest, and tables can be arranged accordingly. However, notes of invitation are a shade more gracious, and somehow seem to give greater social significance to the occasion. If they are sent out well enough in advance, and answered promptly, the hostess will have time to fill in, if necessary, and arrange the right number of players for each table.

Dear Ruth:

How would you and Bill like to play bridge on Friday evening, March the fourth? The Prestons and the Clarks are coming, and as you know, they're excellent players.

I hope you and Bill have no other plans for that evening, and that you can come. We're starting at about eight-thirty. Do try and make it, Ruth—we're looking forward to seeing you!

Affectionately yours,
Betty

An invitation calls only for an acceptance or regret—not for a long, chatty letter giving the local gossip and the family news. So answer as follows—briefly and to the point.

Dear Betty:

Bill and I haven't had a really good game of bridge in months, and we're delighted to come to your party on Friday, March the fourth.

We enjoyed the Clarks and Prestons very much the last time we met them at your house; and we're glad of this opportunity to see them again. I just hope Bill and I can hold up our end of the game—we're rather out of practice!

Thanks for asking us, Betty. We'll be there promptly at eight-thirty.

Affectionately yours,
Ruth

It's always better not to accept an invitation at all, than to accept it and be unable to go at the last minute. This is especially true of bridge invitations; for if you are expected and you fail to put in an appearance, others are left out of the game. So if there's a possibility you may not be able to keep the engagement, say so frankly in a note of regret:

Dear Betty:

I wish I could accept your very tempting invitation to play bridge on Friday, March the fourth—but I hesitate to do so.

Bill has one of his usual deadlines to meet. He has been working night after night until ten or eleven o'clock; and although he says he may be through by the fourth, there's a very good chance that he *won't* be.

I wouldn't like to say "yes," Betty—and then find at the last minute that we can't come. So count us out this time; but many thanks for including us, and I hope you'll ask us soon again!

Affectionately,
Ruth

Many women like to entertain their friends at afternoon card parties; and frequently such parties are preceded by a luncheon. If it's a simple, informal party at home, the invitations are extended by telephone or personal note. But if it's a large bridge luncheon at a restaurant or hotel—perhaps to announce an engagement, or to honor a special guest—engraved invitations are usually sent out.

FOR AN INFORMAL
BRIDGE LUNCHEON

Dear Marcia:

I understand you've been taking bridge lessons recently. Well, here's your chance to show us what an expert you've become!

I'm having a group of friends here for luncheon and bridge next Tuesday, June the eighth. Can you come at one o'clock, and stay for most of the afternoon?

Betty and Susan will be here, and I know they'll be disappointed if you can't come. But I'll be even *more* disappointed—it's such a long time since I've seen you! So please try your best to make it.

Affectionately yours,
Janet

FOR A FORMAL
BRIDGE LUNCHEON

When a mother and daughter entertain at an afternoon party, the names of both appear on the invitation:

Mrs. Thomas Matthew Benton
Miss Anita Benton
request the pleasure of your company
at luncheon
Thursday, the twentieth of September
at one o'clock
The Hampshire House

Please reply to   Bridge
250 Park Avenue

FOR AN INFORMAL
COCKTAIL PARTY

Dear Ruth:

We're having some friends in for cocktails on Friday, June the eighth, from four to six. Can you and Bill come?

Tom and I are looking forward to seeing you, so don't disappoint us!

Cordially yours,
Betty

FOR A FORMAL
COCKTAIL PARTY

When invitations are issued for a cocktail party, the exact time of arrival and departure should be given—otherwise guests may stay too long and interfere with plans for the evening.

Dr. and Mrs. Thomas Matthew Benton
At Home
Friday, June the eighth
from four until six o'clock
250 Park Avenue

Cocktails

FOR AN INFORMAL
TEA PARTY

A simple informal tea party at home is still one of the most gracious and charming ways of entertaining a group of favorite friends and interesting acquaintances. It is also a pleasant way for a bride who does not want to undertake elaborate luncheons or dinners to repay the hospitality of her friends.

A tea or "at home" is a type of reception, and is more strictly *social* in character than other forms of afternoon entertaining. Therefore even a quite small and informal tea party calls for *written* invitations. It's not considered good form to telephone your invitations for this type of party.

Dear Mrs. North:

I have asked some friends to come for tea on Tuesday, April the eighth, at four o'clock. Will you join us?

I know you have just returned from Bermuda, but I hope you're not too busy to come. I'm looking forward to seeing you.

Cordially yours,
Elizabeth K. Benton

If some special entertaining is planned for the afternoon, that fact should be mentioned. An invitation is always more likely to be accepted if a *good reason* for accepting is given!

Dear Mrs. North:

Some of your good friends and mine are coming for tea on Tuesday, April the eighth, at four o'clock. I hope you can join us.

Rosa Cantrell is one of the guests, and she has promised to sing for us. And Mrs. Winston is planning to show her Samoan movies. So *do* come if you can—it promises to be a most interesting afternoon!

Cordially yours,
Elizabeth K. Benton

Acceptance

Dear Mrs. Benton:

It does indeed promise to be an interesting afternoon . . . and I'm delighted to accept your invitation for Tuesday, April the eighth, at four o'clock!

I have heard about Mrs. Winston's fascinating Samoan movies, and I am looking forward to seeing them. And of course it's always a great treat to hear Rosa Cantrell!

You were sweet to include me, and I'm very happy to come.

Cordially yours,
Alice North

Regret

Dear Mrs. Benton:

I just can't tell you how sorry I am that I cannot accept your invitation for tea on Tuesday, April the eighth!

I have a club meeting that afternoon; and although I'd gladly forego it if I could, I have a special report to make and must be present.

Thanks so much for asking me. I certainly hate to miss such a marvelous afternoon!

Cordially yours,
Alice North

FORMAL TEA PARTIES

Teas, like luncheons and other afternoon parties, are generally given by women alone; but sometimes they are given by "Mr. and Mrs." jointly. Such teas are formal and ceremonious, as a rule, and are given for some special purpose like honoring an important guest, presenting a debutante daughter, or announcing an engagement. The invitations for such teas or receptions may be handwritten; but usually they are engraved—especially if the affair is away from home, at a club or hotel.

For a formal tea given at home by a mother and her debutante daughter, the invitations are written or engraved as follows:

Mrs. Thomas Matthew Benton
Miss Anita Benton
At Home
Friday afternoon, October fifth
from four until seven o'clock
250 Park Avenue

For a formal tea given by a mother and her debutante daughter *away* from home, in a hotel, the invitations are exactly the same as the above . . . except that the name of the hotel is given instead of the home address. If a reply is requested, that fact is indicated in the lower left corner, and the address for the reply is given.

When *both* parents receive with a debutante daughter, the invitations are issued by them jointly . . . and men as well as women are invited to the party. Instead of "Mrs. Thomas Matthew Benton" in the invitation above, the top line reads "Dr. and Mrs. Thomas Matthew Benton." The rest of the invitation remains the same.

Sometimes a large formal tea is given at a hotel by the parents of two debutantes who are friends. For an important social function of this kind, invitations are almost always engraved—and read as follows:

Dr. and Mrs. Thomas Matthew Benton
Mr. and Mrs. Walter Jennings
Miss Anita Benton
Miss Suzanne Jennings
At Home
Friday, November the seventeenth
from four until seven o'clock
The Savoy Plaza

When a tea or reception is given in honor of a distinguished guest—or "to meet" a well-known personality—that person's name should appear first on the invitation.

To Meet
Miss Rosa Cantrell

Dr. and Mrs. Thomas Matthew Benton
request the pleasure of your company
Tuesday, the fourth of March
from four until seven o'clock
The Sert Room
Waldorf-Astoria
Please respond to
250 Park Avenue

Formal tea invitations should be sent out ten days to two weeks in advance. The customary phrase is "At Home"—which simply means a social gathering, or reception. If the purpose of the tea is to meet a celebrity, the phrase "request the pleasure of your company" is preferred.

All such invitations are answered as written—in the same third-person phraseology, and with the same formal spacing. As a rule, one accepts an "At Home" simply by attending it . . .

unless a reply is specifically requested. But if one cannot accept, a regret should be sent promptly. All the names that appear on the invitation should be repeated in the acknowledgment. For example:

Mr. and Mrs. Frank North
regret that they are unable to accept
Dr. and Mrs. Thomas M. Benton's
Mr. and Mrs. Walter Jennings'
Miss Anita Benton's
Miss Suzanne Jennings'
kind invitation for
Friday, November the seventeenth
owing to illness in the family

If no name and address for a reply are given on the invitation, it should be sent to the hotel where the reception is scheduled to be held. The envelope should be addressed to all the persons in whose names the invitations are issued.

GARDEN PARTY INVITATIONS

By "garden party" is generally meant a tea or reception held out-of-doors. If it's an important social function and formality is desired, the invitations may be engraved as follows:

Mr. and Mrs. Robert G. Scully
At Home
in the garden
Thursday, June the twenty-fifth
from three to six o'clock

But nowadays most garden parties are charmingly informal, and invitations are by friendly note:

Dear Joan:

Our garden has never been as lovely as it is now! We'd like our friends to see it, so we're having tea on the lawn next Thursday, June the twenty-fifth, from three to six o'clock.

We hope you and Ralph can come. You simply *must* see what a magnificent display of June roses we have this year!

Affectionately yours,
Martha

Acceptance

Dear Martha:

Ralph and I will be delighted to come to tea on the lawn Thursday, June twenty-fifth, at three o'clock.

Your garden is always lovely, but especially so this time of the year—and we're so glad to have an opportunity of seeing it. We're looking forward to it with great pleasure.

Affectionately yours,
Joan

Regret

Dear Martha:

How I wish I could come to your garden party next Thursday! But Ralph and I are going to Boston for a week, and we won't be back in time.

We both love your garden, especially this time of the year—and we're sorry to miss seeing it. But we're even *more* sorry to miss seeing you!

Thanks, Martha, for asking us . . . I'll telephone you when we get back from Boston.

Affectionately yours,
Joan

INVITATIONS FOR HOUSE AND WEEK-END PARTIES

All invitations for house parties, whether for a week end or longer duration, should be by letter. There are many things the guest needs to know, and these should be included in the invitation.

For example, house guests must know the exact duration of the visit: when they are expected to arrive and when they are expected to leave. They should be given some idea of the activities planned, so that they will know what clothes and sports equipment to take with them. They should be told the best way to come, with marked road maps or timetables enclosed for their convenience.

A week-end visit is generally from Friday or Saturday until the following Monday morning. Guests should be invited at least two weeks in advance, to give them time to make all necessary arrangements. If several members of a family are invited, they should all be mentioned specifically by name. The thoughtful hostess mentions what other guests have been invited, to avoid the possibility of bringing uncongenial people together for a week end.

> Dear Jane:
>
> I hope you and Fred haven't any plans for the week end of July twenty-fourth, as we'd like you to spend it with us at Far Acres. It's simply *beautiful* here now, with everything in bloom!
>
> I think we can promise Fred some good fishing this year. The trout are biting better than ever! So bring your fishing clothes; and be sure to bring your tennis things, too, because the Owens are coming and I'm sure you'll want to get out on the courts with them.
>
> There's a very good train Friday night; I've marked it in red on the timetable. It gets you here about seven-thirty, which is just in time for dinner. You can get a late train back Sunday night, or there's an early express that Bob usually takes on Monday morning.
>
> We hope nothing will prevent you from coming, as we're looking forward to your visit . . . and I know the Owens are looking forward to seeing you again, too. Be sure to let us know what train you are taking so that Bob can meet you at the station.
>
> Affectionately yours,
> Martha

Acceptance

Dear Martha:

Fred and I are counting the days to our week end with you at Far Acres! We are delighted that you have asked us; and we certainly won't let anything prevent us from coming.

We plan to take the five o'clock train on Friday night, July twenty-third, as you suggest. And we'll take the early express back to town on Monday morning.

Thanks so much for asking us, Martha! We're looking forward to two wonderful days with you and the Owens.

Affectionately yours,
Jane

Regret

Dear Martha:

How awful to have to turn down your very, very tempting invitation! I can't think of *anything* Fred and I would enjoy more right now than a week end at Far Acres. But I expect my mother just about that time—either on the twenty-third or twenty-fourth of July. She is stopping over on her way to Canada, and plans to spend a few days with us. Under the circumstances, we cannot make any plans for the week end.

But thanks so much for asking us, Martha! I know we're missing a marvelous time! Please remember us to the Owens, and tell them how sorry we are not to have been able to join them for the week end.

Affectionately,
Jane

People who own country houses often invite friends to house parties that may last anywhere from three days to three weeks. The invitation must give the exact date of expected arrival and departure, so that there can be no question about the duration of the visit. And like the week-end invitation, it should indicate the best and most convenient way to come, the sports and activities planned, the clothes likely to be needed, and so forth.

Dear Ruth:

As you know, Anita and I are at Shady Lawn for the summer. Tom is joining us here for two weeks at the end of August; and I'm planning a house party for that time so he'll be able to enjoy tennis and golf with the friends he likes best.

I'd like you and Bill to come, and to bring Marilyn along. We have a new boat this year, and I'm sure Marilyn and Anita will enjoy going out on the lake together.

Can you arrange to come to Shady Lawn on the sixteenth of August, and stay until the thirtieth? There's a very good train out of Grand Central at four-fifteen; it gets you here just in time for dinner. Try to take that train on Friday, the sixteenth, Ruth—and I'll see that someone meets you at the station. If Bill can't get away that early, there's a fast express Saturday morning. I've marked both trains on the timetable I'm enclosing.

I have asked the Norths and the Jennings to come; and Tom's brother may be here for a week or ten days. We should have lots of good bridge; they're all experts!

I'm looking forward to your visit, Ruth—and I know Tom will be delighted to have you and Bill here. So write and tell me you're coming!

With love,
Betty

Acceptance

Dear Betty:

Of course we'll come to your house party! We love Shady Lawn, and we love the Bentons . . . so how can we resist? In fact, Marilyn and Bill are so excited about it that they've talked of little else since your invitation arrived!

We plan to take the four-fifteen on Friday, August sixteenth, as you suggest. Bill may have to leave on the twenty-fifth; but Marilyn and I will stay until the thirtieth.

Thanks so much for asking us, Betty! We're looking forward to some wonderful swimming, fishing and all-around relaxing at Shady Lawn—but most of all, we're looking forward to being with you! We'll see you on the sixteenth.

With love to you and Anita,

                                                          Ruth

Regret

Dear Betty:

What a wonderful invitation—and how difficult for me to turn it down! But Bill can't get away in August this year; so we just can't come to your house party, much as we'd love to.

Bill tried to arrange things at the office, but it was out of the question. It seems that the campaign he is now working on must be ready by September first; and unless he stays right with it, he won't be able to complete it in time.

We certainly hate to miss a house party at Shady Lawn. Marilyn is practically *sick* about it! But I guess you'll have to count us out this year, Betty. . . .

Thanks for asking us, though—and we hope you, Tom and Anita thoroughly enjoy the rest of the summer!

                                                   With love,
                                                          Ruth

INVITATIONS FOR SHOWERS

The setting for a shower may be a luncheon, an afternoon tea, or an evening party . . . and the invitations may be telephoned, or they may be in the form of any attractive shower cards that appeal to you. Written invitations are simply informal notes giving the time, place, type of shower, and so forth.

Dear Miss White:

I am giving a linen shower for Miss Mary Crawford on Saturday, April sixth, at four o'clock. I hope you can come, and stay for a buffet supper afterward.

This is a surprise for Mary, so please don't mention it to her if you see her before Saturday.

I have heard a great deal about you from Mary's friends, and I am looking forward to the pleasure of meeting you.

Sincerely yours,
Suzanne Jennings

Acceptance

Dear Miss Jennings:

I'll be delighted to come to the shower for Mary Crawford on Saturday, April sixth, at four o'clock— and to stay on for the buffet supper afterward. I'll bring something nice in linen for the bride-to-be.

Mary has spoken of you so many times that I almost feel as though I know you. I'm very glad of this opportunity to make your acquaintance.

Sincerely yours,
Helen White

Regret

Dear Miss Jennings:

I'm so sorry I must miss the shower you are giving for Mary Crawford on Saturday, April the sixth. I'll be out of town that week end.

However, I am sending a gift for Mary by mail. Will you please put it with the other gifts for her?

Thanks for inviting me, and I do hope we shall have the pleasure of meeting some day. Mary has told me so many nice things about you!

Cordially yours,
Helen White

INVITATIONS FOR CHRISTENINGS

Most christenings are very informal affairs. Invitations are usually telephoned, or friends are asked when seen. But it is also correct to write brief, friendly notes:

Dear Mrs. Whitney:

Our new baby is to be christened at the Community Church next Sunday at four o'clock. We are planning to call him "Robert." Wouldn't you and Mr. Whitney like to come to the service?

Sincerely yours,
Dorothy Evans

To an intimate friend, the note would naturally be less dignified and reserved:

Dear Kathleen:

That precious young son of ours is going to be christened next Sunday at four o'clock, at the Community Church. Come and see him make his first public appearance. He's simply *adorable*, Kathleen! We're planning to call him "Robert"—I hope you approve.

I'll be looking for you on Sunday—so be sure to come!

Affectionately yours,
Dorothy

Sometimes a business associate is invited to a child's christening and is unable to attend. When business interferes with the acceptance of any kind of invitation, it's gracious to imply you would have been *delighted* to accept otherwise.

Dear Mrs. Evans:

I am leaving for Los Angeles today on business. But it's with great reluctance that I do so, as I had hoped to attend your son's christening at the Community Church on Sunday.

I'm very sorry I won't be able to be there. Allow me, however, to wish you great joy in your son; and to wish the young fellow himself a long and happy life.

Sincerely yours,
John T. McElroy

There are usually two godmothers for a girl and one for a boy —two godfathers for a boy and one for a girl. They are chosen from among the relatives and intimate friends, and generally well before the baby's arrival. However, if someone living at a great distance is asked to be a godparent, a telegram is sent on the day of the child's birth—or very soon afterward.

It's a boy! Will you be godfather?

or

The baby arrived and it's a girl! We'd like you to be godmother.

A letter asking someone to be a godparent should be written with due regard for the seriousness of the occasion. It is no time to be flippant or facetious:

Dear Joan:

Our son is to be christened at the Community Church on Sunday, April the tenth, at four o'clock. We have decided to call him "Robert."

Joan, you and I were confirmed together; it would make me very happy if you would consent to be Robert's godmother. Peter Dawson and Kenneth Ayres will be the godfathers. I think you know them both.

We are planning to have a small dinner party at the house after the service, and we expect you to join us.

> With affection,
> Dorothy

The purpose of godparents is to provide "substitute parents" or protectors for a child, should it be left alone in the world. To be selected as a godparent is therefore somewhat of an honor—certainly an expression of trust and confidence in the person so selected. The request cannot very well be refused; on the contrary, it should be accepted with evident pleasure and pride, and with an appreciation of the responsibilities involved:

Dear Dorothy:

I'm proud and happy to be chosen as godmother for little Robert!

I warn you I shall take very seriously my share of the responsibility for your son's welfare, and shall keep a careful eye on the young man in the years ahead.

I'll be at your house about three o'clock on Sunday so that I can go to the church with you, and perhaps be of some help on the way.

> Affectionately,
> Joan

5

Dance Invitations and Acknowledgments

The days of large, colorful balls and receptions are over; but the dance as a social function remains as popular as ever.

The word "ball" is rarely used on invitations nowadays, except for a large public subscription dance or a charity affair. For ordinary social invitations, formal or informal, the word "dance" is used. The phrase "a small dance" frequently appears on formal invitations, regardless of the size of the function.

Invitations for formal dances are usually engraved, and are sent out from two to three weeks in advance. Following are the most familiar and acceptable forms:

Dr. and Mrs. Thomas Matthew Benton
request the pleasure of your company
at a small dance
Thursday, the eighth of November
at ten o'clock
The Savoy Plaza
Please reply to
250 Park Avenue

The fill-in type of invitation (with the guest's name written in by hand) is somewhat more personal, and for that reason many people prefer it. Instead of "at a small dance" in the body of the invitation, the word "Dancing" may be used in the lower right corner.

Dr. and Mrs. Thomas Matthew Benton
request the pleasure of

Mr. and Mrs. Frank North's

company on Thursday, the eighth of November
at ten o'clock
The Savoy Plaza

Please reply to   Dancing
250 Park Avenue

The most formal and precise invitation of all is the "At Home" with "Dancing" in the lower left or right corner. It may be used whether the dance is for twenty or thirty people in a private house—or for several hundred people, with an entire floor of a large hotel engaged for the purpose:

Mr. and Mrs. Paul Preston
At Home
Tuesday, the third of April
at ten o'clock
The Drake

Kindly send reply to   Dancing
20 Lake Drive

When a dance is given by two couples, the names of both should appear on the invitation. If a reply is requested, the name of the person to whom it should be sent is indicated:

Mr. and Mrs. John Arnold
Mr. and Mrs. Henry S. Schuyler
request the pleasure of your company
at a small dance
Friday, the fifth of November
at ten o'clock
The Lowell Country Club

Please address reply to
Mrs. John Arnold
10 Vernon Square

Dances are frequently given in honor of an important guest or someone who is to be especially honored. The name of that guest should always appear on the invitation. Either of the two following forms are correct and may be used:

Dr. and Mrs. Thomas Matthew Benton
request the pleasure of your company
at a dance in honor of
Miss Doris Fernell
Thursday, the eighth of November
at ten o'clock
The Savoy Plaza

or

To Meet
Miss Doris Fernell

Dr. and Mrs. Thomas Matthew Benton
request the pleasure of

Mr. and Mrs. William Forster's

company on Thursday, the eighth of November
at ten o'clock
The Savoy Plaza

Dancing

Masquerade and costume dances are based on the idea that people like to throw off conventional garb once in a while, and dress up to represent an entirely different character or personality than their own. Such dances are especially suitable for young people home from school for the holidays. Invitations are exactly like any formal dance invitations, except that "costume dance," "masquerade" or "fancy dress" appears somewhere on the invitation to show what kind of dance it is. Two examples follow:

Dr. and Mrs. Thomas Matthew Benton
request the pleasure of your company
at a costume dance for their daughter
Miss Anita Benton
Thursday, the eighth of November
at ten o'clock
The Savoy Plaza

or

Dr. and Mrs. Thomas Matthew Benton
request the pleasure of your company
at a small dance
to be given at their home
on Thursday, the eighth of November
at ten o'clock
250 Park Avenue

Please respond   Fancy Dress

If a special kind of costume is to be worn—representing famous personalities of the past, characters from books, the dress of colonial times, and so forth—that fact should be indicated in the lower left corner of the invitation.

DEBUTANTE DANCES AND
DINNER DANCES

The most popular form of invitation for a dance in honor of a debutante daughter is as follows:

Mr. and Mrs. Walter Jennings
request the pleasure of

Miss Anita Benton's

company at a dance in honor of their daughter
Miss Suzanne Jennings
Wednesday evening, October the seventh
at ten o'clock
One East Sixtieth Street

R.s.v.p.

The formal "At Home" is also correct for a debutante dance, with the name of the daughter at the top of the invitation with those of her parents:

Mr. and Mrs. Walter Jennings
Miss Suzanne Jennings
At Home
Wednesday, October the seventh
at ten o'clock
One East Sixtieth Street

Please respond   Dancing

If the dance is held away from home, at a club or hotel, the following invitation is correct:

Mr. and Mrs. Walter Jennings
request the pleasure of your company
at a small dance in honor of their daughter
Miss Suzanne Jennings
on Wednesday, October the seventh
at ten o'clock
The Ambassador

A dinner dance is by far the favorite type of entertainment for a debutante daughter. Often two groups of guests are invited: one group for dinner and dancing, another for dancing only. In that case two separate sets of invitations are issued: regular dance invitations for those who are to come *after* dinner, and invitations like the following for those who are invited for both dinner and dancing:

Mr. and Mrs. Walter Jennings
request the pleasure of your company
at dinner
in honor of their daughter
Miss Suzanne Jennings
Wednesday, October the seventh
at eight o'clock
The Ambassador

Please reply to   Dancing at ten
One East Sixtieth Street

or

Mr. and Mrs. Walter Jennings
request the pleasure of

Mr. and Mrs. James Winston's

company at a dinner dance for their daughter
Miss Suzanne Jennings
on Wednesday, October the seventh
at eight o'clock
The Ambassador

Please address reply to
One East Sixtieth Street

SUPPER DANCE INVITATIONS

Nowadays supper parties are frequently given to honor a special guest or a debutante daughter, or to introduce a new daughter-in-law. These dances are simple and unpretentious compared to the great "balls" of the past; but the same precise formality is maintained in the invitations. Following is the correct invitation for a debutante's formal supper dance at home:

Mr. and Mrs. Walter Jennings
Miss Suzanne Jennings
request the pleasure of your company
at a supper dance
Wednesday, October the seventh
at half past ten o'clock
One East Sixtieth Street

The favor of a reply
is requested

If the supper dance is held at a hotel, and is for the purpose of presenting a new daughter-in-law to one's friends, either of the following two invitations may be used:

To meet
Mrs. Arthur Blanchard

Mr. and Mrs. Floyd T. Blanchard
request the pleasure of your company
at a supper dance
on Tuesday, September the fifth
at ten o'clock
The St. Regis

R.s.v.p.
One University Place

or

Mr. and Mrs. Floyd T. Blanchard
request the pleasure of

Mr and Mrs. Frederick Sterle's

company at a supper dance in honor of
Mrs. Arthur Blanchard
on Tuesday, September the fifth
at ten o'clock
The St. Regis

Please send reply to
One University Place

Occasionally an afternoon tea with dancing is given for a debutante, or to introduce a son's bride. The invitation is generally a formal "At Home," with the name of the hostess and her guest of honor at the top:

Mrs. Floyd T. Blanchard
Mrs. Arthur Blanchard
At Home
on Tuesday, the fifth of September
from four until seven o'clock
The St. Regis

Dancing

HOW TO ACKNOWLEDGE
FORMAL DANCE INVITATIONS

All formal invitations should be answered in formal, third-person phraseology. The acceptance or regret should be carefully handwritten on one's best white note paper, in the same arrangement as the invitation and following the same wording.

Acceptances

Mr. and Mrs. Frank North
accept with pleasure
Dr. and Mrs. Thomas M. Benton's
kind invitation to be present
for dancing
on Thursday, the eighth of November
at ten o'clock
at the Savoy Plaza

Mr. and Mrs. Philip Duell
accept with pleasure
Mr. and Mrs. John Arnold's
and
Mr. and Mrs. Henry S. Schuyler's
kind invitation for dancing
on Friday, the fifth of November
at ten o'clock
at the Lowell Country Club

Miss Anita Benton
accepts with pleasure
Mr. and Mrs. Walter Jennings'
invitation to a dance in honor of
Miss Suzanne Jennings
on Wednesday, October the seventh
at ten o'clock

Regrets

Mr. and Mrs. Frank North
regret that they are unable to accept
Dr. and Mrs. Thomas M. Benton's
kind invitation for dancing
on Thursday, the eighth of November
at ten o'clock
owing to a previous engagement

Mr. and Mrs. William Forster
regret that they will be unable to attend
Dr. and Mrs. Thomas M. Benton's
dance in honor of
Miss Doris Fernell
on Thursday, the eighth of November
as they will be out of town

> Mr. and Mrs. Frank North
> regret that owing to illness
> they are unable to accept
> Dr. and Mrs. Thomas M. Benton's
> kind invitation to a costume dance
> for their daughter
> Miss Anita Benton
> on Thursday, the eighth of November

Frequently a formal regret is followed up by a personal note a week or so after the dance. This is not an obligation, but it's a courteous and thoughtful thing to do. If the dance was for a debutante or a special guest, it's a friendly gesture to send flowers a few days after the dance, with a brief note saying how sorry you were to miss it.

RECALL OR POSTPONEMENT
OF FORMAL DANCE INVITATIONS

If an invitation must be recalled, it is always more polite to give the reason for it. A simple announcement like the following is usually sent out. It may be either printed on cards, or carefully written by hand on plain white note paper. As a rule, there is not enough time to have such announcements engraved.

> Dr. and Mrs. Thomas Matthew Benton
> regret that they are obliged to recall their invitations
> for Thursday, the eighth of November
> owing to the illness of their daughter

The postponement of a dance may be indefinite, or another date may be specified. For example:

> Mr. and Mrs. Walter Jennings
> regret that owing to illness in the family
> their dance for Wednesday, October the seventh
> is temporarily postponed

or

Mr. and Mrs. Walter Jennings
wish to announce
that the dinner dance in honor of their daughter
has been postponed until
Wednesday, October the twenty-first
at eight o'clock
The Ambassador

Please send reply to
One East Sixtieth Street

It is always best to repeat the hour and the place, even though they are the same as in the original invitation. If an invitation is merely postponed and not canceled, it isn't necessary to give a reason or make an explanation.

SUBSCRIPTION DANCES
AND CHARITY BALLS

When a large dance is given by a club or association, and attendance is by paid subscription, a return card and envelope are usually enclosed. The return of the card with a check for tickets is the only acknowledgment required. No formal acceptance of the invitation need be written . . . nor is a "regret" expected if you do not plan to attend.

Bear in mind that the word "ball" may be used only in invitations like the following—invitations to large public or semi-public affairs:

The Entertainment Committee of the Ferndale Club
requests the pleasure of your company
at a Ball
to be held at the club house
on Friday, the fifth of October
at ten o'clock
for the benefit of
The Community Hospital

Tickets five dollars

or

The pleasure of your company is requested
at the
Annual Masquerade Ball
of the Women's Advertising Club
to be held at the Marshland Hotel
on Tuesday, the fifteenth of November
at half past ten o'clock
for the benefit of
The Guild for the Blind

The subscription is three dollars
for each person

Frequently the invitations to a dance issued by a club list the names of the patrons or patronesses. If there are just a few names, they may appear on the face of the invitation, as shown below. But if there are many names, they should be listed separately on the inside or reverse side of the invitation. Occasionally the addresses of the patrons are also given when tickets are on sale at their homes.

The pleasure of your company is requested
at a
Spring Dance
on Saturday evening, the second of May
at ten o'clock
The Wynnfield Club

Patronesses

Mrs. Robert Bruce	Mrs. Charles Cort
Mrs. John T. Price	Mrs. Earle Higgens
Mrs. Arthur Hervey	Mrs. Charles Gordon

Please send reply to
Dance Committee
The Wynnfield Club

Tickets five dollars
for each person

Invitations to subscription dinner dances usually give the name of the person through whom reservations can be made. For example:

The Graduating Class of 1938
Hahnemann Medical College and Hospital
invites you to attend a
Dinner Dance
at
The Bellevue-Stratford
Wednesday, the fourth of October
at half past seven o'clock

Make reservations through
Miss Margaret Baker   Tickets five dollars
11 Rittenhouse Square   for each person

INVITATIONS FOR
INFORMAL DANCES

Some people still cling to the custom of using visiting cards as informal invitations to dances, teas, musicales, even luncheon and supper parties. They simply scribble the few necessary words in a corner of the card—usually the lower left corner—and let it go at that!

We cannot approve this use of visiting cards for invitations. It's a careless and "sloppy" social habit, and should not be encouraged. Originally intended as a convenient substitute for engraved third-person forms, visiting card invitations have a curt and unflattering connotation. They sound *hurried*. They have neither the dignity of formal engraved invitations, nor the warmth and charm of friendly informal notes.

However, as some people still use visiting cards for invitations, and you will no doubt continue to receive them from time to time, you should know what kind of party they represent—and what kind of acknowledgment you are expected to write.

If you receive an invitation like one of the following, you can expect a not-too-formal party, somewhat more important socially

Mr. and Mrs. Frank Price

Buffet Supper
Sunday at Eight

R. S. V. P

30 Lake Drive

Mr. and Mrs. Robert Maitland

Dancing at 10
Tues. June 14

400 Park Avenue

To Meet
Mrs. Joel Kane

Mr. George Warren

Wed. June 6
Bridge at 4

Highbridge Road

than a simple little supper or dance for intimate friends would be, but not important or elaborate enough to warrant engraved invitations.

These invitations should be answered at once whether a reply is requested or not, and they should be answered by personal note. It may be more convenient to write, "Delighted! Sunday at eight" on your own visiting card and send it to your hostess. And fundamentally, of course, that's no more incorrect than the invitation is. But it's so much more courteous to write a friendly note . . . just as it would have been more courteous to write a friendly *note of invitation* instead of sending a visiting card!

So whenever you receive a visiting card invitation, write a brief but cordial note in response. If it's an acceptance, write with evident pleasure; make it clear you are looking forward to the occasion:

> Dear Mrs. Maitland:
>
> What a pleasant surprise to receive your invitation for Tuesday, June 14th, at 10 o'clock! Dr. Benton and I will be *delighted* to come.
>
> May I add that we are looking forward with great pleasure to seeing you and Mr. Maitland again!
>
> > Sincerely yours,
> > Elizabeth K. Benton

If you cannot accept the invitation, explain why in your note. If there is no real reason, if you just don't want to go, the easiest way out is to say you have another engagement . . . but say it graciously and with apparent regret:

> Dear Mrs. Maitland:
>
> I'm so disappointed not to be able to accept your kind invitation for Tuesday, June 14th. We have another engagement for that evening—one we cannot very well get out of.

Dr. Benton and I sincerely regret not being able to come, and we hope you understand and forgive us under the circumstances.

Cordially yours,
Elizabeth K. Benton

THE FRIENDLY NOTE
OF INVITATION

When you plan a simple, informal dance to celebrate a birthday or anniversary, to entertain a son or daughter home from school, or perhaps merely to repay a group of friends for their hospitality to you—you invite your guests either by telephone or by note. It's always more desirable to write notes if you have the time. They may be as short as you like, but they should be *cordial*. Following are several examples for various types of small dances:

Dear Mrs. Brown:

Will you and Mr. Brown give us the pleasure of your company on Thursday, March eighth, at ten o'clock? We are planning a small, informal dance; and Dr. Benton and I should like very much indeed to have you join us.

We do hope you have made no other arrangements for the eighth, and that we can look forward to seeing you.

Sincerely yours,
Elizabeth K. Benton

Dear Ruth:

Next Friday, September the fifth, is Tom's birthday—and I thought it would be pleasant to have some of his friends here to help him celebrate. Will you and Bill come? We'll have dancing from nine until midnight, and then cut the birthday cake!

Tom and I are both very eager to have you here, so don't disappoint us!

Affectionately yours,
Betty

Dear Suzanne:

Richard will be home for Thanksgiving next week. We are having some of his friends in for dancing on Friday evening, the twenty-third, and I hope you can come.

The dancing will be from nine-thirty to midnight, and we'll see that you get home safely. So *do* come!

Sincerely yours,
Elizabeth K. Benton

Dear Peter:

Mother has asked me to invite a few friends to a small, informal dance she is giving for me next Wednesday, April third, at nine o'clock.

Many people you know will be here—and I hope you can come, too.

Sincerely yours,
Anita Benton

Dear Julie:

If you meet a witch or a ghost on the way here Saturday night, October the sixteenth, don't be alarmed! They'll just be guests on their way to our masquerade.

I'd like you and your brother Bob to come. You can dress here if you like, or you can come all dressed and masked so that nobody recognizes you. I think that's more fun!

Come at nine, Julie. There'll be dancing until eleven, and a buffet supper afterward. I hope that both you and Bob can make it.

With love,
Anita

It's entirely proper to write, "I'd like you and your brother to come" in an informal invitation. But do *not* address the envelope to "Miss Julie Clark and brother." That's distinctly bad form. A note written to one person should never be addressed in any way except to that one person.

Acceptances

Dear Mrs. Benton:

Mr. Brown and I will be delighted to come to your dance on Thursday, March the eighth, at ten o'clock. It was kind of you and Dr. Benton to think of us, and to include us among your guests.

We look forward with much pleasure to seeing you both again.

Cordially yours,
Millicent Brown

Dear Betty:

Of course we'll come and help Tom celebrate his birthday! It sounds like lots of fun.

Friday, September the fifth, at nine . . . it's a date! Bill and I will be there promptly. And thanks so much for asking us!

Affectionately,
Ruth

Dear Mrs. Benton:

I'll be very glad to come for dancing on Friday evening, the twenty-third, at nine-thirty.

I think it was very kind of you to ask me!

Sincerely yours,
Suzanne Jennings

Remember that even between good friends, notes of invitation and acknowledgment should be brief and to the point. Don't let yourself be tempted to write of other things.

Dear Anita:

I'm certainly glad you invited me to your dance on Wednesday, April third, at nine o'clock. I'd have hated to miss it!

Thanks for asking me. I'll sure be looking forward to April the third!

> Sincerely yours,
> Peter Whitney

Dear Anita:

What fun! Masquerades are my favorite kind of party, and I wouldn't miss yours for anything!

Bob and I will be there on Saturday, the sixteenth, at nine o'clock. We're coming all dressed and masked, and we *hope* you won't know who we are!

I'm so glad there'll be dancing, Nita. You know how I love it! Bob does, too- -and he says to be sure and thank you for inviting him.

With love to you and your mother,

> Julie

Regrets

Dear Mrs. Benton:

It was very kind of you and Dr. Benton to invite us for Thursday, March the eighth—and we are extremely sorry that we cannot accept.

Mr. Brown must leave for Los Angeles on the seventh. He tried to postpone the trip for a few days, but was unable to do so.

But thank you so much for asking us, and we hope to have the pleasure of seeing you both soon.

> Cordially yours,
> Millicent Brown

Dear Betty:

It's not easy to say "no" to a party at your house— especially when it's to help Tom celebrate his birthday, but we just can't help ourselves! Bill invited some clients for dinner on Friday, the fifth, and I just don't see how we can get out of it gracefully.

Bill is as disappointed as I am. We certainly wish either *our* dinner or *your* dance were on another evening!

Please give our love and congratulations to Tom on his birthday, and tell him we're sorry as can be to miss his party. We'll have to come and pay our respects another time.

Thanks for asking us, Betty—and our sincere regrets!

Devotedly yours,
Ruth

Dear Mrs. Benton:

I'd love to come to your dance for Richard on Friday, the twenty-third, but mother and I are going to Baltimore for the week end to be with my sister. Both she and the baby have been ill.

Thanks for asking me, Mrs. Benton—I think it was very sweet of you. I'm sure you must know how disappointed I am not to be able to accept.

Sincerely yours,
Suzanne Jennings

Dear Anita:

Gosh, I'm sorry—but my cousin's being married on Wednesday, April the third, and we're all going to Scarsdale for the wedding. I sure wish the bride had picked some other day!

It was swell of you to invite me to your dance, and I hate to miss it. Please give my regrets to your mother, too.

I hope you'll give me the chance to say "yes" some other time, Anita.

Sincerely yours,
Peter Whitney

Dear Anita:

My mother and dad are celebrating their wedding anniversary on Saturday, October the sixteenth, and of course they expect Bob and me to be with them. Dad has tickets for the theater, and I think he has made a reservation for somewhere afterwards—but he won't tell us the details. He says it's a surprise.

Bob and I simply *hate* missing your masquerade—it sounds like such fun! And you know how we both love to dance! But it's just one of those things, Nita. . . . We can't let mother and dad down.

I'll be thinking of you on the sixteenth, and wishing I were there. Bob says to be sure and thank you for asking him; he's as sorry to miss your party as I am.

With love,
Julie

ASKING AN INVITATION FOR
A RELATIVE OR FRIEND

It is never permissible to ask for an invitation of any kind for yourself. Nor is it permissible to ask for a luncheon or dinner invitation for someone else. But if you are invited to an informal dance, and you have someone staying with you at the time——or you would like to take someone along whom you think your hostess would enjoy meeting—it's entirely proper to ask for an invitation.

Dear Mrs. Benton:

I know that you and Dr. Benton are interested in Indian folklore and legend. My nephew, Ralph Harris, who has just written a book about the Indians of New York State, is staying with us—and I would like to bring him to your dance on Thursday, March the eighth. I think you will enjoy meeting him; and I know *he* will enjoy seeing your unusual Indian collection.

May I bring him? I know he'll be delighted to receive your invitation. But if you feel you cannot invite another guest, please say so frankly and I'll understand.

Mr. Brown and I are looking forward with pleasure to the eighth!

Cordially yours,
Millicent Brown

Dear Betty:

Bill's brother has just arrived unexpectedly from California; and as he'll only be here a few days, we don't like to desert him even for an evening.

So may we bring him to your dance on the fifth? He's a most charming and congenial person, and I'm sure you and Tom will enjoy meeting him.

But if you'd rather not have an extra guest, Betty—please say so! We'll get him a ticket for the theater or something, and come help Tom celebrate his birthday anyway!

Affectionately yours,
Ruth

Dear Mrs. Benton:

I would love to come to your dance on Friday, the twenty-third—but I have a house guest this week, and I can't very well leave her alone for the evening.

Her name is Janet Carey. She lives in Virginia and she is my roommate at school.

I know she would be very happy if you invited her to the dance; and I'd like very much to bring her. But if it would be inconvenient for you to have another guest, please tell me!

Thank you for inviting me, Mrs. Benton. I do hope you won't think I'm too presuming in asking to bring my friend.

Sincerely yours,
Suzanne Jennings

The hostess who receives such a note should reply at once, either extending a courteous invitation to the stranger, or explaining frankly why she cannot do so.

Dear Suzanne:

By all means bring Miss Carey with you to the dance on Friday, the twenty-third! I'll be delighted to have her.

Sincerely yours,
Elizabeth K. Benton

or

Dear Suzanne:

I would be very happy to include your friend among my guests for the twenty-third, but so *many* of Richard's friends are coming that I'm afraid there will be very little space for dancing as it is.

I hope you understand, and that you will give me the opportunity of meeting Miss Carey some other time.

Sincerely yours,
Elizabeth K. Benton

6

Wedding Invitations and Announcements

In the start of their social life together, a bride and groom naturally want to be *correct*. They want their wedding to be perfect in every detail, as traditionally beautiful and dignified as they can make it.

With all the many other things to plan and decide in connection with the ceremony and reception, it's nice to know that in the matter of invitations there need be no problem, no difficulty. Here at least it's easy for the bride and groom to make their choice, and to know that their choice is the right one. For whether a wedding is of great social importance or great simplicity, the forms are fixed by custom and long usage . . . and it's necessary only to select the particular invitation or announcement that suits the circumstances.

All the approved engraved forms for church and home weddings are given in this chapter, as well as suggestions for the simple, informal notes that are written by hand when the wedding is a very small and intimate one. But first, here is a general commentary on the etiquette of wedding invitations . . . answers to the questions people ask most frequently on the subject:

1. Everything about a wedding should be in quiet dignity and good taste, including the invitations and announcements. Only white paper of finest quality should be used, and it should be entirely without decoration—except, perhaps, for a family crest or coat of arms embossed without color. Gilt edges, borders, monograms, entwined initials are all in extremely bad taste.

2. Engraved invitations are traditional for all weddings, large and small. But if it's a very simple, informal wedding for just a few relatives, or a quiet wedding due to a recent death in the family, invitations may be by personal note, or even by telephone. In this case, formal announcements are usually sent on the day of the wedding, or soon after, to everyone on the mailing list of both families.

3. Wedding invitations come in two sizes: *large* double sheets which fold once into the envelope, and *smaller* double sheets which slide into the envelope without folding. Both are correct. But it is *not* good form to use cards or single sheets.

4. The engraving is aways in black. The style of lettering depends on personal choice, and on the size of the invitation.

5. Wedding invitations and announcements are usually enclosed in two envelopes, although one may be used. When two are used, the inside envelope is left unsealed (should not be gummed). The invitation, reception card, and whatever other cards or enclosures are required, are placed in this inside envelope. Tissue, if provided by the stationer, is left in place to prevent smudging.

Only the name or names of the persons being invited are written on the inside envelope. If Mr. and Mrs. John Malcolm Stewart and their two children are invited, the inside envelope reads:

Mr. and Mrs. Stewart
(No given name)
Judy and Neal
(Children under 21)

An adult son or daughter living at home should receive a separate invitation. The phrase "and family" should not be used, on the inside or outside envelope. Two adult sisters are addressed as "Misses Jean and Harriet Stewart" on the outside envelope, "The Misses Stewart" on the inside envelope. Two adult sons are addressed as "Messrs. (or "The Messrs.") Neal and Craig Stewart"—with "Messrs. Stewart" on the inside envelope.

Even when several children are included on the inside envelope, the outside envelope is addressed to the parents only. Here, of course, the full name is used; initials should be avoided if possible. It is traditional for wedding invitations and announcements to be addressed by hand; and only black ink should be used.

Place the inside envelope into the outer one so that the name of the guest faces forward. Just insert it with its flap, or back, facing the raised flap of the outside envelope and it will be in the proper position. The use of two envelopes is not for formality only; the outside envelope protects the invitation and enclosures.

6. Start making your guest list well ahead of time; and be sure to order an adequate supply of invitations. It's better to have a few left over than to discover at the last moment that you forgot a distant cousin or an old school friend, and haven't another invitation to send. Relatives or friends in distant places, or in mourning, may be invited even though they are not expected to attend.

7. Wedding invitations should be mailed at least one month in advance; and as engraving takes time, be sure to see your stationer early. You will find it helpful to have the outside envelopes delivered a week or two ahead of time so that they can be addressed and ready to mail by the time the engraved invitations arrive.

8. Announcements should be ordered at the same time as the invitations, and should be similar in style and wording. They are mailed on the day of the wedding or *after* it, to those who did not receive invitations.

9. Invitations and announcements are issued by the bride's parents, even though she may not be living at home. If one parent is dead, the invitations are issued in the name of the remaining parent. If neither parent is living, the invitations

are issued by the nearest relative (like a married brother and his wife)—or by a guardian. In rare cases, when there are no relatives and no guardian, the invitations may be issued by an intimate friend—or the bride and groom may send them out in their own names. In the latter case, the bride's name comes first. When invitations or announcements are issued by someone other than the bride's parents, or a relative with the same name as her own, the bride's *full name* should be used to prevent confusion.

10. Parents who are separated may unite their names on the occasion of their daughter's wedding, if they so wish. Thus the invitations may be issued by "Mr. and Mrs. Frank B. Mitchell"—even though "Mr." and "Mrs." have been living apart for many years. But if parents are legally divorced, and especially if one or the other has remarried, the invitations should be issued only in the name of the parent with whom the daughter has been living. If that parent has remarried, the invitations should be issued in the names of the parent and the new mate. It would be a glaring discourtesy to issue the invitations in the name of a parent alone, when that parent has remarried and the bride has been making her home with both.

    When a bride has lived part of the time with one parent and part of the time with the other, the invitations are usually issued in the name of her mother.*

11. The year is not necessary on wedding invitations, and is not ordinarily used. But if it *is* used, it should be written as spoken: "Nineteen hundred and sixty." The form, "One thousand, nine hundred and sixty" is an affectation and should be avoided.

12. The year *should* be given on wedding announcements—also the city or town in which the ceremony was held. This applies even after an elopement, and regardless of the time that has elapsed between the marriage and the announcement.

---

* Examples of invitations to meet special and unusual circumstances will be found on pages 197 to 206.

But the name of the church or the house address where
the ceremony was performed is not necessary, though it is
frequently given.

13. Numbers, names, street addresses, dates should all be spelled
out in full on an engraved invitation or announcement.
Numerals may be used only if an address is unusually long
and would look clumsy and unattractive if spelled out on
the invitation.

14. If necessary, the street address may be engraved under the
name of the church.

15. The word "to" is used between the names of the bride and
groom on announcements and on invitations to the ceremony. But the word "and" is grammatically necessary instead of "to" on invitations to a wedding breakfast or reception—because by that time the bride and groom are
already man *and* wife.

16. The words "honor" and "favor" are frequently spelled with
a "u" on wedding invitations and announcements. But this
is now looked upon as an affectation in this country, and
the use of the Americanized form (without the "u") is
recommended.

17. The phrase "request the honor of your presence" is always
used for church weddings. It may also be used for home,
club or hotel weddings—but as such invitations include
the reception following the ceremony, the phrase "request
the pleasure of your company" is generally considered more
suitable.

18. "Wedding breakfast" is the term generally used for the
reception following the ceremony if it's before one o'clock
in the afternoon. If it's *after* one o'clock, "reception" is
the correct word to use.

19. At the typical wedding, family and intimate friends are
invited to the reception and the ceremony; less intimate
friends, neighbors, acquaintances and business associates are
invited to the church only. Two sets of invitations may be
ordered for the two groups of guests: one for the ceremony
only, the other for the ceremony and reception. Or the

same invitation may be sent to all guests, with a separate card enclosed for those invited to the reception.

20. When an invitation is for the church ceremony only, a reply is not ordinarily required—and as a rule none is requested. But when the invitation is to both the ceremony and the reception following it, a reply is generally requested. The letters "R.s.v.p." or the phrase "Please reply" may be engraved in the lower left corner of the invitation; or a separate card to be filled out and returned by the guest may be enclosed.

21. Occasionally, when one of the bride's parents is an invalid, the wedding ceremony is very small and private, with only the immediate families present; but a big reception follows for all the relatives and friends. In this case, *reception invitations* only are issued. Invitations to the ceremony are either given verbally to the few who are to be present; or "Ceremony at three o'clock" is written on a small card and enclosed with the invitation to the reception.

ANNOUNCING AN ENGAGEMENT

Engagements are usually announced informally at a luncheon or supper party. Or public announcement is made by writing or telephoning the society editor of the local papers. But occasionally formal announcement of an engagement is sent to members of the family and to friends. The correct wording for an engraved formal announcement follows:

Mr. and Mrs. George Coleman
have the honor to announce
the engagement of their daughter
Harriet
to
Mr. John Anthony Wayne

If the engagement is subsequently broken off, an announcement to that effect must be sent to all who received the original

announcement. That's one reason many people prefer to tell the
news casually and informally, instead of issuing engraved announcements. But if such announcements *have* been sent out
and the engagement is then broken off, an announcement like
the following should be sent to the same people:

Mr. and Mrs. George Coleman
wish to announce
that the engagement of their daughter
Harriet
and
Mr. John Anthony Wayne
has been broken by mutual consent

THE CHURCH WEDDING

Here is the correct form for an invitation to a church ceremony:

Mr. and Mrs. Gerald Weylin
request the honor of your presence
at the marriage of their daughter
Margaret
to
Mr. Donald Blaine
on Thursday morning, the seventh of June
at ten o'clock
St. Thomas Episcopal Church
New York

If preferred, the fill-in type of invitation may be used, with
space for the guest's name to be written by hand.

Mr. and Mrs. Gerald Weylin
request the honor of

Mr and Mrs. Alan Brewster's

presence at the marriage of their daughter
Margaret
to
Mr. Donald Blaine
on Thursday, the seventh of June
at ten o'clock in the morning
St. Thomas Episcopal Church
New York

The reception card to go with the above invitation would read as follows:

Mr. and Mrs. Gerald Weylin
request the pleasure of your company
at breakfast
Thursday, the seventh of June
at half past twelve o'clock
Forty-five Park Avenue

Please respond

Or instead of the above form, a small card may be enclosed with the invitation reading simply:

Breakfast
immediately following the ceremony
Forty-five Park Avenue

Please respond

Remember that *"breakfast"* is the proper term for a reception held before one o'clock . . . *"reception"* is the proper term after one o'clock.

The invitation for an afternoon or evening church ceremony is exactly the same as the invitation for a morning ceremony— except, of course, for the difference in time. An afternoon invitation would read:

on Thursday, the seventh of June
at four o'clock

or whatever the time may be. An evening invitation would read:

on Thursday evening, the seventh of June
at eight o'clock

or

on Thursday, the seventh of June
at nine o'clock in the evening

There are several types of reception cards suitable for afternoon and evening weddings. The simplest and most familiar type is a card reading:

Reception
at ten o'clock
The St. Moritz

Please send response to
Forty-five Park Avenue

Another popular type of reception card leaves space for the guest's name to be written in:

Mr. and Mrs. Gerald Weylin
request the pleasure of

Mr. and Mrs. Alan Brewster's

company immediately following the ceremony
The St. Moritz

Please address reply to
Forty-five Park Avenue

These cards are enclosed in the envelope with the invitation to the ceremony—for those guests who are invited to both the ceremony and the reception. For guests who are invited to the reception only, an invitation like the following is more acceptable:

Mr. and Mrs. Gerald Weylin
request the pleasure of your company
at the wedding reception of their daughter
Margaret
and
Mr. Donald Blaine
on Thursday, the seventh of June
at four o'clock
The St. Moritz

Please reply to
Forty-five Park Avenue

If all guests, or most of the guests, are invited to both the ceremony at the church and the reception following it, a combined invitation like the following may be used:

Mr. and Mrs. Gerald Weylin
request the honor of your presence
at the marriage of their daughter
Margaret
to
Mr. Donald Blaine
on Thursday, the seventh of June
at twelve o'clock
St. Thomas Episcopal Church
New York
and afterwards at breakfast
at the St. Moritz

Please reply to
Forty-five Park Avenue

Occasionally a reception is given for the bride and groom at the home of a relative or friend. The invitation should be in the name of the bride's parents, regardless of who gives the reception. Here is the correct wording for a card enclosed with the invitation to the ceremony:

> Mr. and Mrs. Gerald Weylin
> request the pleasure of your company
> at the residence of
> Mr. and Mrs. John Ridgely
> Nine Hundred Riverside Drive
> immediately following the ceremony

The reply to such an invitation is always sent to the parents of the bride and not to the people in whose home the reception is held.

CHURCH ADMISSION CARD

When the wedding is large, the church small, and the general public is not to be admitted, cards of admission are necessary for the guests. These are usually engraved in the same style as the invitations, and are enclosed with them. The wording is simply:

> Please present this card
> at St. Thomas Episcopal Church
> on Thursday, the seventh of June

For members of the family and intimate friends, the number of the pew may be written on the admission card in ink. If they are not to occupy individually reserved pews but a special area "ribboned" off at the front of the church, the phrase "Within the ribbon" may be written in the lower left corner of the admission card. If admission cards are not necessary, "Pew No. 7" or "Within the ribbon" may be written on a small white card and enclosed with the invitation.

THE HOME WEDDING

The invitation to a *church* wedding is solely for the ceremony, which is why a separate invitation to the wedding breakfast or reception must be enclosed with it. But the invitation to a *home* wedding is for both the ceremony and the reception. Obviously a second invitation to stay on at a house to which the guest is already invited is unnecessary.

Either "honor of your presence" or "pleasure of your company" may be used on the invitation for a home wedding. One is used as much as the other, and both are correct . . . but "honor of your presence" belongs more rightfully to the sacred and solemn dignity of the church.

Here is a typical invitation to a wedding held at the home of the bride:

Mr. and Mrs. Anthony Duncan

request the pleasure of your company

at the marriage of their daughter

Edith Anne

to

Mr. Eugene Griffith

on Tuesday, the tenth of October

at four o'clock

Sixty-four Lake Drive

Chicago, Illinois

The favor of a reply
is requested

If the invitations are issued by the parents of the bride, but the wedding ceremony takes place in a home other than their own, this is the form of invitation to use:

Mr. and Mrs. Anthony Duncan
request the pleasure of your company
at the marriage of their daughter
Edith Anne
to
Mr. Eugene Griffith
on Tuesday, the tenth of October
at four o'clock
at the residence of Mr. and Mrs. John Porter
Twenty-six Ivy Street
Chicago, Illinois

If the ceremony is private and guests are invited to the reception only, the following form is used. Note that the word "and" is used instead of "to"—as by the time of the reception the bride and groom are already married.

Mr. and Mrs. Anthony Duncan
request the pleasure of your company
at the wedding reception of their daughter
Edith Anne
and
Mr. Eugene Griffith
on Tuesday, the tenth of October
at eight o'clock
The Drake
Chicago, Illinois

Please send reply to
Sixty-four Lake Drive

For an outdoor wedding, the same form of invitation is used as for any other home wedding . . . except that the phrase "in the garden" appears just above the address. For example:

on Tuesday, the tenth of October
at four o'clock
in the garden
Sixty-four Lake Drive
Chicago, Illinois

As a rule, a rain card is enclosed with the invitation to an outdoor wedding. This is a small card engraved to conform with
the invitation, and reads simply:

In the event of rain
the ceremony will be held
at Saint Paul's Church

TRAIN AND DIRECTION CARDS

When a wedding takes place at a country home, the transportation of guests is sometimes arranged by the bride's parents.
They may have a special car added to a regular train for the
convenience of the guests; or if it's a very big wedding, they
may charter a special train for the occasion. Train cards are
generally enclosed with the invitation and guests use them in
place of tickets. If it's for a special car, this is the best form to
use:

A special car will be attached to the train
leaving Pennsylvania Station, New York
for Southampton at 10.40 A.M.
and to the returning train
leaving Southampton at 8.20 P.M.

Please present this card in place of a ticket

If it's for a special train, this is the way the card is customarily
worded:

A special train
on the Long Island Railroad
will leave the Pennsylvania Station, New York
for Southampton at 10.40 A.M.
and returning
will leave Southampton at 8.20 P.M.

Please present this card in place of a ticket

When transportation is not provided, a small card is often
enclosed with the invitation to indicate the best trains to take.
This is a thoughtful gesture that guests appreciate. The information may be neatly written by hand on plain white cards; or
engraved cards for the purpose may be ordered at the same time
as the invitations. This is the usual wording:

Train leaves Pennsylvania Station
for Southampton at 10.40 A.M.

Returning train leaves Southampton
for New York at 8.20 P.M.

Route maps and direction cards are also frequently enclosed
with the invitation to a country wedding. A simplified map may
be printed or engraved on a card for all guests coming from a
certain point, like New York. Or a direction card like the following may be used to help guests find their way to the wedding
without too much difficulty:

Automobiles from New York follow
Route 27 to Old Town
then turn right at the white arrow
and follow Hedgerow Road
to Shady Acres

Train and direction cards do not need to be enclosed in separate envelopes. They are merely slipped into the same envelope as

the invitation. However, it's a good idea to use sheets of tissue between the cards and the invitation to prevent smudging. Suitable tissue for this purpose—very thin and in the proper size—can be provided by your stationer.

WEDDING ANNOUNCEMENTS

When a wedding is small and private and no general invitations are issued, it is customary to send out formal announcements on the day of the ceremony or very soon afterward. Such announcements should have all the traditional beauty and dignity of wedding invitations—being engraved on the finest white paper and, like invitations, enclosed in two envelopes.

The announcement is made by whoever would have sent out the wedding invitations. That means the parents or nearest relative, whether actually present at the ceremony or not. For example, even if the bride's mother is an invalid—even if her father is abroad at the time of the ceremony—the announcements are issued in the names of both parents.

Announcements are never sent to those who were present at the ceremony. Nor are they sent *instead* of invitations to relatives and friends living at a great distance. An *invitation* sent to someone far away means, "We would have loved to have you with us!" But an *announcement* means, "We couldn't invite you to the wedding, but we want you to know about it."

Here is the correct wording for a formal wedding announcement:

Mr. and Mrs. Anthony Duncan
have the honor of announcing
the marriage of their daughter
Edith Anne
to
Mr. Eugene Griffith
on Tuesday, the tenth of October
Nineteen hundred and sixty
Saint Paul's Church
Chicago, Illinois

Instead of "honor of announcing" it is also correct to use "honor to announce" or just "announce." For example, here is the form customarily used for announcements after an elopement. Notice that the name of the city or town in which the ceremony was held is given; but the name of the church or the house address where the ceremony was performed is not necessary (though it is frequently included):

Mr. and Mrs. Clyde Peters
announce the marriage of their daughter
Marion
to
Mr. Nelson Crowinshield
on Friday, the twentieth of June
Nineteen hundred and sixty
Carson City, Nevada

If the bride is a young widow or divorcée, the announcement is still made in the name of her parents or nearest kin:

Mr. and Mrs. Clyde Peters
announce the marriage of their daughter
Marion Peters Armstrong
to
Mr. Nelson Crowinshield
on Friday, the twentieth of June
Nineteen hundred and sixty
Carson City, Nevada

But if the widow or divorcée is a woman of mature years, the announcement may be made in her own name and that of the groom, as follows:

Mrs. Helen Wallace Smith
and
Mr. William Tracy Hamilton
announce their marriage
on Friday, the twenty-first of May
Nineteen hundred and sixty
at Saratoga Springs, New York

Ordinarily "Mrs." is not used before the name of a widow or divorcée on an announcement of her remarriage, when the announcement is issued by her parents or other relatives. But it is *always* used on announcements issued by the bride and groom themselves.

ENCLOSING "AT HOME" CARDS
WITH THE ANNOUNCEMENT

If the bride and groom want to let their friends know where they are going to live, they send them cards of address—or as they are more familiarly called, "at home" cards. These are usually enclosed with the announcements of the marriage; or they are sent out separately after the bride and groom are settled in their own home and ready to receive visitors.

The typical at home card is about the size of a visiting card and reads:

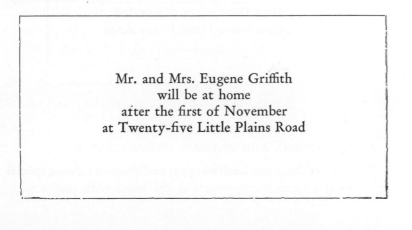

Mr. and Mrs. Eugene Griffith
will be at home
after the first of November
at Twenty-five Little Plains Road

Or a joint visiting card of the new "Mr. and Mrs." may be used, with the address indicated in the lower right corner:

Mr. and Mrs. Eugene Griffith

25 Little Plains Road

At home cards engraved with the bride's new name should not be sent out *before* the ceremony—for the reason, of course, that she has not yet acquired her new name. However, cards without any name may be enclosed with the invitations. These would read:

At home
after the first of November
Twenty-five Little Plains Road

WEDDING INVITATIONS FOR
SPECIAL AND UNUSUAL CIRCUMSTANCES

Not all weddings conform to type; and those involving special or unusual circumstances—such as the bride with one parent, the bride whose parents have remarried, the double wedding for sisters, and so on—require special wording of the invitation.

The forms that follow are for these special cases; and though they are for invitations, they apply also to wedding *announcements* issued under the same circumstances.

INVITATION TO A DOUBLE WEDDING

Mr. and Mrs. Henry Hassett
request the honor of your presence
at the marriage of their daughters
Nancy Joan
to
Mr. Robert Kinnaird
and
Amy Jean
to
Mr. Harrison Colt
on Friday, the second of October
at four o'clock
Grace Church
Brookline, Massachusetts

Sometimes friends or cousins are married on the same day, at the same time, and invitations are issued jointly for both ceremonies. The wording of a double wedding invitation when the brides are *not* sisters should include the surnames of the brides to prevent any possibility of confusion:

Mr. and Mrs. Henry Hassett
and
Mr. and Mrs. John Ward Sheldon
request the honor of your presence
at the marriage of their daughters
Nancy Joan Hassett
to
Mr. Robert Kinnaird
and
Marion Sheldon
to
Mr. Frederick Bowen
on Thursday, the fourth of October
at four o'clock
Grace Church
Brookline, Massachusetts

THE BRIDE WITH ONE PARENT

If a bride's mother is dead and her father has not remarried the invitations are issued in his name alone:

Mr. James Norman Walsh
requests the honor of your presence
at the marriage of his daughter
Edith
to
Mr. Curtis Phelps
and so forth

If the bride's father is dead and her mother has not remarried the invitations are issued in the name of the mother.

But if the mother *has* remarried and the bride has a stepfather, the invitations are issued in the names of both. Following are the two forms that are most frequently used. Both are correct; the choice is entirely a matter of personal preference. The bride's *full name* should always be used; and in the first of the two forms given below, "her daughter" may be used instead of "their daughter."

Mr. and Mrs. Benjamin Crane
request the honor of your presence
at the marriage of their daughter
Mary Alice Thorne
and so forth

or

Mr. and Mrs. Benjamin Crane
request the honor of your presence
at the marriage of
Mrs. Crane's daughter
Mary Alice Thorne
and so forth

If the bride has a stepmother, the invitations may read "the marriage of their daughter," "the marriage of his daughter," or "the marriage of Mr. Walsh's daughter"—depending on which wording best suits the circumstances and the wishes of those most intimately concerned. In this instance, of course, the bride's full name does not need to be used as it's the same as the name in which the invitations are issued.

WHEN THE PARENTS OF THE BRIDE ARE DIVORCED

Parents who are divorced and remarried do *not*, under any circumstances, combine their different names on invitations or announcements for their daughter's marriage. It's not only a question of taste and propriety. The names of divorced parents and their new mates appearing together on a wedding invitation is an affront to the sacred dignity of marriage.

Invitations should be issued in the name of the parent with whom the bride has been living. If that parent has remarried, the invitations are issued in the names of the parent *and* the new mate. If the bride has lived part of the time with one parent and part of the time with the other, the invitations are usually issued in the name of the mother.

Here is the wording to use when the bride's mother is a divorcée who has not remarried:

Mrs. Preston Hodges
requests the honor of your presence
at the marriage of her daughter
Carolyn
and so forth

Here is the wording to use when the bride's mother is a divorcée who *has* remarried:

Mr. and Mrs. Ronald Fischer
request the honor of your presence
at the marriage of her daughter
Carolyn Hodges
and so forth

or

Mr. and Mrs. Ronald Fischer
request the honor of your presence
at the marriage of
Mrs. Fischer's daughter
Carolyn Hodges
and so forth

WHEN THE BRIDE HAS NO PARENTS

As a rule, when a bride has no parents the invitations are issued by her oldest brother, whether he is married or not. Or a sister, aunt, grandparent or other close relative gives the wedding and issues the invitations. If there are no relatives and no guardian, the invitations may be issued by intimate friends. And in those rare cases when there are neither relatives nor friends to issue the invitations, the bride and groom invite their own guests —using the form immediately below:

The honor of your presence
is requested at the marriage of
Miss Laura Ellen Kay
to
Mr. Thomas Field Macfarlane
on Thursday, the eighteenth of June
at twelve o'clock
Trinity Church
Detroit, Michigan

When wedding invitations are issued by a married brother and
sister-in-law of the bride, this is the proper wording:

Mr. and Mrs. Henry Fairchild
request the honor of your presence
at the marriage of their sister
Janet Fairchild
to
Mr. William Pierce
on Friday, the third of October
at four o'clock
Grace Church
Brookline, Massachusetts

Following is the correct form to use when a married sister
and brother-in-law give the wedding and issue the invitations:

Mr. and Mrs. John Alan Wright
request the honor of your presence
at the marriage of their sister
Eleanor Rogers
to
Mr. Frank Pearson
on Wednesday, the first of June
at four o'clock
Saint Paul's Church
Seattle, Washington

When friends give a wedding reception at their home for a bride who has no parents, this is the way the invitation should read:

Mr. and Mrs. Maxwell Burton
request the pleasure of your company
at the wedding reception of
Miss Martha Helstrom
and
Mr. Raymond Frank Peterson
at four o'clock
Six Beach Lane Road
Manhasset, Long Island

Please respond

INVITATIONS FOR A SECOND MARRIAGE

If a widow or divorcée is young, the invitations to her second marriage are issued in the name of her parents or nearest relative; and the form is the same as for her first wedding except that the full name is used. For example:

Mr. and Mrs. Henry Hassett
request the honor of your presence
at the marriage of their daughter
Nancy Hassett Kinnaird
to
Mr. William Kingston
and so forth

If the bride is a mature woman, or if there are no relatives or old family friends to issue the invitations, this form is acceptable:

The honor of your presence is requested
at the marriage of
Mrs. Nancy Hassett Kinnaird
and
Mr. William Kingston
and so forth

The name of the bride always comes first on invitations and announcements issued by the bride and groom.

A divorcée uses whatever name she has taken after the divorce. If she has legally resumed her maiden name, it is entirely permissible for her to use it on the invitations and announcements of her second marriage.

WHEN THE GROOM IS IN THE MILITARY SERVICES

The generally accepted rule at present is that for the rank of Captain or above in the Army—Lieutenant, senior grade, or above in the Navy—the title is used in front of the name. For example:

Captain Arthur Cunningham
United States Army

For officers under these ranks, the title goes on a line directly below the name. For example:

Harold Creighton
Lieutenant, junior grade, United States Navy

If the groom is in the regular Army or Navy, the wording "United States Army" (or Navy) appears in the line below his name. But if he has been called into the Army or given a temporary commission, the positioning is the same but the wording is "Army of the United States"—or for the Navy, "United States Naval Reserve." In the case of a private or non-commissioned officer, the name is on one line and the branch of service is designated below it. For example:

Frank Pearson
Signal Corps, United States Naval Reserve

or

John Hamilton
Coast Artillery, Army of the United States

The title of "Mr." is not used in military invitations or announcements.

Army Officer's Wedding Invitation

Colonel and Mrs. Charles Higgins
request the honor of your presence
at the marriage of their daughter
Marilyn
to
Captain Richard Anderson
United States Army
on Tuesday, the tenth of October
at four o'clock
Christ Church
Santa Barbara, California

Army Officer's Wedding Announcement

Mr. and Mrs. John Curtis
announce the marriage of their daughter
Catherine Alice
to
David Alan Sewall
Second Lieutenant, United States Army
on Thursday, the seventh of September
Nineteen hundred and sixty
Boston, Massachusetts

Naval Officer's Wedding Invitation

Mr. and Mrs. Winston Evans
request the honor of your presence
at the marriage of their daughter
Marion Elaine
to
Theodore Spencer
Ensign, United States Navy
on Friday, the first of August
at twelve o'clock
Saint Paul's Church
New York

Naval Officer's Wedding Announcement

Mr. and Mrs. Thomas Rourke
announce the marriage of their daughter
Adelaide
to
Commander Ralph Cummings
United States Navy
on Thursday, the seventh of June
Nineteen hundred and sixty
Trinity Church
Washington, District of Columbia

RECALLING A WEDDING INVITATION

A sudden death in the family, serious illness or an accident may make it necessary to recall the invitations issued for a wedding. If it's very close to the date set for the wedding, someone in the family should notify immediately all who received invitations. But if there's time, small cards should be printed or engraved and sent to the list of expected guests. The announcement should be formal in wording, but is not necessarily arranged with indented lines. The reason for recalling the invitation is always given:

> Owing to the sudden death of
> Mr. Donald Blaine's sister,
> Mr. and Mrs. Gerald Weylin beg
> to recall the invitations issued
> for the marriage of their
> daughter, Margaret, on Thursday
> the seventh of June.

> or

> Mr. and Mrs. Gerald Weylin regret
> that owing to their daughter's
> illness they are obliged to re-
> call the invitations to her
> marriage on Thursday, the seventh
> of June.

When a wedding is broken off after the invitations have been issued, announcements should be sent out as quickly as possible. If comparatively few guests are expected—or if time is short—someone close to the bride (preferably her mother) should telephone the people who must be notified. No explanation need be given on the telephone or in the announcement; just a matter-of-fact statement that the wedding will not take place is all that's necessary:

> Mr. and Mrs. Gerald Weylin announce
> that the marriage of their daughter
> Margaret and Mr. Donald Blaine will
> not take place.

HOW TO ACKNOWLEDGE WEDDING INVITATIONS

An invitation to a church wedding does not require written acknowledgment—unless a reply is specifically requested, or unless an invitation to the reception is included. But a prompt acceptance or regret *is* definitely required for a home, club or hotel wedding, or for an invitation to a wedding reception.

The answer to a formal wedding invitation should not be written like a friendly note, but should be in formal third-person phraseology. It may be written in straight box form, without indented margins, if that is preferred; but the wording should follow the exact wording of the invitation—even to the repetition of date, place and time. That helps prevent the possibility of a misunderstanding. A *regret,* of course, does not require repetition of the time, as that is unimportant if one does not plan to attend.

It's thoughtless and rude to wait until two or three days before the wedding to mail your acceptance or regret. Always write your reply and mail it *promptly,* within a few days after receiving the invitation. Write it by hand, on the first page of a double sheet of your best white note paper.

Here is the correct form to use for accepting a formal invitation to a reception following the ceremony:

> Mr. and Mrs. Edward Willis
> accept with pleasure
> Mr. and Mrs. Anthony Duncan's
> kind invitation for
> Tuesday, the tenth of October
> at eight o'clock
> at the Drake

Or it may be written without the indented arrangement of the lines:

> Mr. and Mrs. Edward Willis accept
> with pleasure Mr. and Mrs. Anthony
> Duncan's kind invitation for Tues-
> day, the tenth of October at eight
> o'clock, at the Drake.

Whenever possible, the regret should include a reason for not being able to accept:

Mr. and Mrs. Edward Willis
regret that a previous engagement
prevents their accepting
Mr. and Mrs. Anthony Duncan's
kind invitation for
Tuesday, the tenth of October

A combined invitation to the ceremony and reception would
be acknowledged as follows:

Mr. and Mrs. Edward Willis
accept with pleasure
Mr. and Mrs. Anthony Duncan's
kind invitation to be present
at the marriage of their daughter
Edith Anne
to
Mr. Eugene Griffith
on Tuesday, the tenth of October
at four o'clock
and afterward at the wedding reception
at the Drake

Regret

Mr. and Mrs. Edward Willis
regret exceedingly that
owing to the illness of their son
they are unable to accept
Mr. and Mrs. Anthony Duncan's
kind invitation to be present
at the marriage of their daughter
Edith Anne
to
Mr. Eugene Griffith
on Tuesday, the tenth of October
and afterward at the wedding reception

The *announcement* of a wedding does not call for formal acknowledgment, like an invitation. You may write a note of congratulation, if you like (see page 254). Or you may send a wedding gift if that is your generous impulse. But these are entirely of your own pleasure and volition; no response is required.

THE INFORMAL WEDDING INVITATION
WRITTEN BY HAND

Personal notes are written when the wedding is very small and informal, and only a few relatives and intimate friends are invited. They should be written *by hand,* on plain white paper —preferably double sheets like those used for engraved invitations. Colored, decorated or odd-shaped stationery, or correspondence cards, are not good taste even for the most informal wedding invitations.

These little notes of invitation to a small and intimate wedding should always be written by the bride herself. Even if she is extremely busy (as most brides are before their wedding!) she should not ask a sister or a friend to write the notes for her. No one is ever too busy to write a few short notes to those they care enough about to want at a small, intimate wedding ceremony.

There is one exception to the rule that the bride always writes her own notes of invitation. If the bride's mother has an old and cherished friend, she may want to write her about the plans and invite her personally to her daughter's wedding. Here is an example:

Dear Martha:

At last my Helen has set the day! She and David are to be married very quietly at the Community Church on Thursday, June the twelfth, at noon. They have invited just a very few relatives and intimate friends; and they are all coming here after the ceremony for a simple little wedding breakfast I'm planning for them.

Helen had your name at the very top of her guest list, but I said I'd write to you myself. We'll see you at the church at twelve, Martha—and of course we expect you to come back here with us afterward for the wedding breakfast.

I am very happy, as you can imagine. I am already as devoted to David as though he were my own son!

Affectionately yours,
Sarah

*Bride's Note of Invitation
to a Close Friend*

Dear Betty:

David and I have set the date—and we want you to be the first to know it! We're going to be married *very quietly* at the Community Church on Thursday, June the twelfth, at noon. We're asking only a few people— just our nearest relatives and our very special friends.

Can you be at the house about eleven, Betty, and go to the church with us? Then we'll all come back here after the ceremony; mother's giving a little wedding breakfast for us.

Let's hope it's a bright sunny day on the twelfth! With much love,

Helen

To a Relative

Dear Aunt Kate:

David and I are to be married at the Community Church on Thursday, June the twelfth, at noon.

We want you to come to the ceremony, and also to the wedding breakfast afterward at home.

We'll be looking for you, Aunt Kate, on the twelfth!

With love,
Helen

If There Has Been a
Recent Bereavement

Dear Julia:

We have changed our plans for an elaborate church wedding because of the death of my uncle.

Instead, Bill and I are going to be married very simply and quietly at my home on Sunday, June the sixth, at four o'clock. We have invited only those we love best, and of course we want you!

There will be a small supper party at six, so plan to stay on for the evening.

Affectionately,
Grace

To an Old Friend of the Groom
—a Stranger to the Bride

Dear Mr. Knox:

Paul Lawrence and I are to be married on Sunday, May the eighth, at the Presbyterian Church on Main Street in Lenox. The ceremony will be at three o'clock.

I know Lenox is a long way from Philadelphia, but we would both love to have you come if you can possibly make it. Paul has spoken so often and so fondly of his old roommate at Exeter that I feel as though I know you! I am looking forward with very great pleasure to meeting you at last.

So *do* come if you can, and stay on for the small reception at my home in the evening. There is a train that leaves here at 9:20 and would get you back to Philadelphia before midnight.

It will make us both very happy to have you come to our wedding!

Sincerely yours,
Marjorie Willis

TO A BUSINESS ASSOCIATE

OF THE GROOM

The bride writes all the notes of invitation, including those to business associates of the groom. If a business associate is married, the note should be addressed to his wife. For example:

Dear Mrs. Harris:

Frank Peters and I are to be married at my home on Tuesday, October the fourth, at eight o'clock in the evening.

Frank has been so long and so happily associated with Mr. Harris, that the wedding just wouldn't be complete without him! We hope you can both come, and that you will stay on for the small reception following the ceremony.

Sincerely yours,
Catherine Miller

INVITING A FRIEND TO

THE RECEPTION ONLY

Dear Harriet:

Jim and I are going to be married on Friday morning, June the twentieth.

In view of circumstances with which you are familiar, the ceremony will be *very private* . . . with only my sister and one of Bill's friends as witnesses.

But we are having a small reception at the Terrace Club on the evening of the twentieth, at eight o'clock, and we want you to come. We are asking only a few of our best friends. Bill wants me to say he's as anxious to have you come as I am.

So we'll see you, won't we, Harriet—Friday at eight at the Terrace Club!

Affectionately yours,
Madeline

Informal notes of invitation like the above should be answered promptly, briefly and with a definite acceptance or regret. Sometimes relatives or friends telephone to say whether or not they are coming . . . and while that's not incorrect, it may be *inconvenient* for a busy bride and her mother to receive many calls. It is always more gracious to answer a note of invitation with a note.

TYPICAL NOTE OF ACCEPTANCE

Dear Grace:

Of course I'll come to your wedding on Sunday, June the sixth, at four o'clock—and stay on for the party in the evening. I wouldn't miss it for anything!

Thanks, darling, for including me among the friends you like best! My love to you and Jim; and I hope the sixth is a bright, beautiful day for your wedding.

Affectionately,
Julia

TYPICAL NOTE OF REGRET

Dear Miss Miller:

Mr. Harris and I regret exceedingly that we cannot accept your kind invitation for Tuesday, October the fourth.

It was sweet of you to ask us to your wedding, and we'd love to come; but unfortunately we will be in Baltimore on the fourth for our grandson's christening, and we won't be able to get back in time for your wedding.

We hope to meet Frank Peters' bride very soon; and in the meantime, we send you both our best wishes for a lifetime of happiness together!

Sincerely yours,
Dorothea Harris

INVITATIONS TO WEDDING ANNIVERSARIES

If the celebration of a wedding anniversary is simple and informal, the invitations are written by hand or are telephoned. Here is the way a note of invitation to a twenty-fifth anniversary buffet supper might be written:

Dear Alice:

Tom and I will be married twenty-five years next Thursday, June the tenth—and we want our friends to help us celebrate.

We're having a buffet supper with dancing afterward—and we hope you and John can come. Supper will be at eight.

We'll be looking for you on the tenth, Alice!

Affectionately yours,
Betty

Acceptance

Dear Betty:

It's hard to believe you and Tom have been married twenty-five years! I wish I knew your secret of staying so *young-looking!*

John and I will be delighted to come and help you celebrate your anniversary. We'll be there Thursday, June the tenth, at eight.

In the meantime, our love and congratulations to you both—and our best wishes for the long years of happiness still ahead!

Affectionately yours,
Alice

Regret

Dear Betty:

I wish we could come to your party on Thursday, the tenth, but we have already accepted a dinner engagement for that evening and I don't think we could get out of it without considerable embarrassment.

John and I would have loved to come and help you celebrate your anniversary, but we'll be with you in spirit, Betty! And we send you and Tom our congratulations and very best wishes for continued happiness in the years ahead!

Affectionately,
Alice

Frequently a formal reception is given to celebrate a twenty-fifth or fiftieth wedding anniversary. The invitations are engraved, and usually the year of the wedding and the year of the anniversary are given at the top. These significant dates—or even the entire invitation, if so desired—may be engraved in silver lettering for a twenty-fifth anniversary, in gold lettering for a fiftieth anniversary. Following are the two forms generally used for an afternoon reception. The wording is the same for an evening reception, except for the time; and if it's a dinner or a supper dance, that fact is of course specified.

1910-1960

Mr. and Mrs. Edward Paul Sullivan
request the pleasure of your company
on the Fiftieth Anniversary of their marriage
on Thursday, the seventh of October
from four until seven o'clock
The Inn
Andover, Massachusetts

1910-1960

Mr. and Mrs. Edward Paul Sullivan
At Home
on Thursday, the seventh of October
from four until seven o'clock

The Inn
Andover, Massachusetts

These invitations are answered like all other formal invitations: a definite acceptance or regret in the same precise, third-person phraseology—handwritten on plain white note paper of good quality:

Mr. and Mrs. John Wolfe
accept with pleasure
Mr. and Mrs. Edward Paul Sullivan's
kind invitation
for Thursday, the seventh of October
from four until seven o'clock
at the Inn
Andover

7

Letters of Thanks

One kind of letter most people enjoy writing is the letter of thanks or appreciation. It's pleasant to say "thank you" to someone who has been generous or thoughtful.

Every gift, however trifling, should be acknowledged with a note of thanks. Every favor or courtesy—every kindness or attention on the part of a neighbor or friend—every expression of hospitality—certainly every letter of condolence or congratulation—deserves sincere and gracious acknowledgment.

And it doesn't matter if you have already expressed your appreciation in person; a letter of thanks must still be written! It can be as brief and simple as you like; but it should express your appreciation with sincerity and warmth. Remember that half the joy of giving is the anticipation of receiving pleased acknowledgment; and surely the person who has been thoughtful or generous toward you deserves that satisfaction! Forgotten thank-you notes can soon make *you* forgotten when you'd like very much to be remembered.

Sincerity is by far the most important quality of all in a note of thanks. If it's just a run-of-the-mill "duty" note—a brief but uninspired thank-you written because such a note is expected and must be written—it defeats its own purpose. It does not give the pleasure and satisfaction a note of thanks should give.

So be sure your letter has the unmistakable ring of sincerity to it. That's much easier to accomplish when you feel grateful and appreciative than it is later on when the emotion has cooled and the enthusiasm worn off. The whole secret is this: *don't wait too long to write your note of thanks!* Don't procrastinate and keep

217

putting it off. Write your letter quickly . . . while the glow is still with you! Then you won't need to grope for words, trying to sound sincere. The words will come of their own accord, will spring naturally and sincerely from the warmth of your own enthusiasm.

We cannot tell you the exact words to put in your personal letters of thanks. After all, the every essence of sincerity is the expression of your own true feelings and sentiments. But we *can* make suggestions. And that, precisely, is what you will find in this chapter: suggestions we hope will prove helpful and stimulating when you "just don't know what to write!"

WHEN AND HOW TO ACKNOWLEDGE
WEDDING GIFTS

As soon as the wedding invitations go out, the gifts start coming in. And the smart bride starts writing her notes of thanks right away, as each gift arrives. She doesn't wait until the thank-you's pile up and get ahead of her, becoming a problem instead of a pleasure.

The bride who is systematic as well as smart, keeps a little gift book. It may be one of the handsome little books that are published for this purpose and kept as a souvenir . . . or it may be just a blank notebook like children use at school. In it she records each gift as it arrives: what it is, from whom it came, the sender's address, where the gift was purchased, when the note of thanks was written and mailed. Then she never needs to wonder, "Did I ever thank Aunt Mary for the picture?" Or, "Did I ever write and acknowledge Uncle Pete's check?"

Then, too, if the bride is swamped with gifts a few days before the wedding, and it just isn't humanly possible to write all the necessary thank-you's in time, she can take the gift book along on the honeymoon and write the notes while she's away. Of course, if she's only going to be gone a week or two, the notes can wait. But if she's going to be away for a month or more, she should take the list with her and write the notes of thanks as soon as she can. This is a task that cannot be evaded . . . nor should any gracious bride want to evade writing cordial notes to those who showered her so generously with gifts!

The bride acknowledges all gifts, for her husband and herself—including gifts from friends or business associates of her husband whom she has never seen and doesn't know. All notes must be personally written by the bride herself; she cannot relegate someone else to do it for her. If gifts arrive while she is away, her mother may acknowledge them—but only to say: "Helen had already gone when your beautiful gift arrived. She will, of course, write and thank you as soon as she gets back." Or better still, the mother may write to the bride and describe the gift so that she can acknowledge it herself. This isn't necessary, of course, if the bride will be back in a reasonable time.

Printed or engraved cards of thanks won't do for wedding gifts—or any gifts! They are not sincere, and they are not in good taste. A letter and *only* a *letter* in the bride's own handwriting is correct for thanking relatives and friends for their wedding gifts. These thank-you's should be written on formal paper—not on cards or so-called "informals." There is no objection to the use of "informals" for brief notes to friends, acknowledgments of kindness or hospitality, even for invitations to card parties and other simple home functions; but they should not be used for acknowledging wedding gifts.

The bride's notes should be an expression of her own personality; but the following provide a variety of acceptable patterns from which she can easily design her own.

To Relatives

Dear Aunt Kate:

It's hard to believe I've been married two whole weeks, and here we are—David and I—in our own lovely home!

One of the things we enjoy most, Aunt Kate, is using the simply *luscious* bath linens you gave us! It was a generous gift, and David and I send you our love and our thanks.

You must come real soon and see how beautifully
your linens go with the colors in our bathroom!

>　　　　　　　　　　　With love,
>　　　　　　　　　　　Helen

Dear Aunt Mary and Uncle Jim:

When I unpacked your gift today, I was so thrilled I
was practically *speechless!* How did you two darlings
know I love Spode and would rather have it than any
other kind of china? It's such a very lovely pattern; I
can hardly wait to show it off to my friends!

David is as delighted as I am. We have decided that
you shall be our very first dinner guests so that you
can see for yourselves how beautiful our table looks all
dressed up in your Spode!

Thank you for your generous gift and for the sweet
note that came with it. David and I send you our love!

>　　　　　　　　　　　Affectionately yours,
>　　　　　　　　　　　Helen

When a present is sent by a married couple, the note of thanks
may be written to both—as above—or it may be written to the
wife alone, with thanks to both in the letter. For example, here
is a typical note of thanks to a married cousin:

Dear Margaret:

Thank you so much for the perfectly *beautiful* little
boudoir clock you and Bill sent us! It's one of the very
nicest wedding gifts we have received.

David sends thanks too; we hope you'll come soon
and see how lovely the clock looks on our dresser. You
just couldn't have made a better choice!

>　　　　　With love from both of us,
>　　　　　　　　　　　Helen

Bachelor uncles are usually very generous. This letter is to a
favorite uncle who sent an expensive silver tea service:

Uncle Joe, darling!

I'll be the proudest hostess in all New York when I use my handsome tea service! What a simply *magnificent* gift—and how generous of you to select it for David and me! We were quite overwhelmed when we unpacked it this morning. It's standing on the table right near me as I write this note, and I keep looking at it and *gloating* because it's really and truly mine!

Thank you, darling—for David and me. We're expecting you to be a *very frequent visitor* at our house, and don't think for a minute we'll let you disappoint us!

Love from both of us, and a special hug and kiss from me.

Helen

To Intimate Friends

Joan, dear:

Thank you so much for the beautiful candy jar! It looks so attractive on our coffee table—you must come and see for yourself.

David and I deeply appreciate your gift, Joan, and we send you our thanks and our affection!

Devotedly,
Helen

Dearest Carolyn:

I just can't get over the English hunting prints you sent us! They're exactly what David and I want for our dining room; but we didn't think we'd be lucky enough to get them as a gift!

David and I are delighted, Carolyn. Thank you very, very much!

We're looking forward to seeing you at the wedding.

Affectionately yours,
Helen

It's always more gracious to mention the specific gift. For example, don't write, "Thanks for the beautiful gift" but "Thanks for the beautiful lamp." And it's nice to mention something special about the gift if possible—how it just goes with something else, or just fits into a certain decorative scheme, or is in some other way the perfect choice. People like to be told they selected the ideal gift; it's part of the pleasure of giving we mentioned earlier in the chapter.

Dear Betty:

You couldn't have selected a more *perfect* gift for David and me if you had tried! We've been looking for twin lamps for our twin night tables; but we haven't seen anything to compare with the ones you sent. They are gorgeous, Betty—and the turquoise shades will go beautifully with the draperies and spreads we ordered.

It was generous of you to send such a wonderful gift. I just don't know how to thank you! David says to be sure and tell you how delighted *he* is with the lamps, too.

Affectionately yours,
Helen

A gift received from an intimate friend of the groom should be acknowledged by the bride, of course. And although she does not know him well, her letter should be very friendly and cordial . . . as she is writing for the groom and herself. A well-written note of thanks is enthusiastic but not profuse.

Dear Bob:

How very sweet of you to send David and me such a beautiful pair of candlesticks! We're delighted with them, and we just can't thank you enough.

David and I are looking forward to seeing you Tuesday at the wedding.

Thanks again for your *wonderful* gift!

Affectionately,
Helen

To Less Intimate Friends

Dear Margaret:

David and I are delighted with the beautiful vase you sent us. We plan to give it a place of honor in our living room.

It was sweet of you to send such a lovely gift, and we both thank you very much.

Sincerely,
Helen Curtis

Dear Miss Walsh:

Thank you for the lovely, lovely salad bowl! I'm sure it will be one of our most useful gifts. David said to be sure and send *his* thanks, too!

With best wishes from both of us,

Cordially yours,
Helen Curtis

Dear Mrs. Chalmers:

We just *love* the tray you sent us! David says it's one of the most beautiful trays he has ever seen . . . and I certainly agree with him.

Thank you very much!

Sincerely,
Helen Curtis

Neighbors who were not invited to the wedding but who sent a gift should receive an especially cordial note of thanks:

Dear Mrs. Howland:

It was most kind of you and Mr. Howland to send us a gift—and such a handsome one! We are simply *thrilled* with the book ends; they are just what we needed for our library desk.

We hope that you and Mr. Howland will come real soon, and see for yourselves how beautiful the book ends look.

Cordially yours,
Helen Curtis

To a Friend in Mourning

Dearest Emily:

David and I were deeply touched when your gift
arrived today. With all you have on your heart and
mind right now, it was sweet of you to think of us. . . .

Thank you, darling. The luncheon cloth is lovely,
and we appreciate it more than we can say!

Devotedly,
Helen

To a Friend Far Away

Dear Claire:

What a wonderful surprise to receive your gift today
—all the way from Italy! And what a perfectly *beautiful* pair of figurines! I love them, Claire—and I just
don't know how to thank you for them.

David joins me in sending thanks for your lovely
gift, and for your thoughtfulness in remembering us
when you are so far away. We're sorry you won't be
here for the wedding, but we'll be thinking of you!

With love from us both,

Affectionately,
Helen

To a Business Associate of the Groom

Dear Mr. Kingston:

Thank you for the beautiful carving set you sent
David and me. It's a lovely gift, and a useful one—and
we appreciate it very much.

Sincerely yours,
Helen Curtis

If the card accompanying the gift is from "Mr. and Mrs.
Kingston," the note of thanks should be addressed to Mrs. Kings-

ton—even though neither the bride nor groom know her personally. If Mr. Kingston does not customarily address the groom by his first name, it's advisable to use his surname in the note of thanks. The use of first name or surname in any note of thanks depends upon the degree of intimacy between the persons involved.

Dear Mrs. Kingston:

I want to thank you and Mr. Kingston for the beautiful carving set you sent Mr. Johnson and me. It's a lovely gift, and a useful one—and we appreciate it very much indeed!

Sincerely yours,
Helen Curtis

To an Old Classmate of the Groom
—a Stranger to the Bride

Dear Mr. Foster:

David and I think it was most generous of you to send us such a beautiful gift! We love the little carved Chinese figures, and they'll be just *perfect* on our mantel!

I'm delighted to know you are coming to New York for the wedding. David has talked of you so often, and with such great affection, that I'm looking forward to meeting you.

Many thanks for the gift, from David and me!

Sincerely yours,
Helen Curtis

SHOWER GIFTS SHOULD BE
INDIVIDUALLY ACKNOWLEDGED

When an engaged girl is given a shower of gifts by her friends, it's not enough to express verbal thanks at the party. An individual note of thanks should be written to each person who contributed a gift.

Dear Anne:

I was so thrilled and excited on Saturday that I'm sure I didn't thank you adequately for the beautiful guest towels. They are lovely—and exactly the color I would have selected myself!

Thanks so much, Anne. I'm looking forward to seeing you on the twelfth.

Affectionately,
Janet

A special note of thanks goes to the hostess who planned the party and provided the refreshments:

Susan, dear:

You were sweet to give a shower for me, and I appreciate it more than I can say. I don't know how you managed to keep it such a secret! It was a complete surprise to me . . . and a thrill I'll never forget.

Bill and I are overwhelmed by the wealth of lovely linens we have suddenly received. Your tea cloth is especially lovely, Susan. I am *doubly* indebted to you— for the party and for your generous gift!

Thanks from both of us—to a swell gal and a wonderful friend!

With love,
Janet

NOTES OF THANKS FOR
CHRISTMAS GIFTS

Instead of a run-of-the-mill note that merely acknowledges the gift you received and says a casual "thank you"—try to show real appreciation. You can do that by pointing out certain features of the gift that especially appeal to you. Or you can tactfully point out that it's just what you've been wanting—just what you've been hoping for. The point is to make the person who sent the gift feel that it was a very good selection, that you are delighted and pleased with it.

Dear Aunt Mary:

What a simply *gorgeous* Christmas gift! A fitted bag is something I've wanted for a long time, but could never get for myself.

Thank you so much, Aunt Mary. I'll have the bag for years and years, and I'll think of you with gratitude and affection every time I use it.

Lovingly yours,
Carolyn

Dear Irene:

I'm delighted with the bracelet you sent me for Christmas. Imagine! It just matches a pair of earrings my sister gave me. Isn't that a lucky coincidence?

You certainly made an inspired choice, Irene! I *love* the bracelet and can't think of anything I'd rather have had. Thank you very much.

Affectionately,
Carolyn

Dear Bob:

How did you know my favorite brand of candy? It's the one kind I just never can resist!

It was thoughtful of you to remember me at Christmas, Bob, and I appreciate it very much.

Cordially yours,
Carolyn

Dear Mrs. Carter:

John and I have been displaying your Christmas gift with great pleasure and pride.

The cups and saucers are *exquisite*—and we think it was wonderful of you to remember that collecting Spode is our hobby.

Many thanks to you and Mr. Carter for your thoughtful and generous gift, and our best wishes to you for the new year!

Sincerely yours,
Carolyn Brewster

FOR BIRTHDAY GIFT

Dear Alice:

If you had asked me what I wanted for my birthday, I'd have said, "A charm for my bracelet." You just couldn't have selected anything I'd like more!

The little stagecoach is adorable—I can't wait to have it put on the bracelet. Isn't it cute the way the tiny wheels turn?

Thank you, Alice. You have a positive *genius* for selecting the right gift!

With love,
Dorothy

Dear Jean:

You never forget my birthday, do you? No wonder you are my favorite cousin!

The scarf is lovely, and it's just what I needed to go with my new suit. The colors are so soft and flattering!

Thank you, darling—not only for the scarf, but for the very sweet card that came with it.

Lovingly yours,
Dorothy

Dear Arthur:

I'm writing this note on the lovely stationery you sent me for my birthday. It was sweet of you to remember, and I want you to know that I appreciate it.

Many thanks, Arthur—for the gift and for your good wishes!

Sincerely,
Dorothy

Dear Uncle Pete:

I thought I told you I was going to stop having birthdays. . . . After all, a girl doesn't like being reminded she's a year older!

But how can I scold you when you've been so generous? The pen is a beauty, Uncle Pete—and I certainly needed one! Thanks a million for it, and for your affectionate birthday message.

With love,
Dorothy

Dear Nance:

I must admit I have a talented sister. The bag is beautiful—and to think you made it yourself! Why, it must have taken *months!*

Thanks, darling—you're an angel to go to so much trouble for me. I *love* the bag, and it goes beautifully with my new brown coat.

Give my love to Fred and the children, and thank them for their birthday wishes. My love to you, *always!*

Dottie

FOR WEDDING ANNIVERSARY GIFTS

The wedding anniversaries that are most frequently celebrated, and for which friends and relatives customarily send gifts, are:

1 year, Paper, Plastics	30 years, Pearls
5 years, Wood	35 years, Jade
10 years, Tin, Aluminum	40 years, Rubies, Garnets
15 years, Crystal, Glass	45 years, Sapphires
20 years, China	50 years, Gold
25, years, Silver	75 years, Diamonds

Such gifts should, of course, be graciously acknowledged by a written note of thanks. The note is written by the wife, for her husband and herself.

Dear Martha:

Jim and I were so touched and pleased that you should have remembered our wedding anniversary! It gave an extra note of happiness to the day.

The *tôle* tray is charming; I can hardly wait for an opportunity to use it!

Many thanks to you and Paul for your thoughtful remembrance, and for your good wishes on our tenth anniversary.

Affectionately,
Harriet

Dear Edna:

How very sweet of you and Dan to remember our anniversary! We were really quite overcome when your package came this morning. . . .

The salad bowl and plates are beautiful. I think they are the loveliest I have ever seen—and so does Ralph.

It's difficult to realize, Edna, that we have been married for twenty years. It certainly doesn't seem that long since I was a bride, and you were my pretty bridesmaid in pink. Remember?

We send you both our love, and our deep appreciation for your thoughts of us on our anniversary. Do come and see us real soon!

Affectionately,
Sally

Dear Carl:

Your flowers came this morning and turned our living room into a garden. Fifty yellow roses for our fifty golden years! How wonderful of you to remember, Carl . . . and so generously!

Steve and I are humble and grateful for our many years of happiness together. And we are grateful, too, for the many good friends we have accumulated along the way. You rank high among them, Carl . . . our dear and loyal friend through all the years.

So we send you our love on our golden anniversary! And we send you our thanks, Carl, for the beautiful roses.

Affectionately,
Lucy

For a Gift for a Newborn Baby

Dear Aunt Ellen:

With all the many things you have to do, how could you find time to make that beautiful sweater and cap set for the baby? I appreciate it twice as much, knowing you made it yourself.

You must come and see my young daughter. George says she's getting real pretty . . . but of course he's prejudiced, like all fathers. I just think she's *cute—* and very, very precious!

Thanks, Aunt Ellen, for the lovely gift.

Affectionately,
Edith

Dear Mark:

How proud my little Joan will be some day to know that her handsome silver cup came from her godfather!

It's a beautiful gift, Mark . . . and I know Joan will treasure and keep it always, as I have kept *my* baby cup through all these years.

I hope you know how very much Fred and I appreciate your kindness.

Affectionately yours,
Anne

Ruth, dear:

How like you to be so generous! The quilt is the prettiest one I have ever seen, and just what we needed for Roger's crib.

Why don't you come and see the young fellow? He's really quite a character! I know you are busy during the week—but Sunday afternoon's a good time, and we'd love to see you.

Lou sends his best wishes, and we both send many thanks for the gift.

Affectionately,
Gert

Dear Mrs. Langston:

Thank you ever so much for the beautiful little dress you sent the baby. She wore it home from the hospital, and I just wish you could have seen how sweet she looked in it!

You were very kind to send a gift, and Mr. Cummings and I appreciate it very much. We hope you will come and see the baby now that we are home.

Sincerely yours,
Mary Cummings

For a Gift to a Young Child

Dear Marj:

I just wish you could see how Patsy adores the cute little panda with the big black eyes! I'm sure that if she could write, she'd say, "Thank you, Aunt Marj, for sending me this beautiful panda to love! You are the very best aunt in all the world!"

But little Patsy can't write as yet . . . so let me thank you for her. You are always so thoughtful and generous.

Come and see us soon, Marj. It's a long time since you have been here.

With love,
Kate

Dear Mrs. Kelly:

Your adorable cap and mitten set came this morning, right on Patsy's birthday. How wonderful of you to remember her!

Thank you very much indeed—for Patsy and myself.

Cordially yours,
Katherine Donlin

FOR A HOUSEWARMING GIFT

When you move into a new house and give a party for your friends, they usually bring gifts. And you thank them in person, of course; but that is not enough. You should send an individual note of thanks to each guest who brings something for the new house.

Dear Mary:

I don't know how to thank you for the beautiful cake knife! How did you know it was just what I needed?

John and I appreciate your lovely gift, Mary. We enjoyed seeing you on Friday, and we hope you'll come soon again.

Affectionately,
Alice

Dear Mrs. Hoffman:

Thank you very, very much for the pair of lovely little porcelain vases. John and I think they are simply *beautiful,* and we cannot thank you and Mr. Hoffman enough for them!

The next time you come—which we hope will be very soon—you will see them in all their delicacy and charm occupying a place of honor in our living room.

Cordially yours,
Alice Denton

FOR A BON VOYAGE GIFT

Often when people leave for foreign shores, their relatives and friends send *bon voyage* gifts to the ship or plane. These may be books, flowers, baskets of fruit . . . but whatever they are, each gift should be promptly and cordially acknowledged.

Dear Aunt Jane:

What a precious pair of darlings you and Uncle Ned are to send flowers to our cabin! Jim and I feel like honeymooners instead of a staid old married couple. Our cabin looks just like a bridal suite, with all those wonderful roses you sent us.

Jim and I are very, very happy. We always dreamed of celebrating our fifth anniversary at his home in Scotland, but now that the dream is becoming a reality, we can still hardly believe it!

So far the voyage has been smooth and pleasant, and no one has missed any meals. I certainly hope it continues like this all the way across! We'll write you again as soon as we arrive.

Love from both of us, and many thanks for the flowers!

Yours devotedly,
Gloria

Dear Laura:

It was certainly grand of you and Ted to come and see me off! I know it wasn't easy for you to get to the airport at such an early hour, so I appreciate it all the more.

Flying over water can get dreadfully boring after the first few hours, and your book of detective stories

came in very handy. It was sweet and thoughtful of
you to think of it.

The flight was uneventful and we arrived in Paris
on schedule time. Jeanne and Paul met me at the airport, and we went straight to their charming little
house. I know I am going to love it here; I'm looking
forward to two *marvelous* weeks with my sister and
her husband!

I'll write to you again, Laura. In the meantime, my
thanks to you and Ted for your many kindnesses to me
—and my love to you both, always!

Blanche

Dear Mr. Peterson:

Your basket of fruit was waiting in my cabin when
I got on board this morning. And a more magnificent
basket I have never seen!

It was kind and generous of you to do this for me,
Mr. Peterson, and I appreciate it more than I can say.

Sincerely yours,
Martha Ellsworth

THE BREAD-AND-BUTTER LETTER

If you have received hospitality at the home of a friend, for
a week end or longer, courtesy requires that you write a cordial
note of thanks within two or three days after your return home.
The fact that you personally and enthusiastically thanked your
hostess before leaving doesn't count. You must still express your
appreciation *in writing*. This is a so-called "duty" note which is
expected of you and which you *must* write. It has become known
as a bread-and-butter letter, because it thanks the hostess for the
"bread and butter"—or hospitality—she provided.

Kate, dear:

This is to tell you again how very much I enjoyed
the week end at Pine Ridge. Everything was just about
perfect: the weather, the company, the beautiful sur-

roundings—no wonder I'm finding it difficult to get down to business this morning! The office seems so dull and prosaic after Pine Ridge.

I hope you and Fred know how much I appreciate your hospitality, and your many kindnesses to me. I count myself fortunate indeed to have two such generous and charming friends!

Affectionately yours,
Maureen

Dear Mrs. Franklin:

I'd like you to know how much the week at your lovely house in Southampton has meant to me. I not only enjoyed myself immensely, but I feel relaxed and refreshed as I haven't felt in months!

Please give my love to Betsy. It was so nice being with her again—just like our old days together at school!

Many thanks to you and Mr. Franklin for asking me.

Sincerely yours,
Evelyn McCormack

Dear Mrs. Benton:

Thank you very much for those four wonderful days at Shady Acres! Every moment was a delight; i can't remember ever having enjoyed myself so thoroughly *anywhere!*

It was good of you and Dr. Benton to invite me, and I deeply appreciate your hospitality.

Sincerely yours,
Walter Hanley

THANKS FOR GIFTS TO A
PATIENT OR INVALID

If friends send you books, flowers or fruit while you are in the hospital—or ill at home—it is not necessary that you write immediately. But you should write a brief note of thanks as soon as you can, or have someone very close do it for you.

Dear Mr. Martin:

I want to thank you for the beautiful roses you sent Mrs. Granby. She was very happy and pleased when she saw they were from you.

I'm glad to say she is improving rapidly, and I hope she will soon be able to leave the hospital.

We both send you our warmest thanks for the flowers and for your very kind wishes.

> Sincerely,
> John Granby

Dear George:

It's almost worth being ill to receive such gorgeous flowers! Your gladioli have certainly transformed this dismal room of mine into a garden. Thank you, George —for the flowers and for your friendly, cheerful note.

They say I may have my first visitors tomorrow and every afternoon thereafter from three to five. I'm glad you want to come and I look forward to seeing you.

> Sincerely yours,
> Rosalie

Dear Mrs. Thompson:

What a beautiful plant! It is standing on the table right beside my bed, and I'm looking at it—and enjoying it—as I write this note. The gardenia is my favorite flower; and to have a gardenia plant of my own, right at my bedside, is a real treat.

I'm grateful to you for thinking of me in such a lovely way. Thank you, my dear—for the plant, and for being always such a thoughtful and considerate neighbor.

> Cordially,
> Amy Hackett

Dear Mary and John:

Now that I can finally sit up and write letters, I want to thank you both for the flowers and books you sent me while I was ill—and most of all, for your many cheerful notes. You have no idea how much they meant to me!

You've been more than kind, you two, and I won't ever forget it. My love and deepest gratitude, now and always!

Jane

THANKS FOR A FAVOR RECEIVED

The gracious person does not accept favors without an expression of thanks and appreciation. Not every favor requires a written note, of course. If you borrow the lawn mower from your neighbor, or ask a friend to send her piano tuner next time he comes—verbal thanks are sufficient. But if a neighbor or friend goes out of the way to do something special for you or a member of your family, nothing but a cordial note of thanks will do to show how grateful you are.

For example, if a friend takes care of your canary while you are away on a vacation, you thank her in person when you call for your pet . . . but you also write a note of thanks:

Dear Lenore:

It was wonderful of you to take such good care of Chipper while we were away. He looked so bright and happy, singing and swinging in the sunshine of your bedroom window, that I felt as though he belonged there and I shouldn't take him back.

I do hope it wasn't too much trouble for you, Lenore. It was certainly a great favor to us, and we want you to know how grateful we are.

Affectionately,
Diane

If a neighbor loans you some expensive or specialized equipment—like a moving-picture camera or a projection machine—

you should show your appreciation more tangibly than by your verbal thanks alone. Surely a warm note of thanks is indicated for so generous a favor!

> Dear Mr. Rogers:
>
> I am very grateful to you for letting me use your projector last Sunday. Jimmy's birthday party was a huge success because of the movies—and there just wouldn't have been any movies without your projector!
>
> So I want to thank you most cordially for Jimmy, for his young guests, and for Mrs. Blagdon and myself. We think it was *swell* of you to be so generous, and we want you to know how very much we all appreciate it.
>
> > Sincerely yours,
> > Hugh R. Blagdon

If a member of your family is visiting in a distant city, and an acquaintance to whom you gave her a letter of introduction is kind and attentive, you naturally write a note of thanks.

> Dear Mrs. Hackett:
>
> My niece, Jane Barlow, has written to tell me how very kind you have been to her during her stay in Washington.
>
> Mr. Crawford and I deeply appreciate your courtesy, and we hope to have the opportunity of reciprocating when you are in New York.
>
> With many thanks to you for entertaining Jane so generously,
>
> > Sincerely yours,
> > Margaret F. Crawford

THANKS FOR A LETTER OF CONDOLENCE

Every letter of condolence should be acknowledged by personal note. Commercial "thank you" cards are in bad taste and should be avoided, except in the case of a public official or person of prominence who receives an overwhelming number of letters from strangers. In private life, sending an engraved form of thanks to a friend or acquaintance who has expressed sympathy is looked upon as rude and ungracious.

The reply to a note of sympathy or condolence need not be written as promptly as other notes of thanks. It can be mailed any time within six weeks after receipt of the flowers or note of sympathy. It can be brief to the point of saying nothing more than a simple "Thank you for your kind expression of sympathy." Or it can be as wordy as one's feelings and impulses at the time prompt. To an intimate friend, for example, one might write:

Dear Anne:

I shall always remember with gratitude the letter you wrote me when you learned of Claire's death. No one but you, who knew my sister and loved her as her own family did, could have written that letter. It brought me comfort, Anne, at a time when I needed it badly.

Thank you from the bottom of my heart, for your letter and for your many kindnesses to Claire during her long illness.

Affectionately,
Carol

To a friend who has asked in her note of sympathy if she can help in any way, one might reply:

Dear Ida:

Thank you for your kind note of sympathy, and for your offer to help.

I'm afraid there's nothing anyone can do to help us right now. Only time can help us get over the terrible shock of Philip's death.

But it was good of you to make the offer, and I appreciate it more than I can say.

> Always affectionately,
> Gail

A woman who has lost her husband may find it difficult to write notes of thanks even to her most intimate friends. She may ask a son or daughter, or some other close relative, to acknowledge the flowers and the letters of condolence she received.

Dear Mrs. Hartley:

Mother has asked me to write to you, as she cannot do so herself just now.

She would like you and Mr. Hartley to know how much she appreciates the flowers and the letter of sympathy you sent. You have both been very kind.

> Sincerely yours,
> Virginia Baxter

This is the type of letter one generally writes to a neighbor who has sent flowers and made a call of condolence:

Dear Mrs. Davis:

You were very kind at the time of my mother's death.

I want you to know how much your sympathy and thoughtfulness have meant to me, and how grateful I am for all you did.

With heartfelt thanks,

> Sincerely yours,
> Thelma Conners

A girl called home from college by the death of her father, might receive flowers and a note from her classmates. She would write a note to the girl closest to her at school, asking her to thank the others for their expression of sympathy.

Dear Grace:

The letter and the flowers came on Tuesday. Will you please give my thanks to all the girls, and tell them how much mother and I appreciate their thoughtfulness?

I shall try to return to school on Tuesday if mother is feeling well enough by that time.

With affection,
Annette

A difficult note of thanks is the one a man writes at the time of his wife's death to friends they have known intimately for many years, and with whom they have shared many happy experiences.

Dear Kate:

I don't need to tell you and Paul how greatly I appreciate all you have done for me in these trying weeks —and how grateful I am for the comfort and understanding you gave me when I needed them so desperately.

No one knows better than you two what Christine meant to me, and what an aching void my life has become without her. But I am trying to take your advice, Kate—and I hope that returning to my work next week will help fill some of the emptiness.

You and Paul have been splendid. I really don't know what I would have done without you. Thank you for everything.

Affectionately,
Todd

THANKS FOR A LETTER OF CONGRATULATION

When friends take the trouble to write and congratulate you on your birthday or anniversary, on your engagement or marriage, on a talk you gave, a prize you won, or a distinction you earned . . . you owe them a gracious note of thanks in acknowledgment. Whether it's a brief and formal note, or a long and newsy letter, depends upon the circumstances and upon the degree of intimacy with your correspondent. Here, for example, are two notes of thanks for birthday congratulations:

Dear Mrs. Martin:

I just can't tell you how flattered I am that you should have remembered my birthday. It was a real pleasure to receive your charming note this morning.

Thank you so much for your good wishes!

Sincerely yours,
Hilda Rankin

Florence, dear:

What do you mean by "congratulations"? Why should I be congratulated for being a year older?

But thanks for remembering my birthday . . . and for your simply *priceless* letter! I can't remember when I enjoyed a letter as much, Florence. It was just as though you were right here in the room with me, laughing and talking.

Which reminds me—when are you going to pay us that visit you promised? We've had our living room completely redecorated since you were here last Spring, and I'd like you to see it. Furthermore, Tom has some new home movies he enjoys showing off, so come real soon and make the guy happy! I must admit the movies are quite good—almost professional.

It was grand hearing from you, and I'm so glad to know little Dan is better and back at school. Give him my love, and tell him I haven't forgotten that he wants a pup from Nellie's next batch. But Nellie seems to be taking her time!

Our best to you and Bill, and *do* drive out soon to see us!

> Always affectionately,
> Doris

Announcement of an engagement is generally followed by letters of congratulation and good wishes from relatives and friends. Such letters should be acknowledged by a personal note of thanks. A letter of congratulation addressed to the young lady is answered by her; a letter to her fiancé is answered by him:

Dear Aunt Emma:

It was sweet of you to write. Thanks very much for your good wishes.

I'm sure you'll like Alan. He's a grand person, and no one can help liking him! We promise to come and see you and Uncle Fred real soon.

> With love,
> Judy

Dear Louise:

What a wonderful letter! Thanks so much for your good wishes, and for all the nice things you wrote about Alan and me.

I guess I'm just about the happiest girl in the world, Louise. I know now what you meant when you said you and Phil were made for each other. I feel the same way about Alan!

Thanks again for your letter. If the future holds only half the fine things you hope for us, we'll be lucky indeed!

> Affectionately,
> Judy

Dear Aunt Mary:

I'm glad you and Uncle John approve so heartily of my engagement. I knew you would love Judy—everyone does. She's everything you say in your letter—and more! I'm a lucky fellow to have won such a grand girl.

Thanks for writing. I hope to deserve all the happiness and good things in life you wish for me.

Affectionately,
Alan

Dear Tom:

You're right! Judy's the cream of the crop and I'm the luckiest fellow in the world!

Thanks so much for your letter. Judy and I appreciate your congratulations and good wishes.

Sincerely,
Alan

Announcement of a marriage is also generally followed by letters of congratulation and good wishes. These, too, should be acknowledged by personal notes of thanks . . . *never* by printed or engraved "thank you" cards.

Dear Mrs. Snowden:

Thank you ever so much for your charming note of congratulation. My nice new husband and I appreciate your letter, and your good wishes for the future.

We will be at home after November first, and we hope you will come and see how cozy we are in our little apartment.

Cordially yours,
Judith T. Powell

Dearest Elaine:

Of all the letters Alan and I have received since our marriage, we enjoyed yours the most! Thank you, darling, for all those good wishes. If our life together proves half as rosy as you predict, we'll be well content!

You say Alan is to be congratulated, but I think *I'm* to be congratulated, too. He's a wonderful, wonderful husband, Elaine, and I just can't tell you how happy I am!

Thanks again for your good wishes. Alan joins me in hoping you'll come often to see us in Garden City.

With affectionate greetings from us both,

Judy

ACKNOWLEDGING VARIOUS OTHER NOTES OF CONGRATULATION

People who are generous and kindly like to acknowledge every message of congratulation, even though a note of thanks may not actually be required. For example, there is no rule that says you must acknowledge every birthday greeting, every anniversary card, every letter of congratulation on winning a prize or receiving an honor or distinction. But such letters deserve acknowledgment; and the people who write them always enjoy and appreciate a note of thanks in response. It can be a very short note, just a few words or a single brief paragraph; but it should be friendly and sincere.

On a Wedding Anniversary

Dear Cynthia:

Your letter took us back twenty years, and brought so many happy memories to mind! Thank you, dear, for remembering our anniversary and for your kind thoughts of us. Paul joins me in sending our love and appreciation.

Affectionately,
Janice

On the Birth of a Child

Dear Mrs. Hanson:

What a lot of fine big wishes you made for our very tiny new daughter! Thank you ever so much—for Mr. Bradley and myself. We deeply appreciate your good wishes and congratulations.

Sincerely yours,
Vera Bradley

On Graduating from College

Dear Mrs. Kellogg:

Your letter was a pleasant surprise. Thank you so much for your congratulations and good wishes.

I have no immediate plans for the future, but I hope to make advertising my career.

Please remember me to Mr. Kellogg, and tell him I appreciate his good wishes for my future.

Sincerely yours,
Gertrude Hill

Dear Mr. Kimball:

That was a wonderful letter you wrote me! I certainly appreciate your congratulations, and your invitation to come and see you about a job.

But as Dad must have told you by now, I am interested in industrial design and hope to find an opening in that field.

It's quite an exciting adventure, starting out in the business world—and I guess I'll need all the good wishes my friends have been sending me!

Thanks ever so much for your interest, Mr. Kimball, and for your very kind offer.

Sincerely yours,
Edwin Halleck

On Winning a Prize

Dear Mrs. Loomis:

I assure you I was very much surprised when my poster won! Thank you for your congratulations, and for your kind comments about my work.

Sincerely,
Evelyn Palmer

Dear Jeff:

One of the nicest things about winning the inter-state debating contest was getting all those wonderful letters from my friends.

It sure was great hearing from *you*, Jeff. I'm glad to know you have finally decided on medicine; I always said you'd make a swell doctor!

Thanks a lot for the congratulations. I guess I was just lucky.

My kindest regards to your parents,

Cordially,
Al Fisher

On Winning an Honor or Distinction

Dear Mrs. Dwight:

I am humble and grateful for the distinction of being named outstanding mother of Middletown. Nothing could have pleased me more!

Many thanks to you and Mr. Dwight for your kind note of congratulation.

Sincerely yours,
Julia L. Marlowe

Dear Dr. Benton:

Thank you very much for your note of congratulation on my election as president of the state medical association.

It was good of you to take the time and trouble to write, and I sincerely appreciate your kindness.

> Cordially yours,
> Frederick P. Harmon, M.D.

On Publication of a Book

Dear Miss Halloway:

What a pleasant surprise to hear from you after all these years!

I am glad you like my new book, and I appreciate your good wishes for its success.

Thank you very much indeed for writing.

> Sincerely yours,
> Lillian E. Watson

Bear in mind that any thoughtful complimentary attention requires an appreciative note in response. If someone congratulates you on a talk you made, a paper you read, a concert you gave, a painting or photograph you exhibited, write a brief note of thanks. It takes only a moment, but it helps widen immeasurably your sphere of friendly influence and affection.

8

Letters of Congratulation

If you hear of a friend's engagement or marriage, if you hear of the birth of a child, or of an honor or distinction that has come to someone you know—sit down right away, while you are elated and excited by the news, and write a letter of congratulation. Sincerity comes more easily and naturally to your written words at such a time, and your note has a truer ring to it.

So never put off any letter of congratulation that needs to be written. Don't be satisfied to write it in your thoughts, promising yourself to put it on paper at the first opportunity. Write it while the news is still fresh in your mind! You'll find that it pays to keep up with your correspondence. You'll find that all your letters of thanks, of sympathy, of congratulation are much easier to write if you write them on time.

Letters of congratulation should be especially easy and pleasant to write, for we all like to share in the joy of some happy event. These are cheerful messages, in which you can spread yourself to your heart's content. The note may be brief and formal, or it may be chatty and informal—depending on the circumstances. The important thing is that it be *sincere*. The desire to congratulate should be clearly present.

Cultivate the habit of writing notes of congratulation even when they are not actually required of you—to friends who have graduated or been promoted, who have had a birthday or anniversary, or any other occasion that warrants a complimentary message. It's a very charming habit to have, and one that cannot fail to make you more popular with your family and friends. A little note of congratulation can give a big lift, and is often remembered a lifetime with pleasure and appreciation.

CONGRATULATIONS ON AN ENGAGEMENT

Always be sure that the *occasion* for congratulation is mentioned specifically in your letter. Don't write "I've heard the news and hasten to congratulate you" but "I've heard the news of your engagement and hasten to congratulate you."

A young lady is not customarily congratulated either on her engagement or her wedding. It's the *man* who is congratulated; the lady is sent good wishes for her happiness.

Dear Lenore:

I have just learned of your engagement to Shelley Travers. Let me be among the first to wish you both every happiness.

I've known Shelley for years, and I'm very fond of the lad. But I think he's lucky to have won a grand girl like you; and tell him for me, my dear, that I congratulate him!

Affectionately,
Hilda K. Brandon

Dear Lenore:

What exciting news! I'm delighted to hear of your engagement, and I wish you all the happiness in the world.

I don't know your Mr. Travers, but I'm anxious to meet him. I'm sure he must be someone special to have won your heart.

I hope you will both be very happy, always!

Fondly,
Janet

Dearest Lenore:

Your mother has told us of your engagement to Shelley Travers. I can't tell you, my dear, how pleased your Uncle Fred and I are by this news. We have been very close to Shelley's family for years, as you know

—and we have always thought of him as an unusually fine and dependable young man. In fact, we don't know anyone we would rather have you marry than him!

So we send you our love, Lenore—and our wishes for a lifetime of happiness. Give Shelley our love too, and tell him how delighted we are to welcome him into the family.

Always affectionately,
Aunt May

Dear Lenore:

I can't say that Bill and I were exactly surprised by the news of your engagement to Shelley. We've been rather expecting it right along.

We think it's simply *swell*, of course. We never knew two people more suited to each other (except ourselves!).

But seriously, Lenore, Bill and I are very glad for you, as we know how happy you must be. We send congratulations to you *both*; and we wish you every good fortune and every possible happiness in your life together.

Lovingly,
Pat

Dear Miss Bailey:

I have just learned of your engagement to Shelley Travers. He's a fine chap, and a very lucky one! Please give him my congratulations. I hope you will both be very happy.

Sincerely yours,
Milton Ames

Dear Shelley:

That's great news about you and Lenore! She's a wonderful girl in every way, and we congratulate you on your good fortune.

Best wishes from us both on your engagement. We hope you will have nothing but joy and happiness in your life together.

Affectionately,
Ethel and George

Dear Shelley:

I just can't tell you, Shelley, how pleased I am by the announcement of your engagement. From what I hear of the young lady, she is charming and very lovely— and will make you an excellent wife.

Your Aunt Charlotte and I send congratulations, and best wishes for your happiness. We hope you'll bring the young lady here soon so that we can meet her. Please give her our affectionate regards, and tell her she has every good wish from us both.

Fondly,
Uncle Matt

Dear Shelley:

I know how crazy you've always been about that precious Lenore of yours; and from what you've told me about her, she's something to be crazy about! So I guess you're a pretty lucky fellow, and I congratulate you.

Some day I hope to meet Lenore. In the meantime, tell her your old pal sends his best wishes for her happiness. And that goes for you, too!

As ever,
Bob

CONGRATULATIONS ON MARRIAGE

When an announcement of a marriage is received, congratulations are usually sent to the bride and groom. The note is customarily written and addressed to both; but it may also be written to the bride individually, or to the groom individually— as indicated in the various examples below.

Dear Anne and Jerry:

We were thrilled and delighted to receive the announcement of your marriage in Springtown last Tuesday.

Tom and I send you both our love, and best wishes for every happiness that life can bring.

We hope you'll let us know when you return to New York, so that we can give you our congratulations in person.

Affectionately,
Barbara

Dear Anne:

I was pleasantly surprised to receive the announcement of your marriage in this morning's mail.

I hope you will be very happy. Congratulations to Mr. Carter, and my very best wishes to both of you for happiness and everything good in life.

Sincerely,
Katherine Miller

Dear Mrs. Carter:

Let me wish you and Mr. Carter every happiness on your recent marriage.

With best wishes from Mr. Millen and myself,

Sincerely yours,
Sarah G. Millen

Dear Anne:

You will always be little Anne to me . . . even though you're now a staid and dignified married woman! It's hard for me to believe you are old enough to be married. Why, it seems only yesterday I dangled you on my knee!

Give my congratulations to that nice new husband of yours, and tell him I think he's a mighty lucky fellow.

My very best wishes to you, for a lifetime of happiness.

Affectionately,
Wilbur T. Ross

Anne, dear:

So you and Jerry are married! You've certainly taken all your friends by surprise. But I think you were wise to eliminate a long engagement. It's just what I would have done in your place!

Jerry's a grand fellow, and I know you'll always be very happy. Are you getting used to having people call you "Mrs. Carter" as yet?

I'd love to hear all about the wedding. Write and tell me, when you can. In the meantime, I send you my love and best wishes . . . and I hope you and Jerry have a long, happy life together!

Fondly,
Cynthia

Dear Jerry:

I've just returned from California—-to find the announcement of your marriage waiting for me. Congratulations, old boy! I certainly wish you every happiness.

I haven't had the pleasure of meeting the lady of your choice, but from what I hear she must be wonderful. Please tell her your old friend Jim Colton sends good wishes, and hopes she'll always be as happy as she is right now. I look forward to the pleasure of meeting her soon.

The best of everything to both of you!

Cordially,
Jim

My dear Carter:

Congratulations on your recent marriage.

I wish you and your bride the best of luck, and ever-increasing happiness as the years go by.

Sincerely yours,
Robert F. Wheeler

CONGRATULATIONS ON A WEDDING ANNIVERSARY

Dear Harriet:

It doesn't seem possible that it's five years since you and Bob were married! Somehow I still think of you as a bride and groom. Maybe it's because you're just about the most devoted couple I know!

Congratulations to you both, and may the years ahead bring you continued joy and contentment.

Affectionately,
Janice

Dear Helen and Fred:

I looked at the calendar yesterday and suddenly realized it's your tenth anniversary! My, how the years fly by!

Ralph and I send you congratulations, and every best wish for the future. We hope you'll have many, many more anniversaries—each one happier than the last.

I wonder if you know what an inspiration your sweet devotion to each other has always been to your friends?

Always affectionately,
Lillian

Dear Mrs. Dearing:

We have heard that you and Mr. Dearing are celebrating your fiftieth wedding anniversary this week.

It must be a great source of pleasure and pride to have reached this milestone in your long and happy life together, and to be able to look back upon a rich and full life and know you have accumulated so many devoted friends.

Mr. Phillips and I send you warm congratulations, and we hope that there are many more years of happiness ahead for both of you.

Cordially yours,
Myra L. Phillips

CONGRATULATIONS ON A BIRTHDAY

Birthday cards are universally used, and there is no real objection to them. At least they show you have not forgotten the day. But a written message, no matter how short, always means twice as much—and especially on a birthday. A few words in your own handwriting have far more meaning and sincerity than the most eloquent sentiment ever printed on a card. So if you have real affection for your relatives and friends, write them personal notes of congratulation instead of sending ready-made congratulations printed on a card.

Jane, dear:

You may not like to be reminded that you are a year older today—but that's not going to keep me from saying "Happy Birthday!"

Let's see. . . . Is it twenty-seven, or twenty-eight—? Or perhaps I'd better not ask!

Anyway, my love to you on your birthday, Jane —and many, many happy returns of the day! Next time you come into town to do some shopping, call me and I'll meet you for lunch. It's been too long since we had one of our good old-fashioned chats!

Affectionately,
Sonya

Dear Aunt Agatha:

Today is your birthday, and I'm thinking of you and wondering how you are. Have you been well this past month? Hasn't the weather been simply *frightful?*

It's too bad you live so far away, Aunt Agatha. If you only lived a little closer, I could come and say "Happy Birthday" to you in person. But as it is, all I can do is the next best thing: send you my love, my congratulations and my very best wishes for the coming year!

So you see my thoughts are right there in Glencove with you, even though *I* am not!

Lovingly,
Margaret

Dearest Judy:

Is it really your birthday again? Where do the years fly so swiftly? But I'm sure *you* don't mind! The years never show on you, Judy. . . . Why, you look younger today than when I first met you more than ten years ago!

But I didn't write this letter to pay you compliments! I wrote to tell you I'm thinking of you on your birthday, and wishing you everything your heart desires in the year ahead. Congratulations, Judy dear— and many, many happy returns of the day!

With affection,
Elaine

Dear Dick:

A little bird told me it's your birthday. So I'm sending congratulations and my very best wishes—for now and all your birthdays to come!

Sincerely,
Mary Lou

Dear Uncle John:

To everybody else in the world, this may be Columbus Day. But to *me* it's a far more special day than that! It's the birthday of my favorite uncle—the uncle who never *ever* forgot my birthday when I was a child and who always made me so happy!

I wish you weren't way out there in Highbridge, Uncle John. I'd love to see you on your birthday and help you celebrate. But I can't—so I'm sending you a little gift I hope you'll like. With it go my congratulations, and all my love. I hope you'll have many, many happy birthdays, and that you'll never lose the cheerful outlook and gay spirits that have made you so well-loved by all the family.

Bill and the children join me in sending congratulations. Love from all of us.

Cornelia

A letter like the above is bound to make a lonely old man, living far away, feel much happier on his birthday than any printed card—however beautiful its decorations or sentimental its verses!

Here is a suitable birthday note for a young man to send a girl he doesn't know very well:

Dear Miss Heller:

My sister tells me this is your birthday. Please accept my heartiest congratulations. I hope you'll enjoy many, many birthdays—and that each one finds you happier than the one before.

Sincerely yours,
Harold Riker

To someone he knows well, he would naturally write a more informal and spontaneous note of congratulation:

Dear Babs:

So you're a year older today—or don't you want to be reminded? Anyway, congratulations and best wishes and all that sort of thing.

If you feel in the mood for celebrating, will you let me take you to dinner and the movies, as a sort of birthday treat? You name the day. And in the meantime, many happy returns!

Cordially,
Harold

CONGRATULATIONS ON THE BIRTH
OF A CHILD

Everybody's happy when a baby is born. To express your pleasure and share in the joy, you write the proud new mother a note of congratulation.

Dear Helen:

Mother just phoned and told me the wonderful news. You and Phil have a baby boy! I'm so happy and excited, you'd think it were *my* baby instead of yours!

Congratulations, darling . . . and may you never have anything but happiness from your son. He can't help being fine and splendid in every way, with you and Phil for parents.

My love to you both—you proud and happy parents!—and to that little fellow who just arrived. I'm coming to see him as soon as I know I won't be in the way.

Affectionately,
Winifred

Marjorie, dear:

What wonderful news! I know you wanted a baby girl—and I can just imagine how thrilled and happy you must be.

Dan must be just about bursting with pride. Tell him that Carl and I send congratulations and best wishes—and that goes *double* for you, Marj!

We wish you both all possible joy and happiness in your new little daughter.

Fondly,
Claire

A letter of congratulation on the birth of a child should not be facetious unless written by a close friend or a member of the family. Here, for example, is a letter that a friendly good-natured young woman might write to a cousin with whom she has always maintained a close relationship:

Dearest Fran:

All the raves I've been hearing about a certain young person, recently arrived, makes me a bit skeptical. I just don't believe a mite of a baby girl, less than a week old, can be so beautiful. I simply *can't* believe she has all the marvelous qualities everyone says she has!

Seeing's believing—so when can I come and see this amazing small person for myself? Will you have Jim phone and let me know?

In the meantime, congratulations to both of you—and all my love!

Nancy

A letter of congratulation on a new baby, from a male member of the family, should be cordial and gay . . . and a bit on the flattering side:

Dear Marjorie:

Congratulations on the new baby! I hear she is simply beautiful, even at five days old. But she'll have to go a long way to be even half as lovely as her mother!

Bill tells me you are calling her Marianne. It's a charming name. . . .

Hurry and get well so that I can come and see you, and judge for myself whether little Marianne is as beautiful as they say.

Affectionately,
Edgar

Here is the kind of letter a woman might write to a neighbor who has had a new baby:

Dear Mrs. Harper:

Your husband just told me the good news. I'm so glad to hear it's a boy, for now little Barbara will have that baby brother she's been wanting!

Congratulations from Mr. Martin and myself. We wish you joy and happiness with your son.

Sincerely yours,
Nellie Martin

Letters are not generally sent to the father, though an intimate friend may want to send a note like the following:

Dear Phil:

So it's a boy! My heartiest congratulations to you and Marjorie. And my best wishes for everything fine and good in life for the little fellow.

I'll come and see Marjorie and the baby when they are home from the hospital.

Sincerely,
Ken

CONGRATULATIONS ON GRADUATION

Dear John:

Congratulations upon having received your doctorate in philosophy from Princeton University. I know this has meant years of study and hard work on your part, and it's an achievement you can well be proud of.

Your Aunt Emma and I have followed your progress with pleasure and interest; and we are sure, from the fine record you have made, that you will be a success in whatever you undertake.

No doubt you are tired after the strain of the past few months; and if you would like to come to Lake Talbot for a few weeks this summer, we'd be very happy to have you. We remember that you always used to like it here as a boy; and although it may be too quiet for you now, the rest and relaxation might do you a lot of good. And we'd certainly enjoy hearing about your plans, now that you have completed your college course.

Think it over, John, and let us know.

Affectionately,
Uncle Clint

Dear John:

I have just learned of your graduation from Princeton.

Please accept my heartiest congratulations, and best wishes for your future success.

Sincerely yours,
Harriet Cranford

Dear John:

Bill tells me you have successfully completed your course at Princeton and have received your doctorate in philosophy. He's very proud of his big brother, and I can't say I blame him! You've made a fine record, and all your old friends back here in Middletown are proud of you.

I understand you'll be here for a few weeks this summer before going to your uncle's place in the mountains. I am looking forward to seeing you and hearing about your plans for the future.

In the meantime, congratulations and best wishes to you, John!

Cordially,
Alice

Dear Mrs. Malcolm:

We hear that John has graduated from Princeton and that he made a very fine record for himself there. You must be proud of his splendid accomplishment, and we are very happy for you.

Please give John our congratulations, and our best wishes for success and happiness in his chosen work.

Sincerely yours,
Myra T. Clark

Dearest Mary:

It doesn't seem possible that you are grown up—and a graduate of Vassar! It was such a little while ago that you used to come and visit me, just so you could swing on my garden gate. Remember?

I'm very proud of you, Mary dear. I've heard all about your fine achievements at college. Just saying "Congratulations" doesn't seem enough; so I'm sending you a gift that I hope you like and find useful. With it goes my love, and my hopes for your happiness and success in the interesting career you have selected.

Devotedly,
Aunt Jean

Dear Miss Abbott:

May I join in the chorus of friendly congratulations that you must be receiving from all sides today on your graduation from Vassar?

Your parents have told me how brilliantly you have distinguished yourself this past year, and how many honors you have won. They are very proud of you, as they well may be. I'm proud of you, too—and I'm just an old neighbor and friend!

I understand you are going to Chicago to join the editorial staff of a new teen-age magazine. My best wishes go with you, my dear! I know it's the work you love and what you have always wanted to do. I'm sure you'll be a great success.

The best of luck to you!

Cordially,
Marion G. Hazlitt

Dear Mary:

I have just learned of your graduation from Vassar, and your plans to go to Chicago to take an editorial job.

May an old friend congratulate you, and wish you the very best of success?

Sincerely,
Bob Traymore

Dear Mary:

First let me congratulate you on your graduation from Vassar. You certainly distinguished yourself, from what I hear!

Then let me congratulate you on that swell job you got in Chicago. Isn't it *wonderful* to get just exactly the kind of job you've been wanting and hoping for! But you deserve it, Mary—and I'm sure this is the beginning of a very brilliant and successful career for you.

I know you'll be very busy, but I hope you'll find time to write now and then and let me know how you are getting along. I don't need to tell you how interested I am!

With every good wish for the future,

Affectionately,
Carolyn

CONGRATULATIONS ON WINNING AN
HONOR OR DISTINCTION

Dear Mrs. Marlowe:

It gave me the greatest possible pleasure to learn that you were named Middletown's outstanding mother of the year. I know of no one who deserves this great distinction more than you.

Congratulations from Mr. Dwight and myself. All your old neighbors and friends are very proud of you!

Cordially yours,
Jennie T. Dwight

Dear Dr. Harmon:

My warm congratulations to you on your election as president of the state medical association. It's a fine tribute from your colleagues, and a reward you richly deserve for your many years of splendid service to the profession and to the people of the state.

I can't think of any man who would have been a better choice. My very best wishes to you!

Sincerely yours,
Thomas M. Benton, M.D.

CONGRATULATIONS ON A PROMOTION
OR A NEW VENTURE

Dear Mr. Forthright:

I read in this morning's paper that after twenty-five years with Courtway and Pratt, you are branching out for yourself and opening your own advertising agency.

I would like to add my congratulations to the many you must be receiving. With your brilliant background and long record of fine achievements, I'm sure the new agency will be a great success. I sincerely hope you will find in this new venture the happiness and satisfaction you so richly deserve.

Cordially yours,
Lillian E. Watson

Dear Al:

I ran into Carl the other day, and he tells me you were recently appointed managing editor of the Middletown *Star*.

It's great news, Al—and I'm delighted to hear it! I knew it would be only a matter of time before your unusual abilities were recognized.

It's fine to know you have achieved the goal you've been working toward all these years, and I wish you the greatest possible success. In my opinion, the *Star* at last has an editor who can make it the dominant, outstanding daily of the Middle West!

My heartiest congratulations!

Sincerely yours,
Bert Fellows

Dear Jim:

Congratulations on the opening of the Middletown Clinic! We know it represents the dream of a lifetime, and we're so very happy that your dream has at last become a reality.

The institution will perform a great service to the people; and under your capable guidance, it cannot fail to be a credit to the community.

Paul and I send our very best wishes to you and to the members of your staff.

Affectionately,
Helen Lawson

CONGRATULATIONS ON WINNING A PRIZE

Dear Mrs. Palmer:

Imagine my delight to read in this morning's paper that you had won first prize in the poster contest! I didn't know we had such a talented neighbor.

Congratulations! I think your poster is *marvelous;* I've clipped it out of the paper so I can show it to all my friends.

Sincerely yours,
Jennifer Loomis

Dear Walter:

Your mother tells me you have won the singles championship and that you now rank third among the top boy players in the country. I'm sure you must be very happy and proud.

Congratulations from Mr. Clinton and myself, and keep up the good work!

Sincerely yours,
Sarah Clinton

CONGRATULATIONS ON A SPEECH
OR A PERFORMANCE

Dear Roger:

I simply *glow* with admiration when I think of the wonderful speech you made last night at town hall. We have all long been aware of the alarming increase in juvenile delinquency here in Middletown. But no one has ever had the courage to place the blame squarely where it belongs . . . as you did last night.

Congratulations on a brilliant and forceful speech! I'm sure that all the mothers who heard it must be as delighted and as grateful as I am. It's bound to do a lot of good.

Cordially,
Nancy Evans

Dear Miss Vuillimet:

Congratulations on your triumph last night! Everybody in Middletown is talking about your brilliant piano recital.

Mother and I are especially fond of the Tchaikovsky Concerto, and your rendition of it was simply *superb*. I just can't tell you how much we enjoyed it!

Sincerely yours,
Fredericka Hollings

Dear Bill:

I attended the track meet yesterday and I saw you win the 100-yard dash. It was a splendid performance, and I congratulate you! Keep up that kind of running and you'll make the next Olympic team!

Sincerely,
Ted Baxter

9

Letters of Condolence

Among the most difficult letters of all to write are letters of condolence. Many people find them so difficult that they send telegrams, printed cards, flowers—anything to avoid writing a personal note of sympathy!

And yet, there is probably no time when a letter can mean so much and be so deeply appreciated. It always helps to know that friends are sympathetic and understanding. A few sincere, well-chosen words can give comfort even to the most grief-stricken . . . can renew the faith and courage of those cruelly hurt and embittered by their loss.

So even though you send flowers or make a condolence call, always write a letter as well to any relative or friend who has suffered a bereavement. Put your sympathy and understanding on paper—*write down* the way you feel—for the greater comfort such written words can give.

A good letter of condolence is like a handclasp, warm and friendly. It is written with dignity and restraint, not filled with gushy sentiment. It's brief, for this is no time to be wordy. It says only what you truly feel: that and nothing more. It doesn't dwell on details of the illness or death, nor quote "comforting" passages from poetry or the Bible. It doesn't touch on memories that reopen the floodgates of pain and sorrow.

Often, in a note of condolence, it's not so much what you say as what you don't say that counts. Surely there can be neither comfort nor compassion in a letter that says, "She was too young to die!" or "Your life will be desolate without him!" It's better not to write at all than to write so tactlessly. A letter of condolence is written for one purpose only: *to give comfort.* And it cannot give comfort if it's tactless, or thoughtless . . . or very obviously insincere.

It shouldn't be difficult to write a good letter of condolence if you are genuinely moved to sympathy by a friend's misfortune. It shouldn't be difficult to write with kindness and understanding if you feel that friend's grief and share in the tragic impact of it. The important thing is to write promptly, as soon as you hear the news—and before the shock of it has worn off. For if you write while your heart is filled with sadness, your letter will have the ring of sincerity to it. Your letter will be a warm and convincing expression of the sympathy you really feel.

When you sit down to write a note of condolence, don't think about the right words and phrases to use. Don't strive for eloquence and effect. Remember, it's the feeling behind the words that counts, not the words themselves. Think of the person who is gone. Think of the heartache and sorrow of the person to whom you are writing. Put down simply and truthfully what you think and feel at that moment. Never mind the words. Write what's in your heart . . . and the words will come without coaxing.

Just remember that the three most essential qualities of a good condolence letter are *tact, sincerity* and *brevity.* A single sentence that expresses real feeling is better than a whole page of meaningless and insincere eloquence.

Following are examples of condolence letters representing a wide range of circumstances. These are not intended as set forms, to be used word for word; but as models or patterns to help you write comforting and understanding messages of your own.

ON THE DEATH OF A PARENT

Dear Margaret:

News has just come to me of your great loss. I cannot tell you how shocked and grieved I am. I wish I could be with you and comfort you in your sorrow.

I know how you adored your mother. It should be a great comfort to you now to know that you were always so very good and kind to her. Everyone says you were the most wonderful daughter a mother ever had! So don't grieve, my dear; she wouldn't want you to.

You have my love, and my heartfelt sympathy.

Affectionately,
Anne

Dear Margaret:

I want you to know how much I sympathize with you and your family.

Long after today's grief shall pass away, as fortunately it must, you will have as a consoling memory the knowledge of all that you meant and were to your mother. We all know of your unfailing devotion, and cherish and admire you for it.

My thoughts are with you now, and I send you my deepest sympathy.

Affectionately yours,
Edgar Tyler

Margaret, dear:

If only I knew what to say to comfort you! But words cannot say what is in my heart, nor tell you how deeply I feel for you in your sorrow.

I loved your mother, too, Margaret, and I'll never get over missing her. You know I share your grief, but how I wish that sharing it could lighten the burden for you!

I send you all my love, darling, and all my sympathy.

Devotedly,
Jane

Dear Margaret:

I know words aren't much comfort at a time like this. But I'd like you to know I'm thinking of you; and that my family and I send our heartfelt sympathy.

Sincerely,
Jim

Dear Margaret:

Today I heard you had lost your mother. I know the suddenness of it must have been a dreadful shock; and I just can't tell you how sorry I am. Having been so recently through the same sad experience, I know only too well what it means. . . .

I wish there were something I could do or say to soften your grief. But only time can do that, Margaret —and it *will*, as surely as it did for me.

With deepest sympathy to you and all your family,

Affectionately,
Vera T. Hubbard

Dearest Margaret:

I'm sorry to be so far away when you need me. . . . Just be the fine, brave person you have always been. You had your mother with you for many happy years, Margaret, and as time goes on you will find comfort and peace in your beautiful memories of her.

I'll hurry back to New York as soon as I can. In the meantime, I send you my love—and I hope you will turn to me for any help or comfort I can give, now and always.

Your devoted,
Aunt Kate

Dear Miss Conners:

We know how much your mother meant to you and how great your sorrow must be. We sincerely wish we could help share your burden until it gets lighter.

Mr. Burke joins me in sending heartfelt condolences to you and your family.

Cordially yours,
Mary G. Burke

Dear Miss Conners:

Please accept my very deepest sympathy on the death of your mother.

I can well appreciate what a great loss this must be to you.

Sincerely yours,
Frederick T. Warner

Dear Miss Conners:

We have heard the sad news and hasten to offer you our sympathy.

We hope you will call on us if there is anything we can do to help.

Sincerely,
Ellen and Joe Hartley

Dear Paul:

I cannot tell you how shocked I was to hear of your sudden great loss. Everyone who knew your mother loved and admired her.

I wish there were something I could do to help you in your grief; but all I can do is send you my very deepest sympathy.

Affectionately,
Grace

Dear Paul:

I've just heard the sad news, and I hasten to offer my sympathy.

Please call on me if there is anything I can do to help.

Sincerely,
Bob

Dear Paul:

I feel it's almost an intrusion to write at a time like this. But I must tell you how saddened we are by the news, and how deeply we feel for you in your sorrow. It was a privilege to have known your mother; and her loss will be felt by many, for a long time to come.

Fred and I hope that time will quickly soften the blow, and leave you only cherished memories.

Affectionately,
Mary Haskins

Dear Paul:

Your sorrow is shared by everyone who knew and loved your mother. There's little I can say, except that your grief is mine—and I only wish I could take away some part of it.

Affectionately,
Amy

Dear Paul:

Your wonderful mother—my sister—is gone. I know what your grief must be, for I know well what she always meant to you, and how completely devoted you were to each other.

I can't tell you how sorry I am that a continent now separates us. I'd like to be with you, Paul, and I'm distressed by the circumstances which make it impossible for me to fly to New York.

But I'm with you in thought, my boy. And although I share your grief, I urge you to find solace in the realization that you were all and everything to your mother . . . you made her so happy and proud! Everyone knows what a fine son you always were, in every way.

So try not to grieve too much, Paul. Try to believe as I do: that your mother is still right there with you, and that she will keep on being proud of you and your work.

Your aunt sends her love and deepest sympathy. We both hope you can arrange to spend a little time with us soon in Los Angeles. And I *do* hope, Paul, you will always count me a loyal and devoted friend, as well as your affectionate,

Uncle Dave

Dear Mr. Owen:

We have just learned with profound sorrow of the death of your mother.

She was well-loved in this community for her charities and good work, and she will be long remembered by many.

We send you our heartfelt sympathy.

Sincerely yours,
Jan and Tom Stevens

Dear Mr. Owen:

All our thoughts are with you in this hour of grief. Mr. Graham joins me in sending deepest sympathy.

Sincerely,
Ethel Graham

My dear Owen:

I cannot tell you how sorry I am to hear of your great loss. Please accept my sympathy and best wishes.

Sincerely,
Jonathan P. Stevens

Dear Alice:

We just learned of the sudden death of your father. The shock was a great one. But he went as he would have wished—quickly and without suffering. That should be some consolation to you.

We send our deepest sympathy to you and your family. We hope that time will soon heal your sorrow.

Affectionately,
Leslie Blair

Dearest Alice:

I was so shocked to hear of your father's sudden death. My thoughts have been with you all day, as I know what your grief and sorrow must be. I wish there were something I could do or say to help.

You know you have my deepest sympathy—and my love and friendship always.

Affectionately,
Emily

Dear Alice:

I'm so very sorry to hear of the death of your father.

Please accept my profound sympathy. I hope you won't hesitate to call on me if there's anything I can do.

Affectionately yours,
Malcolm Cushing

Dear Mrs. Taylor:

It was a great shock to hear of your father's death. He was a wonderful neighbor and friend, and he'll be missed by many.

Mr. Henderson and I send kind thoughts and sympathy to you and your family.

Sincerely yours,
Agnes Henderson

Dear Mrs. Taylor:

We have heard the sad news and wish to offer our heartfelt sympathy.

You have the consolation of knowing your father went quickly, without suffering. That should help you bear the pain of his loss.

We send you and your family our affectionate regards—and deep regrets for this sudden and unexpected sorrow.

Sincerely,
Hellen and Frank Austin

Dear Jim:

I sympathize with you on the loss of your father, to whom I know you were deeply devoted.

I hope you will find what comfort you can in the fact that he was with you to a fine old age . . . and that you made his life such a happy one. He was so proud of you, Jim—so proud of your splendid accomplishments. That should help soften your sorrow a little.

Lillian joins me in sending affection and sympathy. You know that if there's anything we can do, you have only to tell us.

Sincerely,
Walter

Dear Jim:

Your father told me so many, many times what a rich, full life his had been—and how much more he had to be grateful for than most people. Let that be your consolation now. He was with you for a considerable part of your life; and you were able to make him very comfortable and happy.

You'll miss him, of course—as we all shall miss his friendly smile and gay spirits. But time will bring comfort in the memory of your many good years together. Try to think of that, Jim, and not of your loss.

Ted and the girls join me in sending wholehearted sympathy.

Affectionately yours,
Isabel

Dear Jim:

My thoughts are with you in your bereavement. You have my heartfelt sympathy. Is there anything an old friend can do to help?

Always sincerely,
Raymond

Dear Mr. Hartwell:

I have just learned of your loss and wish to offer my deepest sympathy.

I knew your father for many years, and always admired and respected him. He will be long and well remembered by his many friends.

Sincerely,
Russel T. Kirkwood

Dear Mr. Hartwell:

We were saddened to read of your father's death in this morning's paper. He was a fine old gentleman, well-loved and admired by all who knew him.

We can well appreciate your great sense of loss. But we hope you'll find some small measure of comfort in the good wishes and heartfelt sympathy of your great host of friends—among whom I hope you include Mr. Travers and myself.

With affectionate regards from both of us,

Sincerely,
Marian Travers

Dear Mr. Hartwell:

Please accept my sincere condolences on the death of your father. I was indeed sorry to hear the sad news.

Sincerely yours,
Helen Blake

Dear Mr. Hartwell:

May old neighbors who remember your father with affection send you a message of sympathy?

We were greatly saddened by the news; and we can well imagine what your own grief must be. But we hope you'll find consolation in the monument of love and respect your father left behind in this community. You can be sure that no one who knew him will ever forget him.

With sympathy and best wishes,

Cordially yours,
Maud and Jules Galloway

ON THE DEATH OF A HUSBAND
OR WIFE

If you have a particularly difficult letter of condolence to write, try to put yourself in the place of the person to whom you are writing. Try to imagine how you would feel under similar circumstances, and what you would like said to you at such a time. Then write as simply and briefly as you can. Remember that *tact, sincerity* and *brevity* are the essential qualities of a good letter of condolence. A long, wordy letter that needlessly stirs up the emotions of the bereaved is undesirable and unkind.

A message of sympathy to someone who has just lost a beloved husband or wife is especially difficult to write. The following examples may prove helpful when you are at a loss for words.

Dear Mary:

There are not enough words of comfort in any language for you now. I know that . . . and yet I must write and try to comfort you.

Darling, you must not grieve. Arthur would not want you to grieve. He'd want you to bear up for the children's sake—and for your own.

I hope you can find a little comfort in the many friends who are thinking of you today, who love you and share your grief. There isn't anything I wouldn't do to help you, if I only could!

With love and heartfelt sympathy,

Susan

Mary, darling:

What can I say? What can *anyone* say? There just aren't words to express my overwhelming sorrow at your great loss.

I know you'll be fine and brave for the children's sake; and that you'll find comfort in the memory of the many happy years you shared with Arthur.

All my thoughts are with you, Mary. I only wish that sharing your grief could take some part of it away!

Love and deepest sympathy from Joe and myself,

Betty

Dear Mary:

We are shocked by the sad news. Is there anything Fred or I can do?

Our hearts are filled with sympathy for you in this hour of trial. We send you our love, and our assurance of devoted friendship—now and always.

Lillian

Dearest Mary:

No one knows better than I what you are thinking and feeling, for I have so recently gone through the same bitter experience.

I know well how meaningless words are to you now; and how little even your best friends can do to comfort you. But time is a great healer, Mary—and it will soon soften the pain and bring you peace of mind, just as it did for me.

You have your children, Mary—and you can be very grateful for that. I am all alone. But I have my memories of my beloved husband, and they grow more precious to me with every passing day. You will have that too, my dear. You will have beautiful memories that no one can take away from you, *ever*.

So try and be brave these first difficult weeks. I send you a heart full of sympathy and understanding; and you know you have my love always.

Janet

Dear Mrs. Bishop:

We feel for you in your great sorrow and send you our heartfelt condolences.

It should be some consolation to you to know that everyone who knew your husband admired and respected him. There are many in this community who will never forget him—Mr. Keeley and I among them.

We hope you will count us your friends as well as your neighbors, and call on us if there is ever anything we can do.

> Sincerely yours,
> Ida Keeley

Dear Mrs. Bishop:

I am profoundly sorry to learn of the death of your husband, for whom I had the greatest admiration and regard.

Please accept my deepest sympathy.

> Sincerely yours,
> Gerald P. Searle

Dear Tom:

Words can't express our shock and grief at the sad news. We know how great your sorrow must be, but we beg you to bear up and be brave for your family's sake. You know Ellen would want you to. . . .

We send you our sympathy and affection in this hour of trial, and we hope you won't hesitate to call on us if there is anything we can do.

> Fondly,
> Kate and Charles

Dear Tom:

It was a great shock to hear of Ellen's death. I know that nothing I can say will help you; but I want you to know you have my heartfelt sympathy.

> Affectionately,
> Carl

Dear Tom:

The news of your great loss has just come to us. John and I realize what this means to you, and our hearts are filled with sorrow. Will you let us know if there is anything we can do to help?

With affection and deepest sympathy,

Laura

Dear Tom:

There's not much we can say at a time like this. But Marge and I want you to know how deeply we feel for you in your sorrow—and how much we would like to help. Will you call on us if there's anything we can do?

With profound sympathy,

Sincerely,
Jerry

Dear Tom:

Ellen was my best friend, and I loved her dearly. But it's with you that my thoughts are today, for I know how you must be grieving.

Ellen wouldn't want you to grieve, Tom. You know that, don't you? You made her very happy, always. She used to tell me you were the most wonderful husband in the world. Try to find some comfort in that—and in the memory of your many fine years together.

Will you have someone telephone me if there's anything you'd like me to do? George and I send you our affection and deepest sympathy in this dark hour.

Judith

Dear Mr. Bailey:

Mr. Comstock and I are profoundly sorry to hear of your great loss. We wish there were something we could do. If there ever is, now or in the future, will you count us your friends and call on us?

Sincerely yours,
Thelma Comstock

Dear Mr. Bailey:

It is with great sorrow that I have just learned of the death of your wife.

I know there is little I can say to lessen your grief; but I'd like you to know you have my deepest sympathy in your bereavement.

Sincerely yours,
Horace Mitchell

Dear Mr. Bailey:

Upon my return to New York today, I was shocked to learn of the death of Mrs. Bailey.

I can well realize what this great loss means to you, and I send my sincerest sympathy. I hope that time will quickly ease your sorrow.

With warmest personal regards,

Sincerely yours,
Eric Larkin

Dear Mr. Bailey:

News of Mrs. Bailey's death has just reached me, with all the attending shock such news carries.

May I add my little word of consolation to that of the countless who knew and admired her?

My husband asks to be included in these condolences.

Sincerely yours,
Florence Whitmore

ON THE DEATH OF A CHILD

How heartbreaking the death of a child can be! And how cruel a long, wordy message is at such a time, especially if it probes into the details of the child's illness or manner of death. It's far better not to write at all than to write carelessly or thoughtlessly to grief-stricken parents. Remember that the only purpose of a letter of condolence is to give comfort. It should sympathize and console . . . but it should not recall any memories nor stir up any emotions that increase the heartbreak. A note to bereaved parents should be short, very short—and should scrupulously avoid mention of any subject that could possibly give pain.

Dear Julia:

I'm thinking of you, darling . . . and hoping you'll be as brave as you've always been.

My love and deepest sympathy to you and David.

Affectionately,
Joan

Dearest Julia:

Our hearts are heavy today with the grief of your great loss. Bob and I couldn't feel any worse if it were our own child.

We send you and David our most heartfelt sympathy. How we wish there were some way we could soften the blow and take away some of your sorrow!

Devotedly,
Florence

Julia, my dear:

We know only too well the shock and grief you and David are suffering today, for it's only a little more than a year since our own son was taken.

Our hearts are filled with sympathy for you both. We hope that time will soon ease the pain. In the meantime, Julia, you must be strong and brave—for the sake of David and the other children. They look to you for guidance and comfort.

With all our love,

Martha and Henry

Dear Julia:

There are no words to express our grief at the sad news. Our hearts are filled with sorrow for you and David.

Is there anything we can do? You know how grateful we'd be if you let us help in some way.

Joel and I send our love, and our deepest sympathy to you both.

Affectionately,
Charlotte

Dear Julia and David:

We know there's little consolation in a note, even from friends who love you well and share your grief.

But Fred and I want you to know our thoughts are with you every minute; and there isn't anything we wouldn't do to ease your pain and sorrow if we only could!

We hope you'll try to bear up for the sake of the other children. They need your faith and courage to help them through this bad time.

With love to you all,

Affectionately,
Mabel

Dear David:

I've just heard the sad news, and I can't tell you how sorry I am.

You and Mrs. Tuttle have the heartfelt sympathy of all your friends here at Hall-Brent. We feel your loss keenly, and we wish there were some way we could lighten the burden of your great sorrow.

Will you let me know if there's anything I can do? I hope you know you can always count on my friendship and affection.

Sincerely,
Ted Baker

Dear Dave:

I was mighty sorry to hear about the little fellow. That's certainly bad news. My sympathy and kindest thoughts to you and Mrs. Tuttle.

> Sincerely,
> Jack Brady

Dear Mrs. Andrews:

I was shocked to hear of the great sorrow that has come to you and your household. I send my deepest sympathy to you and Mr. Andrews.

> Sincerely,
> Edna Williams

Dear Mrs. Andrews:

Mr. Davis and I are profoundly sorry to hear of your son's death.

We realize what a sad blow this has been; and we send you and Mr. Andrews our heartfelt sympathy. We wish it were within our power to soften your great sorrow.

> Sincerely yours,
> Rose Davis

Dear Mr. and Mrs. Andrews:

I hope you will forgive me for intruding on your grief. Although I'm a new neighbor and almost a stranger to you, I must tell you how deeply I feel for you in this great sorrow.

Mr. Mulhall and I extend to you our warmest sympathy. Please count us among those who share your grief and whose hearts are heavy for you today.

> Sincerely yours,
> Dorothy K. Mulhall

Dear Mr. Andrews:

I have just learned with deepest sorrow and regret of the death of your little boy.

I realize the inadequacy of words to comfort you in your great grief. But I'd like you and Mrs. Andrews to know my thoughts are with you in your bereavement; and I stand ready and eager to help in any way I can.

With sympathy and warmest personal regards,

Sincerely yours,
Edwin Corbett

ON THE DEATH OF A RELATIVE

When someone loses a relative, it's kind and thoughtful to write a brief note of sympathy. If you knew the person who died, you may want to include a word of praise in your message. Otherwise a simple expression of sympathy, a word or two of comfort, are all that are necessary.

Dear Jim:

I know how devoted you were to your brother, and I just can't tell you how stunned and distressed I am by the sad news.

Please extend my sincere sympathy to your mother, and tell her how deeply I feel for her—and all of you —in this great sorrow.

Sincerely,
Margot Walsh

Dear Claire:

I wish I knew how to comfort you on the loss of your sister. She was so sweet and charming! No one who knew her will ever forget her.

But you must accept this great blow with courage, Claire—for the sake of your mother. She needs you so desperately now, and will look to you for comfort in the months ahead.

I send you both my love and deepest sympathy, and only wish it were possible to take away some of your grief.

Affectionately,
Celia

Dear Mrs. Phillips:

We were very sorry to hear of the death of your sister. Although she was very ill, and you were more or less prepared for it—we know how great your loss is and we sympathize with you in your bereavement.

Mr. Willard joins me in sending condolences to you and your family.

Sincerely yours,
Amy R. Willard

Dear Fred:

Your sister died as she lived, simply and quietly . . . with the love and respect of all who knew her.

I hope you are finding some small measure of comfort in the fact that she went quickly, without suffering.

But I know well how much you'll miss her, Fred, and I send you my deepest sympathy. Eleanor asks to be included in this message, and sends you her affectionate regards.

Sincerely,
Roger

Dear Mr. Forrest:

Word of the recent death of your brother has just come to me, and I hasten to offer condolences.

I had the privilege of knowing your brother in years past, and I realize your great loss. He was a fine and brilliant man, and he will not soon be forgotten by the many who admired and respected him.

Please convey my sympathy and my warm personal regards to all your family.

Cordially yours,
Gerald M. Larkin

Dear Paula:

I have just this moment learned of the sudden death of your brother, Eric. I can't tell you how shocked I am by this sad news. I know what he meant to you and your sister, and I send you both my deepest sympathy.

I'm sure that many hearts must be heavy with sorrow today; for I never knew anyone with such a host of friends as Eric. He'll be keenly missed by everyone who knew him.

Is there any way I can help, Paula? You know I would gladly do anything I can.

> With love,
> Emily

Dear Miss Travers:

I have just been told of your aunt's death; and knowing your devotion to each other, I realize what a great loss this is to you.

I'd like you to know how sorry Mr. Patton and I are; and how deeply we sympathize with you in your bereavement.

With kindest thoughts from us both,

> Sincerely,
> Jennifer R. Patton

Dear Mrs. Drummond:

We read in this morning's paper of the death of your talented young nephew. We share with many the shock and sorrow of this tragic news; and our hearts go out in sympathy to you and your family.

Mr. Rankin and I send our heartfelt condolences; and we hope you will find some consolation in the record of brilliant achievements he leaves behind him.

> Sincerely yours,
> Bessie G. Rankin

Dear Myra:

My mother just telephoned and told me your niece died this morning. I'm terribly sorry to hear this sad news. I knew she was desperately ill; but like everyone else, I hoped and expected she would recover.

Please extend my heartfelt sympathy to your family. If there is anything I can do, you know you have just to mention it.

Affectionately,
Doris

WHEN DEATH IS A RELEASE

There are times when death is clearly "for the best," and may be looked upon almost as a blessing rather than a great sorrow. Under these circumstances, the expression of sympathy or condolence should be for the long illness or suffering of the deceased, rather than the immediate death.

Here are typical examples of such letters, written when death was a release from long and hopeless suffering.

Carol, dear:

All my thoughts are with you and your mother today. My heart is filled with sympathy for you both— for the long year of suffering, and for your sorrow now that Jean is gone.

I loved your sister, Carol; I'm sure you know that. I shall miss her more than I can say. But I know how she suffered this past year, and I'm grateful that her suffering is over at last. I try to find comfort in that thought, and I hope you will, too.

Affectionately,
Lucy

Dear Ted:

I can only repeat in this note what you already know: that Jim and I are profoundly touched by all the sorrow that has come to you in these past few years. Our thoughts and sympathies were always with you, for we knew how terribly Emma suffered—and how hopeless her condition was.

Be grateful that her long suffering is over, Ted—and try to feel, as all your good friends do, that it was for the best.

With all our affection,

Fondly,
Grace

Dear Mrs. Carleton:

Yours has been a long and tragic sorrow; and now that it is over at last, I am sure that time will soon bring comfort and peace.

Mr. Jamison and I want you to know how deeply we sympathize with you for all you have endured through the years, and now. We assure you of our affectionate regard, and hope you will let us know if there is anything either of us can do—as neighbors and friends.

Sincerely yours,
Laura Jamison

Dear Dick:

You have been through a great deal these past few months, and all my thoughts and sympathies are with you now.

I hope you will look on Barbara's death as a release from cruel and hopeless suffering. John and I feel deeply for you in your present sorrow, but we are grateful that the long ordeal is over.

Try not to look back, Dick. You have your two fine sons to think about. So keep your eyes on the future and the life that lies ahead.

Always affectionately,
Carolyn

Dear Mr. Winters:

When I learned of your wife's death today, I was not as shocked as I might have been if I had not known of her long and tragic illness.

I'm deeply sorry for all the grief and sadness you've had, now and in the past . . . and I offer my sincere condolences.

I hope that time will quickly bring the peace of mind so long denied you.

With best wishes,

Sincerely yours,
Henry T. Bishop

WHEN SOMEONE IS KILLED
OR COMMITS SUICIDE

When death strikes cruelly and without warning, it leaves shock and anguish to those left behind. Only relatives and close friends should write; others should not intrude upon the horror and heartache of sudden death.

To a Woman Whose Husband Was
Killed in an Automobile Accident

Dear Christine:

We are stunned, as all your friends are, by the tragic news. Jerry and I send you our heartfelt sympathy, and we beg you to let us help you in any way we can.

Will you have someone call us if there's anything we can do? In deepest sorrow and affection,

Yours devotedly,
Sue

To a Woman Whose Husband Was
Killed in a Plane Crash

Dearest Mildred:

There are no words to express my shock and grief. I wish I were there to comfort you in your anguish.

Be brave, darling—for little Tommy's sake. You know that Bill would want you to carry on. I'll come to you as soon as I can.

With all my love, your heartbroken

Sally

To a Mother Whose Child Was
Killed in a Street Accident

Mary, darling:

Ed and I are too grieved and shocked even to try and express our sympathy.

Our hearts are filled with sorrow for you and Pete. We hope and pray that time will quickly soften this terrible blow.

We send you our love, and we're standing by to help in any way we can. Have someone call us, darling, if you want us.

Devotedly,
Jane

To a Man Whose Wife Died
in Childbirth

Dear Fred:

We're heartbroken by the sad news. We know there are no words to comfort you now; but we want you to know we're thinking of you every moment, in sorrow and devotion.

Bill and I hope you'll accept this cruel blow with the courage and faith Anne would expect of you— for the sake of the little one.

You know you can count on us, Fred—now and always—for any help within our power to give.

With love and sympathy,

Isabel

To a Woman Whose Parents Were Killed in a Railroad Accident

Dear Claudia:

I just can't believe the terrible news. I wish with all my heart I could help or comfort you in some way.

It may be some slight consolation to you to know that your grief is shared by everyone in Middletown.

With deepest sympathy to you in your great loss,

Affectionately,
Kathryn

To a Man Whose Wife Committed Suicide

Dear Roy:

How could this have happened to you, who least deserved it?

Your friends all know your love and tireless devotion to Lenore. Only the agony of her long and painful illness could have driven her to such madness.

So don't ever blame or reproach yourself, Roy dear. You did everything you could for her—and all your friends are filled with sympathy and affection for you in your trouble.

I hope you'll let me help if there's anything I can do. Alan joins me in sending love and heartfelt sympathy.

Edith

To a Woman Whose Crippled Son Committed Suicide

Dearest Cora:

We all know the torment of grief you have suffered so bravely, for so many years—and we cherish and admire you for it.

This last great shock seems almost too much to bear; but time is a wonderful healer, Cora darling—and when the anguish is over and your pain has eased, you will have the comfort and peace of mind so long denied you.

For Paul is at rest, dear. His agony is over. You and Fred did everything humanly possible for him; and you must never, never reproach yourselves in any way.

Jim and I send you both all our love and sympathy in this dark hour. If there's anything we can do to help, you know you have only to tell us.

Devotedly,
Irene

SOME FAMOUS LETTERS OF CONDOLENCE

Often it helps, in writing your own letters, to know what others have written to family and friends in time of tragedy or bereavement. Here, for example, is a beautiful and touching letter written by William Godwin to his daughter Mary on the death of her husband, Percy Bysshe Shelley. The young poet was drowned in a storm at sea. The letter is dated August 9, 1822:

My poor girl! What do you mean to do with yourself? You surely do not mean to stay in Italy? How glad I should be to be near you, and to endeavour by new expedients each day to make up for your loss! But you are the best judge. If Italy is a country to which in these few years you are naturalized, and if England is become dull and odious to you, then stay.

I should think, however, that now you have lost your closest friend your mind would naturally turn homewards, and to your earliest friend. Is it not so? Surely we might be a great support to each other, under the trials to which we are reserved, What signify a few outward adversities, if we find a friend at home?

Above all, let me entreat you to keep up your courage. You have many duties to perform; you must now be the father as well as the mother; and I trust you have energy of character enough to enable you to perform your duties honourably and well.

Ever and ever most affectionately yours,

The day her beloved sister Emily was buried, Charlotte Brontë (the author of *Jane Eyre*) wrote in sorrow and tender understanding to a friend who had been close to them both:

The anguish of seeing her suffer is over; the spectacle of the pains of death is gone by; the funeral day is past. We feel she is at peace. No need now to tremble for the hard frost and the keen wind. Emily does not feel them.

Princess Alice of England, the devoted daughter of Queen Victoria, wrote the following letter to her mother on the anniversary of her father's death:

Darmstadt, December 11, 1866

Beloved, precious Mama,—

On awakening this morning, my first thoughts were of you and of dear darling Papa! Oh, how it reopens the wounds scarcely healed, when this day of pain and anguish returns! This season of the year, the leafless trees, the cold light, everything reminds me of that time!

Happily married as I am, and with such a good, excellent and loving husband, how far more can I understand now the depth of that grief which tore your lives asunder!

Alice

When Charles Dickens' infant daughter died, his wife was ill . . . and he broke the tragic news to her gently, tenderly, in a letter that has become a classic of its kind. He didn't actually tell her the child was dead; he prepared her slowly for the shock, let her realize for herself that there was no hope.*

You would suppose her quietly asleep, but I am sure she is very ill, and I cannot encourage myself with much hope of her recovery. I do not (and why should I say I do to you, my dear?) I do not think her recovery at all likely. . . . Remember what I have often told you, that we never can expect to be exempt . . . from the afflictions of other parents. . . .

When Robert E. Lee was president of Washington College, a student was drowned—and he had the sad duty of writing a note of condolence to the boy's father. Here is the first paragraph of his letter:†

Washington College,
Lexington, Virginia.
March 19, 1868.

My dear Sir:

Before this you have learned of the affecting death of your son. I can say nothing to mitigate your grief or to relieve your sorrow; but if the sincere sympathy

---

* This is merely a brief excerpt. For the complete letter, see Schuster, *A Treasury of the World's Great Letters,* p. 307.
† From: Capt. Robert E. Lee, *Recollections and Letters of General Robert E. Lee* (New York: Doubleday & Co., Inc , 1904, 1924).

of his comrades and friends and of the entire community can bring you any consolation, I can assure you that you possess it in its fullest extent.

By far the most famous condolence letter ever written—and, in fact, one of the most famous letters in American history—is the one Abraham Lincoln wrote to Mrs. Lydia Bixby, consoling her on the loss of five sons in the Civil War.

Executive Mansion
Washington, Nov. 21, 1864

To Mrs. Bixby, Boston, Mass.

Dear Madam,

I have been shown in the files of the War Department a statement of the Adjutant General of Massachusetts that you are the mother of five sons who have died gloriously on the field of battle. I feel how weak and fruitless must be any word of mine which shall attempt to beguile you from the grief of a loss so overwhelming. But I cannot refrain from tendering you the consolation that may be found in the thanks of the republic they died to save. I pray that our Heavenly Father may assuage the anguish of your bereavement, and leave you only the cherished memory of the loved and lost, and the solemn pride that must be yours to have laid so costly a sacrifice upon the altar of freedom.

Yours very sincerely and respectfully
A. Lincoln

10

Notes of Sympathy on Illness, Injury, and Material Loss

Not all letters of sympathy are written on the sad occasion of death. They are written also to cheer friends who are ill, or who have been injured in an accident. They are also frequently written to relatives or friends who have suffered material loss by fire, flood, theft or other unfortunate circumstances.

A note of sympathy, like a note of condolence, should be tactful and *sincere*. If the illness or loss is a relatively minor one, the letter may be written in a light and bantering vein. But when a person is gravely ill or has suffered a really serious loss, any attempt to be facetious is in very bad taste and should be avoided. Even though your bright and witty letter may be written with the best intentions in the world, to cheer the invalid or unhappy victim of misfortune, you can be sure it will be resented. For people take their troubles seriously, and expect you to do likewise.

That doesn't mean your note of sympathy should be gloomy or pessimistic. Quite on the contrary! It should bring courage and comfort to the person who receives it . . . should be like a mental handclasp, warm and friendly, and filled with promise for the future.

It's not at all difficult to write a good note of sympathy—one you can be sure will be received with pleasure and appreciation— if you are able to put yourself in the place of the person to whom you are writing. Just try to imagine yourself gravely ill or injured. Try to imagine how you would feel if your valuables were stolen or your property destroyed by fire. Would you welcome jokes or bright sayings from your friends at such a time? Or would you want kindness and understanding—would you want sincere and well-meant sympathy?

Just write as you would like to be written to under the same unhappy circumstances, and your letter will give the comfort and cheer for which it is primarily intended.

TO THOSE WHO ARE ILL

Always try to write to a sick person as though complete recovery were just around the corner—and he, or she, will soon be up again, sound and well as ever. Minimize the illness, if you can; don't dramatize its seriousness. And just in case you think that's farfetched, here's an actual excerpt from a letter written to someone in my family:

> I'm so sorry to hear of your illness. I know how serious
> it is, because one of my best friends died of it.

Surely that's the perfect example of what not to say in a letter of sympathy!

The spirit behind your message should be, *Sorry to hear you're not well. But you will be very soon, of course! Just want you to know I'm thinking of you.* . . . Say it any way you like, but that should be the meaning behind your words. Unless a note of sympathy makes the person who receives it *feel better*—unless it gives that person a mental lift and a more cheerful outlook—it should be dropped into the wastebasket and not the mailbox! For a gloomy or thoughtless letter can do more harm than good to someone already depressed by illness or suffering.

A note of sympathy may be quite brief, just a paragraph or two. Or it may be long and chatty, like the letters you write to friends who are *not* ill. The length of the letter is not important. But what you say in your letter is very important indeed to the person confined to a lonely room, ill . . . and perhaps in pain. Your letter should be like a warm and friendly visit with that person, bringing brightness and cheer into the sickroom, bringing at least momentary escape from the loneliness or pain.

When writing to an invalid or convalescent you know well,

try to bring the outside world to him by writing of the things in which he is interested and with which he is familiar. For example, if he's a golf enthusiast, tell him about the 90 your neighbor shot the other day. If his hobby is tropical fish, tell him about the exhibit you saw recently . . . or the article you read in a magazine . . . or the new kind of tank just developed for Siamese fighting fish. If necessary, go out of your way to get some interesting tidbit of information to include in your letter. Remember that you are able to get around and the sick person is not. He'll appreciate news of the outside world, especially in his own field or hobby.

To a woman whose great love is gardening, you might write about the flower show . . . or tell her how lovely her garden looked as you went by it that morning . . . or confide plans for your own garden next Spring. Or you might mention that you saw her children recently, and how lovely they looked—or how surprised you were to see how big they were getting. You can always find something to write about that's of interest to the patient, if you really want to. If you are writing to someone who has no special interests or hobbies, you can always write about people. Everyone is interested in people: what they are doing, where they are going, what they have accomplished.

The following examples cover a variety of circumstances, and are written with different degrees of intimacy. Some are formal and reserved in tone, but cordial—the type of notes you might write to neighbors or acquaintances with whom you are friendly but not intimate. Others are chatty and informal in tone, and are the type of notes you would send to relatives or close friends.

Bear in mind that the most important thing is to write *optimistically*, with the cheerful assumption that the sick person is well on the road to recovery.

Dear Mrs. Corbin:

I was so sorry to learn of your illness. You must hurry and get well! Everybody in the neighborhood misses you, and we're all hoping you'll be back soon.

Mr. Burke joins me in sending best wishes for your speedy recovery.

Sincerely yours,
Mary T. Burke

Dear Mr. Warner:

I was mighty sorry to hear you were in the hospital. But your son says you're making fine progress, and that's wonderful news to everybody around here!

Keep up the good work. Mrs. Johnson and I hope you'll regain your health and strength in record time, and that we'll soon see you back in your own house, as well as ever.

Until then, our very best wishes!

Cordially yours,
George Johnson

Dear Mr. Pratt:

Word of your illness has just reached Middletown, and your many friends here are thinking of you—and hoping for your quick return to health. We won't be content until we hear that you are completely recovered and yourself again!

I understand you will be in the hospital for a few weeks. I'm sending you some books to help make the time pass more quickly. I hope you'll enjoy reading them.

Mrs. Lawson sends her best wishes. We expect to see you back in Middletown real soon, hale and hearty—and with all your old vitality!

Cordially yours,
Henry T. Lawson

Dear Miss Turner:

Your mother has just informed us of your emergency operation last Tuesday. We were surprised and very sorry to hear about it, but happy to know everything is progressing nicely and that you'll soon be up and around again.

We certainly hope your convalescence will be swift and uneventful, and that you'll be back with your family in no time.

With best wishes from all the Wheelers,

Sincerely yours,
Amy G. Wheeler

Dear Roger:

Yesterday Jim Ryan told me about your wife's illness. I am very sorry to hear about it, and I hope she will soon regain her health.

Please give her my sympathy and very best wishes.

Cordially,
Phil

Dear Dr. Howell:

Mrs. Dunne and I are extremely sorry to hear of your illness. We often wondered how you could keep going as you did, day and night. It was bound to catch up with you sooner or later!

We *do* hope you won't rush your recovery—that you'll think of yourself, for a change, and get a good rest before you return to your practice. We're sending you some books we think you'll enjoy.

With best wishes for your quick and complete return to health,

Sincerely yours,
Gilbert Dunne

Dear Mr. Foster:

I'm delighted to hear that you are well on the road to recovery and will be able to leave the hospital in a week or so.

We've all missed you around here. It will be wonderful to see you up and around again—your old cheerful self!

With best wishes for a speedy convalescence,

Sincerely yours,
Elaine Falcon

Dear Edith:

We missed you so much at the meeting last week! You have no idea how much you mean to your many friends.

So hurry and lick that old flu germ, will you? Another meeting without you is *unthinkable!*

Your mother says you're feeling a lot better, and I'm so glad to hear it. But I hope you'll be entirely better by the time this note reaches you.

Did you hear about Elsie Keith? She won the prize for architectural design. Isn't that wonderful? She's going to New York next week to receive the award.

And, oh yes! Betty Larkin's engaged to Phil Walten. What do you think of a surprise shower for her at the club house? Don't you think it would be fun?

The girls asked me to send you their best wishes, Edith. We all hope you'll soon be completely well.

Affectionately,
Grace

Dear Joe:

I've just this minute heard that you are in the hospital. I think you are very wise to find out once and for all what's causing your trouble, and get it over with.

I hope that by the time this note reaches you, you'll be feeling a great deal better. I'm sure that now it won't be long before you are entirely and completely yourself again.

By the way, Joe, the boys are postponing that fishing trip until you can join us. We've decided it wouldn't be nearly as much fun without you. So hurry and get well!

Affectionately,
Harry

Dear Mary:

I hear you are making such a rapid recovery that you'll soon be out of the hospital and back with your family and friends. That's wonderful news, Mary! I've missed you so much. You've been on my mind constantly, ever since you went to the hospital. I just can't tell you how sorry I was that you had such a difficult time of it.

But all that's over now, and you'll soon be as good as new! I met Dr. Carleson at my sister's house yesterday (her little boy has the mumps) . . . and he tells me you are his prize patient. He says you rallied beautifully, and that from this point on you'll show steady improvement—until you have all your old health and strength back again.

I saw John yesterday, too. The poor man is like a lost sheep without you! He says he's counting the very *hours* until you come home. Janet was with him; my, how she has grown in the past year! You have a lovely daughter, Mary . . . as gracious and charming as she is sweet to look at. You must be very proud of her.

This morning I walked by your house on the way to the post office, and I stopped for a moment to look at your garden. I still say it's the most beautiful garden in town! Your roses are magnificent this year. And I do hope you'll get home before the lilacs are gone—they're simply *gorgeous!*

Frank sends his best wishes, and he says to be sure and tell you how delighted he is to hear about your fine progress. Keep it up, Mary—and come home real soon to those who love and miss you.

Affectionately,
Lillian

TO THOSE WHO HAVE BEEN INJURED

A note written to someone who has been injured in an accident should be as brief as possible, and genuinely sympathetic. It is better not to write at all than to write out of curiosity. The spirit behind your message should not be, "How did it happen? Whose fault was it? Were there any witnesses?"—but "I'm so sorry to hear about it! I hope you weren't badly injured and that you'll soon be all right again." In other words, your concern should not be for the details of the accident but for the condition and well-being of the person who has been injured.

Dear Miss Jenkins:

I was indeed sorry to hear of your fall, and of the injury to your hip. I am told it's not a very serious injury, and I'm sure that's as great a relief to your family as it is to your many friends.

I sincerely hope you will make a quick recovery, and that you'll soon be up and around again—-as well as ever!

Cordially yours,
Vincent R. Mitchell

Dear Mrs. Farrell:

My husband and I were shocked and distressed to read about the terrible accident in which you were involved. We were somewhat cheered, however, to learn from your son that you were not among the more seriously injured.

Please accept our sympathy on your unfortunate experience, and let us know if there's anything we can do to help. We hope you are already on the mend, and that you'll soon be completely recovered from your injuries.

Sincerely yours,
Natalie Collins

Dear Mr. Brown:

I met your brother today, and he told me about the accident you had. I'm certainly sorry to hear about it.

I understand that your injuries are painful, but not serious—and that you'll be able to leave the hospital in about a week. That, at least, is something to be thankful for!

If I can be of any service, will you let me know? In the meantime, I'm sending some books and puzzles to help pass the time until you are well enough to go home.

My sympathies to you, and best wishes for a speedy recovery.

Sincerely,
Bert Clifford

Dear Tom:

I just can't tell you how sorry I was to learn of your accident. Your family tells me that you are progressing nicely, and that you'll be out of the hospital in about ten days. I'm certainly relieved to know that!

In the next day or so you'll receive a little package from Margaret and me. I hope you like it, and that it will help to pass the time more pleasantly.

With every good wish for your swift recovery,

Sincerely,
Bob

Dear Ruth:

It was certainly a shock to read in last night's *Press* that you were injured in an automobile accident and taken to the hospital.

Mother and I were terribly upset about it. We hope that your injuries are not serious and that you will soon be up and around again. We won't come until we're sure that you want visitors; but in the meantime we'll keep in touch with Ellen so we'll know how you are getting along.

We send you our love and our sympathy, Ruth. We're sorry you were hurt, and we won't be content until we hear that you are completely well again.

Affectionately,
Phyllis

Dear Mrs. Gilbert:

I feel I simply *must* write this note and tell you how much you are in the hearts and minds of everyone in Middletown.

We were shocked and saddened beyond words by news of the crash. But we were grateful, too, that your injuries were not worse.

The affection and best wishes of the entire town are with you, and everyone's hoping for your quick and complete recovery.

Sincerely yours,
Cora Stanley

Dear Marjory:

I've just learned that young Pete was hurt in a football game. I'm ever so sorry to hear it, and I hope his injuries are not serious.

I know just how you feel because I had the same experience with George a few years ago—remember? I guess it's just something all mothers of growing boys must expect!

Please let me know if there's anything I can do to help. Perhaps you'd like to send Patsy here for a week or so, until Pete is better. We'd love to have her, and I'd see that she got to and from school safely. Just phone me, Marj—and I'll come and get her.

Tell Pete I'm sorry he was hurt, and that I hope he'll soon be fit as a fiddle again.

Affectionately,
Harriet

Dear Mr. Willet:

I was extremely sorry to hear about Mrs. Willet's accident. I hope it is not serious, and that she will soon be entirely well again.

Please give her my very best wishes.

Sincerely yours,
Jonathan Kent

TO THOSE WHO HAVE SUFFERED
MATERIAL LOSS OR DAMAGE

People who have suffered material loss or damage generally appreciate a brief message of sympathy from their friends. But it should not be a probing letter, filled with questions—a letter prompted more by curiosity than kindness. It should merely express sympathy, and perhaps offer help. Here are a few examples:

Dear Mr. Thompson:

I was extremely sorry to hear of the fire which destroyed your beautiful house in Far Acres. I know well how much that house meant to you and Mrs. Thompson, and I hasten to offer my sympathy.

With best wishes to you both,
Sincerely yours,
Roger Whitney

Dear Madeline:

I can't believe the lovely little cottage in Cornwall is gone! I was shocked and grieved when Bill told me about the fire. But he says you've been an awfully good sport about it—as, of course, you would be! You're always such a good sport, about everything.

Some day you and Bill will have another cottage to take its place. And in the meantime you have your memories of all the many happy summers you spent at

Cornwall. Nothing can ever take that away from you, Madeline! I know *I'll* never forget the wonderful times I've had there as your guest.

All my love to you, dear—and my sympathy for ~vhat I know is a great loss to you and Bill.

> Affectionately,
> Cora

Dear Sally:

Your sister phoned this morning and told us about the fire which damaged your house last night. Jim and I know how distressing this experience can be, as we went through it ourselves. If there's any way we can help, will you call on us? You are more than welcome to use our basement for storing things until the damage to your house is repaired.

We hope the damage is less than you think, and that your lovely house will soon be good as new again.

> Sincerely,
> Betsy Wall

Dear Tom:

I've just heard about the great damage to your house and grounds by the recent heavy floods in Middletown. I'm certainly sorry about it, and I wish you'd let me help if there's anything I can do.

I realize that words are little consolation at a time like this. But I'd like you to know that I'm thinking of you, Tom . . . that you and your family have my deepest sympathy in your trouble . . . and that you can count wholeheartedly on my friendship, now and always.

So will you let me know what I can do—how I can help?

> Affectionately,
> Bill Stevens

Dear Mrs. Smithfield:

All your friends are shocked and grieved by the great loss suffered by your family in the recent flood. To lose a lovely home so cruelly and suddenly is a tragic experience; and no letter can adequately express our sympathy for you.

But there is at least some consolation in the fact that you and your family are safe. We knew that your house was directly in the path of the flood; and you can't imagine how relieved and grateful we were to hear that you had reached your sister's house safely and had escaped the full fury of the storm.

All your many friends and former neighbors in Middletown are anxious to help in every way possible. We are sending a box of blankets, sweaters, warm socks and other things you may need to help you through the emergency. We are also sending some books and toys to help cheer the children and keep them from thinking too much about their unhappy experience.

Will you tell us what else we can do? In the meantime, we send you our best wishes—and we hope you will meet this cruel but temporary setback with the courage and faith we know you possess.

> Sincerely yours,
> Anna G. Sloan
> (For the Mothers' Club
> of Middletown)

Dear Mr. Arnall:

Your brother has told me of the heavy loss you suffered in the hurricane that brought so much destruction to your city last week.

I'm sincerely sorry to hear about it, and I hope you'll call on me if there's any way I can help in the emergency.

Mrs. Price joins me in sending sympathy and best wishes to you and your family.

Cordially yours,
Henry M. Price

Dear Agatha:

I was dismayed to read about the robbery in this morning's paper. I know what your collection of jade means to you, quite apart from its material value. I certainly hope that the police catch up with the thieves and get the collection back.

All my sympathy to you in this unhappy experience!

Affectionately,
Joyce

Dear Ted:

I hear that thieves broke into your house and got away with a lot of valuables. That's certainly bad news. But I'm glad you and Jean weren't in the house at the time as you might have suffered personal injury. That would have been much more distressing to your many friends!

So don't let it get you down, Ted. Maybe the police will recover your property. And if not, I'm sure you and Jean will take the loss in your stride and not let it distress you too much.

Sincere sympathy to you both, and my best wishes— now and always!

Affectionately,
Steve

TO THOSE WHO HAVE LOST
A WELL-LOVED PET

Under ordinary circumstances, it is not necessary to write a note of sympathy to a friend whose cat has died, or whose dog has been run over. But if the cat or dog is a well-loved member of the family (as so many pets are!) it's kind and thoughtful to

write a few words of consolation to the person who most keenly
feels the loss.

Dear Diane:

Bill just told me about Chipper, and I'm so sorry to
hear about it.

I know how precious that little golden-throated
canary was to you, and how badly you must feel. But
Chipper lived to a good old age, Diane. Surely you
couldn't have expected to keep him much longer. . . .

So cheer up, and think of the *new* canary Bill promised to get for you. Let's both try to think of a cute
name for it!

Fondly,
Leonore

Dear Emily:

I've just heard about Mitzie. She was such a beautiful
cat, and such a loyal and devoted companion! I can
well imagine how much you'll miss her.

But cats can't live forever, Emily—not even *very
special* cats like Mitzie! She was getting quite old, you
know. So try not to feel too badly about losing her.
You wouldn't have enjoyed watching her get more and
more feeble.

With affection, and sincere sympathy to you in your
loss,

Sincerely,
Susan

Alan, dear:

Your mother has just told me about Puck. Please
don't feel too badly about it! Cruel things like that
sometimes happen, and we must learn to face them
bravely.

It was an unfortunate accident, but no one was to
blame—except, perhaps, poor little frisky Puck himself. I understand he ran right out under the wheels

and was gone before you could even shout his name. So at least he didn't suffer, Alan—and that's something to be grateful for.

This morning I went to the kennels where I bought Puck for your birthday. They have one of his brothers there—a friendly, affectionate little dog with the funniest spot on his nose you ever saw! I fell in love with him at first sight, and I know you will, too. Will you come and look at him with me tomorrow after school? And if you like him, he's yours!

So cheer up, Alan darling. I'll call for you tomorrow at four. And on the way to the kennels, I'll tell you the wonderful, wonderful name I've thought of for your new dog!

With love,
Aunt Lillian

II

Letters of Introduction

The purpose of a social note of introduction is to bring together people you feel reasonably sure will find pleasure and enjoyment in each other's company.

For example, if you have a friend going to a distant city where you have other friends—and if you believe it would be mutually pleasant and agreeable for these people to meet—you offer to write a note of introduction. Or if someone you know and like is going to Nassau for a vacation, and you happen to have very good friends who live in Nassau, you might say: "Be sure to stop in and see the Ridgways! I know you'll enjoy meeting them. Here—I'll give you a letter of introduction."

Notice that the letter is offered, not requested. No one should ever *ask* for a letter of introduction—nor should anyone write such letters carelessly or indiscriminately. It's an unkindness to your distant friend to give a letter of introduction to someone you do not know well . . . someone who may turn out to be a nuisance or a bore. It's equally inadvisable to send a letter of introduction to a casual acquaintance . . . someone who may not be at all interested in meeting your friend and who may look upon your letter as a presumption.

So make it a point never to write a letter of introduction unless you know both persons intimately and well. Even then, write it only if you feel sure that the meeting will be of interest or benefit to both of them. Ask yourself if the persons concerned have anything in common. Ask yourself if they would really enjoy meeting each other—if they are likely to get along easily and well together. If there is any doubt in your mind, don't write a letter of introduction.

For bear in mind that an introduction by letter imposes obligations and responsibilities far more binding than any spoken introduction. It's a demand upon a distant friend's courtesy, hospitality and time—a demand that cannot be denied without repudiating the friendship of the person who wrote the letter, and bluntly ignoring the person who presented it.

Before you write any letter of introduction, therefore, be sure that your friend wants it—and be sure that the person to whom it is written will want to receive it. Then write it briefly and to the point. It should give the name of the person being introduced —the reason or purpose for the introduction—and any other information that is relevant or important. As it is actually a letter of request, asking that kindness and hospitality be shown to a complete stranger, it should include an expression of thanks for any courtesies extended.

A letter of introduction may either be handed to the friend for whom it is written, to be presented personally—or it may be sent through the mail like any other letter. If it is to be delivered personally, the envelope should be left unsealed. Obviously nothing of an intimate nature should be included in a letter given to one friend for presentation to another. However a second and private letter may be written and sent by mail, giving more information about the person who is on the way with a letter of introduction. Examples of these various types of letters follow.

TO BE PRESENTED IN PERSON

Dear Jim:

The bearer of this note, Mr. Robert Mitchell, of Chicago, plans to be in Asheville for about a month. Besides being a personal friend of mine, he is radio director of a number of top-ranking shows; and knowing how interested you are in radio advertising, I'm sure you'll enjoy meeting him.

I have long wanted you and Bob to know each other, and I'm glad of this opportunity to bring you together.

I'll appreciate anything you can do to make Bob's stay in Asheville more enjoyable—and I know he will, too.

With kindest regards to you and Ellen,

Cordially yours,
Kenneth Dawson

Dear Elsie:

This will introduce Janet Blake who is going to spend the winter in Washington gathering material and doing research for a new book. She plans to spend her days at the Congressional Library, and her evenings with congenial people. I told her I know of no one more congenial than you!

I'm sure you'll like Janet, and that you two will enjoy each other's company immensely. I don't need to tell you how much I'll personally appreciate any courtesies you show her.

Sincerely yours,
Edith Preston

Dear Catherine:

I'm giving this letter to Gerald Breen, a very good friend of ours. He is going to be in Chicago for a few days, and I'd like you two to meet as you happen to be interested in the same thing: child welfare.

Mr. Breen is making a study of juvenile delinquency, and I told him about the wonderful work you are doing among the underprivileged children of Chicago. He is very eager to talk with you about it.

I'm sure you'll enjoy meeting Mr. Breen, and I'm equally sure he'll be delighted and charmed to meet you.

Affectionately,
Alice

Dear Mr. Thompson:

This note will introduce James Fenton, of whom you've heard me speak many times. I've always been most anxious for you two to meet, as you have so many interests and hobbies in common that I feel sure you'll enjoy knowing each other.

Mr. Fenton will be in Middletown next week, and I've made him promise to look you up. He hesitated to "impose on a stranger," as he called it; but I pointed out that each of you has heard me talk about the other so often that you are practically acquainted! Besides, you are both chess experts—and for that reason alone you should meet!

I will appreciate any courtesy you show Mr. Fenton during his brief stay in Middletown, and I am sure he will too.

Please give my best wishes to Mrs. Thompson. I hope to see you both again before very long.

Sincerely yours,
Arthur T. Rhinelander

Dear Mrs. Hathaway:

The young lady who hands you this note is Miss Virginia Andrews—the daughter of one of my oldest and dearest friends. She will be in New York for the next year or so to study fashion design.

Virginia is a charming and talented girl, and I feel so certain you will enjoy her company that I have insisted that she call and present this note. She has never been in New York before; and I'll be very grateful for any help or advice you can give her. I know she, too, will deeply appreciate any courtesy.

Very sincerely yours,
Martha B. Emmons

Dear Bill:

I am writing this letter for my good friend and former neighbor, John Larkin. He and Mrs. Larkin are moving to Cleveland, and will live within walking distance of your house.

I know that you and Wilma will like the Larkins very much . . . and I know they'll like you. That's why I am writing this letter. I think you should meet —not because I happen to be a mutual friend, but because you have so many interests in common. The Larkins are musical. They are excellent bridge players. They love to entertain. But I'll let you and Wilma discover all their many other neighborly charms and qualities for yourselves!

By the way, didn't you once tell me your daughter was interested in writing radio scripts? Well, get her to talk with John about it. John used to teach radio writing at Middletown University.

Thanks, Bill, for any kindness you may extend to the Larkins on my account. I feel certain you'll soon love them for themselves, and that before long you and they will become the very good neighbors and friends *we* have always been here in Middletown.

With best wishes to the family from all of us,

Affectionately,
Bruce

TO BE SENT BY MAIL

When a letter of introduction is sent by mail, it imposes less of an obligation on the person who receives it. For example, if you write to a distant friend and say, "My former neighbors, the Boltons, are going to live in your city and I think you'd enjoy knowing them"—it's up to the distant friend to decide whether or not she wants to know them. She takes the initiative, saving the newcomer this embarrassment. And inasmuch as the letter was not presented personally, she is free to make advances or not, as she feels inclined.

Dear Peggy:

I've just learned that old friends of mine, Jane and Ira Hall, are now living in Chicago, at 70 Lake Shore Drive. That's practically next door to you, isn't it?

The Halls are very charming people, and I think you would enjoy knowing them. I told them all about you; so if you call them, they'll recognize the name right away and know who you are.

I hope you *will* call them, Peggy. They're really wonderful people to know, and lots of fun to be with. Bob and I have certainly missed them since they moved away!

When are you and Fred coming to New York again? It seems ages since we saw you!

Affectionately,
Lorraine

Dear Harry:

I have often spoken to you about Phil Evans and the many interests you and he have in common . . . even to the point of both of you having sons at Exeter. And you've often said you'd like to meet him.

So I'm writing this note to let you know Phil is in New York for a few weeks and is stopping at the Hampshire House. If you call him there, I'm sure he'll be delighted to arrange a meeting. He knows who you are and will recognize the name when you call.

I know how busy you are, Harry, and I realize that this suggestion may come at a very inopportune time. So please don't regard it as an obligation. But if you have any free time while Phil's in New York, do try to see him—as I'm sure both of you will thoroughly enjoy the meeting.

Cordially yours,
Charles Benton

Dear Joe:

My brother-in-law, Roy Fowler, will be in Boston all next week—at the Statler Hotel. I've often wanted you two to meet, and this seems like the ideal opportunity.

Roy is research director of an advertising agency. I told him about the book you are writing on the history of buying trends in America, and he was completely fascinated—as I knew he would be! He said he'd like to know more about it; and I think you might find it interesting and helpful to discuss it with him.

So call him if you can, Joe—but not if it's an inconvenience. If he doesn't hear from you, he'll understand that it's because you are tied up. I suggest this meeting only because I know you two are bound to enjoy each other's company.

Cordially,
Homer

Dear Marcia:

I was interested to hear that you and Bill will be at the Whitehall in Forest Beach during the month of February. My sister and her husband will be there at the same time—and you simply *must* meet them as I know you'll all enjoy one another's company.

My sister is Mrs. Wilbur J. Sloan. She used to be Janet Turner, the swimming star. She and her husband are excellent bridge players; and they play the same kind of golf as you and Bill—in the low 90's.

I've already written to Janet and told her that you will be there. She'll be expecting you to ask for her at the desk or to leave a message in her box. She has heard me speak of you many times, Marcia, and she's most anxious to meet you.

I *do* hope you'll get together, as I know you'll enjoy being with the Sloans as much as they'll enjoy being with *you*. Have a wonderful time!

Affectionately,
Barbara T. Owen

"FOLLOW UP" LETTERS OF INTRODUCTION
GIVING ADDITIONAL INFORMATION

Frequently when a letter of introduction is given to a friend to be delivered in person, another letter is written at the same time and sent by mail. The purpose is to say that the letter of introduction is on the way . . . and to give any additional information that may seem necessary or desirable. Here are some examples of such "follow up" letters:

Dear Jim:

In the next day or so you will receive a telephone call from Robert Mitchell of Chicago. He is a very good friend of mine; and as he is planning to be in Asheville for a month or more, I gave him a letter of introduction to you.

I know how busy you are, Jim, and I don't want you to regard this as an obligation. But I feel certain you'll enjoy meeting Bob Mitchell; and I'll wager that once you meet him, you'll want to keep on seeing him! For Bob's good company anywhere—at bridge, golf, tennis, or just talking. I should say *especially* talking! Bob's just about the most brilliant and entertaining conversationalist I know.

I'm writing this note so that you'll know who Bob is when he calls. I'll appreciate any kindness you and Ellen may show him as a stranger in Asheville; but please don't put yourselves out or feel that you are commited in any way at all. If I didn't feel you'd be as delighted to meet Bob as he will be to meet you, I wouldn't have given him a letter.

I hope you and Ellen are well, and I look forward to seeing you on your next visit to Chicago.

Sincerely yours,
Kenneth Dawson

Dear Elizabeth:

Our very good friend, Harvey Cromwell, will be in New York for the month of June—before going abroad to make a survey of housing conditions in England and France.

I have given him a note of introduction to you. Jim and I will deeply appreciate anything you can do to make his brief stay in New York pleasant.

Affectionately,
Margaret

Dear Mrs. Carter:

Dr. James Gibson will be in Buffalo the week of June tenth to attend the medical conferences. I am giving him a note of introduction to you.

Dr. Gibson has been our family physician for many years, and we are utterly devoted to him. He is a talented musician as well as the best-loved doctor in town . . . and that's why I'd like you two to meet. I know you'll enjoy his playing as much as he enjoys your singing. He and Mr. Carter have an interest in common, too—as they are both ardent golfers. Perhaps they can manage a game together during Dr. Gibson's brief stay in Buffalo.

At any rate, I'd like you to know who Dr. Gibson is so that you'll recognize the name when he calls. I'm sure you and Mr. Carter will find much pleasure in making his acquaintance. And I know he'll thoroughly enjoy meeting both of *you!*

Needless to say, I'll deeply appreciate anything you may do to make Dr. Gibson's first visit to Buffalo more interesting and pleasant.

Cordially,
Edna B. Whitmore

Dear George:

A former neighbor of ours, Edward Brockton, is moving to Evanston in about a week or so. I gave him a letter to you, as I think you'll enjoy knowing him.

Ed is a commercial artist, and a very good one. As a hobby he makes fascinating animated movies for children. You must get him to show them to your youngsters some time; they'll love them!

I'm writing this note so you'll know a little more about the Brocktons than my letter of introduction tells you. They're really grand people, George—and I know you and Jane will like them very much. They were our neighbors in Middletown for more than eight years, and we were mighty sorry when they moved away.

I feel certain that when you get to know the Brocktons they'll become your very good friends—as they are ours.

Thelma sends best wishes to you, Jane and the children.

Cordially,
Jim Tyler

Dear Catherine:

You will receive a call, in a few days, from a Mr. Gerald Breen. Fred and I have known him for many years and are very fond of him. He expects to be in Chicago for a short time, and we have asked him to get in touch with you. He has a letter of introduction.

Mr. Breen is a lawyer who is especially interested in juvenile delinquency and child welfare. He has an article in this month's *Sentinel* called "Are Parents Delinquent, Too?" I told him all about you, and the work you are doing among the underprivileged children of Chicago—and of course he's extremely interested. He said he'd like very much to talk with you about it while he's in Chicago and has the opportunity.

So will you see him if it's convenient, Catherine—and tell him whatever you can? I'm sure you'll enjoy meeting him; he's interesting and very likable.

When are you coming to New York again? We had such fun last time you were here that we're looking forward with great pleasure to your next visit.

Affectionately,
Alice

A FAMOUS LETTER OF INTRODUCTION

The following letter of introduction was written by the gifted composer, Felix Mendelssohn, to a friend in London. Although it was written more than a hundred years ago, it has none of the pompous phraseology of that period . . . and remains the classic letter of its kind: simple, charming and very much to the point.*

Berlin, March 10, 1844

My dear friend,

The bearer of these lines, although a boy of thirteen, is one of my best and dearest friends and one of the most interesting people I have met for a long time. His name is Joseph Joachim. He was born in Hungary at Pesth, and he is going to London.

Of all the young talents that are now going about the world, I know none that is to be compared with this violinist. It is not only the excellence of his performances, but the absolute certainty of his becoming a leading artist—if God grants him health and leaves him as he is—which makes me feel such an interest in him. . . .

He is not yet very far advanced in composition, but his performances of the Vieuxtemps, Bruch and Spohr concertos, his playing at sight (even the second violin parts of difficult quartets I have heard him play in the most masterly manner), his accompanying of sonatas, etc., is in my opinion as perfect and remarkable as may well be.

I think he will become a yeoman in time, as both of us are. So pray, be kind to him, tell him where he can hear good music, play to him, give him good advice, and for everything you may do for him, be sure that I shall be as much indebted to you as possible. Farewell.

Very truly yours,
F.M.B.†

---

* G. Selden-Goth, *Felix Mendelssohn-Bartholdy Letters* (New York: Pantheon Books, Inc., 1945).

† Felix Mendelssohn-Bartholdy.

Book III
Your Personal Correspondence

I

The General Rules of Personal Correspondence

Your personal correspondence is made up of the letters you write to family and friends. These are the letters you *want* to write and *enjoy* writing, as compared with your social correspondence which is made up for the most part of "duty" notes and letters of obligation.

The purpose of personal correspondence is to bring news and share experiences with those who are near and dear to you—to "visit" with those you like, and miss, and with whom you want to keep in contact. They are the letters you write to distant friends, to husband or wife away from home, to children at school or camp . . . the letters that reach out across space and bring you close to those you love and from whom you are separated.

Once in a national drive to promote letter writing, the post office department used the slogan: *Someone feels better when you send a letter!* Your personal correspondence is made up, or should be made up, of letters that make people feel better. A good personal letter is written with joy and received with delight. It's intimate and informal, with all the natural ease of good conversation. It's *you* on paper—what you are doing, reading, thinking, feeling—your very personality tucked into an envelope and mailed with love or affection to someone far away!

Lord Chesterfield, undisputed social arbiter of the eighteenth century, considered the ability to write good personal letters so important that he never stopped urging his son to develop to the utmost his skill and facility in this direction. Always, over and over again—through more than twenty years of correspondence between father and son—his advice remained the same: *Write as you speak! Write as though you were seated in a room with me, talking in plain, simple language about the things you have seen and done and thought and experienced since you wrote me last.*

Here is a typical excerpt from one of Chesterfield's famous letters to his son. It was addressed to "Dear Boy" and ended simply with the word "Adieu."

> Your letters, except when upon a given subject, are exceedingly laconic, and neither answer my desires nor the purpose of letters: which should be familiar conversation between absent friends. As I desire to live with you upon the footing of an intimate friend, and not of a parent, I could wish that your letters gave me more particular accounts of yourself, and of your lesser transactions.
>
> When you write to me, suppose yourself conversing freely with me by the fireside. In that case, you would naturally mention the incidents of the day; as where you had been, whom you had seen, what you thought of them, and so forth.
>
> Do this in your letters! Acquaint me sometimes with your studies; sometimes with your diversions; tell me of any new persons or characters that you meet in company; and add your own observations upon them. In short, *let me see more of you in your letters.*

The next time you sit down to write a personal letter, remember Chesterfield's advice to his son. Put as much of yourself as you can into your letter. Write as you speak, of things you know are interesting to your correspondent. Use words that come readily and easily to your mind, for your letter should be natural and unstudied—like the flow of conversation. Your letter should be good plain talk on paper, bringing your image, your voice, your gestures to the mind of the reader.

Unlike social correspondence, there are no fixed or standard forms for letters to family and friends. The most *natural* letters are the best in personal correspondence. You can even take liberties with the long-established customs and traditions, if you like . . . being as different and original as you please. For example, you don't need to start your letter in the usual familiar way, with a salutation:

> Dear Helen:
>
> We've been having very bad weather here. It's been raining very hard for a week, without letup. I hope you are having better weather in New York.

You can start your letter *without any salutation at all,* if that appeals to you—making it as informal and conversational as the following:

> What awful weather we've been having, Helen! It's been raining cats and dogs for the past week. How's the weather in New York?

That doesn't mean just being yourself is all there is to successful personal letter writing. It isn't quite as simple as that! After all, very few of us are "born" letter writers who can put ourselves on paper with the greatest of ease and charm. For most of us, good letter writing is neither easy nor natural. But by following a few well-tested ideas and suggestions, *anyone* can write more interesting letters—*anyone* can write the kind of letters that family and friends love to receive.

DO YOU WANT TO WRITE GOOD LETTERS?

The first and most important thing is to consider your *attitude* toward letter writing. If you groan when you receive a letter that requires an answer—if you say to yourself, "Gosh, must I answer this?"—your attitude is wrong. You cannot hope to write really good letters, letters that are fresh and stimulating and alive, as long as you continue to feel that way.

Before all else, therefore, you must want to write good letters. You must be willing to make the necessary effort to write the kind of letters people receive with eagerness and joy. That's

Rule Number 1 for all personal letter writing: *you must want to write good letters.* You must look upon it as a pleasure, not as an irksome duty. You must consciously make yourself be interested in the letters you write and in the people to whom you are writing.

ANSWER EVERY LETTER PROMPTLY—
IT'S EASIER FOR YOU

The next most important thing is to answer all your correspondence promptly, so that your letters reflect the mood and impulse in which you resolved to write. The impulse may come from within yourself, perhaps from thoughts of your distant friend—or it may be in response to a letter you have received and that needs to be answered. In either case, your letter is bound to be more interesting and readable if you write it before the impulse fades . . . before the warmth of friendly intention cools and evaporates.

One year the postmaster of New York, in a radio address during National Letter-Writing Week, said: "We've all heard the timeworn apologies for failure to write, but how often do we really have a good excuse? It's a common trait to be careless in keeping up with one's correspondence. . . ."

Don't be careless! *Keep up with your correspondence!* Remember what we said earlier in this book, and now repeat for emphasis: *Don't wait too long to answer your letters. Write while the glow is still with you! Then you won't need to grope for words, trying to sound sincere. The words will come of their own accord, will spring naturally and sincerely from the warmth of your enthusiasm.* Any letter is easier and more pleasant to write if it's written on time and you don't need to make apologies or explanations for its delay.

LETTER WRITING CAN BE AN ENDLESS SOURCE
OF PLEASURE AND SELF-EXPRESSION

Letter writing can be such fun, if you let it be! It can enrich your entire life—can provide an endless source of pleasure, of self-expression, even excitement and adventure.

It isn't necessary to be in constant personal contact with your friends to enjoy communication with them. The poet Emily Dickinson and her great admirer, Colonel Thomas Wentworth Higginson, met rarely—perhaps only two or three times in all; but for a quarter of a century they maintained a truly extraordinary friendship through their correspondence. Tchaikovsky and Nadejda von Meck *never* met; theirs was a strange and beautiful romance that found expression in their fascinating letters* and in Tchaikovsky's tragic, haunting music. Write because you *want* to write . . . to maintain more interesting and enduring friendships . . . to share your ideas and experiences. Write for your own pleasure and fulfillment, not out of a sense of duty or obligation to distant friends.

Personal letter writing can provide you with a most gratifying form of self-expression. It enables you to transfer your thoughts, ideas, emotions and experiences to others . . . by means of the written word. Writing to someone about an idea or problem you may have, putting it down on paper, often helps to clarify it in your own mind. And when you are worried or in doubt, it can be sheer relief to sit down and write a letter to someone you love and trust.

Beethoven, we are told, "poured out his heart" in letters. Unhappy Schubert found solace and peace writing letters to his many friends. Young Chopin—restless, ambitious, unsure of himself—bolstered his lagging courage by writing enthusiastic letters to his friends:

> Although I have only been here a year (he wrote from Paris to a friend at home) all the artists of the city show me much friendliness and consideration. . . . Accomplished players take lessons from me. . . . I might almost imagine that I was already the perfect artist!

Not everyone can write for publication; but everyone can enjoy, through letter writing, some of the same deep inner sense of satisfaction that an author feels in creative expression.

* Catherine Drinker and Barbara von Meck Bowen, *Beloved Friend* (New York: Random House, Inc., 1937.)

YOU DON'T NEED LITERARY STYLE
TO WRITE INTERESTING LETTERS

It isn't necessary to have a distinguished or "literary" style to write the kind of letters people love to receive. A simple, kindly letter, written from the heart, is as welcome as the most brilliant epistle . . . perhaps even more so! It's the *feeling* behind your letter that counts, the warmth and understanding. So don't hesitate to write letters—lots of them!—because you feel you don't write well. Lincoln was often unsure of his spelling; he was sometimes careless with grammar and punctuation. Yet Lincoln's warm heart and generous love of mankind are reflected unmistakably in all his letters, making even the least of them shine with greatness.

Bear in mind that your style improves with practice, in letter writing as in all kinds of writing. The more you write, the more easily you will write—and the more interesting and readable your letters will be. Balzac always advised young writers to correspond freely with family and friends, for "letter writing forms one's style." Every good letter you write increases your skill and facility for writing the next one.

HOW LONG SHOULD A LETTER BE?

People frequently ask how long a personal letter should be. That depends entirely on what you have to say. It isn't necessary to write long letters. If you were talking face to face with your correspondent, you wouldn't deliver a prolonged monologue. You would say what you have to say . . . and stop. And that's exactly what you should do in letter writing. You should begin and stop writing with the same ease of transition as you begin and stop talking in conversation.

The length of your letter is not at all important. It can be as brief as the warm but hurried "hello" when busy friends meet, greet and part. Or it can ramble on and on for pages in the easy intimacy of friends who have stopped for a heart-to-heart chat. It's the *tone*, or *spirit*, of your letter that counts, not the number of pages you fill with writing.

In general, letters to family and friends should be neither so

brief as to give the impression of haste—nor so long and rambling as to cause confusion and boredom. Just be sure your letter
carries the feeling of friendly, informal conversation . . . and
let the length of it take care of itself. The really important thing
is to have something to say, something interesting and pleasant
to communicate—even if it's nothing more than "I miss you—
I'm thinking of you—and I'm writing to let you know you are
on my mind!"

YOUR LETTERS CAN HAVE
GREAT INFLUENCE ON OTHERS

Think for a moment of the letters you customarily write to
family and friends. Are they just a few hurried, scribbled words
on a sheet of paper? Or are they the kind of letters that are
received with eagerness, read with great pleasure and satisfaction
. . . letters that have meaning and importance for those who
receive them?

The letters you write can have a far greater influence than
you may believe possible. A simple little note from you may
give new hope or courage to someone sadly in need of it. A brief
letter, written with love and understanding, may ease the tension
of worry or fear for someone far away. Letters often help people
make a choice or a decision . . . sometimes even help determine
a way of life. . . .

A busy doctor received a letter from a woman he had seen
just once, and didn't even remember. She wrote from China,
describing a garden enclosed by a high wall. On one side of the
wall was a brass plate, with a legend in Chinese characters.
Translated, the legend said: "Enjoy yourself. It's later than you
think."

"I called myself a silly old fool for being disturbed by a letter
from a woman I couldn't even remember," wrote the busy
doctor who thought everything would fall to pieces if he took
a vacation.* "But before I knew it I found myself saying again
to myself: 'Well, maybe it *is* later than you think; why don't
you do something about it?' "

* Frederic Loomis, "In a Chinese Garden," *Reader's Digest*, November, 1946, p. 110.

He *did* do something about it! And what he did not only changed his entire life, but the lives of many others who passed his way.

A woman, about to divorce her husband, received a letter from a friend—once fabulously rich—who had lost all her worldly possessions and was now living in Alaska. She and her husband had gone there to start life anew.

"It's so terribly lonely here," she wrote. "The life is bleak and primitive. But Ted and I have each other, and that's all that really matters to us now. We have discovered all over again how much we love each other; and we are happier now, with nothing, than we were years ago with everything money can buy."

The woman about to divorce her husband read that letter twice. She put it away, then took it out and read it slowly for a third time. "We have discovered all over again how much we love each other." She took stock of her own life. She thought of her husband and how devoted he once had been . . . and still could be. Quietly she dropped her plans for a divorce, made plans for another kind of life together.

These are not figments of the imagination. They are based on real letters, written by real people. They are exceptional, of course; only a tiny percentage of the vast numbers of letters written daily have any such vital significance. *But any letter you write can have a great and lasting influence on the person who receives it* . . . and usually that happens when you least expect it to have any influence at all. Therefore every letter you write should be given care and thought, should be something more than just a few scribbled words. Every letter you write should have some meaning for the person who receives it . . . even if it's only to give a little glow of warmth and pleasure, a spiritual "lift," to an otherwise dreary day.

SO TAKE YOUR LETTER WRITING SERIOUSLY!

There is perhaps no form of communication more revealing than an intimate letter to a friend. The type of person you are

. . . your character, your inner thoughts and feelings . . . are often more clearly disclosed by your letters than you realize.

"In a man's letters, you know, his soul lies naked," wrote Samuel Johnson. "His letters are only the mirror of his heart."

Even people who don't know you at all, can know you very well through your letters. Often they tell more about you than your appearance or your conversation. . . .

So take your letter writing seriously! Don't be satisfied to "dash off" a few lines when a real letter is called for. Let every letter you write, however brief, be truly worthy of the name. Let it have meaning and substance for the person who receives it. And above all, let it represent you to best advantage.

A good letter can be one of the most wonderful and delightful of all written things. So in your personal correspondence at least, make it a point to write because you want to write, for your own pleasure and fulfillment . . . and for the joy and satisfaction of your friends.

SOME INTERESTING PERSONAL LETTERS

Not all the great letters of the past can be judged great by today's standards. In fact, many are insufferably boring and affected . . . and were clearly written with an eye on posterity. Such letters should certainly not be used as patterns for contemporary style.

But the following letters are by no means in that category. They are chosen for their straightforward simplicity, for their warmth and friendly charm. They represent interesting examples of good personal letters, written by famous people.

Longfellow to a Young Girl *

Nahant, August 18, 1855

To Emily A.

Your letter followed me down here by the seaside where I am passing the summer with my three little

* Curtis Gentry, *Fifty Famous Letters of History* (New York: Thomas Y. Crowell Co., 1930), p. 153.

girls. The oldest is about your age; but as little girls' ages keep changing every year, I can never remember exactly how old she is and have to ask her Mamma who has a better memory than I have. Her name is Alice, I never forget that. She is a nice girl and loves poetry about as much as I do. The second is Edith with blue eyes and beautiful golden locks which I sometimes call her "Nankeen hair" to make her laugh. She is a very busy little woman and wears gray boots. The youngest is Allegra; which you know means merry; and she is the merriest little thing you ever saw—always singing and laughing all over the house.

These are my three little girls and Mr. Read has painted them all in one picture which I hope you will see some day. They bathe in the sea and dig in the sand and patter about the piazza all day long and sometimes go to see the Indians encamped on the shore and buy baskets and bows and arrows. I do not say anything about the two boys. They are such noisy fellows it is of no use to talk about them.

And now, dear Miss Emily, give my love to your papa and good night with a kiss from his friend and yours.

> Henry Wadsworth Longfellow.

Lincoln to an Old Friend

> Springfield, August 24, 1855

Dear Speed:*

You know what a poor correspondent I am. Ever since I received your very agreeable letter of the 22nd of May I have been intending to write you an answer to it. You suggest that in political action, now, you and I would differ. I suppose we would; not quite as much, however, as you may think. You know I dislike slavery, and you fully admit the abstract wrong of it. So far

---

* Joshua F. Speed, one of Lincoln's oldest and dearest friends, and one of his most intimate correspondents. Though they differed radically on the matter of slavery, they never lost their regard and affection for each other.

there is no cause of difference. But you say that sooner than yield your legal right to the slave, especially at the bidding of those who are not themselves interested, you would see the Union dissolved. I am not aware that anyone is bidding you yield that right; very certainly I am not. I leave that matter entirely to yourself. I also acknowledge your rights and my obligations under the Constitution in regard to your slaves. I confess I hate to see the poor creatures hunted down and caught and carried back to their stripes and unrequited toil; but I bite my lips and keep quiet.

In 1841 you and I had together a tedious low-water trip on a steamboat from Louisville to St. Louis. You may remember, as I well do, that from Louisville to the mouth of the Ohio there were on board ten or a dozen slaves shackled together with irons. That sight was a continued torment to me, and I see something like it every time I touch the Ohio or any other slave border. It is not fair for you to assume that I have no interest in a thing which has, and continually exercises, the power of making me miserable. You ought rather to appreciate how much the great body of the Northern people do crucify their feelings, in order to maintain their loyalty to the Constitution and the Union. I do oppose the extension of slavery because my judgment and feeling so prompt me, and I am under no obligations to the contrary. If for this you and I must differ, differ we must.

You say, if you were President, you would send an army and hang the leaders of the Missouri outrages upon the Kansas elections; still, if Kansas fairly votes herself a slave State she must be admitted, or the Union must be dissolved. But how if she votes herself a slave State unfairly, that is, by the very means for which you say you would hang men? Must she still be admitted, or the Union dissolved? That will be the phase of the question when it first becomes a practical one.

In your assumption that there may be a fair decision of the slavery question in Kansas, I plainly see you and I would differ about the Nebraska law. I look upon that enactment not as a law, but as a violence from the beginning. It was conceived in violence, is maintained in violence, and is being executed in violence. I say it was conceived in violence, because the destruction of the Missouri Compromise, under the circumstances, was nothing less than violence. It was passed in violence, because it could not have passed at all but for the votes of many members in violence of the known will of their constituents. It is maintained in violence, because the elections since clearly demand its repeal; and the demand is openly disregarded.

You say men ought to be hung for the way they are executing the law; I say the way it is being executed is quite as good as any of its antecedents. It is being executed in the precise way which was intended from the first, else why does no Nebraska man express astonishment or condemnation? Poor Reeder is the only public man who has been silly enough to believe that anything like fairness was ever intended, and he has been bravely undeceived. . . .

You inquire where I now stand. That is a disputed point. I think I am a Whig; but others say there are no Whigs, and that I am an Abolitionist. When I was at Washington, I voted for the Wilmot proviso as good as forty times; and I never heard of any one attempting to unwhig me for that. I now do no more than oppose the extension of slavery. I am not a Know-Nothing; that is certain. How could I be? How can any one who abhors the oppression of negroes be in favor of degrading classes of white people? Our progress in degeneracy appears to me to be pretty rapid. As a nation we began by declaring that "all men are created equal." We now practically read it "all men are created equal, except negroes." When the Know-Nothings get control, it will read "all men are created equal, except negroes and foreigners and Catholics." When it comes to this, I shall prefer emigrating to some country where they make no pretense of loving liberty,—to Russia, for instance, where despotism can be taken pure, and without the base alloy of hypocrisy.

Mary will probably pass a day or two in Louisville in October. My kindest regards to Mrs. Speed. On the leading subject of this letter, I have more of her sympathy than I have of yours; and yet let me say I am

Your friend forever,
A. Lincoln

Mendelssohn to his Parents*

Rome, November 8, 1830

Today I must write to you about my first eight days in Rome; how I arranged my time, how I look forward to the winter; and what effect my heavenly surroundings have had on me . . . My mood is so tranquil and joyous, and yet so earnest, that it is impossible to describe it to you. What it is that thus works on me I cannot exactly define; for the awe-inspiring Coliseum, and the serene Vatican, and the genial air of spring, all contribute; and so do the kindly people, my comfortable apartments, and everything else. But besides that, I am different. I am healthier and happier than I have been for a long time, and take such delight in my work, and feel such an urge for it, that I expect to accomplish much more than I anticipated; indeed, I have already done a good deal. If it pleases Providence to grant me a continuation of this happy mood, I shall look forward to the most delightful and productive winter.

Picture to yourself a small house, with two windows in front, in the Piazza di Spagna, No. 5, which has warm sun the whole day long, and rooms one flight up, where there is a good Viennese grand piano; on the table some portraits of Palestrina, Allegri, etc., along

---

* G. Selden-Goth, *Felix Mendelssohn-Bartholdy Letters*.

with the scores of their works, and a Latin psalm-book, from which I am going to compose the *Non Nobis;* that is where I now reside. The Capitol was too far away, and above all I dreaded the cold air, from which I certainly have nothing to fear here when I look out of my window in the morning across the square and see every object sharply defined in the sunshine against the blue sky. My landlord was formerly a captain in the French army, and his daughter has the most splendid contralto voice I ever heard. Above me lives a Prussian captain, with whom I talk politics. In short, the situation is excellent.

When I come into the room early in the morning, and see the sun shining so brightly on my breakfast (you see a poet has been lost in me), I immediately feel thoroughly comfortable; for it is now far on in the autumn, and who, in our country, can still expect warmth, or a bright sky, or grapes and flowers? After breakfast I begin my work, and play, and sing, and compose till about noon. Then Rome in all her vastness lies before me like a problem in enjoyment. But I go deliberately to work, selecting a different historical object every day. Sometimes I visit the ruins of the ancient city; another time I go to the Borghese Gallery, or to the Capitoline Hill, or St. Peter's, or the Vatican. That makes every day memorable, and as I take my time, each impression becomes more firmly and indelibly fixed. When I am at my morning work I dislike leaving off, and wish to continue my writing, but I say to myself: you must also see the Vatican; and when I once get there, it is just as hard to leave again. Thus each of my occupations gives me the purest pleasure, and one enjoyment follows on the heels of the last.

If Venice, with its past, seemed to me like a mausoleum, where the crumbling, modern palaces and the perpetual reminders of former grandeur made me feel somewhat out of sorts, and sad, Rome's past seems to me like the embodiment of history. Her monuments are exhilarating, they make one feel at once serious and stimulated, and it is a joyful thought that man can erect something which, after a thousand years, can still give enjoyment and strength to others. . . .

One of my home pleasures is the reading—for the first time—of Goethe's "Journey to Italy." I must admit that it is a source of enormous pleasure to me to find that he arrived in Rome the very same day that I did; that he also went first of all to the Quirinal, and heard a Requiem there; that he was seized with the same fit of impatience in Florence and Bologna; and that he also felt so tranquil, or, as he calls it, solid here. Everything that he describes happened to me precisely the same way. . . .

And so every morning brings me fresh anticipations, and every day fulfils them. The sun has again just shone on my breakfast, and I will get to work. . . .

                                        Felix M.B.

2

Friendly Letters

Friendly letters are simply the exchange of thoughts between friends—written communications between persons who, for the moment, happen to be separated. The more natural and spontaneous such letters are, the more *conversational* in tone, the greater pleasure and satisfaction they are likely to give.

Therefore the one quality above all others you should strive to achieve in your letters to friends is an ease of expression, as simple and unaffected as your way of speaking. The best letters are those that pick up the threads of friendship and carry them forward as though no separation had occurred—letters that are like personal visits, intimate and chatty, and rich with the warmth of your personality.

It requires no special knack or ability to write such letters. Your attitude is what counts. If you feel friendly toward the person to whom you are writing . . . if you feel cordial, and close, and eager to share the news of the day . . . you will find yourself writing easily and well.

"Our intellectual powers increase with our affection," says Emerson.* "The scholar sits down to write, and all his years of meditation do not furnish him with one good thought or happy expression. But it is necessary to write a letter to a friend, and forthwith troops of gentle thoughts invest themselves on every hand with chosen words!"

So make it a point to write when you feel especially friendly and affectionate toward the person to whom you are writing. Try to imagine yourself meeting that person in the street . . .

* In his essay *On Friendship*.

344

your face lighting up with pleasure . . . your hand going out in cordial greeting. Imagine yourself saying, "Well, *hello!* I'm glad to see you!"

That's the feeling a good personal letter should have: a feeling of warmth and friendly greeting. It should clearly be written because you *want* to write and *enjoy* writing, not because a letter is due and it's your "turn" to write.

HOW TO BEGIN A FRIENDLY LETTER

The old saying that "all beginnings are difficult" is certainly true as applied to letter writing. The beginning of a letter is usually the most difficult part of it. But once the first sentence is written—and especially if it's an *interesting* first sentence that gets the reader off to a good start—the rest of the letter tends to run on smoothly, one point leading to another as in conversation.

It's wise to organize your thoughts before you start to write. Decide what you want to say in your letter, then plunge right in and say it without a lot of unnecessary preliminary remarks. For example, don't start off with: "I received your letter and am sorry not to have answered it sooner." If you knew how many people start their letters with just that exact sentence, you would never use it again! Equally overworked are such opening sentences as: "I've been meaning to write for a long time" . . . "I know I should have written long before this" . . . "I would have written sooner, but there just wasn't anything to write about."

Try to avoid opening your letter with an apology or excuse for delay in writing. Such beginnings are not only commonplace and trite, but rude. When you say in a letter, "This is the first opportunity I've had to write" or "I meant to write sooner but I've been so busy"—what you are actually saying is, "I haven't written before because there were so many other more interesting and important things to do." You wouldn't dream of saying anything so discourteous to a friend; why imply it in the very first sentence of your letter? How much more gracious and flattering it is to write, "I've thought of you so many, many times during

these busy months!" . . . or "If you only knew how often you
are in my thoughts!"

As undesirable as an apology in your opening sentence is an
announcement, right at the start, that this is a hurry-up letter
written while waiting for the cake to bake or the children to
come home from school. It's certainly no compliment to your
correspondent to say, "I just have time to scribble a few words
before John comes home for dinner" . . . or "I'll have to rush
this letter, as the office is just about ready to close." A letter that
is obviously dashed off in a hurry is not very likely to be received
with joy or read with pleasure.

The opening sentence of a letter is very important, and
should receive careful thought. For the tone of the first sentence
can determine the effect of the entire letter on the person who
receives it. No one can possibly be thrilled by a letter that starts
out with the blunt and uninspired statement: "There's no news;
everything's just about the same." Nor is there any promise of
enjoyment in a letter that begins, "I said I'd write, so I will."
Such remarks are dull and pointless, and should be avoided. They
only bore the reader . . . and what's even worse, may annoy or
offend him.

So watch that opening sentence! Always try to start off with
something interesting, some important news, some information
your reader will be glad to receive. If possible, start off with a
compliment—a word of appreciation or praise. You might say,
"What a treat to receive your letter . . . you always write
such interesting news!" Or, "It's always a thrill to see your
handwriting; I enjoy your letters so!" Such compliments compel
attention much better than the old familiar rubber-stamp
phrases that are used over and over again as the start of friendly
letters—phrases that have lost all life and sparkle: "How are
you?" . . . "I received your last letter" . . . "I owe you a letter so I thought I'd write."

Avoid particularly starting your letter with any word that
ends in "ing" . . . like "Having heard that you are in New
York, I am writing to say . . ." or "Learning of your illness, I

hasten to send my sympathy." Such participial openings always tend to make a letter sound stilted and formal.

Here are some interesting first sentences taken from letters written by famous people, most of them to intimate relatives or friends. They show how lively and colorful the opening sentences of letters can be.

Things have happened quickly since I last wrote you.
Edward M. House

It was a perfect delight to see your well-known handwriting again! *Mark Twain*

Truth is such a rare thing, it is so delightful to tell it.
Emily Dickinson

Nothing could have given me greater pleasure than to get news of you! *Pierre Curie*

My heart is singing for joy this morning!
Anne Sullivan Macy

I cannot sleep, and so talk to you, precious beloved friend! *Peter Tchaikovsky*

I shall not forget how good you were to take time to write to me! *Walter H. Page*

I am very much pleased with your letter.
Theodore Roosevelt

And is it a year since we parted from you?
Charles Lamb

I send you a little line, and shake your hand across the water. *William Makepeace Thackeray*

I am going to be married! *Lord Byron*

I love your verses with all my heart, dear Miss Barrett! *Robert Browning*

I am deeply touched by your remembrance.
William James

You'll be thunderstruck to hear what I've been asked
to do.   *Helen Keller*

My heart is so full that I must tell you about it!
                                                          Felix Mendelssohn

Thank you, thank you without end, for the photograph . . . it made me very happy, made my world
glow and my heart light and warm. *Nadejda von Meck*

There is no man in the world who could have given
me the heartfelt pleasure you have, by your kind note.
                                                          Charles Dickens

You are the first friend to whom I write this morn-
ing.   *John Ruskin*

I am very much gratified that you, in a foreign
country, and with a mind almost overoccupied, should
write me.   *John Keats*

It is astonishing how much the state of the body influences the powers of the mind.   *Michael Faraday*

There are moments in life when high position is a
heavy burden.   *Napóleon Bonaparte*

Yes, my dear friend, I have told you, and I repeat it:
I love you dearly.   *Du Barry*

Whatever you do will always affect me . . . one
way or another.   *Lord Chesterfield*

WHAT TO WRITE IN A FRIENDLY LETTER

There is only one real reason for writing a friendly letter . . .
and that is the mutual pleasure to be derived from it.

Therefore letters to friends should be written on a gay and
cheerful note, whenever possible. They should tell of pleasant
and amusing things, not of sickness, heartache, family problems
or other disturbing or distressing things.

That doesn't mean every letter you write must be filled with
joy and cheer. Some of the best letters ever written tell of great
tragedy or sorrow. In fact, many letters are written expressly for

the purpose of sharing an unfortunate or unhappy experience with a friend.

But we are not here discussing such special letters, based on tragic or unhappy circumstances. In the general run of friendly correspondence, it's always best to write of pleasant and agreeable things. No one can be said to enjoy a letter that's filled with "peeves" and complaints. No one can derive real pleasure from a letter that's one long recital of worries, troubles and grievances.

So try to keep the tone of your friendly letters cheerful and lighthearted. Don't write when you are discouraged or depressed; wait for a happier frame of mind. Don't write when you are angry or annoyed; or if you do write, wait until the next day to mail your letter. You may not want to mail it when you read what you have written.

The letters you write to friends should be warm and cordial —should be newsy and alive. They should be filled with the kind of information that is of interest to your correspondent, the kind of news he or she will enjoy hearing. Write of actual people and places . . . of amusing, exciting or unusual things you have seen, heard or done. Don't scorn even the weather, for it's an interesting subject despite all the jokes we hear about it. People like to know what kind of spring New York has had . . . how much rain there's been in California . . . whether it's been a pleasant winter in Florida.

Don't waste a friend's time with a long letter about unimportant trivialities, of no possible significance to anyone but yourself. But if you have heard a good story or a lively joke, remember to tell it in your letter. Or if someone you both know has won a prize, or had a baby, or built a house . . . pass on the news. If you are in Shanghai and you are writing to someone back home, *write about Shanghai* (not about how homesick you are or how your husband's hair is falling out!). If you are writing to someone from your home town who is living in Shanghai, don't just ask how he likes it there and when he expects to return; *give him news of the town and the people in it.* Any news about familiar persons or places is important news to someone far from home.

The letters you write to friends should be narrative in style, not just a series of questions like: "How are you? How do you feel? How are the children?" But on the other hand, if you receive a letter containing a number of questions, be sure to answer them. For even the most intimate friends may be offended if the questions or comments contained in their letters are ignored. It's a good idea to keep all letters from friends until you have answered them. Reread each letter just before answering it, and try to give whatever news or information is requested.

WHAT NOT TO WRITE IN A
FRIENDLY LETTER

Try not to discuss illness in your letters to friends—though, of course, if you or a member of your family has been seriously ill, you should certainly not try to conceal that fact. It's just as important to be truthful and straightforward in your letters as in your conversation. But don't go into a long and tedious discourse on the nature and treatment of the illness. Don't give all the unimportant and uninteresting details. That can be as boring as backing someone into a corner and telling him all about your operation! Only the victim is really cornered in a conversation; he can't very well escape unless he is willing to be rude and ignore you. It's different with a letter. Nobody is obliged to read a letter that bores or annoys him. It can always be tossed into the wastepaper basket. So if you want your letter to be read with interest and pleasure, *keep the unpleasant details of your illness to yourself.*

Don't write at length about your children . . . except, perhaps, to a doting grandparent or to an intimate friend who has children of her own. Remember that the bright sayings of children never sound quite so bright outside the boundaries of their own indulgent homes. Nor does the average person care to read a long letter about Junior's first unintelligible word or his first amazing tooth. Save that kind of letter for grandma! She adores hearing about every detail of the baby's progress, but nobody else does.

It is not advisable to write of domestic difficulties or business reverses in the letters you write to friends. There may be occasions, of course, when you feel you must confide in someone—must write about your troubles to someone you know will sympathize and understand. But don't make it a practice to broadcast your personal affairs in your letters.

Don't discuss your servant problems in letters to friends, for such problems are of no interest to anyone but yourself. It may relieve your injured feelings to write a long tirade on your maid's insolence or incompetence; but it won't make an interesting or enjoyable letter. Furthermore, it's quite as bad taste to complain about servants in your letters as in your conversation . . . and as boring.

Always try to avoid bad news in your letters, if you can. But if you must give such news, tell it all. Don't hold back part of it, with the idea of sparing your friend as much as you can. That defeats its own purpose; for it can be very upsetting to receive bad news that is only half-told, that leaves a lot of disturbing questions unanswered.

Try also to avoid the impact of shock in the first sentence. If you have had an accident, for example, don't start off with a blunt statement of that fact, such as: "We had a bad accident in the car on the way back from Maine." It's much more thoughtful and considerate to write, "Well, we're back home again, after three wonderful weeks in Maine! It was the best vacation ever. We had a little more excitement than we bargained for, as we had an accident on the way home. But don't be alarmed as we are all fine! Nothing more than a few bruises and scratches to show for it. The car was badly damaged though . . ." and so on. Even in the case of a serious accident with major injuries to members of the party, the news can be eased into the letter without too much shock to the reader.

"We have just had the most terrible excitement; but thank God, everyone is safe and well. So don't be worried by the news in this letter," wrote blind Helen Keller to her friend, Mrs. Macy—telling of the fire that nearly destroyed her home and

could easily have taken her life.* "Everyone is safe and well
. . . don't be worried . . ." she wrote, before even mentioning
the fire.

CONSIDER THE PERSON
TO WHOM YOU ARE WRITING

No letter is a good letter if it fails to interest the reader.
Therefore don't write exclusively about yourself, but *keep your
correspondent in mind*. What are his interests, his hobbies? What
exciting news can you give him? What would he most enjoy
hearing about?

Naturally you wouldn't write the same kind of letter to a
neighbor's teen-age boy away at school as you would to a dignified, elderly friend of the family. You must consider the person
to whom you are writing. For people are different; their tastes
and interests are different; and obviously the best letters are
those written from the reader's point of view, with the reader's
interests and problems in mind.

A boy likes an exciting letter, full of news. He enjoys hearing
who won the local sports events—what his former friends are
doing—little anecdotes about dogs, horses, pets—descriptions of
unusual or interesting places and people.

A girl likes the same kind of letter, newsy and full of information . . . keyed, of course, to her own interests or hobbies.
She especially likes to know what other girls of her age are doing,
and what they have accomplished. She enjoys letters that tell
her about hobbies or collections—about movies or movie stars
—about parties or pretty clothes.

Women like to know about fashions, people, plays, books.
Men are interested in sports, politics, business, world affairs.
Older people love letters that tell them about the very young
. . . letters that describe birthday parties, picnics, school plays,
graduations, all the gay, exciting highlights of childhood. But
the *really* old live a great deal in the past, and enjoy most the

---

* Nella Braddy, *Anne Sullivan Macy* (New York: Doubleday, Doran & Co., 1933),
p. 254.

letters that tell about people and places they once knew . . . letters that bring back happy memories.

All people, young and old, like to feel important! Remember that, whenever you write a letter. People not only like to feel important, but they resent very much any implication that you consider yourself superior. So make it a point never to boast about yourself or your accomplishments in letters to friends. Don't make the mistake of trying to impress the person to whom you are writing with your knowledge or skill. You'll write a much more successful letter if you minimize your achievements . . . and subtly let your correspondent know that you recognize and respect his superior knowledge and judgment. You'll write a much more successful letter if you *make your reader feel important.*

"What kind, beautiful souls live on this earth!" wrote the great composer, Tchaikovsky, to his beloved friend, Nadejda von Meck. "Meeting such people as you on the thorny road of life, one grows to feel that humanity is not as selfish and wicked as the pessimists say. . . . Among a million others, if such a one as you appears, it is enough to save a man from despair." *

Surely that letter must have made Madame von Meck feel happy and proud! It must have made her feel very important.

HOW TO CLOSE YOUR LETTER

When you have said everything you want to say in a letter, take your leave promptly—but graciously. Don't tag on a lot of pointless remarks, like an uncertain visitor standing in the doorway ready to go but not quite knowing how to say "good-by." Remember what we said in an earlier chapter:† It's a wonderful quality in letter writing to know what you want to say—to say it—*and to stop.*

Your closing sentence is important. As your last thought, it's likely to make a strong impact on your reader's mind, and remain long in his memory. So watch that closing sentence, and

* Bowen, *Beloved Friend.*
† Page 58.

write it carefully! Try to avoid such offensive phrases as: "I must close now as I have something important to do" . . . "That's all for now, I'm in a big rush" . . . "I guess I'll close as there's nothing else to write." Such expressions are rude and abrupt, and are certainly no way to take leave of a friend. Avoid also any use of the phrase "In haste" as that clearly says you are busy, or bored, or impatient . . . that you want to get the letter over and done with.

Try to give your letter a gracious, a friendly, closing—like a handclasp and a smile. Let your last thought be, not of yourself, but of the person to whom you are writing. For example, "I'll write again very soon, Claire, and keep you informed of Bob's progress." Or, "I'll look up that recipe you want, Anne, and send it to you next time I write." Or, "I loved your letter, Bess, and I hope you'll write soon again!"

Here are some examples of interesting closing sentences, from the actual letters of famous people:

> God bless you, dear Barbara—you are very precious to us.
> *George Eliot*

> Think of me, sometimes, when the Alps and ocean divide us—but they never will, unless you wish it.
> *Lord Byron*

> Adieu, my love; keep well and be just to yourself and to me.
> *Napoleon Bonaparte*

> Be happy, my dearest ones—I will write, be sure!
> *Elizabeth Browning*

> Heaven bless my love and take care of him!
> *Mary W. Godwin*

> *Au revoir.* I don't want to say 'Good-bye' because I don't want this letter to end. Devotedly yours.
> *Nadejda von Meck*

> Whatever blessed and happy thing God can send to His children, may He grant to you, and give you beautiful and never-to-be-forgotten days.
> *Felix Mendelssohn*

There is nothing that I will not brave for your sake.
. . . Adieu, my dear heart! *Voltaire*

You are everything to me. *Sarah Bernhardt*

Good-bye, my dear friend. . . . Good-bye. Yours
until death. *Peter Tchaikovsky*

We send continents of love to you and yours.
Mark Twain

So come along; I will show you every nook and
corner of my Paradise. *Anne Sullivan Macy*

The world will not take up its knitting and sit
quietly by the fire for many years to come.
Walter Hines Page

EXAMPLES OF LETTERS
TO PERSONAL FRIENDS

When you sit down to write a letter to a friend, remember
that the best letters are newsy, informal and easy to read . . .
as natural and spontaneous as conversation. If possible, they
should take up where you left off in conversation with the person to whom you are writing, on the same subject or subjects
you discussed when you were together. A good letter is simply
good plain talk on paper . . . unstudied and unstilted . . .
easy-flowing . . . *interesting.*

Friendly Letter from One Man to Another

Dear Fred:

Remember that television set we were talking about
last time you were here, the one in the Chinese cabinet
that matched the screen we bought in Hong Kong?
Well, Anne and I decided to give it to each other for
our anniversary. It has just been delivered, and I'd
like very much for you to see it. Can you come on
Monday, the 10th?

By the way, I ran into Jim Ellis the other day. He's living near you now, so I gave him your address and he said he would call you. He is a research engineer and is doing some very interesting work. Get him to tell you about it.

Jim tells me his brother Pete just came back from Mexico City; he went there to open a branch office for his company. Didn't you say that Chalmer-Holt was thinking of opening a branch office in Mexico? It might be a good idea to look up Pete Ellis and talk with him about it. You remember Pete, I'm sure. He was a junior the year we graduated, and he lived in the Delta Sigma Pi house right next to ours. I think he played end the year Bill Hickey was captain of the team. Anyway, he's a real nice guy, and I'm sure he'll be glad to tell you whatever you want to know about Mexico.

I just finished reading *The Cat's Claw*, a real creepy mystery—the kind you like. I thought of you while I was reading it, and if you want to borrow it I'll be glad to give it to you when you are here. That reminds me! You promised to lend me your copy of *The Readers' Treasury*. Will you bring it along when you come on the 10th?

Anne says to come about 8:30 for coffee and dessert. She has asked her sister, Jean, to come too; and perhaps we can have a rubber or two of bridge.

How is your hay fever this year, Fred? I don't seem to be bothered by it nearly as much this year as last. Maybe it's because they cleared away most of the ragweed around here.

We're looking forward to seeing you, Fred, so don't disappoint us! Unless you call or write to the contrary, we'll be expecting you. Regards from Anne.

                                        Cordially,
                                        Jack

Friendly Letter from One Woman to Another

Many letters are boring because they put too much stress on one subject. The most interesting letters, the letters that are eagerly received and read with keen enjoyment, are those which cover a wide variety of subjects . . . letters that are alive with news of the day and sparkling with the writer's personality.

Here, for example, is the kind of letter one woman might write to another who is an intimate personal friend. It can be long and chatty, and filled with all sorts of pleasant little anecdotes. But it shouldn't run on and on in a tiresome narration of unimportant details. It shouldn't contain gossip, or scandal or any private confidences that may cause embarrassment if read by an outsider:

Good morning, Helen!

It's a very, *very* good morning, here in Glendale. The sun is pouring in my window; the air is crisp and frosty outside; and there's a bright haze on the hills for miles around. I thought of you first thing, when I saw what a beautiful day it was; for it's just the kind of perfect Autumn morning you love.

So here I am writing to you, Helen, instead of attending to the dozens of things that need to be done. But let them wait! I just feel like "visiting" with you this morning, and telling you all the news—and for once I'm going to obey that impulse.

The baby is just ten months old today. He's a darling and doesn't give me any trouble at all. Right now he's sound asleep in his crib, that cute rattle you sent him in his fist, and the sweetest, most mysterious smile on his face! I wish you could see him.

Ted brought home a cat last week, of all things! As though a baby, a house, a garden and a big overgrown kid for a husband weren't enough to take care of! But you know how Ted is about animals. : . . I guess I should be glad he didn't bring home an alligator or a bear cub as a pet! The cat is called "Minx"—and she really *is* a minx with her yellow eyes and big bushy tail! She follows me around all day, and I actually think she's jealous of the baby. I hope she never scratches him. If she does, out she goes—whether Ted likes it or not!

Have you heard about Mary Ellen and young Doctor Peters? They're going to be married next month. You should see the adorable house they're building out near Alley Pond Road! Mary's such a flighty little thing, I just can't picture her a doctor's wife. But maybe she'll settle down and become more serious, now that she's going to be married.

How about spending a week end with us in Glendale while the weather is still so heavenly? Ted and I would love to have you, Helen. And don't give us that line about being too busy! You work much too hard for your own good, and you really owe it to yourself to take a little vacation now and then.

Besides, we want to show off our young son and heir. He has acquired two new teeth and a lot of fuzzy new hair since you saw him last—to say nothing of the most angelic smile this side of heaven!

So come and see him, Helen—and us—and the cat! Come and enjoy some of this brisk Autumn weather, away from the dusty city! *You* name the date, and we'll welcome you with open arms. Love from all of us,

Kate

Letters to Friends in Distant Places

Friends far from home are interested in everything that has happened in their absence. They want all the news, down to the last detail. If someone has put a new iron fence around his property . . . or bought a new car . . . or had a baby . . . that's NEWS of first importance. Information about familiar people and places makes any letter thrilling and exciting to receive.

Dear Paul:

Just wait till you hear all the news I have to tell you! So much has happened these past few weeks that I could fill a book telling you all about it.

In the first place, remember that big old red brick house at the top of Cornish Hill, where the Redfields used to live? Well, before the Redfields, the Pettys lived there—and it seems that *five generations* of Pettys lived right in that same house without changing the interior or the furnishings very much. Now the trustees of the estate are turning the house into a museum. I understand it's full of antiques that people will pay good money to see. They are going to call it the Petty Mansion; and with the money they charge for admission, they're planning to build a beautiful park around the house and grounds. Everyone in Cornish is delighted, of course.

And as though that weren't enough excitement for this sleepy little town, Fred Waters has just won ten thousand dollars in a prize-novel competition. You remember Fred, don't you? He used to be a reporter on the Cornish *Times*. Nobody ever dreamed he had any real talent . . . yet his book was judged the best of over a thousand manuscripts submitted! It's called *Late April* and it's about a girl who hated men until she was middle-aged, then suddenly went to the other extreme and became man-crazy. I haven't read it yet; but my brother Alex read it and liked it very much. I'm enclosing some clippings about it from the *Times*.

We had quite a little excitement here last week. On Tuesday evening, two men in a black sedan stopped at the Crystal Gas Station on Main Street and held up the attendant. They got away with over two hundred dollars. The very next day we had a mysterious fire. The Jenkins' house burned down—you know, that beautiful old white Colonial house on Magpie Road. Nobody knows how the fire started; the Jenkinses were at the movies at the time and there was no one at home.

Anyway, it burned right down to the ground and nothing was saved—not even one piece of furniture. The fire made too much headway before the alarm was turned in. I'm certainly sorry for the Jenkinses; they lost all their possessions, including the letters and pictures of their son who was killed in the war. Maybe they can replace the other things, but they can never replace those precious letters and pictures of their son.

Well, I guess I've given you all the news, Paul. . . . Oh, there's one thing more! The Stassons are selling their store and moving to Arizona. Their little boy (the one who has asthma) was very sick this winter and the doctor recommended a change of climate. They're leaving about the first of April.

When are you coming back to Cornish, Paul? Or are you getting to like Montreal so much that you don't want to come back? We all miss you very much; Alex says he hasn't had a decent game of tennis since you went away. I hope you took a lot of pictures this time, so that you can show us where you've been and all the interesting things you've done.

Write soon and let us know when we can expect you. So many people are always stopping Alex and me and asking, "When is Paul coming back?" Well, *when is he?*

Affectionate greetings from all the family,

> Cordially,
> Annette

Dear Joan:

It seems such a long, long time since you left Middletown! Can it only be a year? It doesn't seem possible when I think of all that has happened here . . . and all the brilliant, exciting things you have accomplished in New York!

Oh, yes—I know all the wonderful things you've done, Joan, even though you *are* so modest in your letters! I've heard all about the new fashion ideas you created for teen-agers, and how several of the big department stores are now featuring "Joan Juniors." And I've heard about your idea for a television fashion show. I think it's a *marvelous* idea, Joan! I hope you'll tell me about it next time you write. Are you going to be in it yourself, or are you just going to plan and direct it?

You've certainly made a big stir in the one year you've been in New York. We're all very proud of you, here in Middletown! There was a write up about you in the Courier last week—I'm sure your mother must have sent you a clipping. They called you "The most promising young designer in America today." How does it feel to be famous? (I'll never know!)

Now for news of our mutual friends: Myra Crockett and Jim Haskins are engaged. They're going to be married sometime in December. Jim is manager of the Hillcrest now—and I understand he's doing very well. He and Myra are going to Bermuda on their honeymoon. I met Myra at my sister's house last week, and she said to be sure and send regards to you next time I write.

Alice Foster is going to Florida for two months, to recuperate. You know she's been very sick—I think I mentioned it in my last letter. She asked for your address and said she would write to you from there.

Kathy Wendall gave up teaching. You know she never liked it. She's a librarian now; and in her spare time she's working on an anthology of poetry for children. That's the kind of work she loves, and she's very happy.

Remember that Fisher boy, the wild one who was always getting into trouble? Well, he's the town hero now! One of the little Harris twins wandered away from her back yard and on to the railroad tracks. Her mother went to look for her, and saw her on the tracks the same instant she saw a train coming. She screamed and ran . . . but she fell before she could reach the baby. Bob Fisher heard her scream, sprinted over the fence, and grabbed the baby out of danger just in time. Some people who saw it happen say that the Fisher boy definitely risked his life to save the baby. So now he's a hero! Mayor Hill made a speech and presented him with a medal, and Mrs. Harris gave him a hundred-dollar bond and a big kiss. It was all very touching, and the most exciting thing that has happened around here in months.

But I suppose this all sounds very small-town and provincial to you, now that you're a big career gal in New York! No, that isn't fair. . . . I know your heart is still in Middletown, and that you miss your old friends as much as we all miss you.

Tell me, Joan, is New York as wonderful as they say? Have you had time to do any sightseeing or are you too busy for that? I wouldn't care how busy I were, if I were in New York—I'd take in all the sights, including Coney Island and the Statue of Liberty! Maybe that's why I'll never be a big success like you!

Well, Joan, it was grand hearing from you; I enjoyed your letter more than I can say. I hope you'll write soon again. And don't forget! I want to know all about that fascinating television fashion show you are planning!

Mother, dad and Dick send warmest regards.

Affectionately,
Carol

Dear Carl:

What a pleasant surprise to receive your letter from Rome! That's one place in the world I've always wanted to see . . . and still hope to see some day. But reading your wonderfully interesting and vivid descriptions is the next best thing to being there myself.

I knew that St. Peter's was the largest church in the world, but I didn't know that the pope's residence was the largest palace in the world. Thanks for the sketches, Carl—they're delightful. You must be having a lot of fun wandering around Rome with your sketchbook. Mother is thrilled with the sketch of the new bridge against the old city; she's having it framed and plans to hang it in the living room. I'm glad you are concentrating on modern life and scenes instead of painting the old ruins, like almost every artist who goes to Italy!

Remember Tom Alpert? I ran into him the other day at the Brush and Pen Club. He's with an advertising agency now—a visualizer in the art department. He doesn't do any finished work at all, just the rough "visuals" or layouts. He apparently likes what he's doing very much, and he says he's making more money now than ever before. That's important to Tom, you know; he has an invalid mother, and a younger brother at college, and he takes care of both of them.

You know Ray Walters, don't you? He's the chap who's engaged to Ed Phelan's sister. Well, he and Ed went to New Hampshire for some skiing last week, and ten minutes after they arrived Ray slipped on the ice and broke his ankle. Now he's hobbling around on crutches, and everybody's kidding him about it and warning him to keep off skiis . . . but the poor guy wasn't even *on* skis when it happened! Try and make anyone believe that!

How long are you staying in Rome? Will you get to see any other parts of Italy while you are there, or do the terms of the scholarship call for remaining right in Rome all the time? You didn't tell us anything about your work at the Academy. I hope it's as interesting and helpful as you expected it to be.

Thanks again for the sketches, Carl—and for your really *fascinating* letter. Anyone who writes as well as you do should write often, so don't wait too long be-

fore writing again and telling us some more about
Rome and your experiences there. I promise to send you
all the local news in return!

Best wishes from all of us,

> Cordially,
> Dale

Letters from Distant Places
to Friends Back Home

There is no better opportunity to demonstrate your ability as
a letter writer than when you are far from home, viewing new
sights and scenes, and writing to friends of your impressions and
experiences. Don't fill your letter with a lot of nostalgic questions about home: "What's new at the office? Have you been
busy? How's everyone?" That kind of letter is dull and unin-
spiring, whether it's written from romantic Bermuda or the
Bronx! Try to make your reader see what *you* are seeing,
through *your* eyes. Try to picture as clearly as you can whatever is new, exciting, different—so that the friend to whom you
are writing can share in your experiences and in your enjoyment.
A good plan is to jot down little incidents as they occur, brief
descriptions of unusual places or people. Then take out your
notes and read them before you write, to refresh your memory
and to make your letters more lively and descriptive.

Dear Bess:

This is one time I wish I had the skill of a writer,
so that I could really do justice to the exotic, almost
incredible beauty of Hawaii! It's the most *heavenly*
place I have ever been! I just don't know how to begin
to describe it to you.

We are staying at the Royal Hawaiian Hotel in
Honolulu until we can find a suitable house or apartment. Frank says it will take six months or more to
establish a branch office, so we'll probably be here that
long at least—maybe more. I don't mind (except that
I'll miss my family and friends, of course!). I really

love it here, Bess; and I know I'm going to have a marvelous time while Frank is busy organizing his office.

The Royal Hawaiian is a beautiful hotel. It's made of pink coral, and when you look at it from a distance —with the sun shining on it and the colorful gardens all around—it looks fabulous and unreal. It's right on the beach at Waikiki, and from our windows we can look out and see the long rolling breakers, the surf riders, Diamond Head in the distance.

Last week end Frank wasn't busy so he took me sightseeing. I was surprised to discover that Hawaii is just one of the islands, and that there's a whole chain of them. Honolulu, which is the capital, isn't even on the island of Hawaii, but on Oahu. Then there's Molokai, where the famous leper settlement is, Maui, Kauai, and some other smaller islands that I haven't learned to pronounce or spell as yet! An interesting thing about Maui is that when you look down on it from a plane, it looks exactly like the head and shoulders of a beautiful woman.

Frank took me to see the pineapple fields and the banana plantations; but I told him I was more interested in native life so he took me to a village on one of the smaller islands. It was very interesting. I saw how the natives spear fish, and weave baskets and eat poi with their fingers (though I have an idea most of it is an "act" put on for the benefit of tourists)! I understand there aren't many pure Hawaiians left; most of them have intermarried with Japanese and Americans, and few of the picturesque old customs and habits of the people are still observed.

But they still do the *real* hula here—a graceful and charming dance—not at all like the coarse and suggestive version of it you see on Broadway! We took movies of a group of Hawaiian girls doing the hula, and we'll show them to you when we get back. You'll see how lovely it is, and how utterly different from the popular idea of a hula dance.

I could go on and on, Bess, telling you of all the fascinating things we've done and seen in the short time we've been here. But I guess I'll just have to save some of it for my next letter. I *must* tell you one thing more, though: On Sunday we took what is called "the weirdest walk in the world"—right across the top of a volcano! It was weird, all right! We walked over what were once fiery, bubbling cauldrons of lava; but all the craters are now extinct, except one. That one is called Kilauea, and it's still very much alive! We walked right to the edge of it and looked down, and we could see the lava churning and boiling way down below. It gave me a sort of queer feeling, like standing at the edge of eternity. . . .

I won't even *try* to describe my feelings the day we visited Pearl Harbor! I thought of all those Jap planes sneaking in, blowing up our ships and killing so many people. It made me mad all over again to stand on the spot where it all happened and to picture how terrible it must have been.

But I really must end my letter now, Bess, or I'll go on forever! I'll write again soon, and be sure *you* write and tell me all the news. I'm enclosing some pictures of Honolulu; they'll tell you much better than I can how beautiful it is here.

Please remember me to your mother and sister. Frank sends best wishes to all of you.

> With love,
> Edith

Dear Pete:

Here I am in New York, all comfortably settled in my sister's house and ready to start on my new job right after the first of the year.

New York is just what you said: a glittering, painted hussy with a big heart! I've been wandering around a lot by myself, sight-seeing; and now that I'm getting used to the crowds and confusion, *I like this town!* It's friendly, and full of life . . . and it suits me to a T.

I took your advice and bought a guidebook. It's a really good one, with all the places of interest marked on little maps so you can find them easily. Gosh, Pete— there are so *many* things to see! I think I could be here a year and not see them all. But I'm trying to see as much as I can, and at least get the "feel" of the city before settling down to the really important business of making good on my job.

I've done most of the usual things, of course—like going to the top of the Empire State Building, taking a guided tour through Radio City, and even riding on a rubberneck bus through Chinatown and the Bowery. But I think it's fun just to browse around the city and discover things for yourself—things you don't find in a guidebook. For example, I was in Times Square yesterday and I saw a sign that said "Trained Flea Circus." That was a new one on me! I went in to see it, and honestly Pete, it was better than a barrel of monkeys! I must take you to see it when you come to New York. The fleas were all dressed up in fancy costumes. They ran races, played football, danced to music and did all sorts of clever tricks.

But here I am raving about a flea circus when I should be raving about the bridges and skyscrapers, the shops and churches, the museums, art galleries, parks . . . Wall Street and the Great White Way . . . all the things that make New York the "wonder city" of the world! I love it all, Pete—even the immense crowds that practically rip the buttons off your coat when you try to get into the subway.

I've been to a couple of pretty good shows, but it's hard to get tickets for the really big hits. I've also been to the Music Hall, and to the Museum of Science and Industry. Next week I want to go to the Hayden Planetarium. and I'd like to see one or two good basket-

ball games. I went to a hockey game at Madison Square
Garden last Sunday night and saw the New York
Rovers beat Washington 6 to 1.

Well, that's about all for now, Pete. I'll write again
when I can tell you about the job. By the way, I sent
you that sheet music you wanted. Let me know if there
are any other numbers you'd like. And be sure to remember me to your mother and Anne.

Sincerely,
Jack

Vacation Letters to Friends

Dear Carla:

You ask me how we like the little house we rented
in Maine. Carla, we *love* it! This is going to be the most
wonderful summer we have ever had—by far!

As you know, Ted and I rented the house sight un-
seen, just from a description of it. We had hoped for a
clean and cozy little place where we would be comfortable, and where the children could swim and fish and
have fun. It turns out to be all of that, and more! It
turns out to be a real storybook cottage by the sea,
lovely beyond words, peaceful and picturesque.

The house is high on a bluff overlooking the sea. It's
completely isolated, with the sea in front, the woods
behind and magnificent gardens all around. We can
look out for miles over the water; and sometimes whole
days go by and all we see are the gulls, or the glint of a
white sail in the distance. It's incredibly quiet and
peaceful, and just the kind of vacation we needed.

The children like it here as much as we do. We
thought at first it might be lonely for them; but
they're having the time of their young lives! All day
long they are on the beach, or out in the boat, or fishing, or exploring the rocky inlets and coves. The water
is very cold (a little too cold for us!)—but the boys

don't seem to mind it and practically *live* in their bathing suits from morning to night.

We are about 10 miles from Ellsworth, where there are movies and nice shops; and only about 15 miles from Bar Harbor in the opposite direction. About twice a week we go shopping and sight-seeing. There are wonderful places to eat all through this section of Maine; and sometimes we drive as much as 30 or 40 miles for dinner! It gives us a chance to see the rocky coast, and the countryside and the snug little villages.

Yesterday we went to Southwest Harbor, a quaint little fishing village like something out of a novel about New England. We had lobsters that were brought in from traps in the harbor, boiled for us in big lobster pots right on the beach, and eaten with such zest as one never experiences in an ordinary restaurant! Behind us was the village with its tiny houses and lovely gardens—many of the houses a hundred years old, and more! Before us was a wild, curving edge of coast, with the sea breaking against the rocks and sending up tall plumes of spray. It was cool and blowy, and there was a tang of salt in the air, and the lobster was hot and delicious, and we felt—well, Carla, we felt as though we had discovered the *perfect* vacation spot at last!

I'm glad to hear that Eileen likes it now at camp. I knew she would, once she got used to it. *All* children are a little homesick the first time they're away. I still remember the first frantic note we got from Bobby, blotched and tear-stained, begging us to come and get him. But when we went there about a week later, he was having such a fine time that he hardly even noticed us!

We had a nice letter from Phil and Mary last week. They are going to Windemere for the month of August. They are planning to leave the baby with Mary's mother in Vermont. I think that's wise, don't you? Mary hasn't been at all well and she needs a complete rest.

Ted says to be sure and tell you how good he is at
making fires (the braggart!). At the moment he's
down on the rocks gathering driftwood with the boys
for a campfire on the beach tonight. There's going to
be a full moon, and we thought it would be nice to
have a picnic supper outdoors.

Next time you write, Carla, will you give me Eileen's
address at camp? I'd like to send her some little books
and things from here. And be sure to let us know what
day you and Joe will be driving through Bangor. It's
not too far from here, and we can arrange to meet you
for lunch or something.

Love from all of us to all of you, and looking forward to another of your delightful letters,

                              Suzanne

Vacation letters to friends are not necessarily as long and
newsy as the one above. In fact, most people send picture post-
cards instead of writing personal letters. But even a brief note
is better than a card to an intimate friend who enjoys hearing
from you.

Dear Tom:

You were right! The Laurentians have nothing on
the White Mountains! I am making Pinkham Notch
Camp my headquarters, as you suggested; but I'm
hoping to make all the best trails and jumps around
here before my two weeks are up.

Did you ever run the famous Richard Taft trail?
Some fellows here are going there on Saturday, and I
may join them. Say, I've been on that aerial tramway
you told me about. It's a honey!

I met a fellow here who says he knew you at Dartmouth. His name is Sid Fellows, or Fellowes. He's coming up again for the winter carnival, so you may meet
him here.

The weather has been cold but clear, and perfect for skiing. There's a nice congenial crowd at the camp and I'm having a swell time. Believe it or not, I don't even miss the office! But give my best to the gang, Tom, and write to me if you get the chance.

Dick

Letter of Cheer to a Friend Who Is Ill

Even a few cheerful words can carry the warmth of your personality to the bedside of a friend who is ill. But a long, news-filled letter is so much more welcome. A person confined to bed always enjoys reading about what's going on in his or her familiar outside world.

Dear John:

What's the idea of being sick? Don't you realize how all your friends miss you?

I met your sister yesterday, and she says you are much better now—in fact, well on the road to recovery. That's fine! But what we all want to hear, John, is that you are up and around, completely well and your old self again.

So hurry those old germs out of your system, will you? Remember there's a golf tournament at the end of the month, and you don't want to miss that!

By the way, I met Chris Hayden at the club last Sunday. He told me that Westinghouse is sending him to Manila—did you know about that? He's leaving early in March, and his family is following at the end of June when school closes. I don't think Chris is too happy about it; he doesn't like the idea of uprooting his whole family and giving up his house here.

I heard a story that may amuse you, John. Three drunks staggered into a bar for another round of drinks. One of them just managed to reach the edge of the bar and prop himself against it. Another got as far as the juke box and hugged it with both arms, unable to maneuver the rest of the distance. The third fell flat on his face in the middle of the floor.

The drunk who was draped over the bar ordered two drinks.

"Two?" asked the bartender.

"Yeah. One for me, one for my friend over there by the juke box."

"What about your friend on the floor?"

"Nope! None for him," was the answer. "He's gotta *drive!*"

I had lunch with Ted Evans the other day. He says they miss you very much at the office, and that it won't be the same until you are back at your desk again. The way Tex said it was: "John's the spark plug of the department; without him around, everything just *stops*." How does it feel to be so important?

I'm sending you some books and magazines to help pass the time. Your sister says you like mysteries, so I'm including the latest Crime Club selection. I hope you haven't read it.

Now hurry and get well, John! Don't forget our annual fishing trip is due soon. We're waiting for you to get better so that we can set the date.

Marge asks about you all the time, and sends her best wishes.

Sincerely,
Roger

Christmas Letter to a Friend

Any time is a good time to write a cheerful, friendly letter to someone far away. But remembering days and occasions important to others—not by means of printed sentiments, but by personal notes—touches the heartstrings and wins affection as nothing else can. Try it and see! Write a birthday or anniversary letter to someone you like, instead of just sending a card. Christmas and New Year are especially appropriate times to write to distant friends . . . to let them know that, however far away they may be, they are still very close to your heart.

Dear Ruth:

Here it is Christmas again . . . and you are still in California, and I am still in New York . . . with a whole continent between us! But you are as much in my thoughts today as though you were just around the corner. It would take far more than a continent between us to make me forget the many happy Christmases we had together, and the many pleasant memories we share.

Do you remember the Christmas party you had that first year you and Ed were married? Do you remember you had a big tree in the living room, and a tiny one right beside it—and everybody wondered why? Then you and Ed began opening the packages around the little tree and taking out booties, and mittens, and Teddy bears—and everybody knew you were going to have a baby! I always thought it was such a sweet way to announce it.

That was eleven years ago, Ruth. Your Judy must be quite a young lady now. And Jimmy was born the year you moved, so he must be seven. I wish I could see them; but I guess it will be a long time before Joe and I get to California.

Joe is just doing obstetrics now. He gave up general practice about a year ago, and I thought he'd be able to take it a little easier. But he is busier than ever, Ruth, and so conscientious that he won't go away even for a week end for fear a patient may need him and he won't be there!

Is Ed still with Technicolor? Did he ever get started on that history of the movies he was going to write?

It seems such a long time since I've heard from you, Ruth—I *do* wish you'd let us know how you all are, and what interesting things you are doing.

But anyway, my dear—I just want you to know that we're thinking of you on Christmas day, and remembering all the good times we used to have, and wishing you weren't so very far away! Joe and I send our love to all the family—and the hope that you'll have a gay and merry Christmas, and a very happy New Year!

Always affectionately yours,
Leila

3

Family Letters

The same general rules that apply to *friendly* letters apply to *family* letters—except that in correspondence with members of the family, people are usually more intimate and informal, and more concerned with personal affairs.

The charm of any letter lies in its freshness and originality, and in its expression of the writer's personality. Therefore no set rules can govern the contents of a family letter any more than they can govern the contents of a letter written to a friend.

Just be sure that you are never careless or thoughtless when writing to a member of your family. Try not to say anything in your letter that is ungracious or unkind. Make it a point never to write anything to a member of your family that you wouldn't or couldn't say directly to that person in conversation.

A good general rule to bear in mind is that you should never sit down and force yourself to write to a member of your family, merely because a letter is "due" and expected. It's much better to write when you feel like writing, when you want to write and enjoy it. Then you are more likely to write an engaging and delightful letter . . . and write it with greater ease of expression.

But on the other hand, never ignore a letter from someone in your family who is worried about your health, or concerned about your welfare or progress. Such letters should be answered promptly and fully. It isn't kind to keep someone who cares about you waiting for information important to his or her peace of mind.

THE EVER-WELCOME LETTER FROM HOME

To children away at school or camp—to someone away on vacation, or living and working in a distant city—there are few things so eagerly welcomed and thoroughly enjoyed as a *letter from home*. A long, cheerful, news-filled letter makes any day a better day, gives a real lift to the spirits. Often a letter from home goes a long way to help dispel loneliness and banish the "blues."

When John Quincy Adams took office as Secretary of State, he wrote to his mother: "My spirits will often want the cordial refreshment of a letter from you. . . . Let me not thirst for them in vain!"

When Goethe was in Rome, he begged his mother: "Write to me soon and at length how you are, and whatever news there may be." For when one is far from home, "everything is interesting that concerns friends and dear ones!"

More than any other letter, perhaps, the letter from home should be in a blithe and happy mood. It should be full of simple, homey, familiar things. It should tell about the little incidents of daily life . . . and especially about anything unusual or interesting that may have happened. Whenever possible, clippings, cartoons, news items or snapshots should be enclosed—for they add greatly to the enjoyment of a letter from home.

The main function of a family letter is to give news, to tell what has happened since the last letter was written—and to say, in effect, "Hello, there! How are you? I miss you and I'd like to have a nice long chat with you. Since I can't do that, I'm doing the next best thing: I'm writing you this letter!" Bear that in mind when you sit down to write to a relative far from home . . . but close to your heart. Don't nag, scold, complain or find fault! Don't burden your distant relative with unnecessary tales of woe! Give all the news you can . . . and your affection . . . and the warmth of your familiar, well-loved personality. *But don't give the disappointment of a letter from home that is dull, boring, unpleasant or discouraging to read.*

One thing more: Although your letter to a relative away from home should be filled with news of family and friends, it should not concern itself *exclusively* with home affairs. Your letter should show unmistakable interest in the things your son, cousin, brother or aunt is doing . . . in his or her progress and well-being . . . the job, school, sports, hobbies, friends and other highlights of his life away from you.

Here are examples of letters from home—not intended as exact models, but to stimulate your imagination and give you ideas and suggestions to help you write interesting letters of your own:

To a Daughter Living and Working in Another City

Dearest Gail:

I was so very, very happy to get your nice long letter this morning! Thank you, darling, for not making me wait too long. I was so worried about that cold of yours; but now that I know you are completely better, I won't worry any more! Just don't go back to the office too soon . . . promise, darling? After all, you can write your scripts just as easily and well at home.

You'd be surprised to know how interested everybody is in your job. Folks keep stopping me all the time to ask about you. They want to know what shows you write, and whether they can hear them on the air. I can't help feeling proud when I tell them about "Comets of Crime" and "Little Emmy." Their expressions are so funny when they say, *"Really?* Does Gail write those famous shows?" I guess it's hard for them to realize that the little tomboy they used to know is now a very serious-minded and successful television writer!

That reminds me, dear: I met Mrs. Murray when I was out shopping yesterday, and she told me that Agnes is graduating this June and would like to get a job in an advertising agency. You know she had some experience writing radio commercials for the local stores. Mrs. Murray wondered if you could help her get a job, or at least tell her how to go about getting started. I said I didn't know, that Agnes would have to write to you herself. So you may get a letter from her one of these days. . . .

I'm sending you a blouse for your new suit, Gail. I know you can get anything you want in New York; but I happened to see this one in Grayson's window and it's just the kind you like—with a Peter Pan collar and long sleeves. It's a lovely, delicate shade of turquoise, with tiny pearl buttons, and I think it will go beautifully with your suit. But if you don't like it, return it and I'll take it back to Grayson's.

You asked about Martha. She doesn't expect her baby until the end of July. I just heard that the girls are planning a baby shower for her at Emily's house sometime next week—I don't know the exact date. But I thought you might like to send her something from New York. It would be a nice surprise for Martha, and I know it would please her very much. You could send it right to Emily, or send it to me and I'll have Bobby take it over the day of the shower.

Bobby is doing very much better in school now. He got 90 in his last Latin test—which only goes to prove he can get good marks when he tries. But I *do* think his eyes may have had something to do with it, Gail. He seems to be able to concentrate much better since he started wearing glasses. You know, that boy must have grown *two inches* since you saw him last. Why, he can actually wear dad's clothes now! He'll be taller than dad, I think. But I wish he would fill out—he's still as thin as a rail!

Dad is fine. The only thing that seems to be bothering him these days is that he's losing his hair. (And they say men aren't vain!) By the way, dad may have to fly to New York soon to see about that Borden property; if he does, I'll go with him and see for myself how you are.

Now take real good care of yourself, darling—and don't overdo it. You know how I worry when you aren't well! Your idea for a Television Theater is wonderful, and I'm sure it will be a great success; but must you do *everything* in such a hurry? Can't you take another week or two to work out your plans? There I go delivering a long-distance lecture! But I know how you *drive* yourself, dear—and I wish you would take things a little easier and try to get more rest.

Dad and Bobby send you their love. We all miss you, darling . . . I guess we'll *never* get used to seeing so little of our Gail! Your letters help, so write soon again.

Devotedly,
Mother

To a Husband Away
on Business

Frank, dear:

You've been gone exactly two weeks today, but it seems more like two years to me! I've been so lonely without you.

But I'm glad to hear you had such a successful trip this time. That order you got in Detroit is simply *marvelous!* I don't blame you for being so elated about it.

Are you coming directly home, dear, or do you plan to make some stops on the way? I hope you'll be home in time for Patsy's birthday party next Sunday. She's counting on you to show movies to her little friends. But if you can't make it, I'll get my brother to come in for an hour or so—he knows how to work the projector.

Patsy keeps asking every day when you'll be back. She says you never finished that story you were telling her about the train that lost its "toot." You better hurry and think up a good ending for it—you know how Patsy is! She won't be happy until she knows exactly what happened to the "toot" and how the little train got it back again!

Everything at home is fine (except that we miss you so much!). I've been busy with the spring cleaning. Yesterday I had Cora come in to wash the kitchen walls, and she did a very good job of it. The kitchen looks as though it's been repainted. I made some new yellow curtains, and they look real pretty—if I do say so myself!

The weather here has been lovely, Frank. It's almost like summer today, balmy and warm. I let Patsy go to school with just a little sweater on instead of her coat. Everything's beginning to get green, and before you know it your favorite magnolia tree will burst into bloom. I can see it beginning to stir and waken already. . . .

I went to see your mother yesterday. Her cold is all gone, and she looks very well. Your sister Jean looks wonderful! She took off about fifteen pounds since she began dieting, and it's very becoming. But now she's complaining that none of her clothes fit!

Let me know exactly what day you'll be home, dear. I want to have your favorite dinner . . . including pineapple upside-down cake! And make it *soon*, because Patsy and I are very lonely for daddy.

Love and kisses to you, darling—

Lynn

To a Married Sister
Living at a Distance

Dear Beth:

Tomorrow is your birthday, and here you are a thousand miles away! I certainly wish you lived a little closer, so we could see each other more often. It's not much fun when a favorite sister marries and goes off to another part of the country!

But anyway, "Happy Birthday, darling!" . . . even though I can't give you twenty-six whacks and an extra one for good luck. I send twenty-six kisses instead, and an extra kiss to wish you luck, happiness and everything good—not just for next year, but for *always!*

Mother and dad have sent you something special for your birthday. I'm not going to tell you what it is, but I know you'll be thrilled. I sent *my* gift last week, and no doubt you have received it by now. I hope you like it. Janey is embroidering a bridge cloth for you . . . but you know Janey! She'll probably finish it by Christmas. It's very pretty, though; it's yellow, and it has hearts, clubs, spades and diamonds embroidered in the corners in red. Janey's proud as punch of her handiwork, and she shows it to everyone who comes into the house. "It's for my married sister in Boston," she tells everybody.

She's a brat, Beth—but an awfully cute one! Do you know what she did the other day? She sneaked an atomizer and a bottle of "Blue Heaven" out of my room and sprayed her cat! She said Tansy didn't smell nice, the way a ladycat should. Poor Tansy! Mother wouldn't let her in the house for two days. And now *I* can't use "Blue Heaven" because it reminds me of the way Tansy smelled and I get sick to my stomach!

I'm still with Colton-Fisher; but one of these days I'm going to tell J.C. just what I think of him . . . and walk out. I don't know why I put up with his tempers and tantrums. Dad wants me to leave and take that job Uncle Ed offered me, but I don't like the idea of working for a relative. Just between you and me, I wish I could meet someone like Henry and get married. Or is it unladylike to admit anything like that, even to a sister?

Do you think you'll be coming for a visit soon, Beth? I wish you would! I know it's difficult for Henry to get away, but couldn't you leave him just for a little while? Your old room is a handsome guest room now, with new lamps and draperies and even a chaise longue by the window! But the only guest we ever want in it is *you.*

Write soon and tell us all the news. Is Henry just as busy as ever? I'm enclosing an editorial about the United Nations which dad clipped out of the paper this morning. He thought Henry might enjoy reading it. I'm also enclosing the recipe for Baked Alaska that you wanted mother to send. She says to be sure and let her know how it turns out.

Many happy returns, darling—from all of us!

With love,
Kay

To a Brother in a Distant City

Dear Mark:

I think what you need is a few weeks in Coatesville! Why don't you drop everything and come on home for a vacation, and for a visit with the family? You owe it to yourself, Mark—and to us, too. We haven't seen you now in nearly two years. You know we have lots of room since the boys were married, and we can put you and Agnes up for as long as you want to stay.

You've been driving yourself too hard, Mark—that's what the trouble is. You just can't keep up that pace and not expect to feel the effects of it. Let Ted and Ernest take over, and come on to Coatesville and be lazy for a while. Forget about business and *relax*—isn't that what the doctor said you should do? Here you could really take it easy . . . and see all your old neighbors and friends . . . and we could play chess in the evenings, the way we used to.

So think about it, Mark—and let me know. You could fly from Chicago to Pittsburgh, and I'd meet you in the car. Jennie and I have our hearts set on it, so don't disappoint us. You know it's kind of lonely for us now, with all the kids married and gone . . . and it would be a real treat for us having you and Agnes here.

Besides, old man, I really need your help! As I told you in my last letter, we're building a big community center here in Coatesville, and I'm on the building and plans committee. You've had a lot more experience along those lines than I have, and I'd sure welcome the chance to talk things over with you and get your opinion about some of my ideas.

You'll be surprised when you see all the changes in Coatesville. It's been getting a real face lifting! But I'm not going to tell you a thing about it; you'll have to come and see for yourself.

There have been a few changes in the family, too. You know about Betty Filler, don't you? She eloped with a boy named Walker; I don't think you know him. But he's a nice young chap—in the lumber business with his father. And of course you know about Kate's twins—cutest pair of tricks you ever saw! Everybody's kidding Ira because he wanted a son but got two daughters instead. By the way, Ira's building a new house, out near Munsey Park. You must see it; it will be one of the show places of Coatesville.

Now don't write and say you can't come, Mark! The whole family is looking forward to seeing you this summer. I'll be waiting for a letter telling me when to expect you.

And listen—don't worry about what the doctor said! A heart murmur isn't anything serious. You know that Uncle Dave has had a heart murmur since he was a boy, and he's huskier right now at 72 than I am at 50. So don't let it get you down. . . . Just be smart and take it easy from now on.

Love from Jennie and from all of us,

Claude

To a Son in a Foreign Country

Dear Stan:

The little Swiss music box arrived this morning,
and I *love* it! Thanks, darling. You are sweet to keep
thinking of me and sending me such unusual, charming little things from all over Europe. But you
shouldn't be so generous, dear! You need your money
for your own expenses, so don't keep spending it on
me.

Stan, your letters are *beautiful!* Your father and I
especially enjoyed the last one from Bern. We could
almost see the Alps through your eyes—the lofty
peaks, the shining valleys. Judging from your letters,
you must be enjoying Switzerland even more than
France.

Are you going to be in Bern the rest of this month?
You didn't say in your letter when you expect to leave
for Italy. As I understand it, you will be in Geneva
for about a week or so before going to Rome. Is that
right? You must be sure to let me know where letters
and packages can reach you.

By the way, I must send you some soluble coffee.
Your description of the "so-called coffee" at your
hotel is amusing, but I hate to think of you starting
the day without a good cup of coffee. Did you like
the shirts I sent in my last package? Were they the
kind you wanted?

Your "Report from Paris" was in the *Courier* yesterday. I think it's one of your most interesting reports
so far. There was also a paragraph about you, telling
how you won the traveling scholarship and were tour-
ing Europe as a student correspondent. I'm keeping a
scrapbook of all your clippings, Stan. Some day when
you are a famous newspaper man (as you surely *will*
be!) you'll enjoy reading them and reliving these first
exciting experiences. Your father and I are so glad for
you, Stan—so happy and proud that you were given
this splendid opportunity!

Everything at home is just about the same. Nothing very new or interesting has happened since you went away. I saw Florence yesterday, and she looks lovely as ever. She told me about the portfolio of water colors you sent her; she's delighted with them!

Your father is well, but very busy—as usual. He promised to take a few days off toward the end of the month, and we may drive to Kingston to see Aunt Emily. By the way, I must tell you something very funny: Aunt Emily has a hen that lays an egg on her porch every morning at eight o'clock . . . then pecks at the door until she comes out and picks it up! She doesn't know how or why the hen got started delivering an egg for her breakfast every morning, but she says it's a convenient little quirk of nature and she hopes the hen keeps it up. I hope so, too—until we get there. I'd like to see it for myself.

Well, son—good-by for now. But I'll write again in a day or two. And I hope *you'll* keep writing those nice long letters home; we enjoy them so! Dad says to ask you what language they speak mostly in Switzerland— German or French. Somebody asked him the other day and he didn't know.

Much love from both of us, darling—and thanks again for the music box!

Mother

Letters to Children Away
at School

Boys and girls away from home—at school or camp, or visiting relatives or friends—like letters full of news of home and the familiar little incidents of everyday life. They *don't* like "preachy" letters—letters that warn, scold, find fault and endlessly criticize.

Letters from parents to children away from home should be gay and cheerful and affectionate . . . should be filled with little anecdotes and endearments . . . above all, should keep alive the love and awareness of home. A letter that makes a child feel unhappy or discouraged fails in its purpose, whatever that purpose may be. It isn't necessary to preach or scold; a point can be made tactfully—and often a great deal more effectively—by relating an incident or telling a story. After all, children are personalities in their own right. They resent being talked down to as inferiors . . . and are often made moody and dispirited by the wrong kind of letter from home.

Bear these facts in mind when writing to your boy or girl at school. Remember that your letters are tremendously important, and can have lifelong influence on your child's character and personality. Try to write on a *basis of equality*, not as a parent alone but as a friend and confidant. Avoid writing in anger or impatience—whatever your child may have done or however he may have failed you. It may relieve your feelings to threaten and scold, but surely that is not the important thing! The important thing is the effect of your words upon the child, his spiritual and emotional response to them. *No letter is a good letter that makes a child feel resentful or unhappy.*

So be sure any letter you write to a son or daughter away at school is a friendly letter, warm with affection and understanding. Be sure it's an *encouraging* letter, showing utmost faith in the child . . . even when stern correction or reproof is necessary.

> Dearest Joel:
>
> I went to Brentano's this morning to get the books you wanted, and when I got back I found your letter waiting for me. Thank you, dear, for writing so promptly! I was anxious to know how you came out in your exams, and I'm delighted to hear that you did so well. But I knew you would, Joel. . . . I have every confidence in you, and I know you will always apply yourself to your studies and try to be near the top of your class.
>
> If you only knew how happy your letters make me! This last one is especially interesting—just the kind of letter I love to get from you—all about your work at school, and your friends. It's a wonderful letter, Joel—

almost like having *you* here in the room with me for a little while!

I can just imagine how thrilled you are to be on the football team. Dad will be very pleased when he hears about it. No doubt he'll write and tell you so himself tonight, after he reads your letter. Yes, you may get whatever equipment you need, Joel. I agree with you that it's better to buy things like that in Exeter rather than send them from New York. You really have to try them on to get the proper size. So just get what you need, dear, and have the store send the bill home.

Don't worry about your fish—I'm taking very good care of them. I feed them regularly every morning, and I always put the food in the little glass ring, just the way you showed me. Yesterday when I went to feed them—guess what? There were about a dozen tiny new babies scooting around. I got them right out and put them into another tank before the big fish could eat them. They're awfully cute, Joel; but I can't tell yet just what they are. They look like guppies, but dad says they might be platties or swordtails. When they're a little bigger we'll be able to tell what they are, and I'll write and let you know.

Did you know that Dennis Thompson is a tropical-fish fan now? I guess you got him started with that pair of gold guppies you gave him last time you were home. He was here the other day to look up something in your Innes book, and he didn't stop talking about the pair of Siamese fighting fish his father gave him for his birthday. I remember how excited *you* were the first time you got a pair of them!

Clare is going riding again on Saturday in Central Park. You wouldn't know your sister, Joel—she's grown so much in the past two months! In fact, she has outgrown her riding breeches, so she's using your old jodphurs now—the ones you had at camp, remember? I had them cleaned and they fit her perfectly. I bought her a new green jacket to go with the jodhpurs, and she looks *adorable* in the outfit! Clare misses you very much, dear. . . . I wish you would write to her once in a while. I tell her that your letters are for *all* of us, but she's always disappointed when the mail comes and there's nothing for her. If you could hear how wistfully she asks, "Didn't Joel write to me?"—I'm sure you would send her a letter every now and then, even if it's only a few words.

I do hope you won't let football practice interfere with your school work, now that you're on the team. But I'm sure you are too sensible for that! Dad and I want you to do the best you can in whatever you undertake, and we'll be proud and happy if you distinguish yourself in football or any other sport. But not at the expense of your studies! We hope you will continue the fine progress you have been making and not let your enthusiasm for football take too much of your time and effort.

I am sending you a box of those peanut cookies you like so much. In your next letter be sure to let me know if there is anything you need, like socks or underwear.

My love to you, dear . . . and many thanks for your nice long letter. I'll be eagerly waiting for the next one!

Devotedly,
Mother

Dear Paul:

Your marks have just come, and by George—I'm delighted! You really have worked hard, haven't you? I must say I'm very pleased with the steady improvement you have shown, especially in Latin and Math.

Now I'm not saying that a 70 in Latin is *good*—don't misunderstand me! But it's certainly a lot better than the failing mark you got last time; and it shows that you are really trying. That's the important thing to me. As long as you keep trying and improving, I'll be satisfied.

That was a fine mark you got in history, Paul. And 90 in English is better than your last rating in that subject. But I'm especially pleased with your showing in Latin, because you've been failing in it right along. I think the trouble has been that you dislike and *resent* Latin, and therefore have trouble concentrating on it. Naturally it's easier to concentrate on subjects you enjoy and find interesting.

You know, Paul, I'd feel much worse if you had difficulty with a subject like science or math. After all, such subjects require *intelligence*. But a fellow doesn't need much intelligence to master Latin! It's just a matter of memorizing, as I've told you in the past. All that's necessary is to buckle down to the job and lick it. That's what you are apparently doing now . . . and that's why I'm so pleased with you.

Everything at home is fine. Your mother is well, and very happy about the good report from school. She says to tell you she sent your hockey stick yesterday; you should receive it in plenty of time for the practice game on Saturday.

The girls are trying to teach Sinbad some tricks, but without much success. I must say he's a most uncooperative pup! All he wants to do is chase cats and chew bedroom slippers. But the girls are determined to keep at it until they teach him how to beg and "play dead." They read about a dog in England that can talk, and they say Sinbad ought to be able to do *something*.

Take good care of yourself, Paul. Your mother and I may drive up to see you soon. In the meantime, we all send you our love—and we hope you keep up the good work!

Affectionately,
Dad

Dearest Eileen:

It's Saturday—the day that used to be *our* day! Remember how we used to plan little trips and excursions, something different every week—and how I'd never, *never* let anything interfere?

How I miss those Saturday jaunts with you, darling! They were always such fun. But I know you are busy and happy at school, and making friends . . . and I know you are doing very well in your studies. So I try not to mind, and not to miss you too much.

Your last letter was *sweet*. I'm so glad you like the curtains I sent. I thought they were bright and cheerful, and would go well with the maple furniture. Would you like me to send you a little hooked rug for next to the bed, dear? It would look cozy and homelike, and be nice to step on when you get out of bed in the morning. I noticed when I was visiting you that your roommate had one. She's a lovely girl, Eileen! I'm certainly glad you have someone so friendly and pleasant to room with.

Dad is very pleased to know that you are going out for basketball. It has always been one of his favorite sports. I can't say I'm too keen about it, though. Basketball is such a rough game! But I know you are sensible and will take care of yourself.

The Easter holidays are not far off, Eileen—and you'll be coming home for two weeks. How wonderful it will be to have you here, if only for a little while. I'm getting your room ready—with fresh curtains, a new bedspread, and a very special surprise! I'm not going to tell you what it is, but I know you'll love it.

I saw your friend, Barbara Collins, yesterday. She asked about you and was delighted when I told her you would be home April 19th. She's having a sweet-sixteen party on the 25th and said to be sure and tell you not to make any plans for that date.

Do you know that old yellow sweater you always liked, the one that got too small for you? I unraveled it and I'm going to make a new one for you—a slipover. I may have it finished by the time you get home.

I'll be watching for your next letter, darling. Make it soon—and make it another nice *long* one like the last! Love and kisses from dad and

Mother

Dear Patsy:

It was a real treat to have you home for Thanksgiving. Mother and I were so glad you had the entire week end instead of just one day like last year.

I want you to know, Pat, that I am very pleased with your efforts this year. Your marks are much better than they have been; and they show me that you are really trying. You can easily be at the top of your class if you want to be. You have the ability; all that's necessary is to make the effort.

But that isn't why I started to write this letter! I want to tell you that I've opened an account for you at Burke's, and now you can order books directly from them. That applies to books you want for relaxation as well as books you need for your school work.

I think it would be better to get the ice skates in Ardmore. You have enough money in your account at school, so draw what you need to buy the skates. Mother would like you to send your old ones home; they'll be just about the right size for Helen.

The weather continues mild and pleasant here. There has been no real winter yet, and it surprises me to hear there has been so much snow at school.

I wish you'd give some thought to joining the debating club, Pat. I think you should. It's a fine thing to be able to get up before an audience and express yourself clearly and well. Of course I don't want you to do anything you don't enjoy or in which you can find no interest. But I certainly want you to take advantage of as many as possible of the opportunities offered at Ardmore.

Keep well, my dear, and let us hear from you often. We are looking forward to having you home again during the Christmas holidays. Love from mother and Helen, and from

Dad

Letters to Children Away
at Camp

Dearest Larry:

I felt very blue after you left for camp. The house felt so empty and lonely when I got back from the station. But I'm glad you will escape the hot city this summer, and that you will have fun and good times at Wing Lake.

You looked very nice in your camp outfit, Larry. It was wonderful to see you all marching into the train, singing and happy, and eager to start another summer's adventure. I was *glad* to see you go, darling—even though I knew I'd start being lonely the minute the train pulled out!

I guess you are all nicely settled in camp by now. Is it just as lovely in Wing Lake as it was last year? I love that view from the dining hall, looking out over the lake! I must remember to take some pictures of it when I come to see you this summer.

I hope your trunk was waiting for you when you arrived. And I hope you put everything away neatly the way you promised. Do you think you have enough blankets, Larry—or will you need more? You know it gets real cool at night, so cover up well. You don't want to get a cold and miss out on swimming!

My, I've been giving you a lot of advice, haven't I? And here you are a real big fellow now, perfectly capable of taking care of yourself. But mothers are silly that way. . . . You understand, don't you, Larry? Just have fun, my dear, and enjoy all the interesting camp activities, and come back to us all tanned and healthy.

Dad and I will probably come to see you in about two weeks. We'll bring Ginger along, because he's a very sad pup since you went away. He isn't living up to his name at all! He just mopes around, wandering in and out of your room looking for you. I can just imagine how excited he'll be when he sees you at camp!

Do you like your counselor? He seems to be very nice. Write and tell us about everything, Larry. You know how much your letters mean to us when you are away. Dad and I send you all our love!

Mother

Dear Tommy:

How are you getting along at camp? I hope you are having fun, and enjoying your friends and all the activities.

So you passed the "crib" test! That's fine, son. Now you'll be able to swim out in the lake. Your mother and I are very proud of you for learning to swim so quickly—and so well.

We miss you very much at home. But it is a good thing you are away, as it is stifling here and very unpleasant. We will come to see you next week end, and mother would like to know if there is anything you want us to bring along.

We are all fine. Your baby sister is getting fat and chubby, and very pretty. She keeps mother busy, which is a good thing—otherwise she'd miss you too much!

Next time you write, Tommy, tell us more about what you do at camp. Have you been on any hikes with your group? Are you learning how to play tennis? We enjoy hearing about all the interesting and exciting things that go to make up your day at camp.

So write again soon, son, and make it a real long letter next time!

Affectionately,
Dad

Dearest Gail:

You sound as though you are having a marvelous time at camp this summer. The picnic on Bald Moun-

tain must have been fun; and I'm sure the costume
dance on the lawn was enchanting. I wish I could have
seen it! You must have looked lovely in your Hawaiian
costume.

I had your snapshots developed and they turned out
very well. Your father says to tell you that you've improved a great deal since last summer. You get your
subjects in better focus now, and your pictures are
sharper. The views of the lake are really *beautiful;*
there's one especially good view of the camp taken
from the opposite shore. I like it so much I'm going to
have it enlarged; then if you want to, you can have
it framed for your bedroom.

As I mentioned in my last letter, I'm having your
room redecorated while you are away. Will you let
me know which of the enclosed samples of wallpaper
you like best? Only one wall will be papered (the one
behind your bed); the other walls will be painted to
match the background of the paper. Alice Harper just
had her bedroom done that way, and it looks very
attractive.

I'm very happy about my new rock garden. I wish
you could see it, Gail—it's so brilliant and colorful,
just like a painting. It's certainly worth the effort we
put into it this Spring. And the roses! They've *never*
been as beautiful as they are this year. I certainly get a
lot of joy out of the garden.

We had a letter from Jackie yesterday. He's learning
to swim and handle a canoe, and he's very thrilled
about it all. After those first few weeks of homesick-
ness, he seems to be developing into a fine little camper.
Your father and I are going to drive up to see him next
week end, and on the way back we'll stop off to see you.
Is there anything you'd like us to bring?

I know how busy you are every minute of the day,
Gail—but write to Jackie, won't you? Remember he's
just a little fellow, and this is the first time he's been
away from home.

I hope you will continue to have a wonderful time, dear. Give my regards to Miss Foster. Your father and I look forward to seeing you next week, and in the meantime we both send you our love.

Devotedly,
Mother

EXCERPTS FROM LETTERS TO CHILDREN
WRITTEN BY FAMOUS PEOPLE

Often it is interesting and helpful to read what others have written. We have included, therefore, the following ex erpts from letters to children, written by famous men and won en:

Your teacher informs me that you recited a lesson the first day you began very much to his satisfaction. I expect every letter from him will give me fresh proof of your progress; for I know you can do a great deal if you please, and I am sure that you have too much spirit not to exert yourself, that you may make us every day more and more proud of you.

Alexander Hamilton to his son Philip, age 9, away at school.

The object most interesting to me for the residue of my life will be to see you developing daily those principles of virtue and goodness which will make you valuable to others and happy in yourself, and acquiring those talents and that degree of science which will guard you at all times against ennui, the most dangerous poison of life. A mind always employed is always happy. This is the true secret, the grand recipe, for felicity. . . . Be good and be industrious, and you will be what I shall most love in the world. Adieu, my dear child.

Thomas Jefferson to his motherless 14-year-old daughter, Martha, in a convent near Paris.

Finish every day and be done with it. . . . You have done what you could; some blunders and absurdities no doubt crept in; forget them as soon as you can. Tomorrow is a new day.

> *Ralph Waldo Emerson to his young daughter at school.*

I must write a line to tell you how much I continue to love you. . . . I hope you continue fond of reading, and that you will make a wise choice in your books, on which your future character will much depend.

> *Hannah More to Edward Freeman, age 7, later one of England's greatest historians.*

Your letter, my dearest niece, with the one before it, came quite safely, for which I return many thanks and kisses. I rejoice too, dear Dolly, to see how well you write and express yourself, and am as proud of all your acquirements as if you were my own daughter.

> *Dolly Madison, to her beloved niece and namesake, age 16.*

Great learning and superior abilities, should you ever possess them, will be of little value and small estimation . . . unless virtue, honor, truth and integrity are added to them.

> *Abigail Adams to her 10-year-old son, John Quincy Adams, later the sixth President of the United States.*

It is very long since I have met with such an agreeable surprise as the sight of your letter, my kind young friend, afforded me. Such a nice letter as it is, too. And what a pretty hand you write. I congratulate you on this attainment with great pleasure, because I have so often felt the disadvantage of my own wretched hand-writing.

> *Mary Lamb to a favorite*
> *young friend, Barbara*
> *Betham, age 14.*

If anybody would make me the greatest king that ever lived, with palaces, and gardens, and fine dinners, and wine, and coaches, and beautiful clothes, and hundreds of servants, on condition that I would not read books —I would not be a king. I would rather be a poor man in a garret with plenty of books than a king who did not love reading.

> *Thomas Macaulay to his*
> *niece, Margaret Trevel-*
> *yan, age 7.*

I have not for a very long time been more pleased than I was this morning at receiving your letter. . . . Your letter was a very good one, and told us all that we liked to hear. It was well expressed and you must have taken some pains to write it.

> *Charles Darwin to his 12-*
> *year-old son, William, at*
> *Rugby.*

My own little darling! I found a nice letter of yours waiting for me here, and hope to have another by the next mail. You cannot think what pleasure they give me. They are just as I love to have you write, telling me what you have seen that amused you, and where you have been.

> *James Russell Lowell to his*
> *daughter, Mabel, age 7.*

Time flies. It is now thirteen years that you came into this world of trouble. I therefore can hardly venture to call you any longer a little Princess. . . . You must give your attention more and more to graver matters. By the dispensation of Providence, you are destined to fill a most eminent station; to fill it *well* must now become your study. A good heart and a trusty and honorable character are amongst the most indispensable qualifications for that position.

> *Leopold I of Belgium to his*
> *niece, Princess Victoria,*
> *later Queen of England.*

I put a New Testament among your books, for the very same reason and with the very same hopes that made me write an easy account of it for you when you were a little child: because it is the best book that ever was or will be known in the world, and because it teaches you the best lessons by which any human creature who tries to be truthful and faithful to duty can possibly be guided.

> *Charles Dickens to his son,*
> *Edward, when the young*
> *man left England to live*
> *in Australia.*

I am delighted to have you play football. I believe in rough, manly sports. But I do not believe in them if they degenerate into the sole end of any one's existence. I don't want you to sacrifice standing well in your studies . . . and I need not tell you that character counts for a great deal more than either intellect or body in winning success in life.

> *Theodore Roosevelt to his*
> *son, Ted, away at school.*

VACATION LETTERS TO THE
FOLKS BACK HOME

When you are traveling, or away on a vacation, write letters that give *interesting information* to the folks back home. Don't just fill your letter with a lot of rhetorical questions such as "How are you? What's new? Have you missed me?" Don't be content just to tell the folks you are "having a wonderful time."

Why are you having a wonderful time? What makes this vacation, or this trip abroad, or this visit with friends out of town, especially interesting and enjoyable? Tell your folks what you have done and seen. Write to them about the people you have met . . . and about the unusual, amusing or exciting things that have happened since you saw or wrote to them last. Share your pleasures and experiences, just as you would if you were back home telling them all about it.

If you are really serious about your correspondence, keep a scrapbook or diary. Take a few minutes each day to jot down the incidents, impressions and anecdotes you want to remember. Make a note of the exact names of places and personalities. You will then have a rich and accurate source of information from which to draw when you sit down to write.

Dear Rose:

I'm so sorry now that you decided not to come with me! Nassau is charming, and I know you would have *loved* it.

The flight from Detroit to Miami was *very bumpy*. We ran into a rainstorm about half an hour after taking off; and from then on it was rough flying almost all the way. I was airsick—for the first time!— and I can't say I enjoyed the sensation. But the flight from Miami to Nassau was smooth and pleasant, and I enjoyed it very much.

The hotel is beautiful, Rose. It's at the far end of the island, facing the sea—with a private beach and spacious grounds and gardens. There's just about every facility you can think of: tennis, golf, riding, archery, ping-pong! My room is small, but comfortable and attractive; and the important thing is that it faces the ocean. At night I can look out and see the reflection of the moon and stars on the water and the lights of ships far at sea.

Swimming is simply marvelous here! The water is brilliant and clear, and so nice and warm. I practically live in a bathing suit; and I'm as tanned as though I'd been in the sun for *weeks* instead of just a few days!

The Bahamas have a real South Sea atmosphere, Rose —with palms and tropical gardens and coral sands— and a wonderful climate. It's about like our June back home, only even more delightful. This would be the perfect place for mother and dad to spend the month of February, instead of always going back to Orlando. I think it would be an interesting change for them. And I *know* dad would enjoy the fishing; it's supposed to be just about the best in the world! Talk to them about it and see what they say. I could make all the arrangements for them while I'm here.

Some people at the hotel chartered a boat for next Saturday, for a day of fishing—and they invited me to go along. I'll probably be seasick, but I'm going anyway! It will give me a chance to see some of the other islands.

Remember how everybody said I'd be bored in Nassau, that there's nothing to do or see? Well, there's plenty to do—and plenty to see! Yesterday there were professional tennis matches at the hotel, and an exhibition of high diving. The day before there was a yacht regatta, conducted by the two yacht clubs. It was a colorful and fascinating sight, and I took a lot of movies to show when I get home. There's even a race track here, for those who are interested. But don't worry, Rose! I can't afford to lose any money so I won't place any bets.

I met a very interesting Englishman the first day I arrived, and he's been most attentive ever since. His name is Henry Ivers, and he's in the export business. He has been here many times, and he knows the islands well, so I ask him everything I want to know!

By the way, there's a couple here from Cleveland Heights. They are practically nextdoor neighbors of the Falgers, and they remember Bill when he was a little boy. Isn't that fantastic! Be sure and tell Bill about it. Their name is Kimball, and he's a photographer. They're a charming couple; and not only do I enjoy their company, but I'm getting some expert advice on how to make good pictures.

I wish you'd give some thought to joining me here for a couple of weeks, Rose. The baby would be perfectly safe with mother, and you know how she *adores* taking care of her. What do you say? You really need a rest . . . and we could have such fun together. I'll be waiting impatiently for your answer, and I hope it's "yes!"

With Love,
Anne

From a Bride on Her Honeymoon to Her Parents

Dear Mother and Dad:

I wish you could see Boca Raton! It is fabulously beautiful. Tom and I just couldn't have picked a more perfect place for our honeymoon! We know now why it is called a "Secret Paradise."

I'm so happy, darlings! Tom is a wonderful, *wonderful* husband. I know that the magic and beauty of this past week, our first week together, will always remain with me. It can never fade, not if I live to be a hundred!

Does that sound sentimental? Well, I *am* sentimental today. It's our anniversary, you know. Tom and I have been married exactly one whole week!

Wasn't the wedding beautiful? Thank you, mother and dad. . . . I'll never forget it! It's the kind of wedding I always dreamed about, ever since I was a little girl. You looked *lovely*, mother! I do hope the pictures turn out well.

I know you both like guava jelly, so we sent you a big jar of it yesterday—right from the hotel. I hope it arrives safely and that you enjoy it.

There's a linen shop here and we bought ourselves a lovely dinner cloth. . . . It's such fun buying things together for our own home! Tom and I are thrilled with all the marvelous wedding gifts we got. I've been trying to write notes of thanks for some of the things that came just before we left; but it's no use. Boca Raton is so enchanting, and there's so much to see and do and enjoy, that I can't concentrate on *anything* but having fun and being happy!

I'm not going to try to describe Boca Raton because I know I can't do justice to it. I'm enclosing some cards instead. They show the magnificent fountain and gardens in front of the hotel—the famous Cloister Lounge—the swimming pool and the patio—the golf course and Cabana Club. Tom is taking a lot of pictures to show you when we get back. There was a professional tennis match yesterday between Vincent Pritchard and William Trask, and Tom took movies of it. He also took movies of Arthur Murray and one of his instructors doing the rumba.

I'll write again in a few days. My husband—your nice new son-in-law—sends his love. Write to us soon!

> Devotedly,
> Lenore

Letter to a Relative Who Has Written after a Long Silence

If you have received a letter from someone who has not written in a long, long time . . . and if you missed hearing from that person . . . say so simply and frankly, but don't scold. Instead of, "Why didn't you write sooner? I really should be very angry at you!"—try to say it in a way that's complimentary.

Dear Kathleen:

How I've missed hearing from you! Your letters are always so interesting and full of news. Please don't wait so long before writing again!

I'm delighted to hear about Bob. You must be very proud of him. Tell him that Fred and I wish him the best of luck, and hope that this is just a start . . . that he will have one big success after another.

Your baby sounds adorable! Is he really a year old already? My, how the time flies! I wish we didn't live so far from each other, Kathleen. I'd love to see your baby; and I certainly wish we could see more of you and Bob! Remember the good times we used to have when you lived in Middletown?

I expect to be at Vaughan's on Tuesday and I'll send you the seeds you want. It sounds as though you are going in for gardening in a big way this Spring!

By the way did you hear about the Hansens? They sold their house in Middletown and bought a big farm near Pine Ridge. They bought themselves a *headache,* if you ask me! Frank is no farmer, and Millie is certainly not the rugged type. Everybody thinks it's a big mistake; but you know Frank Hansen when he gets his mind set on something!

I see Janet occasionally. She comes to Middletown to visit her mother. But I almost never see Emily any more. The last I heard of her she was studying music in Philadelphia. Could be! You never know where Emily is going to turn up next.

That about winds up the news from this end, Kathleen. It was grand hearing from you, and I'll be looking for another letter before long. Fred sends his best to you and Bob.

Affectionately,
Arlene

Letter to a Relative Who Has Asked for Advice

When a relative writes and asks for advice, give it honestly and sincerely—and to the best of your ability. Make it the subject of your entire letter. Don't cloud the issue by writing about a number of other matters.

Dear Joe:

You asked for my advice and I am going to give it to you: *This is not the time to start a new business.* I think you should wait until conditions are better, until the downward spiral is stopped and the prospect for small new businesses is more promising.

I'd like to quote to you from an editorial in this morning's *Wall Street Journal*. It says: "The death rate among businesses this year will climb like a kite in a spanking spring breeze! . . . Only a miracle can pull a number of new small businesses, particularly retail establishments, through the new year without a collapse."

So there's the answer to your question, Joe. You'd be taking a big chance; and I don't think you have the right to take that chance with Martha seriously ill and young Joe about ready for college.

Now I'm not saying you should stay in the groove indefinitely. I don't think any man should let himself get into a rut of living or thinking. I believe in change, and I understand fully the impulse that makes you want to strike out against regimentation and find new interest and adventure in a business of your own.

But this just isn't the time for it, Joe! So I say *wait* . . . perhaps six months, or a year, or maybe even longer. Be patient, and make your plans; then when the time comes you'll be ready. And I'll be ready then, too, Joe—to help you financially and in any other way I can.

If you want to talk this over more fully, I'll be glad to meet you for lunch some day next week. But I strongly advise against trying to buck the trend.

Agnes and I send affectionate greetings to all the family. We hope Martha will soon be well and strong again.

Sincerely,
Don

4

Love Letters

There are few letters more eagerly awaited, more joyously re-ceived, than love letters. They banish lonely hours, reassure lonely hearts. They keep the precious glow alive, and sustain de-votion when loved ones are apart.

"What cannot letters inspire?" asks Heloise of Abelard in one of the most passionate and enduring of all the love letters of history. "They have souls; they can speak; they have in them all that force which expresses the transports of the heart; they have all the fire of our passions, they can raise them as much as if the persons themselves were present; they have all the tenderness and the delicacy of speech, and sometimes even a boldness of expression beyond it."

The most essential quality of a love letter is *sincerity*. And to be sincere, it must come from the heart, spontaneously. It must be a simple and unaffected expression of your feelings. It may be impulsive, restrained, romantic, gay, sad, impassioned, boast-ful, pleading, jubilant or despairing. It may be any or all of these. But whatever else it is or is not, *it must be sincere*. It must ring true.

Therefore love letters should follow no set rules. They should be unstudied and unstilted. They should be fresh and alive. So write what you truly think and feel; write what you want to say . . . what you want your loved one to know . . . not in flowery or poetic language, but in simple words that come from the heart.

Don't be ashamed of your sentiments when you write a love letter. Don't be embarrassed or constrained by your feelings. *Write as the heart dictates.*

Just be careful not to write anything that can be misunderstood or misconstrued. And never be guilty of saying anything in a love letter that you would be mortified to have others see . . . anything that's shocking or offensive. There need be no sacrifice of good taste to achieve sincerity and an honest expression of your deepest feelings and emotions.

EXAMPLES OF LOVE LETTERS

FROM WOMEN TO MEN

My darling:

I have just been talking with you on the telephone. Do you always feel elated and inspired after we have talked together? *I* do! Only tonight I feel lonely, too . . . and I wish with all my heart you were here beside me, instead of in Baltimore!

Sweetheart, I hope it won't be long before you are permanently located in New York. Please talk to Mr. Harris again—*soon*. Just think, darling! If you were transferred to the New York office we could see each other all the time, every day—instead of just once every two weeks!

Your letters are wonderful. They make me so happy. I know you couldn't write as you do unless you really and truly loved me. And that's all 1 want to know . . . that's all that means *anything* to me now.

I'm glad you can come on Friday next week instead of Saturday. I'll meet you at the station, as usual. My mother wants us to have Sunday dinner at home this time, Jack; do you mind? She says she hardly ever gets to see you—that in fact she hardly *knows* you—and that she just won't have her daughter marrying a complete stranger! I think she has a point there, young man! So let's not plan anything special for Sunday. We'll have dinner with the folks, and then go for a long walk or a drive. There are so many things I'd like to talk over with you. . . . I always forget half the things I want to say when we're talking on the phone!

But what I want to say most of all, darling, is that I *adore* you, and I miss you with all my heart! I'll be counting the hours until you come to New York. *Write soon,* and tell me again what I love to hear—that you'll love me for ever and ever!

> Your devoted,
> Nancy

Dearest Tom:

It's wonderful to get a nice long letter from you, first thing every morning. It starts my day right! Thank you, darling. . . . Did anyone ever tell you that you're a pretty grand person?

Your letter this morning is sweet. But don't be jealous, dear! You have no reason to be. I love only you— and shall never love anyone else, *ever!*

My sister is having an anniversary party next Saturday and she wants us to come. I told her you had tickets for the ice show, but she was so disappointed that I promised I'd at least *ask* if you wanted to return them and go to her party instead. Do you, dear? Now don't say "yes" unless you really want to! It doesn't matter to me—I'll be happy and content either way, as long as I'm with you.

There I go talking in song titles again! *"As long as I'm with you. . . ."* Remember? It was on the air the other night, and we listened to it together. I think it's a lovely song, and the words sound almost as though they were written for us. I feel as though *I* could write the lyrics for a love song, Tom—I'm so thrilled and happy, and so "filled with dreams for two!"

But now you'll think I'm being sentimental and silly. . . . Well, maybe I am, darling! That's what being in love with you does to me.

Are you still so busy, dear? You didn't say in your letter whether you are still working late, like last week.

You must be glad that Keenan case is settled at last. It certainly dragged on and on and *on!*

I have a new dress for Saturday night. It's red, and I bought it especially for you! Let me know about the party soon, Tom, so I can tell my sister whether or not we'll be there.

Good-by now, darling. . . . Don't ever stop loving me!

Devotedly,
Lou

Paul, darling:

Do you know what I've been doing all evening? I've been looking at our wedding gifts, and thinking what a lovely home we are going to have . . . and how unbelievably, outrageously *happy* I am!

Do you really love me, darling? I wonder how many millions of times that question has been asked! But there is just no other way to say it: *Do you love me?*

You have captured my heart completely, Paul— you know that, don't you? There will never be room in it for anyone but you. How happy we'll be when we're together, sweetheart—in our very own home— for always!

There! You see. . . . You are marrying an incorrigible romantic. You'll have to keep assuring me endlessly of your love, all through the years. And you'll have to whisper "sweet nothings" in my ear even when we're old and gray. Do you mind?

But cheer up! I have a practical side, too. For example, I am keeping a nice neat little record of all the gifts we have received and who sent them. I'll start writing thank-you notes next week on the nights you are busy.

By the way, we got a beautiful gift from the Warrens yesterday. It's a polished wood salad bowl with a silver base, and a serving fork and spoon to go with it. Now we'll be able to serve salads in the *grand* manner!

What time will you be here on Saturday, Paul? Mother invited some friends for cocktails at five, and she would like you to be here if you can manage it. If not, we'll expect you for dinner at about eight. There won't be any guests; just the family. But my sister and her husband are coming in later, and we can play some bridge after we get through addressing the announcements.

Goodnight, my dear. I hope there will be a long, long letter from you in the morning. Nobody—but *nobody!*—writes such beautiful letters as you.

With all my love,
Betty

Dear Bob:

One of these days I'm going to write a letter with only three words on it: *"I love you!"* But I'm going to repeat those three words over and over again, a thousand times! Then maybe you'll stop writing such silly letters. . . .

Thanks for the perfume, darling. You really shouldn't keep sending me gifts all the time. It's less than a month since you sent me those lovely handkerchiefs. No wonder the family says you're spoiling me!

But I *like* being spoiled, Bob! I like getting such beautiful letters . . . and knowing you love me . . . and being engaged. . . .

I'm even beginning to practice saying, "Mrs. Creighton"—just to get used to the sound of it! *"Mrs. Robert Creighton."* It's a pretty name, darling. I love it—and I love *you.* (There! I said it again. Now are you satisfied?)

This has been a hectic week at the office. I can't ever remember being so busy! But Mr. Maxon is leaving for Washington in the morning, and that will give me a chance to relax a little . . . and get caught up on my regular work. There are always so many meetings and conferences when he's in town, and so much extra work to do.

What have you decided about Chalmers Rand, Bob? Are you going to make the change, or stay where you are? Dad thinks you'd be foolish to turn it down— not because it means more money, but because it's a much bigger opportunity. Dad does business with Chalmers Rand, and he says it's a swell outfit. But you know best, Bob. . . . Whatever you do is okay with me.

I'm looking forward to the week end, dear. The plans for Saturday sound marvelous! But are you sure you want to take that long drive out to your sister's place on Sunday? You know you'd still have a long trip back to Boston in the evening . . . and I think that's far too much driving for one day. You'd be exhausted . . . and I'd worry about you falling asleep at the wheel. . . . Why don't we plan to go there some Saturday instead? Then you can stay at my house overnight, rest up the next day, and go back to Boston in the evening. Doesn't that sound more sensible?

This has turned out to be a much longer letter than I expected. All I started out to say was that I love you, darling—and thanks for the perfume—and won't it be wonderful when we're married!

                                                      Edna

My darling:

Thanks for your beautiful, *beautiful* letter! I, too, shall always be in love with you—if we live to be a hundred!

Mother and I were out shopping all day yesterday; that's why I wasn't home when you called. After all, a girl can't get married without a trousseau! I bought some gorgeous things, dear; just wait until you see them. And mother bought us an exquisite dinner cloth with 12 napkins to match! She is going to monogram them for us. Isn't she *sweet?*

My sister Joyce telephoned this morning. She's thrilled about being maid of honor. She's going to wear pink—she looks lovely in it with her blond hair. I'm going to ask the bridesmaids to wear a delicate shade of blue. Don't you think that will be pretty?

I know you hate all this "pomp and ceremony" as you call it . . . but sweetheart, a girl's wedding day is the most important day of her life! I want *our* wedding to be perfect in every way—I want it to be *beautiful*—so that we'll always recall it with pleasure and pride.

Sea Isle sounds wonderful—but New Orleans enchants me, too! *You* decide, dearest. You've been to both places and you know more about them than I do.

I'll expect you early on Saturday. There are a *million* things to talk about! Be sure to bring your list, sweetheart; we must send out the invitations by the middle of next week at the latest.

I adore you, darling—and I'm the happiest girl in the world! Take good care of yourself and don't work too hard. Love and kisses,

Elaine

Dear Fred:

It's easy to say I forgive you. The fault was as much mine as yours. Sometimes I'm too quick to take offense where none was intended. Dad's always telling me I'm too sensitive, only *he* calls it "thin-skinned!" He says it's a trait I must learn to control or I'll never be happy. I guess he's right. . . .

Of course I love you, Fred! And not "just a little." I love you *deeply,* and with all my heart. I'm sure you must know that, dear. I was miserable after our quarrel, and I've been longing all week to see you and straighten things out.

Wouldn't you like to come here for dinner on Sunday instead of going out somewhere? The folks are going to a church bazaar, and we'd have a nice long afternoon to talk and listen to records. I'd enjoy that, Fred. . . . We could go out somewhere in the evening if you want to.

I'll be waiting for your call on Friday at the usual time. I'm so glad you wrote, darling. Don't ever stop loving me!

Kate

Dearest:

I'm delighted to hear you had such a successful meeting in Chicago. I knew they'd like your plans for the new factory; they looked wonderful to me. But of course *everything* you do looks wonderful to me, sweetheart!

You've been an angel this week; you've written practically every day. I'd be disappointed now if you *didn't* write every day when you're out of town. See how you've spoiled me!

But I'm disappointed anyway, darling, by the news in your last letter. Must you really go to Los Angeles? Couldn't Mr. Kennedy come to New York to discuss his old stadium? I had been counting on you being home for the dance at Clearview on the twelfth. Oh, well . . . that's what I get for marrying "the brilliant and extremely competent young Mr. Harkness." That's what they called you in this morning's *Tribune*. I'm enclosing a clipping of the article as I thought you might enjoy reading it. Have I mentioned lately that I'm very proud of you, dear, and that I think you are the best architect in the country (to say nothing of the most *precious* husband in all the world!).

When are you going to be able to stay home long enough to become acquainted with your young son?

He's so sweet, dear! I don't know what I'd do without him, now that you are away so much. I took him to the doctor for his regular periodic checkup, and he's fine. Nothing wrong with him—except that he misses his daddy.

Hurry back to us darling. We love you so!

Lillian

Examples of Letters
from Men to Women

Darling Peggy:

You can't imagine how happy I was last night! It seemed as though you were closer to me than ever before. Maybe I'm wrong. Maybe it was just my imagination. But after I left you, I just walked and walked . . . as in a dream . . . thinking of all we said to each other, and the plans we made. . . .

I think you are a wonderful girl, Peggy. And I'm very much in love with you. I'm always happy when I'm with you, but last night I was happier than ever! I felt for the first time that you cared for me, too.

Do you, Peggy darling? Or were you just being kind? Oh Peggy, sweetheart, I just couldn't bear it if you didn't love me, you mean so much to me now!

Next week will be a difficult one for me—four full days of exams. But I'm not worried. I know I'll pass them all with flying colors, now that I'm happy.

Don't forget about the game on Saturday, sweetheart. I'll call for you about one. Pete and Marge are going, and if you want to we can go in Pete's car. Otherwise I'll see if I can borrow Dad's car for the day. Wear that cute red jacket, Peggy—you look adorable in it!

Write to me soon, darling—one of your sweet letters that always makes me so happy. I send you all my love!

Jim

Dearest Sally:

It's June first. That means our wedding is only three weeks away! I'm so happy, I just can't think of anything else.

Isn't it marvelous, my sweet, that with all the millions and millions of people in the world, you and I should have met . . . and fallen in love . . . and now we'll soon be married! Or do you think it was all planned that way, long ago—perhaps even before we were born?

Anyway, precious, I think I'm the luckiest man in the world! I'm going to devote my life to making you happy. *I promise!*

Darling, we really should decide between Lake George and Lake Placid right away—otherwise we're likely to spend our honeymoon in little old New York! I'm enclosing the booklets you asked me to send. Will you look them over right away, and decide which it will be? Then let me know and I'll wire for reservations. Phone me as soon as you can, pet—we should have attended to this long ago! But there's always my brother's hunting lodge in Canada, if we can't get reservations elsewhere. Bob's been asking me for weeks if we wouldn't like to use it for our honeymoon.

I'll help you address the announcements this week end. Don't try and do them all by yourself. As for the notes of thanks—just write as many as you can, Sally. The rest can wait until we get back and are in our own home.

"Our own home. . . ." Doesn't that sound wonderful, sweetheart! I wonder if you are as happy as I am. I know we're going to have a marvelous life together, Sally. . . . I love you more than I ever dreamed it would be possible to love anyone!

Love me too, precious! Don't ever *stop* loving me! You are the most important thing in life to me now— you know that, don't you?

All my love and a million kisses!

                                        Don

Dear Jane:

How does a matter-of-fact professor of mathematics *like me* tell a wonderful girl *like you* that she's everything he ever dreamed about? How does he tell her that she's beautiful, charming and precious—that she's everything good and fine—and that he loves her very, very much?

Is there some special language of love, my dear? If there is, I'm not familiar with it. I have no eloquence at my command. I know only that you have brought new meaning into my life, and that my every dream and thought and hope of the future is now inescapably bound up in you.

My dear, we have known each other a very short time—as time is measured. It is less than six months since I met you at the faculty tea and your father introduced us. But it seems to me now as though I must have known you always—as though there were never a time when your lovely image was not in my heart and mind.

What I'm trying to say—very clumsily, I think—is that I love you. I wish I could say it more romantically; but no one, dear Jane, could say it with deeper feeling nor mean it more sincerely.

I love you . . . and I hope with all my heart that you return the feeling! I think you do; if I didn't think so, I wouldn't have had the courage to write this letter. Our companionship these past weeks, and the many long and intimate talks we have had, lead me to hope and believe you care as I do. . . .

I am sending you a ring that belonged to my mother. Wear it when I meet you next Sunday, Jane. It will be all the answer I need, the answer I'm longing for. But if you return it, I'll understand; and I'll try not to unburden my heart to you again.

Either way, my dear—I love you and always will.

Joel

Betty, darling:

I do not blame you for writing as you did. I would not blame you if you never saw me again.

But sweetheart, I didn't mean what I said! You know that. You *must* know how I love you.

Please write and say you forgive me, Betty. I'll be miserable until I know. My life would be less than nothing without your love. . . .

Darling, did you ever read the love letters that Napoleon wrote to Josephine? I wish I could write like that! In one of his letters he says: "To love you alone, to make you happy, to do nothing which would contradict your wishes, this is my destiny and the aim of my life."

That expresses my feelings toward you exactly, Betty dear. I want to devote my life to you—and to make you happy.

So write soon, sweetheart, and say you forgive me —and that you love me just a little.

                                        Steve

Dearest:

Only a few more days, and I'll be home! I'm counting the hours, my sweet, and I hope they *fly*. Every hour is an eternity when I'm away from you. I think there ought to be a law against sending a man away from his wife for weeks at a time!

This has been a very successful trip, darling. I signed up more than fifty new dealers in the Chicago area alone. Peterson is going to be very pleased when he sees my report.

But *I'll* be very pleased when I'm *home!* That's all I can think of right now. It seems like months since I saw you, sweetheart. Does it seem like that to you, too? Or have you been so busy with your music that you haven't even missed me? See—I love you so much I'm even jealous of your music!

I bought you something very nice in Chicago, but I'm not going to tell you what it is. I'll give you a hint, though. It's something to wear, and it's something you have wanted for a long time. . . .

I'll probably leave here on Thursday—or Friday at the very latest. I'll wire when I know what plane I'm taking. Don't have any guests, precious. I want to have dinner with you alone the first night I'm home.

Do you love me? More than anyone?

Devotedly,
Chris

Excerpts from the Love Letters
of Famous Men and Women

I am very uneasy, my love, at receiving no news of you; write me quickly four pages—pages full of agreeable things which shall fill my heart with the pleasantest feelings. I hope before long to crush you in my arms and cover you with a million kisses.

Bonaparte to Josephine

Since I left you I have been sad all the time. . . . Ah, when shall I be able to pass every minute near you, with nothing to do but love you; and nothing to think of but the pleasure of telling you—and of proving it?

Bonaparte to Josephine

My last letter to you, my dear love, has informed you that I arrived safely in this country. . . . One might suppose that I am very happy. But *you* are not with me . . . and there is no happiness for me far from you.

Lafayette to his wife

My thoughts go out to you, my Immortal Beloved. . . . Oh, God! Why is it necessary to part from one whom one so loves! Your love makes me at once the

happiest and the unhappiest of men. . . . My life, my
all, continue to love me!

Beethoven to his sweetheart

Love me, dear, as I shall forever love you! That is all
I ask from life. But don't promise to, unless you can
keep your word. Your own welfare is far more precious to me than my own.

Adrienne Lecouvreur to Clavel

I am a prisoner here in the name of the King; they
can take my life, but not the love that I feel for
you. . . . No, nothing has the power to part me
from you! Our love will last as long as our lives.

Voltaire to Olympe Dunoyer

Adèle, my adorable and adored Adèle! I have been
asking myself every moment if such happiness is not
a dream. . . . At last you are mine! Soon—in a few
months, perhaps, my angel will sleep in my arms, will
awaken in my arms. . . . My Adèle!

Victor Hugo to Adèle Foucher

Goodbye, my life, my soul, my heaven on earth! I
leave you to good friends. . . . Goodbye, Lucile—
my Lucile. . . . The shores of life recede from me. I
see you still, Lucile, my beloved. My bound hands
embrace you, and my head as it falls rests its dying
eyes upon you.

.Camille Desmoulins to his wife
(on the eve of his execution)

How is it that I have deserved thee; deserved a purer
and nobler heart than falls to the lot of millions? I
swear I will love thee with my whole heart, and
think my life well spent if it can make thine happy.
. . . Oh, my darling! I will always love thee.

Thomas Carlyle to Jane Welsh

I always think of you and I have a thousand things
to say to you. The most important . . . is that *I love
you to distraction, my dear wife!*

Heinrich Heine to his wife

I have no limit now to my love. . . . You have
ravished me away by a power I cannot resist. My love
is selfish. I cannot breathe without you.

John Keats to Fanny Brawne

How I love you! Rising in the morning, my first
thought is of you, and all day I am conscious that you
are near; your presence seems to inhabit all the air
about me . . . your nearness is a never-ending delight!

Nadejda von Meck to Tchaikovsky

Is it necessary to tell you that I love you with all my
heart? Never before have I met a soul so closely re-
lated to mine or one that so sensitively responded to
my every thought, every heart beat. Your friendship
has become the cornerstone of my existence.

Tchaikovsky to Nadejda von Meck

Paris is a morgue without you. Before I knew you, it
was Paris, and I thought it heaven; but now it is a vast
desert of desolation and loneliness. It is like the face
of a clock, bereft of its hands.

Sarah Bernhardt to Victorien Sardou

Jane Welsh loved Thomas Carlyle devotedly . . . and was
forever begging assurance that he was her "own true and affectionate husband." The following was written in a passion of
relief upon receiving a letter and gift from him on her birthday,
after thinking he had forgotten the occasion:

Seaforth, Tuesday, July 14, 1846

Oh! my dear husband. Not a line from you on my
birthday, the postmistress averred! I did not burst out
crying, did not faint—did not do anything absurd, so
far as I know; but I walked back again, without speaking a word; and with such a tumult of wretchedness
in my heart as you, who know me, can conceive. And
then I shut myself in my own room to fancy everything that was most tormenting. . . .

And just when I was at my wit's end, I heard Julia crying out through the house: "Mrs. Carlyle, Mrs. Carlyle! Are you there? Here is a letter for you."

And so there was after all! The postmistress had overlooked it, and given it to Robert, when he went afterwards, not knowing that we had been. I wonder what love-letter was ever received with such thankfulness! Oh, my dear! I am not fit for living in the world with this organization. I am as much broken to pieces by that little accident as if I had come through an attack of cholera or typhus fever. I cannot even steady my hand to write decently. But I felt an irresistible need of thanking you, by return of post. Yes, I have kissed the dear little card-case; and now I will lie down awhile, and try to get some sleep. At least, to quiet myself. I will try to believe—oh, why cannot I believe it, once for all—that with all my faults and follies, I am "dearer to you than any earthly creature."

Your own,
J. C.

My dearest beloved Emma, dear friend of my bosom. The signal has been made that the Enemy's Combined Fleet are coming out of Port. We have very little wind, so that I have no hopes of seeing them before to-morrow. May the God of Battles crown my endeavours with success; at all events, I will take care that my name shall ever be most dear to you and Horatia, both of whom I love as much as my own life. And as my last writing before the Battle will be to you, so I hope in God that I shall live to finish my letter after the Battle. May Heaven bless you!

Lord Nelson to Lady Hamilton
(before the Battle of Trafalgar)

My own love: I do not know by what compulsion I am to answer you, but your porter says I must, so I do. By a miracle I saved your five pounds and I will bring it. I hope, indeed, oh my loved Shelley, we shall indeed be happy. I meet you at three and bring heaps of Skinner street news. Heaven bless my love and take care of him!

Mary Godwin to Percy Bysshe Shelley
(a few hours before eloping with him)

POSTSCRIPT ON
PERSONAL LETTER WRITING

When you are writing to someone who is far from home, someone who is perhaps lonely and homesick, be sure it is a *happy* letter, a gay and cheerful letter. Guard against any thoughtless little undercurrents of discontent or complaint which may creep in. Disregard your own feelings, and think only of the person who is to receive your letter.

In this connection, I ask you to read the following short story. It will put you in the right mood for writing letters to loved ones far from home.

LETTER TO A SOLDIER

*By Latham Ovens**

She dipped her pen in the blue-gray ink. It reminded her of the blue-gray lights that danced in his eyes when he smiled. It had been like that since he went away. Little things, keeping him with her, making his absence seem like a dream.

Quickly, eagerly, she dipped her pen again and wrote: "My Dearest." But she couldn't go on from there. Words that had tumbled into her mind to say to him wouldn't tumble out again onto the paper before her.

She pressed her lips together in a tight little line. This would never do. She wasn't much of a writer; but then, he knew that. He wouldn't expect a masterpiece of literature in her letter. He'd want her to set things down just as she'd say them if he were here.

If he were here!

---

* Reprinted through courtesy of the author.

She shut her eyes as if to close out the thought. But it did no good. Closing her eyes just brought the memory of him into sharper focus. She could see the familiar boyish determination in his face, feel his strong arms around her. She opened her eyes quickly then, to blot the image out.

She'd write her letter—tell him of the awful emptiness of missing him. She'd write that she was sick with longing. She'd tell him that he must come back—leave everything and come straight back to her.

She had tried to keep him from going to the war at first. And he had listened to her, and agreed with her, and promised that he would never leave. And they'd closed their eyes and their ears to the war. And they'd tried to live in the little world that was encircled by each other's arms.

But it didn't work. She had known it wouldn't.

It wasn't anything he'd said, of course. But his arms were a little less tight when he held her; and his kisses were less strong and impulsive; and some of the light had been dimmed in his blue-gray eyes.

So she'd sent him off to war, and her heart went with him.

But she mustn't write of this in her letter. No. She must tell him only she was well, and keeping very busy, and she missed him very much.

Then tell him, quickly, that she knew it wouldn't be much longer before they'd be together again. Soon, the war won, he'd be coming back to her again. Tell him that. Tell him she was *sure* of that!

She got that much down on the paper, her pen racing across its surface, trying to keep up with the thoughts that came tumbling from her mind in quick confusion.

Yes, these were the things that she must tell him. The well chosen, carefully censored words in her mind. Not the little, secret, hidden words that filled her heart.

Don't tell him of the night hours spent lying across her bed, looking out her window to where the moonlight cut a bright silver path across the lawn. Don't remind him of how they used to walk that path together, down to the river's edge, with nothing to break the silence of their contentment but the gentle *lap-lap* of the water against the bank.

No, don't tell him that. Tell him, instead, she was feeling well, and keeping busy. And tell him, carefully, that she missed him very much.

Tell him only the things that won't worry or distract him. A soldier has a job to do. A big job. A brave job. He'd do it well, she knew. She mustn't intrude her loneliness to take his mind off that.

She mustn't let him guess the unhappy, bitter ache that crept up into her throat, and tightened there, each day that passed without a word from him. She must tell herself, as she had told herself so many times, to be patient. She must remember this is war. Remember a soldier has so many things to do. Keep in mind the distance and uncertainty of mails. *But oh, dear God, please let him write tonight!*

The pen dipped into the blue-gray ink, then hesitated just above the paper. She gripped it hard between her fingers to keep it from moving recklessly across the page, recording all the things it mustn't say.

Guiding the pen in slender, careful strokes, she told him first about the weather. About how it had rained so hard every one thought the fields were ruined. About how the sun came out afterward, in time to save the fields, and the crops this year were better than they'd ever been.

She told him about the family, and about his brother. She told him the house and the long green lawn and the river were all very much as they had been. They hadn't changed a bit.

She wanted to ask him if he had changed.

She wanted to ask if the war and the battles, and the sting of defeat and the glory of victory, had made any change in him. In her heart she knew they must have. And she wondered if every woman worried this way about her man at war. She wanted to ask him if soldiers worried like that, too, about their womenfolk at home. But she guessed they hadn't time.

She couldn't very well tell him about her prayer— the one that she whispered softly into her pillow each night: *"Dear God, please take Your very best care of him. Don't let them harm him. Don't let them change him in any way. Give him the strength and courage to do what it is his duty to do. Then please, dear God, bring him safely back to me!"*

This was the sort of thing you could whisper into your pillow. Something personal, between you and God. But you couldn't write it down in a letter. Not even in a letter to a soldier. Not even in a letter to him.

And all the while she was thinking this her pen was writing safer things. Telling him how the flowers in the garden were in bloom again. How the tall grass out near the stables had been cut and trimmed. How the horses all looked well this year.

And having told him all this, she signed the letter, the pen moving easily across the bottom of the page: "Your affectionate wife, Martha."

Then she folded her letter into an envelope and sealed it down firmly with a bit of sealing wax dipped in the candle's flame. And across the front, in big bold letters, she addressed it:

General George Washington
Headquarters of the Continental Army,
Valley Forge, Pennsylvania.

Book IV

*Your Business
and
Club Correspondence*

I

The General Rules of
Business Correspondence

A very large part of the business of the world is conducted by means of correspondence. Therefore it is extremely important to be able to write good business letters—letters that represent one's self and one's firm to best advantage.

No intelligent, forward-thinking business man would long tolerate a rude, careless or untidy salesman or representative. Yet thousands of letters go out every day that reflect discredit upon the firm they represent, letters that antagonize as surely as an offensive or bad-mannered individual. Such letters can do more harm than good, for often they destroy the very confidence and good will they seek to establish and maintain.

Before all else, therefore, consider the physical aspects of your business correspondence. Take pride in the letters you send out, just as you take pride in your own appearance. Sign and send out only letters that are well typed, well spaced, faultlessly neat and inviting to the eye . . . *letters that make a good first impression.* Here are the essential qualities that go to make up an attractive, well-groomed business letter:

1. *Good Quality Stationery*

It is advisable to use the best quality of paper you can for business correspondence. Single sheets of plain white bond paper are the best, unruled, with the letterhead printed or engraved in black. The most convenient size, and the size most generally used, is 8 1/2 x 11 inches—though some firms now use 7 1/4 x 10 1/2 inch paper for general correspondence.

The letterhead should contain the name of the firm, the

address, and the nature of the business (unless the name itself gives that information). Telephone numbers, cable addresses, branch addresses and other such data may be included in the letterhead; but there should be no ornate advertising material on letterheads used for general correspondence.

Envelopes, of course, should match the letterhead in quality and weight; and any printing or engraving that appears on the envelope should conform with that on the letter sheet. Standard size envelopes are 6 1/2 or 6 3/4 x 3 1/2 inches. The large official or legal size envelope is 10 x 4 1/2 inches.

Quality and dignity should be the distinguishing characteristics of your business stationery. Never use loud, effeminate, highly tinted, bizarre, odd-shaped or in any way unconventional stationery for the general run of routine business letters. Such stationery is an affectation and in bad taste . . . more likely to antagonize the reader than to win his confidence and respect.

2. *Neat Typing*

All business correspondence should be typed, and at least one carbon copy made and kept on file. Whether you type the letters yourself or have them typed for you, be sure they are faultlessly neat and clean—without smudges, finger marks or erasures— otherwise they will not represent you to best advantage. Never be guilty of sending out over your signature a letter that is soiled, creased or torn, or that is in any way marred or unsightly. Avoid worn typewriter ribbons, as they produce an uneven effect that is certainly not appealing to the eye. And always keep the type of your machine shining bright and clean; for blurred type is not only difficult to read, but is very likely to smudge and spoil the appearance of your letter.

3. *Even Spacing*

No letter can look attractive if it is carelessly spaced and arranged. Whether long or short, your business letter should present an even, well-balanced appearance—neither crowded at the top of the page nor sitting lopsidedly on one side of it.

Try to estimate the length of your letter and visualize its position on the page *before you begin to type it*. Then plan your margins accordingly, so that they provide an even frame or setting for your letter . . . making it look well placed and properly balanced on the page.

Bear in mind that wide margins make your letter more readable and inviting; so if your letter is a very long one, plan on using *two* sheets instead of crowding it all on one. The second sheet should be of the same size and quality as the first, but without the letterhead. When such additional sheets are used for a letter, they should be numbered at the top, either in the center of the page or in the right-hand corner. But don't use an additional sheet for only one or two concluding lines of a letter; in that case it's better to try and get it all on the preceding page. Never continue a business letter on the *back* of the sheet, using both sides of the letterhead.

Most business letters are single-spaced, with double spaces between the paragraphs. However very short letters look better when they are double-spaced, with either double or triple spaces between the paragraphs. The paragraphs may be indented or not, as preferred. But if they are indented, they should all line up exactly the same distance from the margin. Don't start one paragraph a half-inch from the margin, another an inch or more from the margin—as that gives your letter a careless and untidy appearance.

4. Short Paragraphs

All letters—but especially business letters—should look easy to read and inviting to the eye. As long wordy blocks of type are anything but inviting, make an effort to keep your sentences and paragraphs *short*. Use a new paragraph for each new thought or idea, and express that thought as simply and briefly as you can.

In business letter composition, "Every sentence and every paragraph should be made to *achieve* something. There can be no accidental notes, as in music. There can be no entertaining experiment, as in the laboratory. There can be no decorative lighting, as in electrical exhibitions. Every syllable and every punctuation mark must be made to count definitely toward the accomplishment of a desired end." *

Whatever the purpose of your letter, it has a much better chance of achieving that purpose if short, swift-moving sentences and short, swift-moving paragraphs make it easier to look at and more inviting to read.

5. *Correct Grammar, Spelling and Punctuation*

Last but not least of our five essentials for an attractive, well-groomed business letter is *accuracy*. No letter should ever be permitted to go out with a misspelled word, a typographical error, or an incorrectly or poorly constructed sentence. This may seem comparatively unimportant to you at the moment, if you happen to be more concerned with the tone and spirit of your letter and what you want it to accomplish for you. But make no mistake about it! Poor grammar, misspelled words, lack of punctuation or the improper use of it, prejudice the reader against you and help to destroy the effectiveness of your letter.

So don't take chances! These, at least, are faults you can easily avoid. If you are uncertain about the spelling of a word, or the grammatical use of a word, *look it up*. It pays to check each letter carefully before it goes out and correct any errors that may cost you the confidence and respect of your correspondent.

The proper use of punctuation is especially important, for it helps to clarify and emphasize your thoughts, and makes your letter easier and more pleasant to read. Here is what R. H. Morris Associates, Correspondent Consultants, say about the importance of punctuation in business letters:

> A high percentage of our letters are involved and confusing because of our infrequent or incorrect use of commas and periods. It is not uncommon to find a sentence in many of our letters that contains from 35

* John B. Opdycke, *Take a Letter, Please!*

to 50 words unbroken by a comma. *Such sentences are too long.* Few readers can follow them with real interest.

We should all make a sincere effort to correct this faulty habit, because a letter that is not clear—one that does not "read easily"—seldom accomplishes its purpose. It usually requires additional, time-wasting, costly back-and-forth correspondence to explain your original intent.

Good letter writers, like renowned authors and orators, choose their words carefully and thriftily. They have learned to make every word count. So should you. A *wordy* letter is a *weak* letter. Therefore, *sweat for simplicity of expression.* Always strive to write *clearly and to the point*—so your letters will be forceful, interesting and effective.

The mind can only accept one thought at a time. Too many words and ideas thrown at your reader in helter-skelter fashion, without proper punctuation, must confuse rather than clarify your thought.

THE PARTS OF A BUSINESS LETTER

Every well-constructed business letter is made up of six parts. These are:

1. THE HEADING
    which in a business letter is the *date only,* as the address is in the letterhead
2. THE INSIDE ADDRESS
    which is the name and address of the person to whom the letter is written
3. THE SALUTATION
    which is the complimentary greeting
4. THE BODY OF THE LETTER
    which is the subject matter or message
5. THE CLOSE
    which is the complimentary conclusion or "good-by"

6. THE SIGNATURE
    which may include the official capacity in which
    the letter is written

This is the same general structure or form as the social letter, discussed in an earlier chapter.* The only difference is in the use of an *Inside Address*, which always appears on business letters but is not ordinarily used in social correspondence. The position of the *Inside Address* may be either, as indicated above, immediately preceding the salutation; or it may be written at the end of the letter, below the signature, in the lower left-hand corner.

The following outline shows the six parts of a business letter:

1. HEADING   November 10, 19—

2. INSIDE   Mr. Martin L. Schiff,
   ADDRESS   45 Broadway
                    New York 4, N.Y.

3. SALUTATION   Dear Mr. Schiff:

4. BODY   Thank you very much for your offer to co-
                 operate with us on the Wendell case.

                     We shall keep you informed as to the prog-
                 ress of the case, and call upon you when your
                 testimony is needed.

                     Mr. Davis will be in New York on Decem-
                 ber first, and he will telephone you for an ap-
                 pointment.

5. CLOSE   Very truly yours,

6. SIGNATURE
                                      John B. Brandt

                                      John B. Brandt

Business letters are almost always written on business letterheads giving the name and address of the firm, and as a rule the

* For a detailed analysis of the parts of a letter, see pages 53 to 67.

nature of the business. The heading of the letter therefore consists only of the date, as shown in the outline above. But if
paper without a letterhead is used, the heading should include
the address—as follows:

> 20 Wall Street
> New York 5, N.Y.
> December 5, 19

The heading may be either in *block* form, as above—or in *step*
form, with each line indented:

> 20 Wall Street
> New York 5, N.Y.
> December 5, 19

In general, it's best not to use abbreviations of cities or states,
unless they are well-known and familiar like N.Y., N.J., Mass.,
etc.* The name of the month should always be spelled out in
full. When in doubt as to whether or not to abbreviate anything
in a letter—*don't*. Even though abbreviations may be clear
and understandable, they lack distinction. A letter in which all
words are spelled out is always more dignified and attractive-
looking.

Try to have the beginning of the date and the beginning of the
complimentary close line up exactly, as that makes your letter
look more evenly balanced on the page.

THE INSIDE ADDRESS

The inside address should be the same as the name and address
on the envelope. It should be in line with the left-hand margin;
and although it may be either in *step* or *block* form, the latter
is preferred. The amount of space between the date and the
inside address depends on the length of the letter. Commas may
be used between lines or not, as you prefer; the tendency today
is to omit punctuation at the ends of the lines.

* For the correct abbreviations of states, see page 74.

All the following forms of inside address are correct and in general use:

1. To a specific individual in a firm

> Mr. Frederick B. Whalen
> Middletown Oil Company
> 416 Main Street
> Middletown 6, Oklahoma

2. To a specific individual, giving his title or position

> Mr. John Haley, Cashier
> Ajax Lumber Company
> 240 Broadway
> New York 7, N.Y.

3. To an anonymous official in the firm

> Advertising Manager
> Holton-Peet Company
> 50 State Street
> Chicago 10, Illinois

4. To the firm itself, to be opened by anyone

> Holton-Peet Company
> 50 State Street
> Chicago 10, Illinois

5. To the firm, attention of a specific individual

> Ajax Lumber Company
> 240 Broadway
> New York 7, N.Y.
>
> Attention of the Cashier
> or
> Attention of Mr. John Haley

The "attention" line should be centered above the body of the letter, and it may or may not be underscored.

As previously mentioned, the inside address is sometimes placed at the end of the letter instead of the beginning . . . especially in official correspondence. In this case, the correct position is about two to four lines below the signature, to the left, in line with the margin.

THE SALUTATION

The salutation immediately precedes the body of the letter and lines up evenly with the left-hand margin. There should be two spaces between the inside address and the salutation, and between the salutation and the body of the letter. The correct punctuation to use after the salutation is the colon (:).

In business correspondence, the forms of salutation most commonly used are:

> Dear Sir:
> Dear Madam:
> My dear Sir:
> My dear Madam:
> Dear Mr. Brown:
> My dear Mrs. Hartley:
> Gentlemen:

Whether married or unmarried, a woman is always addressed as "Dear Madam," *never* as "Dear Miss." "Gentlemen" is preferred to "Dear Sirs" and is more generally used, although both are correct. The plural form is used even when the firm name is a single individual, as:

> John Hayden, Inc.
> 20 Maiden Lane
> New York 38, N.Y.
>
> Gentlemen:

It is also good practice to use "Gentlemen" when writing to a firm that consists of both men and women, or even a firm consisting of women alone. (The form "Mesdames" is obsolete and should not be used.) "My dear Sir" or "My dear Madam" is more formal than "Dear Sir" or "Dear Madam"—although the use of "My" in the salutation is gradually dying out, especially in business letters. Note that when "My" *is* used, the word "dear" is not capitalized.

When writing to a personal business friend, it is permissible to use an informal salutation such as "Dear Fred" or "Dear Mary."

Form letters may be addressed to "Dear Reader," "Dear Doctor," "Dear Music Lover," "Dear Customer"—or to whatever group the subject of your letter is addressed. However such salutations lack warmth and personality, and there is a growing tendency to omit salutations entirely from form and circular letters.

THE BODY OF THE LETTER

A business letter is always written for a specific purpose—and that purpose should be kept clearly in mind, from the first word to the last. Not a single sentence should be included that in any way obscures the basic purpose of the letter, or makes it any less swiftly and sharply understandable to the reader.

Before you begin the body of your letter, ask yourself: "What is my objective? What do I hope to accomplish by this letter, and what is the best way to go about it? What facts or ideas do I want to convey—what impression do I want to give my correspondent? How am I most likely to get the result or create the response I want?"

Then plan your letter, as a speaker plans his speech or a writer the chapter of a book. Think your letter through before you begin to write. *Know what you want to say;* and once you have decided on the BIG IDEA of your letter—stay with it! Don't ramble. Don't write about irrelevant or personal things (they don't belong in a business letter)! Stick to the facts. Tell your correspondent what he wants to know—or what you want him to know. Don't waste words on generalities—or on obvious and unnecessary remarks which merely clutter up your letter and cloud the main theme. Say what you have to say simply, clearly and to the point—making every sentence work toward the purpose for which the letter is written.

Bear in mind that business letters are often read under pressure, when people are busy and dozens of other interests compete for their attention. So streamline your letters to make them more effective. Keep them brief and fast-moving, with short sentences and short paragraphs. Start a new paragraph for each point you wish to stress, arranging the paragraphs in logical order so that your letter "reads easily" and moves, step by step, toward the aim or purpose you wish to achieve.

Both the opening and closing sentences of a business letter are very important. The opening sentence should indicate the subject or reason for the letter, and should compel the reader's interest and attention. The closing sentence should leave the reader with a single clear-cut thought or idea, and should inspire whatever action or response is desired.

THE COMPLIMENTARY CLOSE

The correct position for the complimentary close is two spaces below the body of the letter, to the right of the page, in line with the date block at the top.

There are a number of closings with varying degrees of intimacy and formality from which to choose. Your best choice, of course, is the phrase most appropriate for your purpose. For example, you wouldn't be likely to close a letter of complaint with "Very cordially yours,"—nor would it be suitable to write "Yours respectfully," to a clerk or a casual business acquaintance. "Yours truly," is the form most frequently used in general business correspondence, and is the best form to use when in doubt. But here are some others from which to choose:

> Yours very truly,
> Very truly yours,
> Yours sincerely,
> Sincerely yours,
> Very sincerely yours,
> Always sincerely yours,
> Faithfully yours,
> Yours faithfully,
> Very faithfully yours,
> Cordially yours,
> Yours cordially,
> Very cordially yours,
> Most cordially yours,

"Respectfully yours," is used, as a rule, only by a tradesman writing to a customer, or by an employee writing to an employer. It is also frequently used in letters to church dignitaries and high public officials, although "Faithfully yours," is now considered a more acceptable form for that purpose.

"Gratefully yours," should be used only when one has cause to be grateful—as, for example, when writing to thank a surgeon who has successfully performed a serious operation, or to a lawyer who has won a difficult case.

"Warmly yours," is an undesirable phrase and should be avoided. So should such closings as "Yours for more business," and "Yours for a better year." Abbreviations such as "Yrs." for "Yours" and "Tly" for "Truly" (you'd be amazed how many people use them!) make a letter look sloppy and hurried.

Try particularly to avoid the use of those familiar old participial phrases such as "Hoping to hear from you soon," and "Trusting this is satisfactory." They tend to make any letter sound stereotyped and dull. Avoid also the use of "I am" and "I remain" preceding the close of the letter, as they are equally out of date and serve no useful purpose.

THE SIGNATURE

Every business letter should be signed by hand, in ink—and whenever possible, by the person who has written it. A typed signature alone is not good form; the use of a rubber stamp is anything but effective; and a signature in pencil or crayon is a rudeness to the person who receives the letter.

The name should always be written out in full, as initials may be misleading or confusing. The signature should not vary from one letter to another. George F. Smith should remain George F. Smith in all his business correspondence. He should not sometimes become G. Smith, sometimes G. Ford Smith. Of course if a man is writing a business letter to someone who is also a personal friend, he may sign just his first name—George.

The signature should always be written clearly and legibly, especially when there is no typed version of it. It's very annoying to receive a letter signed with an indecipherable scrawl that might work out to be any one of half a dozen different names! Many a letter remains unanswered for no other reason than that the busy person who receives it has no time to solve the mystery of the signature. It doesn't take much more time to write your name clearly than to dash it off carelessly; and surely it's worth the little extra effort.

Most business letters, however, have the writer's name *typed* several lines below the complimentary close, leaving space between for the handwritten signature. This prevents the possibility of mistake or confusion, however illegible the written signature may be. For example:

Very truly yours,

John F. Martinson

John F. Martinson

Frequently the name of the firm represented is used in the signature, with the name of the person writing the letter immediately below it:

Very truly yours,
Dorrance Advertising Agency

Peter Halleck

Peter Halleck, Treasurer

The following forms are also correct, and their choice is merely a matter of personal preference:

Sincerely yours,
The Mason-Cortley Company

BY *George C. Fraser*

George C. Fraser

Yours truly,

Wheeler Jones, Jr

Wheeler Jones, Jr.
A. J. Harper Company

Sincerely yours,

Frederick B. Prentice

Frederick B. Prentice, Editor
Trade Book Department

Cordially yours,

Leon B. Harris

Eastern Advertising Manager

Very truly yours,
R. H. Macy & Co., Inc.

Per   *(Miss) Mary Landis*

Estimating Office

When a letter is dictated, it is customary to give the initials of the person who dictated the letter as well as the stenographer who typed it, for identifying purposes. The initials are placed below and to the left of the signature, in line with the left-hand margin. If Peter Halleck has dictated a letter to Margaret Foster, any one of these four methods of initialing may be used: PH/MF, PH:MF, PH-MF or PH/mf. Occasionally the full name of the person who dictated the letter is used, with the initials of the stenographer following, as for example: Peter Halleck/mf.

The following last paragraph, complimentary close and signature of a typical business letter are given to show how the identifying initials are used:

I am sorry for the delay, and will see that you receive a complete set of proofs immediately.

Very truly yours,
Dorrance Advertising Agency

Peter Halleck

Peter Halleck, Treasurer

PH/mf

If something is enclosed with the letter—such as a bill, check, proof or copy of another letter— attention should be called to it by writing "Enclosure" or "Enclosures" below the initials in the lower left-hand corner. For example:

PH/mf
Enclosures

The phrase "Dictated but not read" is a discourtesy and should not be used.

ADDRESSING THE ENVELOPE

All letters should be carefully addressed, otherwise they may be lost or delayed.* Be sure that the name of the firm, the name of the individual, street number, city, zone, state are all given correctly. Apart from the possibility of misdirection, remember that nobody likes to receive a letter in which his name is misspelled. It's one of the quickest ways possible to antagonize your correspondent.

Begin typing the address slightly below the middle of the envelope, a little toward the left—but leaving enough space to get even a long name or address in without crowding. Either straight block or indented step arrangement may be used. Postal authorities prefer the step arrangement as it's easier to read.

Special directions such as "Attention of" or "Personal" should be typed in the lower left corner of the envelope.

* See pages 68 to 76 for detailed information concerning the addressing of envelopes.

Mailing instructions such as "Air Mail" or "Special Delivery" —if they are not already stamped or printed on the envelope— should be typed at the upper right side, under the postage stamp or stamps.

John D. Rockefeller, Sr. once said: "The ability to deal with people is as purchasable a commodity as sugar or coffee. And I will pay more for that ability than for any other under the sun."

The ability to deal with people is greatly increased by the ability to write good letters. And anyone can write good letters by applying a few simple basic principles.

In the first place, make it a point to answer all business letters *promptly.* An answer long delayed is not, as a rule, well received —is in disfavor even before it arrives.

When you answer a letter, keep it in front of you. Check or underline the parts of the letter that require an answer. Get all the necessary data and information you will need to write a complete and intelligent reply. *Be sure of your facts before you write;* for no one can write a satisfactory letter without full command of the subject.

If it's a letter of inquiry, asking for specific information or seeking an adjustment, answer it fully and completely—leaving nothing to the imagination. Tell the reader exactly what he wants to know. Don't write vaguely, making alibis instead of stating facts. Don't make it necessary for your correspondent to write again, for more specific details. Make yourself thoroughly familiar with the matter under discussion . . . review any previous correspondence on file . . . and know exactly what you are going to say *before* you start to write or dictate. This may seem unimportant to you; but if you try *thinking through* your letters before you start to write, you will find that it helps you express yourself with greater ease and confidence . . . and keeps you from rambling, from becoming too wordy and involved.

WRITE YOUR LETTERS FROM
THE READER'S POINT OF VIEW

One reason why so many letters fail to achieve the purpose or secure the results for which they are written is simply this: They are self-centered, are self-seeking, and are completely self-interested.

It's very important to adopt a "you" attitude in your correspondence—to project yourself to the other side of the fence and try to see things from the point of view of the person to whom you are writing. What are his needs and desires—his interests—his problems?

If there is any one great basic principle of success in the writing of business letters, it can be summed up as the ability to see things through the other fellow's eyes as well as your own.

So try to approach all business correspondence from the standpoint of the reader, subordinating your own interests or those of your firm. Whatever your objective—whether you are trying to sell something, secure information, clear up a misunderstanding, collect a bill, or build up confidence and goodwill—you can be sure your letter will be much more effective if it's written in terms of "you" instead of "we" or "I." For example, compare these opening paragraphs from two letters sent out by competing insurance companies:

1. We are very proud of our reputation as experts in the field of estate planning. Among our clients are some of the country's outstanding business and professional men.

2. You are, of course, well aware of the importance of estate planning to you and your family. But do you know that recent changes in the tax structure may have serious impact on your present estate program?

Surely the second approach is of more personal interest to the reader, and is therefore more effective.

BE SURE IT SOUNDS SINCERE

It's all well and good to flatter the ego of your correspondent, but your letter won't carry weight unless it *sounds sincere*. You cannot win confidence with empty words. Your reader won't be impressed unless he believes what you say . . . and he won't believe what you say if your words have a false ring to them.

So when you sit down to write a business letter, no matter what kind of business letter it may be, try to feel a genuine interest in your correspondent and his problems. Try to put yourself in his place and write the kind of letter you would like to receive under similar circumstances. Don't make the mistake of thinking you can get by with mere flattery and pretense.

For no letter is a successful letter, however cleverly written, if it leaves an element of doubt in the reader's mind, if he feels he is being fooled, bluffed, patronized or exploited. No letter is a successful letter if it doesn't *sound sincere*.

ENTHUSIASM IS CONTAGIOUS

In any business letter that has a selling job to do—whether you're selling a product, service or idea—*be enthusiastic*. Let your correspondent see that you believe what you say, that you yourself are sold completely on the product or idea. In other words, sound a positive note in your letters whenever you can. Eliminate all negative thoughts. Don't even suggest that the reader may have any doubts or misgivings.

Take the advertising writer as an example! Every really good copy writer believes wholeheartedly in the products about which he is paid to write. He always uses them himself, if he can, and raves about them to his friends—insisting to everyone, including himself, that they are truly amazing and exceptional. He deliberately hypnotizes himself into believing that the product about which he happens to be writing at the moment is the best product of its kind in the world. For he cannot write enthusiastic copy unless he himself is sold on the product. And he knows he must write enthusiastic copy to be successful; for enthusiasm is contagious—it "catches on"—it makes people buy.

Bear that in mind when you are writing a letter that must

sell, convince, impress, or in any way *win over* a correspondent to your way of thinking. If you write with enthusiasm, the reader will sense that you believe what you are saying—and your letter will be much more likely to get the response you want.

COURTESY COUNTS IN
LETTER WRITING, TOO

It's not only in face-to-face contact with people that good manners are important. Courtesy counts in letter writing, too. Tact, kindness, consideration for the rights, feelings and sensibilities of others—all carry weight in business correspondence, and often make the difference between a successful letter and one that's a "flop." All other things being equal, it's the courteous and graciously written letter that usually wins out and gets the desired results.

So make a conscious effort to be well-mannered in your letters. Don't abuse, condemn, criticize or ridicule the person to whom you are writing, no matter what the circumstance. Say what you have to say tactfully, without giving offense; for nothing is to be gained by antagonizing your correspondent. *You can be sure that an angry, impatient or sarcastic letter will not get you the results you want.* It may relieve your feelings to "get it off your chest"—but it won't do either you or your company any good.

On the other hand, it's often possible to win over the most stubborn or disgruntled individual by expressing yourself with dignity and restraint. It isn't necessary to be rude, curt or abrupt; you can say what needs to be said *courteously*. You'll find that it always pays to be tactful and polite, in business letters as surely as in your personal contacts.

HOW TO PREJUDGE THE
EFFECTIVENESS OF YOUR LETTER*

1. Does your letter *look neat?* Is it faultlessly typed, well spaced and balanced, free of noticeable erasures or errors?
2. Does it look *easy to read?* Is it concise, with short sentences and paragraphs?

* Courtesy of R. H. Morris Associates, Correspondence Consultants.

3. Is the opening paragraph *pertinent* and *interesting* . . . does it refrain from "acknowledging" and "advising" . . . thus inviting further reading of the letter?

4. Is the letter *clear* and *forceful,* not involved or cluttered up with meaningless, stereotyped words and phrases?

5. Does it sound *natural* . . . not stilted, officious or affected?

6. Have you kept your *reader's point of view* . . . his desires, needs and requirements, well in mind? Approached him from *his* side of the fence, not yours?

7. Have you told your reader *what he wants to know?* Have you answered fully and completely all his questions, asked or implied?

8. Have you avoided saying anything that might be *misconstrued?*

9. Does your letter sound *sincere?* Does it sound as though you are really trying to be helpful and considerate of your reader's feelings, wishes and needs?

10. Have you said what you should say, *specifically and to the point?* Is your letter concise . . . brief without omitting important details, but not so brief that it appears curt?

11. Does each sentence and paragraph follow in natural sequence so your letter *reads easily—doesn't ramble?*

12. Have you made it as *easy as possible* for your reader to follow your bidding . . . are you sure you haven't asked him to do the impractical or unpleasant?

13. Have you used sound, logical *reasons why* your reader should do as you suggest or ask?

14. Are your closing lines *strong* and *forceful,* likely to cause your reader to react favorably to your suggestions or proposals?

15. Is the letter *friendly,* likely to build *good will,* as well as accomplish its purpose?

16. Is it the kind of letter *you yourself would like to receive* if you were in the reader's position? Is it fair and considerate, written in the right tone?

These are the points by which your reader will consciously or subconsciously accept or reject your message. If you can answer "Yes" to these questions when checking each letter you have written, you may be sure you have done a good job.

2

The Tone and Language of a Good Business Letter

No letter is a good letter if it fails to make friendly contact with the reader—if it fails to win his interest and hold his attention. Even letters of complaint, collection letters, routine letters of inquiry or adjustment—and above all letters that must sell products, services, ideas or good will—should be friendly in tone and spirit.

There is no reason why a business letter should sound stiff and formal, like a legal document . . . without life or sparkle. There is no reason why *any* letter, written for any purpose, should be cold, impersonal, forbidding. Yet so many letters are! For some reason the very atmosphere of a business office seems to induce the use of stilted, rubber-stamp words and phrases. Surely the difference between spoken and written language is most pronounced in business correspondence!

I have on my desk before me right now a letter from one of the biggest department stores in New York. The signature on the letter is a familiar one to me. The person who wrote that letter is brilliant, witty, a wonderful after-dinner speaker. Yet here is the opening paragraph of the letter:

> Please be advised that your communication of recent date is at hand. We wish to state that the matter will be given our prompt attention. We regret that you have been put to an inconvenience, but assure you it was unavoidable.

Those sentences might have been lifted bodily from any typical business letter of 1900 or thereabouts! There's no life to the words, no freshness. There's no real feeling of interest or sincerity. It's just another routine letter, written in the routine way, without much thought . . . and certainly without any attempt to establish a warm, human, friendly contact with the reader.

The very best letters are conversational in tone, like people meeting and talking things over face to face. They are interesting to read, cordial in spirit, sometimes witty and often imaginative . . . *and always natural.*

Imagine a salesman calling you on the telephone and saying: "I am in receipt of your letter of recent date concerning our new washing machine. I wish to state I am now in a position to demonstrate it at your earliest convenience." People just don't talk that way, and your letters shouldn't sound that way. Use the language of everyday conversation in your letters—the language in which people think, dream and talk. Use the words people themselves use in the streets, on the farms, in the shops and in their homes.

In a previous chapter we stressed the importance of sincerity. Your letter isn't likely to sound sincere if you use antiquated stock expressions that have long since lost all freshness and vitality. "You never hear it spoken, but you read it every day— this rubber-stamp language of the dead, dead past." * Hackneyed expressions have no real meaning for the reader. They carry no vital message across—convey no clear image or picture. So avoid them like the plague! They only make a letter sound pompous and boring. They make a letter sound cold, impersonal and insincere. In fact, according to R. H. Morris Associates, they sometimes make a letter sound like this!

> We beg to advise you, and wish to state
> That yours has arrived of recent date.
> We have it before us; its contents noted;
> Herewith enclosed are the costs we quoted.
> Attached you will find, as per your request,
> The forms you wanted, and we would suggest,

* L. E. Frailey, *Smooth Sailing Letters* (New York: Prentice-Hall, Inc., 1938).

Regarding the matter and due to the fact
That up to this moment your decision we've lacked,
We hope that you will not delay it unduly,
And we beg to remain, yours very truly,

If you do nothing more than eliminate the dull, stereotyped words and phrases that sprinkle most business correspondence— if you write with freshness, sparkle and originality—you are bound to write more successful letters. Don't hesitate to write exactly as you speak; the more your letter expresses your personality, the more warmth and appeal it will have for the reader. You don't need to use long "impressive" words; simple language is always the best—and an occasional word of slang, or even a coined word or phrase, adds color and life to your letter.

Always try to talk directly *to* your correspondent, not as though you were talking through a third person. Use his name now and then to maintain an intimate, friendly relationship. ("That's why, Mr. Peters, I think it would be best to . . . ") Put a smile into your letter if you want to; there's no law that says business correspondence must be gloomy and solemn . . . must put the reader to sleep! *Smiles build good will.* Just be sure your letter is in good taste—that it is neither too flippant nor too familiar—and that it takes serious things seriously.

The following stilted phrases are the ones most commonly used in business correspondence—and often in social and friendly correspondence as well. Make a real effort to avoid using them, to *wake up* and *modernize* your letters:

along these lines

and oblige

as per

assuring you of our interest

as the case may be

attached hereto

attached herewith

at your convenience

awaiting further orders

awaiting your reply

contents duly noted

deem it advisable

due to unforeseen circum-
    stances

enclosed herewith

enclosed please find

esteemed favor

for your information

hoping to hear from you
hoping this meets with your approval
hoping to receive
in receipt of
in reply wish to state
in view of the fact
look into the matter
our records indicate that
permit me to say
pleased to inform you
referring to your letter
rest assured
same shall receive prompt attention
take this opportunity to
thanking you in advance
this letter is to inform you
this will acknowledge receipt of
trusting this is what you desire
trusting to hear from you
under separate cover
upon investigation
up to this writing
we beg to advise
we beg to remain
we exceedingly regret
we note from your letter
we take the liberty of
your kind favor
your letter has come to hand
yours of recent date

Instead of this	*Say this*
Enclosed you will find	We enclose
At an early date	Soon
At the present writing	Now
In re. the matter of	Regarding
Trusting you will send	Please send
We are writing to tell you	This explains
We shall advise you	We shall let you know
Your letter is at hand	We have your letter
As per your letter	According to your letter
We take pleasure	We are glad
Owing to the fact that	Because
As to your suggestion	Regarding your suggestion
Even date	Today
In due course	Soon
Under date of November 10th	On November 10th
In view of the circumstances	As
As a matter of fact	In fact
In the amount of	For
In the event of	If
In the near future	Soon
Under the circumstances	Because

Instead of this	*Say this*
Costs the sum of	Costs
Due to the fact that	Because
For a period of a week	For a week
Until such time as	Until
In a satisfactory manner	Satisfactorily
At the earliest possible moment	As soon as possible (or "immediately")
At all times	Always
Attached you will find	Attached are (or "We attach")
We would request that you	Please
By return mail	At once
On receipt of	When we receive
The party you suggested	The person you suggested
The writer has investigated	I have investigated
We are ready at this time to	We are now ready to
The above-mentioned merchandise	The merchandise
According to our records	Our records show (or "We find that")
Please so advise us	Please let us know
In the course of	During
We extend our thanks for	Thanks for

MEANING OF ABBREVIATIONS
USED IN BUSINESS LETTERS

It is not advisable to use abbreviations in correspondence, unless they are very familiar and commonplace. There is less likelihood of mistakes and confusion if words are spelled out in full. The trend is more and more to avoid abbreviations entirely; however many are still in general use—and as long as they *are* in use, you should know their meaning.

A1	first class, highest quality
@	at
acct. (or a/c)	account
A.D.	in the year of our Lord
adv.	advertisement

agt.	agent
a.m. (or A.M.)	before noon
amt.	amount
anon.	anonymous
app.	appendix
atty.	attorney
avoir.	avoirdupois
Ave.	Avenue
bal.	balance
bbl.	barrel
B.C.	Before Christ
B/L	bill of lading
bldg.	building
blvd.	boulevard
Bros.	Brothers
B/S	bill of sale
bu.	bushel
bx.	box
C.	hundred
C.B.	cash book
C.E.	Civil Engineer
Cent.	centigrade
cf.	compare
c.i.f.	cost, insurance and freight
Co.	Company; county
c/o	in care of
c.o.d.	cash or collect on delivery
coll.	collect
Corp.	Corporation
C.P.A.	Certified Public Accountant
cr.	creditor; credit; crate
cu.	cubic
cwt.	hundredweight
D.	five hundred
dept.	department
disc. (or disct.)	discount
do.	ditto
dr.	debtor, debit
doz.	dozen
ea.	each

e.g.	for example
et al.	and others
etc.	and so forth
exch.	exchange
exp.	express
f.o.b.	free on board
ft.	foot; feet
gal.	gallon
h.p.	horsepower
hr.	hour
ibid.	in the same place
i.e.	that is
imp.	imported
in.	inches
Inc.	Incorporated
inv.	inventory
Jr.	junior
lb.	pound
Ltd.	Limited
M.	Thousand
m.	noon; mile; minute; meter
mdse.	merchandise
memo.	memorandum
mfr.	manufacturer
mgr.	manager
misc.	miscellaneous
mo.	month
ms.	manuscript
mss.	manuscripts
mtg.	mortgage
N.B.	take notice, note well
no.	number
O.K.	all right, correct
oz.	ounce
per	by
%	percent.
pkg.	package
p.	page
pp.	pages

pr.	pair
pc.	piece
pk.	peck
p.m. (or P.M.)	afternoon
P.O.	Post office; Postal Order
Pres.	President
P. S.	postscript
R.R.	railroad
recd.	received
R.F.D.	Rural Free Delivery
rm.	ream
Ry.	Railway
sec. (or secy.)	secretary
Sr.	senior
S.S. (or SS)	steamship
St.	Street
Sts.	Streets
stet	let it stand
supt.	superintendent
tr.	transpose
trea.	treasurer
via	by way of
vid.	see
viz.	namely
vol.	volume
vs.	versus (against)
w.b. (or W/B)	way bill
wt.	weight
yd.	yard
yr.	year

Some organizations have long and difficult names which are commonly abbreviated for purposes of convenience. Among the more familiar abbreviations you may come across in business correspondence are the following:

A.F.L.	American Federation of Labor
A.P.	Associated Press
C.A.A.	Civil Aeronautics Authority
C.C.C.	Commodity Credit Corporation

C.I.O.	Congress of Industrial Organizations
F.B.I.	Federal Bureau of Investigation
F.C.C.	Federal Communications Commission
F.E.P.C.	Fair Employment Practices Commission
F.H.A.	Federal Housing Authority
F.T.C.	Federal Trade Commission
H.O.L.C.	Home Owners' Loan Corporation
I.C.C.	Interstate Commerce Commission
I.T.O.	International Trade Organization
N.L.R.B.	National Labor Relations Board
R.F.C.	Reconstruction Finance Corporation
S.E.C.	Securities and Exchange Commission
T.V.A.	Tennessee Valley Authority
U.N.	United Nations
U.P.	United Press
U.S.E.S.	United States Employment Service
V.A.	Veterans' Administration

THE OPENING PARAGRAPH

The way you begin a letter is very important—unless, of course, it's just a routine matter-of-fact order or acknowledgment which doesn't need to win over or impress the reader. Because of its strategic position, the opening sentence is often the determining factor between success or failure. For upon it may depend the reader's *acceptance* of the letter: whether it is read with interest and attention, or merely scanned and thrown aside.

A good opening sentence is like the headline of an advertisement. It instantly attracts the reader's attention, stimulates his curiosity or desire, *makes him want to read on.*

A poor opening sentence "begs to acknowledge" or "wishes to state"—says what is obvious, unnecessary or trite—makes no bid whatever for the reader's attention.

Naturally, the opening differs with the various types of letters you write. If it's a simple letter of order, inquiry or acknowledgment, you don't need an especially interesting or original opening. In fact, the more direct and businesslike it is, the better. All that is required of it is that it state its purpose clearly, and (when appropriate) show a friendly interest in the reader's problems and needs. But not even the most simple routine letter need start out with an impersonal, stereotyped opening, like the following:

> Yours of the 15th regarding delay in shipment just received. We exceedingly regret this matter.

The same thing, expressed in a natural, conversational tone, puts the reader in a more receptive frame of mind:

> We are sorry to learn, from your letter of March 15th, that you have not yet received the chairs you ordered.

When a letter has a specific job to do . . . such as selling a subscription to a magazine or applying for a job . . . the opening paragraph must be more than merely warm and friendly in tone. *It must be interesting.* It must be exciting, provocative, newsy, imaginative—must instantly get under the skin of the reader—touch a life nerve—make him read on.

Here are a few of the more familiar ways of giving a letter an interesting start. There are many others. You'll find it stimulating and helpful to make a study of the letters you receive, and to keep a file of the opening sentences that impress you most. Add others of your own to the list; and refer to it when you need help getting a letter off to a good start. But bear in mind that just compelling the reader's attention isn't enough; your opening paragraph must have direct bearing on the subject of the letter, must lead logically into what you want to say.

1. *Ask a Question*

A blunt statement of fact is never as provocative as a question. For example, if you were writing a letter to sell subscriptions to a weekly news magazine, you might start off with: "To be well-informed, you should know what is going on in all parts of the world today." But you will intrigue more readers and get better response if you put it in the form of a question: "How would you like to be the most interesting, best-informed man in your community?"

2. *Make a Startling Statement*

Most people are intrigued by a startling or unusual statement of fact, something they didn't know before. They are likely to continue reading a letter that starts off with: "This may shock you, but it's true! Most people have had, or will some time have, anemia." You should be sure of your facts, of course; for an incorrect statement discredits your entire letter.

3. *Tell a Story or Anecdote*

When an anecdote is interesting or exciting, and ties in with the subject of the letter, it's an excellent way to get started. A good story always gives life and sparkle to a letter. For example, an ordinary run-of-the-mill letter on fire insurance might start off like this: "A recent national survey shows that property values have risen. If you haven't increased your fire insurance, you should do so at once." That's dull, "sleepy," uninspired. Compare it with this colorful opening paragraph:* "When Mrs. O'Leary's cow kicked over a lamp on the night of October 8, 1871, she set off the great Chicago fire. It was a *170 million dollar fire!* Many lives were lost and much property destroyed. However, that tragedy was the starting point of intensive safety measures and fire prevention programs that have steadily increased down through the years."

4. *Quote an Authority*

The opinion of a person of reputation carries weight, and makes an effective opening for many types of letters. If you were writing to the head of a department store, for example—explaining about a new system of inventory control—you might start off with: "According to Dr. John T. Hammond, noted economist, the most important single factor in successful merchandising is *inventory control.*"

---

* From a letter sent to policyholders by the Hardware Mutual Insurance Company of Minnesota.

5. *Quote a Famous Saying of the Past*

People are always interested in the great of the past, in their ideas and ideals . . . and their famous sayings. The lead for a letter sent out by a bank to encourage thrift might use as its opening sentence: " *'I shall study hard, save my money, become a great man!'* wrote Benjamin Franklin as a young lad."

6. *Dramatize the Results of a Survey or Test*

If you use the results of a survey or test for an opening paragraph, be sure to key it to the interests or problems of the reader. Give it a human, emotional appeal instead of expressing it coldly in terms of facts and figures. For example: "Do you realize the danger you are in, *right in your own home?* According to a survey conducted by the Council on Public Safety, more people die of accidents in their own homes than anywhere else." Here is how *Fortune* magazine used the results of a survey in the opening paragraph of a letter sent to subscribers: "One of the most startling opinions ever turned up on the *Fortune* Survey came in answer to this simple question last Fall: Do you think married women whose husbands make enough to support them should or should not be allowed to hold jobs if they want to? The opinion, from both sexes, was an overwhelming *No!*"

7. *Highlight a News Story*

A tie-in with important news of the day gets your letter off to a good start, and makes it timely. A brokerage house customer's man, writing to his client, might say: "I think you will agree with me that the recent surprising political events foreshadow an era of greater freedom for business enterprise than has been possible in many years. As an investor, it is important that you know how this will affect your holdings."

EXAMPLES OF EFFECTIVE OPENINGS

FOR VARIOUS TYPES OF LETTERS

Do you know that less than 3% of American families have incomes of $10,000 a year or more?

If you love your home, here's some news you'll be thrilled to hear!

Can you think of any better time than *right now* to start thinking about your summer vacation?

We are very sorry that you have decided to discontinue the protection of your policy.

Have you ever stopped to think that a magazine leads a *double life* in a doctor's office?

Sorry! It's our mistake and we apologize. Our driver will pick up the chairs tomorrow and deliver the ones you ordered.

We are sorry the draperies are not satisfactory. Our draper will call on Thursday morning, April 4th, to remeasure them.

We have good news for you! At last we have been able to match your Haviland china; and we now have six cups and saucers in the pattern you want.

I'm sorry, but I cannot accept the desk which was delivered here on September 3. It is not the desk I ordered. The walnut is a darker tone, and the design on the drawers is different.

I purchased an end table from you on October 2, and was promised delivery within a week. It is now more than two weeks, and the table has not yet arrived.

Have you forgotten that you still owe us some money? I don't like to remind you—but it is a rather long time, you know.

Here's that old bill again! How about paying it, and keeping your credit good? Or if you can't pay it now, won't you let us know when we can at least expect some part of it?

I hate to be insistent, but we simply must have some payment on the bill you owe us, otherwise we cannot extend any further credit. The amount still due is $356.70.

I'm sorry you had to write me again about my bill. I know it's long overdue, and I shall make every effort to pay it before the end of the month.

It's a real pleasure to send you our booklet on decorative tile. We hope it will give you the information you want.

I must say I am surprised by your letter of October 2. I thought we were being most generous and fair.

There's a chill in the air—and that's a danger signal! It means your car needs cold weather servicing, *right now*.

Our representative is heading your way—and he has some news for you! News that's *very important*, and that you must not miss.

Thank you, Doctor, for all your kindness to us—above and beyond the call of duty. I enclose my check for $100, and never was a bill paid more gratefully!

I am happy to enclose my check for $150—which is little enough to pay for a boy as fine as Junior!

Thank you for your order. The books are now on their way to you, and should reach you within a few days of this letter.

You will be glad to know that your application for admission to the Advertising Club has been approved.

THE CLOSING PARAGRAPH

The closing paragraph of a business letter should leave the reader with a single clear-cut thought or idea—and should inspire whatever action or response is desired. It's here that you make your final bid for the reader's confidence and good will. It's here that you either get the order, sell the idea, win the reader over to your way of thinking, leave a good last impression, or do just the opposite . . . depending on what you say and the words you use in your closing paragraph.

Avoid weak, namby-pamby closings like "Hoping to hear from you soon" and "Trusting this meets with your approval." Avoid negative, uncertain closings like "We feel this is to your advantage" and "We hope you will find it satisfactory." If you aren't sure of yourself, your reader won't be. So make a strong exit! Use positive language. Ask for a direct course of action. Take it for granted that your correspondent will agree to the adjustment, accept the explanation, respond to the idea, send in the order, or make the payment that is long overdue. In other words, *push the button that animates your reader and gets quick response.*

A treacherous little word to avoid in closing paragraphs is the word *if.* Don't give your correspondent the choice between two decisions, unless either decision is a satisfactory one. Instead of "Please let me know if you can see me" write "Please let me know when you can see me." Instead of "If you will sign and return the enclosed card," make it positive, tell him what you want him to do, hurry him into action: "Sign and return the enclosed card to me now, today—before you forget!"

There are many types of business letters that do not necessarily strive for a particular response or course of action. The closings of such letters should strive to maintain confidence and good will. ("We hope you will enjoy your purchase for many years to come.") Or they should thank or compliment the reader. ("Thank you for sending your check so promptly," or "Congratulations on the fine job you have done!")

EXAMPLES OF EFFECTIVE CLOSINGS
FOR VARIOUS TYPES OF LETTERS

Please send a complete report, and we'll do everything we can to help.

Congratulations on the fine showing you have made for the firm!

Thank you for letting us know about it. We shall take care of it at once.

We are depending on you to help us in this undertaking. Please don't let us down!

You have been most patient and considerate and we are grateful.

May we have information at once please? We cannot proceed without it.

As soon as we hear from you, we'll be able to make the adjustment.

Be sure to let me know if I can be of any further service to you.

We are always delighted to hear from our customers, and we hope you'll take the time to write us again.

Will you send confirmation of this order at once so that we can begin shipment?

May we have your check for $35.68 without further delay? Thank you.

We hope you will send a check at once for at least part of the amount due us.

I'll be looking for your check tomorrow morning. Don't disappoint me!

The stamped, addressed envelope is for your convenience. Sign and mail it to me *today*.

I'm enclosing a handy card for you to use. It requires no postage. Mail it right away, before you forget!

Make sure you don't miss this unusual offer. Send back the enclosed renewal form *in a hurry!*

Please let us know exactly what adjustment will be satisfactory to you.

I hope this proves how eager we are to make amends, and to please you in every way we can.

We shall be very grateful for any information you can give us.

Thank you for your order. We hope you and your family derive great pleasure from the use of your projector.

We hope this is the beginning of a long and happy association.

You can certainly pride yourself on your handling of this case!

Please let us know your decision before the meeting on August 8th.

You may expect to hear from us within a week.

We are sorry we cannot be more helpful, but there is no way we can get the information for you.

I'll telephone tomorrow morning for an appointment.

I'll be glad to come for an interview any time you say. My telephone number is Boulevard 8-9300.

Can you come in for an interview on Thursday morning at 11 o'clock?

THE USE OF POSTSCRIPTS
IN BUSINESS LETTERS

In social and personal correspondence, a postscript is just an afterthought, suggesting careless or disorganized thinking. It is usually unnecessary and often unsightly—and should be avoided.

But in business correspondence, a postscript is often purposely added to draw attention to some point or to emphasize a special offer. This is good practice, and is especially effective in sales letters. The postscript should be brief, and should contain only one clear-cut message. It may be used either with or without the "P.S." Here are some examples of typical business-letter postscripts:

Don't forget! June 10th is the deadline.

P.S. A discount of 2% will be given on all orders received on or before June 30th.

Extra Money-Saving P.S.: If you use *Today's News* in your waiting room, its cost is deductible on your income tax as a business expense!

P.S. Be sure to use the enclosed card; it requires no postage.

Remember! This offer is good until March 15th only.

P.S. I can be reached any morning before 10 at Chesapeake 2-4500.

P.S. My present employers know about this letter.

THE TEN COMMANDMENTS FOR WRITING A GOOD BUSINESS LETTER*

1. *Write as You Would Talk:* Use plain, homespun, everyday English which is more interesting and convincing than tongue-twisting, unfamiliar words.

2. *Be Courteous and Friendly:* Good manners always pay handsome dividends even in a letter. It's hard to resist someone who is trying to be sincerely friendly.

3. *Be Natural:* It has been wisely said: "The secret of writing a good letter requires the ability to put yourself in an envelope and seal the flap." This means, of course, that you should write as one human being to another. Do not take yourself or your position so seriously that your letters sound stilted, officious or superior to your readers.

4. *Learn to Visualize Your Readers and Be Helpful:* Acquire the knack of putting yourself in your readers' place. Base your appeal on how you are trying to help *them*—not yourself.

---

* Courtesy of R. H. Morris Associates, Correspondence Consultants.

5. *Keep an Open Mind:* Appreciate your readers' point of view. Respect their rights, wishes and needs.

6. *Practice Real Diplomacy:* Don't assume a "teacher to pupil" tone. A true diplomat makes others feel how much they know—*not* how little; how important they are—*not* how unimportant.

7. *Be Willing to Admit Mistakes:* Don't argue or try to justify an error. The most effective way to disarm an irate person is to admit frankly any cause for complaint.

8. *Write Clearly and to the Point:* Use short, crisp sentences. Finish with one point before going on to another. Avoid long, involved paragraphs. Say what you have to say interestingly and completely —*then stop*. Be cordial—not curt.

9. *Tell Your Readers What They Want to Know:* It is so easy to be misunderstood, doubted or misconstrued. Therefore, don't be vague or evasive. Don't expect your readers to read between your lines or to interpret your intentions. Be specific and complete.

10. *Dramatize Your Letters: Don't* expect dry, stereotyped letters to produce results. Paint glowing word pictures of *how* your readers will benefit by following your suggestions or proposals. Show them *reasons why* they should act for their own benefit.

These are the ten requisites for writing good business letters. If your letters conform to these points you can consider them well written—a real credit to you and to the company you represent.

3

Examples of Routine Business Letters

What counts most in any business letter is simply this: *Does it do its job?* Does it do it courteously and efficiently, in a way that reflects credit on the individual or the firm it represents?

No business can long endure without the confidence and good will of its customers. And letters play a very large part in establishing and maintaining good will. Dozens of different kinds of letters must be written every day, the letters of general business activity. Orders must be acknowledged, inquiries made, complaints answered. Letters must be written to customers, clients, lawyers, credit managers, buyers, representatives, manufacturers. . . .

The routine letters of business are not expected to be clever or imaginative. They are expected only to do well the job for which they are intended. They should never waste the reader's time nor tax his patience. They should never be rude, crude, curt or offensive. Letters that antagonize are a liability to any firm; they never influence anyone—they only destroy good will.

Following are examples of various types of business letters, of the kind that are written every day in the week. For purposes of convenience, only the first letter is given in complete form, with date and inside address included. All other examples are given without date and inside address—it being understood, of course, that these should always be included.

LETTERS OF ORDER AND CONFIRMATION

All letters ordering merchandise should give explicit information, specifying a catalog or model number when available—and giving the shade, size, type, quantity or whatever other data is necessary to identify the merchandise. An incomplete or confusing order wastes time . . . and time is valuable in business.

April 14, 19—

The Upjohn Company,
Kalamazoo, Mich.

Gentlemen:

Please send the following as quickly as you can, and charge to our account:

6 bottles of 100 each of ferrated
    liver concentrate tablets

6 bottles of 100 each of ferrated
    liver concentrate capsules

12 bottles of 100 each of Unicaps

12 bottles of 4-oz. size of citrocarbonate

Yours very truly,

Gentlemen:

This is to confirm my telephone order this morning for the following items:

6 Jr. Sewing Machines, Model 2B

12 Travel Kits, Model 4M

12 Folding Clothes Racks

24 knitting bags, Style 40, 12 blue, 12 green

Please ship this merchandise the quickest way possible, and charge to our account.

Sincerely yours,

Gentlemen:

Can you supply us at once with 12 dozen white sports shirts for boys, sizes 10 to 16? We are interested in shirts that retail for about $4.

We would like a quotation and approximate shipping date; and would greatly appreciate your immediate response.

Yours very truly,

Gentlemen:

How soon can you deliver 1000 folders of the same size and quality as the samples we enclose?

In your reply, please include quotations on lots of 1000, 2000 and 5000.

Yours truly,

Gentlemen:

Please send samples and quotations on one million metal paper clips.

At the same time let us know if you can supply 50 Ace staplers, model 102—giving us a quotation on this also.

We would like to have the information by the end of this week if possible.

Very truly yours,

Gentlemen:

I wish to order the following items from your Spring catalog:

A-6   Infant's dotted Swiss dress, pink,
      size 2, Price $4.95.

B-11 Boy's V-neck sleeveless sweater, tan or
      maize, size 32, Price $5.95.

M-42 Nylon hose, 3 pairs of Wood Rose in size 9,
      51 gauge, $1.65 a pair

This comes to $15.85, and I enclose a check for that amount.

Sincerely yours,

Gentlemen:

Please send me two pairs of men's striped broadcloth pajamas, at $7.50 a pair, as advertised in yesterday's *Times*. I would like one pair in blue and one in green, in size C. Charge to my account.

Yours truly,

Gentlemen:

Your estimate for painting my bedroom and sitting room is satisfactory. I should like to have you proceed with the work as soon as possible.

Yours truly,

Dear Mr. Fredericks:

I have decided to accept the proposal submitted by you on April 12th for the construction of kitchen cabinets in my home. It is understood that the work is to commence no later than June 1st, and is to be completed within two weeks.

Mrs. Curtis and I like the revised plans very much, and we'd like you to know we appreciate your efforts to carry out our somewhat unusual ideas.

I enclose my check for $50 in accordance with the terms of your proposal.

Sincerely yours,

Dear Sir:

Will you please send me the floor plan and rates of the Royal Hawaiian, indicating the accommodations you can let me have for the month of February.

I require one double room with bath for my husband and myself; and a connecting room, if possible, for my young daughter.

We plan to arrive on January 30th and leave on February 28th.

Sincerely yours,

Gentlemen:

I would like to reserve* a double room and bath for the week of Sept. 7th to Sept. 14th.

---

* For letters connected with travel, including additional letters of reservation, see BOOK VI, TRAVEL CORRESPONDENCE.

Please confirm the reservation by air mail as we are leaving here in a few days.

                                        Very truly yours,

Dear Mr. Turner:

We have reserved a double room and bath in your name for the week of Sept. 7th to Sept. 14th. The rate is $20 a day.

We look forward to your visit and hope your stay will be a very pleasant one.

                                        Sincerely yours,

Dear Dr. Brewster:

We are delighted with your letter telling us of your plan to visit the Inn again this year. We hope to have the pleasure of welcoming you and Mrs. Brewster; but we regret that we no longer have space available in July and August.

The demand for accommodations has been exceptional this season, and far exceeds the supply. It is a great disappointment to us not to be able to take care of many old friends for the exact periods they would like to be here.

Perhaps you can arrange to visit the Inn in June. Some very fine rooms are still available for that month. And Spring, you know, is one of the most delightful seasons of all in the Poconos!

                                        Cordially yours,

Dear Mr. Hartley:

Many thanks for your order which has been forwarded to our plant for immediate manufacture.

I take pleasure in assuring you that I will personally follow through on your order, and see that each piece is made exactly according to specifications.

You can depend on delivery on or before December 5th, as promised.

                                        Sincerely yours,

Gentlemen:

Thank you for your order of February 10th. It is being shipped today.

We enclose an invoice and bill of lading.

Yours very truly,

Dear Mr. Peters:

This is in answer to your inquiry of March 4th.

We can ship immediately 1000 folders of the same size and quality as the sample enclosed. A price card is enclosed for your convenience.

We await your instructions, and will rush the folders to you as soon as your order arrives.

Sincerely yours,

Dear Mr. Jasper:

Thank you for your order of December second. We are prepared to ship the gloves at once, and they should reach Denver not later than Monday or Tuesday of next week.

We are delighted to know that your customers like our gloves, and that you disposed of the last shipment so quickly. Thank you for telling us!

Cordially yours,

Dear Mr. Brown:

We wish to thank you for your order of three bottles of saddle oil.

Ours is a strictly cash business and we have no facilities for sending goods C.O.D. Will you therefore send a check for $6.20 to cover the cost plus the shipping charges?

We hope this does not inconvenience you. We shall see to it that the saddle oil goes out at once, as soon as your check arrives.

Very truly yours,

Gentlemen:

We are sorry to have to tell you that we cannot fill your order for 200 pairs of black doeskin gloves.

We can send you all the white, tan or yellow gloves you want; but there is a temporary shortage of black due to difficulty with the dyes.

Thank you very much for your order—which we hope you'll give us an opportunity to fill when black doeskin gloves again become available.

Sincerely yours,

LETTERS OF COMPLAINT AND ADJUSTMENT

The purpose of the usual letter of complaint is to get better merchandise or service, or to effect a satisfactory adjustment of some kind. You are more likely to get what you want if you are *courteous* in your letter. Nothing is gained by being sarcastic or insulting. That only makes your correspondent want to double up his fists and fight back, though he *won't*, of course, if he values your good will above his own pride and feelings!

So just state your case . . . say what the trouble is and how you expect it to be corrected. Be specific and to the point, but be pleasant about it. You will find that a friendly and courteous letter gets better results, as a rule, than an angry or impatient one.

Gentlemen:

Many of our customers have been complaining about your ball-point pens. They are clearly not giving satisfaction, and we have had to refund the purchase price on many of them.

We have had trouble only with the last shipment. The pens received before were satisfactory and we had no complaints from customers.

Please check to see if there was an error in the making of these pens. We suggest that you check also to see if they are being packed with adequate protection for shipping.

We have 3 ½ gross of the pens left, and we'd like you to send a new shipment at once to replace them. We'll wait for instructions from you before returning the others.

Yours very truly,

Gentlemen:

We are sorry to have to complain about your usually very fine merchandise.

The last shipment of 10 dozen Mary Jane blouses, ordered on March 23rd, is unsatisfactory and we cannot accept it. The collars are noticeably uneven on some of the blouses; and there are open seams on many of the sleeves.

We are sure this was just carelessness in checking, and that you will send another shipment of blouses promptly to replace this faulty one.

Yours very truly,

Dear Sir:

The addressing machine we bought from you on May 2nd has broken down completely. We have been unable to use it, and unable to have it repaired.

Since you have no service man in this territory, we are returning the machine to you via fast freight. We know you will send us a new one promptly as your machines are guaranteed for a year.

Sincerely yours,

Gentlemen:

We are sorry to say that the shipment of 24 bridge tables received today at the Hartford depot (New York, New Haven & Hartford R.R.) is so badly damaged that we are unable to accept it.

This is as disturbing to us as we know it must be to you, as we have been waiting for these tables for some time now—and have promised delivery to a number of customers.

Please see what you can do about rushing another shipment to us, in satisfactory condition. We would appreciate a wire telling us when we can expect it.

Yours truly,

Dear Mr. Perkins:

I cannot understand why there are so many mistakes in our billing recently. Is there any way this situation can be corrected?

I'm sure you'll agree that a little more care and accuracy on the part of your accounting department will benefit both of us.

Sincerely yours,

Gentlemen:

The walnut dining room set ordered on February 17 arrived in good condition, except for one side chair.

This chair was apparently damaged in the shipping. The legs are badly scratched, and one of them has a deep nick in it.

I know you won't want me to keep the damaged chair. I'll expect a new one to take its place; and in the meantime, it's packed and ready to be sent back to you—as soon as I receive your instructions.

Sincerely yours,

Gentlemen:

On December 12th I ordered a girl's raincoat with hood attached, red and green plaid, size 8, price $7.95.

Today I received a plain red raincoat, without a hood. Although it's the right size, and the same price as the one ordered, I cannot keep it as my daughter especially wants the one with the hood.

Please have your driver pick up this raincoat; and either deliver the one ordered or refund the money.

Yours truly,

Gentlemen:

I have not yet received the wrought-iron porch furniture which I purchased on May 15th. Delivery was promised in two weeks, but it is now nearly a month.

Please let me know when I may expect to receive it.

Yours truly,

The writing of adjustment letters, in answer to complaints, requires a very special technique. Such letters must be written without anger or impatience—must be written very skillfully and courteously to avoid *further antagonizing the complainant.* This holds true whether the complaint is a fair one or not. One of the most effective ways to disarm an irate person and win him over to your way of thinking is to admit freely a cause for complaint. Arguments and accusations only make things worse, as a rule. But "talking it over" in a friendly way—explaining how or why it happened, and being very reasonable and understanding about the whole thing—often settles the trouble pleasantly, and without loss of good will.

Dear Madam:

We can understand your annoyance at not having received the stationery you ordered on March 3rd.

Orders for printed stationery take three to four weeks for delivery; and our salesmen have been instructed to so inform customers. Apparently you were not told it would take that long; and we are certainly sorry for the oversight.

However, your stationery is now ready and will be sent to you at once. You should receive it about the same time as this letter.

We hope you will forgive us for the delay—and that you will thoroughly enjoy your purchase!

Sincerely yours,

Dear Mrs. Curtis:

We are most distressed by your letter of April 16th.

We admit you have cause for complaint, and we are sorry you were put to such trouble and inconvenience by the carelessness of one of our clerks. But surely you are too fair-minded to condemn our entire organization for the mistake of a single individual!

Of course we'll reframe the paintings, if you wish. Shall we have our driver call and pick them up?

Perhaps you would like to come in and talk things over with us personally. You have been a good customer for so long, we certainly don't want to lose your friendship now.

Cordially yours,

Dear Madam:

Thank you for your very courteous letter.

We are sorry the plant stand arrived in poor condition. It was apparently damaged during shipment.

We are sending you another table at once—doubly well-packed, this time, to make sure it reaches you safely! The driver who delivers it will pick up the damaged table.

We hope that you have not been inconvenienced, and that you will enjoy your purchase for a long time to come.

Sincerely yours,

Dear Mr. Stoughton:

We certainly owe you an apology!

The collection letter was sent by mistake, instead of the usual form reminding you that your account was due.

We hope you will forgive us, and we assure you it won't happen again. You know your credit is good with us for all the merchandise you want, now and always.

Cordially yours,

Dear Mr. Fraser:

We're sorry you found it necessary to return our last bill for correction.

You are right about the 10% discount, of course. But the $32 is not an error; it represents charges for air-express deliveries made at your request during the month of December.

We'll see that our billing department makes no mistake about the discount in the future.

Yours very truly,

LETTERS OF INQUIRY AND ACKNOWLEDGMENT

A letter of inquiry is written to obtain information or to make a request. It should be direct and specific; but most of all, it should be reasonable in its demands upon the time and effort of the person to whom it is addressed. Friendship should not be imposed upon. An inquiry requiring clerical help should be accompanied by an offer to pay for the expenses involved. Anyone seeking personal or confidential information should make his purpose clear and show himself to be a person of responsibility.

Always enclose a stamped addressed envelope when writing to a stranger for information. This isn't necessary, of course, if you are writing for information about a trip you expect to make, or books you expect to buy—and the company to which you are writing stands to benefit by the correspondence. But if you are writing for information that is of importance *only to you*—if you want to know how to pronounce a certain word, what to do or say under certain circumstances, or perhaps what to do about certain personal problems or difficulties—you should enclose a stamp or a stamped addressed envelope.

All letters of inquiry should be acknowledged, except those

obviously written by a crank. The reply should be courteous and friendly, whether it grants the request or not. If information is withheld, the reason should be given as tactfully as possible. A simple statement of company policy is often the best way out. The refusal to give information or grant a request is always more gracious if another more likely source is suggested.

Dear Mr. Tavis:

We are making a survey of the buying habits of the American public.

Could you let me know whether you have sold more *modern* furniture this year than *period* furniture? Or was it the other way around?

We will be grateful for your answer and will, of course, keep it in strictest confidence.

Sincerely yours,

Dear Mrs. Clinton:

I wonder whether you would be willing to review for the *Midwestern Quarterly* Professor Countway's new book, *The History of Musical Instruments?*

We should like a review of 500 to 700 words, by the first of February if possible. If you are willing to write it for us, and will let me know, I shall send you the book at once.

I wish I could offer you some other payment, but at present our faithful reviewers work without fee.

Sincerely yours,

Gentlemen:

We have heard that you are making a tabulating machine that is faster than the Model V we are now using.

We need two additional tabulating machines for our accounting department, and would like to know more about the new model.

Will you please send us whatever information is available? We should particularly like to know how it differs from Model V, other than in its speed—what the price is—and when you can make shipment.

Yours very truly,

Dear Mr. Franklin:

The Middletown High School is having a "College and Career Night" for its 2000 students on Thursday evening, May 5th.

We should very much like to have you come to speak to a group of students interested in advertising.

We should like a brief talk presenting the necessary qualifications and preparation for a career in advertising, with emphasis on the opportunities it offers today. This would be followed by a period of informal discussion.

We hope you will say "yes"—as we know any talk you give will be stimulating and helpful to the students.

Cordially yours,

Gentlemen:

Do you have a booklet on interior decorating?

I am interested in doing over two rooms in my house, using plywood for the walls and built-in bookcases.

I thought you might have a booklet available showing interesting or unusual use of plywood in the home. If so, I'll be very pleased to receive a copy.

Yours very truly,

Gentlemen:

I am writing for permission to reprint a letter which appears on page 179 of *Northern Nurse* by Elliot Merrick, published by Scribner's in 1942.

I should like to use it in a book on letter writing, to be published by Prentice-Hall in October. It illustrates perfectly a point I wish to make: that to *receive* interesting letters one must *write* interesting letters.

I'll be glad to make any payment required for reprint permission; and of course adequate acknowledgment will be given both to Scribner's and to the author.

Yours very truly,

Gentlemen:

I'd like to know where I can purchase the *Betty Parnell* dress advertised on page 132 of the September issue of Vogue.

Yours truly,

Dear Mrs. Miller:

Thank you for your inquiry about the *Betty Parnell* dress shown in the advertisement in the September Vogue.

Clark & Company of Middletown is the store nearest you that carries this dress.

Should you decide to buy it, I take this opportunity to wish you many happy moments as you wear it!

Cordially yours,

Dear Mr. Hoyt:

I'm so sorry I cannot accept your invitation to speak at the school on Thursday evening, May 1. I should like to very much indeed, but I have a previous commitment for that evening.

However, I am passing your request on to the American Association of Advertising Agencies as they usually have speakers available. You will no doubt hear from them in a few days.

Sincerely yours,

Dear Dr. Benton:

We are pleased to learn of your interest in *Boca Raton*.

The booklet we are sending you with this letter will give you an idea of the size, beauty and completeness of the club. It provides 650 sleeping rooms; and has facilities for all sports, entertainment and shopping within its own boundaries.

Boca Raton will open on December 12 and our rate sheet is now in the process of being printed. As soon as it is ready I will send it to you; and I'll be happy to make reservations for whatever accommodations you require.

I look forward to the pleasure of meeting you when you come to Boca Raton, and I shall do everything I can to make your stay pleasant and comfortable.

Cordially yours,

Dear Mrs. Watson:

Thank you for your letter and your interest in our work.

We enclose copies of the material you wish to use from our Correspondence Manuals, and which you have our permission to reprint.

There will be no charge for the use of this material, and the credit line you suggest is satisfactory.

Best wishes for the success of your new book!

Cordially yours,

LETTERS ABOUT CREDIT

Much of the business of the world is conducted on a credit basis. This involves a great deal of correspondence: letters applying for credit, investigating credit rating, extending or refusing credit and so forth.

Letters giving credit information should be straightforward and truthful, based only on fact. Letters refusing credit should be tactfully written, the emphasis being on some broad general principle or on company policy rather than anything personal.

Here are examples of the usual types of letters about credit used in business:

Gentlemen:

We wish to open a credit account with your company.

Please let us know what information and references you require.

Very truly yours,

Gentlemen:

We enclose a check for the merchandise ordered on May 12.

We should like our name put on your books as a charge customer, being billed once a month instead of each time we send an order.

If you will let us know what information you require, we'll be glad to send it.

Yours very truly,

Gentlemen:

I'd like to open a charge account with your store.

I have accounts with Lord & Taylor, Altman's, Best & Company and Bonwit Teller.

Yours truly,

Dear Madam:

We are delighted to welcome you as a charge customer. Your name is now on our books, and you may feel free to order merchandise at any time.

To complete our records, will you please fill out the enclosed forms and return them to us?

We hope you will enjoy your association with this store; and we shall, of course, make every effort to serve you courteously and well.

Sincerely yours,

Dear Mr. Randolph:

We take great pleasure in adding Turner & Peart to our list of credit customers.

The standing and reputation of your firm are such that we do not require the usual forms of application. All we need for our files are the names of two firms with which you do business on a credit basis.

As you know, this is just a routine procedure in opening new credit accounts.

Cordially yours,

Gentlemen:

Thank you very much for your order, which has received our careful attention.

As your name is not on our books, we are enclosing a credit application. Please fill it out and return it to us at once so that shipment will not be held up.

We hope this marks the beginning of a long and pleasant association between us.

Cordially yours,

Dear Mr. Bowen:

Your request to be placed on our books as a credit customer is a real pleasure. We are delighted to add your name to our list of accounts.

We enclose a credit card to be filled out and returned for our files. This is just routine business procedure, as you know. We are honored to have you as a credit customer, and we'll be glad to fill any order—at any time.

Thank you for your expression of confidence in us.

Sincerely yours,

Gentlemen:

We appreciate your letter of October 4.

Since you say you have opened a credit account for us, we assume you are shipping the goods we ordered— and that we can expect them promptly.

We enclose your credit information blank and two business references.

Sincerely yours,

Gentlemen:

Thank you for your courteous letter. I understand the need for credit references and am glad to give them.

Two firms with which I have accounts and to whom you may refer are Smith, Emmett & Co., Inc. and Arnold & Dupree—both of Dallas.

I'd appreciate a quick checkup on these references, as I'd like to receive the order in time for our Easter sale.

Yours very truly,

Dear Mr. Burton:

Thank you for your letter giving references in connection with your application for credit.

It's embarrassing to us to realize we did not make ourselves entirely clear in our last letter. Our house policy requires *trade references*—that is, the names of firms who have supplied you with goods on credit terms.

Will you please send us two such references; and in the meantime you may order what you like, as your name has been entered on our books as a credit customer.

Sincerely yours,

Dear Mr. Haskins:

We have received a request from Mr. William Turner, of Dallas, to be placed on our books as a charge customer. Mr. Turner asks credit up to $3000 for a period of three months.

Will you tell us what you can about Mr. Turner? We would like to know his financial standing, the extent of his business, and his reputation for meeting obligations. Your reply will be kept in strict confidence.

We shall be very grateful indeed for your help.

Sincerely yours,

Gentlemen:

We have had business dealings with Taylor-White for many years, and have always found them to be completely reliable.

The company is sound financially, and has the reputation of meeting obligations promptly.

We do not hesitate to recommend them as a safe credit risk.

Cordially yours,

Gentlemen:

We are glad to give you a reference for the Ray Bolton Company.

This firm is well known to us, and we have had considerable business dealings with them through the years.

Ray Bolton is a highly reputable and trustworthy firm, sound financially and prompt in the payment of bills. You should have no hesitancy about extending credit to them.

Sincerely yours,

Gentlemen:

The firm mentioned in your letter of April 8th is not well known to us.

As far as we know, this is a respectable and trustworthy firm; but as we have had little business dealing with them in recent years, we cannot vouch for their credit standing.

We're sorry that we are not able to be more helpful.

Sincerely yours,

Gentlemen:

We are sorry to say that we cannot vouch for the reliability of the Spencer-Crane Company. Our own experience with them has not been satisfactory.

During the three years Spencer-Crane have been on our books, they have repeatedly failed to meet their obligations on time; and they have caused us much trouble with regard to payments. Right now they owe us $318.55 for purchases made over a period of six months.

We give you this information in confidence, in the hope it will be of help to you.

Cordially yours,

COLLECTION LETTERS

Collection letters are generally written in a series, one letter following the other at periodic intervals, with increasing degrees of urgency and insistence.

The best collection letters do not bully, threaten, call names. They are firm, but *tactful*. They assume that the debtor wants to pay, give him a chance to explain why he does not or cannot pay, stress the advantages of maintaining good credit rating . . . make it possible for him to pay graciously and without resentment.

Often the first collection letter fails to get results; but the second or third one may. Therefore *persistence is important*. But it isn't necessary to write a long series of angry, threatening letters. If three or four letters have been sent and ignored, it's reasonable to assume that the firm or individual either can't or won't pay the bill. In that case, a last brief letter may be written giving the correspondent "fair warning" that other steps are about to be taken. This should be in the nature of a *notice*, not a *threat*.

Following are examples of collection letters in varying degrees of insistence. The first four represent a series:

Dear Mrs. Franklin:

In checking our accounts, we find there is a balance of $42.50 due us for purchases made in September.

As you have no doubt overlooked this bill, we are bringing it to your attention.

Will you please send your check at once so we can clear this indebtedness from our books and bring your account up to date.

Yours very truly,

Dear Mrs. Franklin:

As you are usually very prompt in paying your bills, we wonder why you have overlooked your September account.

Is there some reason why you are not paying this bill? Would you like to come in and talk it over with us?

The amount is for $42.50, and it is now more than three months overdue.

We'll be looking for your check in the next day or two; or for a letter telling us when we may expect at least part of the amount due us.

Yours very truly,

Dear Mrs. Franklin:

We are disappointed not to have received any word from you in answer to our letters concerning the bill of $42.50 which you owe us.

As you know, the terms of our agreement extend credit for one month only. This bill is now four months overdue. Surely you don't want to lose your credit standing with us and with other stores—nor do we want to lose you as a customer.

We therefore urge you to send a check at once. We urge you to keep your account on the same friendly and pleasant basis it has always been in the past.

Of course if there is some reason why you cannot pay this bill, or can pay only part of it now, we'd be very happy to talk it over with you . . . and perhaps we could be helpful.

Yours very truly,

Dear Mrs. Franklin:

We can't tell you how sorry we are you haven't answered any of our letters about the $42.50 you owe us. We must now regretfully assume you do not want to pay, and we have no other choice than to turn the matter over to our collection attorneys.

This is most distasteful to us, especially in your case —and we are therefore making *one last request* for your check, or for a letter of explanation.

We are holding up proceedings for five days in the hope of hearing from you. Please don't disappoint us!

Yours very truly,

Dear Mr. Ellis:

We don't like to remind a good customer like you that a bill is overdue.

However you have probably overlooked the balance of $32 due on January 15; and we know you would want us to bring it to your attention.

If your check is already in the mail, Mr. Ellis, just forget this letter—and forgive us for writing it!

Sincerely yours,

Gentlemen:

This is to remind you that the amount of $325 was due on your account on January 1.

We know that reminders like this are annoying, and we certainly don't like to send them. But we cannot function efficiently unless our accounts are kept up to date. We hope you understand.

And we hope there's a check from you for the full amount in the next day or two!

Sincerely yours,

Dear Mr. Johnson:

We're still waiting for that $56 you promised to send the beginning of the month. It's now more than four months overdue.

Your credit is still good with us, Mr. Johnson, and we hope it always will be. But won't you please settle that old bill and get your account straightened out on our books?

We know you want to; and we hope you'll find it convenient to do so soon.

Sincerely yours,

Gentlemen:

We cannot understand why you have ignored our two previous letters. If there's anything wrong, won't you write and tell us about it—and perhaps we can be of some assistance.

We know you want to maintain your fine credit standing in the industry, and we want to *help* you maintain it. If you cannot pay the long overdue bill of $683 at this time, let us know what the trouble is, and when you think you'll be able to pay some part of the bill. In that way you won't be jeopardizing your good name and the reputation you now have for reliability.

We cannot impress upon you too strongly the need for answering this letter at once, and sending a check in payment of your bill if you can possibly do so.

Very truly yours,

Dear Mr. King:

Look! We've been very patient about that $400 you owe us since last June. Don't you think we deserve some word from you explaining what the trouble is?

We'll be expecting a letter from you in the next day or so—or better still, a check for some part of the amount.

Please don't disappoint us *this* time, Mr. King!

Sincerely yours,

ACKNOWLEDGING COLLECTION LETTERS

If you are unable to meet a bill on the day it is due—or if you are waiting for a change or correction to be made in a bill before you pay it—*write and say so*. Explain the circumstances fully and courteously. You will find your creditor much more reasonable, much more willing to co-operate with you and give you an extension of time, if you tell him exactly what the situation is.

Gentlemen:

We are placed in a most uncomfortable position! We are obliged to ask for an extension of time on your bill for $921.45.

We had depended on a check from a client to take care of this bill. But we have just been informed that this check will not arrive until April 15th.

We must therefore ask for a two weeks' extension of time on your bill. We are sorry for the delay and hope it will not inconvenience you.

Sincerely yours,

Dear Mr. Barton:

I am sorry that illness and unexpected expenses have made it impossible for me to pay my bill on time.

However, I am sending you $20 on account—and I'll make every effort to pay the balance before June 30.

Thank you for your courteous and understanding letter.

Sincerely yours,

Gentlemen:

This is in answer to your second letter requesting payment of the $876.50 bill sent on January 6.

Let me point out *again* that as soon as you adjust this bill to take care of the $50 for glassware smashed in transit, we will send payment in full.

Yours very truly,

Gentlemen:

The reason we have not paid your bill of August 15 is because of an overcharge of $60, which we pointed out to you in a previous letter.

As soon as you send a corrected bill, we shall be glad to send payment in full.

Yours truly,

Dear Mr. Richards:

I'm sorry you had to write me again about my bill. I know it's long overdue, and I shall make every effort to pay it before the end of the month.

You have been most patient and considerate, and I am grateful.

Sincerely yours,

MISCELLANEOUS BUSINESS LETTERS

Gentlemen:

Thank you for your letter of May 20.

We have already placed an order for summer sportswear, but we are interested in carrying your line for the Florida season.

Will you have your salesman drop in to see us when he is in this territory?

Very truly yours,

Dear Mr. Bradley:

We are sorry we cannot comply with your request for lower prices at this time.

Our prices are now at the lowest possible point consistent with our standards of quality. We cannot change the price without changing the product. Naturally we cannot change the product if we expect to maintain the confidence and trust of valued customers like yourself.

We hope you understand our position. We ask you to accept our prices, as quoted . . . and to continue our pleasant and mutually profitable relationship on the same basis as before.

Sincerely yours,

Gentlemen:

We have given your letter of June 12th very careful consideration.

As we have done business with each other so pleasantly for many years, we should like to comply with your request for lower prices.

However, our own overhead has increased sharply in recent months and we cannot reduce prices 15% without lowering our standards of quality . . . and that we are not prepared to do.

We suggest an overall reduction of 5% in price, throughout the line.

We hope this is satisfactory, and that we can continue our long and friendly association.

Sincerely yours,

Dear Dr. Wilson:

We are pleased to notify you that the Directors of the Universal Couplings Corporation—in which you have an interest—have declared a dividend of 10¢ per share payable March 24th to stockholders of record March 18th.

We are informed that this dividend is being paid out of royalties which the Corporation has recently received from its foreign licensees.

The market in the stock at this writing is 1½ bid and 2¼ asked.

Very truly yours,

Dear Mr. Countway:

Mr. Thomas Harley has suggested that you should receive a copy of *Scoop Stories of the Year* which we are sending you today.

We hope this little book will provide you with some interesting reading.

Cordially yours,

Dear Mrs. Watson:

This note is to thank you for your valuable assistance. Yours is a most interesting story, and I am sure it will fit nicely into the pattern of my article.

The forms will be open for another two or three weeks, so if you think of anything we didn't discuss which would make interesting reading—I'll be glad to have it.

I'm returning the pictures and clippings you let me use.

I hope you know how grateful I am to you for your courtesy and help.

Sincerely yours,

Dear Mr. Crosley:

Mr. Rogers is in Des Moines and expects to be there until at least May 15.

I have sent him your letter, and no doubt he will answer it from there.

Sincerely yours,

Martha K Condon

Secretary to Mr. Rogers

Dear Mr. Martin:

Is my face red!

I wrote you yesterday saying that a balance of $67 was still due on your account. I now find that your check for this amount was received on August 5, but was credited to another customer by mistake.

Thank you very much for the check—and please excuse the embarrassing mistake!

Very cordially yours,

Dear Mrs. McCarthy:

Have you moved recently? Or could it be that the salesgirl made a mistake in writing out your check?

We ask these questions because your name at the above address does not appear on our records as a charge customer.

If the error is ours, of course we want to correct it. Or if you charged the merchandise thinking you were in some other store where you have an account, perhaps you want to talk with us about opening an account here.

In either case, will you drop in and see us in the next day or so? Or if it's more convenient, telephone Middletown 4300, Extension 55.

Yours very truly,

Dear Mrs. Brandt:

What's wrong? Have we offended you in any way? Have we failed in courtesy . . . service . . . value?

You have not used your account here for nearly six months, and we are most concerned about it. We certainly hope it is not because of dissatisfaction with the store. If it is, we should like to know about it— and correct it if we can.

So would you please take a minute or so to write your comments on the back of this letter? We'll appreciate it very much indeed.

Sincerely yours,

4

Letters That Sell

A good sales letter is like a good advertisement. It compels the reader's attention—makes him stop, look, read and *buy*.

All selling—whether over the counter, in newspapers or magazines, on the air or by means of a letter—should be keyed to the interests, problems, needs or desires of the prospect. The reader of your sales letter should be able to see at once, clearly and unmistakably, the promise of real benefit to himself or to his family. Cold logic, dry facts, uninspired statistics . . . these have their place, of course . . . but their place is not in a sales letter that must go into a busy office or home and either compel instant attention or land in the wastebasket.

If you will study and analyze all the really *good* sales letters you receive, the letters that convince and persuade you almost against your own will, you will find that they are keyed to what I call "The 7 Basics of Mass Selling." Every good sales letter you write, whatever its nature or purpose, should conform to this 7-point structure. The body of the letter, the wording, the approach, the strategy of appeal, may all be as original and different as you like; but the structure should be basically this:

1. *Compel attention!* Make contact with the reader— attract his interest or curiosity with your very first sentence.

2. *Offer a definite promise!* Make it imperative for the person to read on, to find out more about his service, product or idea that can mean so much to him or to his family.

3. *Aim at some simple fundamental human instinct!* Never mind how the product is made or how many people bought it last year. The reader wants to know, "What does it mean to *me?*"

4. *Feature the "plus" value of your product or idea!* Find the point of difference between your product and others of a similar nature—and show that difference to be an advantage.

5. *Prove what you say!* Back up your claim or claims with facts. Sell fast with fast-selling sentences! Make the reader say "Yes! Yes!" in his mind. (If he says "Yes, that's true!" three times in the course of reading your letter, he's *sold*.)

6. *Persuade the reader to grasp the opportunity or advantage you offer!* The effect of a good sales letter on a prospect should be . . . *not* "What a wonderful letter!"—but "What a wonderful opportunity! I mustn't miss it!"

7. *Close with an urgent request for action!* Give the reader something to do—give specific directions or instructions. An order blank or return post card enclosed with the letter helps get action.

Of these seven basics, Number 3 is by far the most important. Your letter must appeal to some deep-rooted human instinct or emotion, otherwise it isn't likely to get the results you want. There must be a *motive* behind the impulse to buy. There must be a fundamental need or desire—a compelling self-interest.

Give a man a pen to try, and what does he write? His own name!

Give a man a group picture in which he appears, and what does he look for? His own face!

It's as simple as that. People buy a product or subscribe to an idea because it offers something they want or need for *their own* profit, pleasure, success or well-being.

Bear that in mind when writing a sales letter. Remember that people are interested in your product only in terms of what it means to them or their loved ones.

Here is an advertising expert's* check-list guide to what people want, the advantages they are most interested in gaining. One of these should be the basic appeal of your sales letter, whether you are selling a bar of soap or a Steinway piano.

1. Better Health
2. More Money
3. Greater Popularity
4. Improved Appearance
5. Security in Old Age
6. Praise from Others
7. More Comfort
8. More Leisure
9. Pride of Accomplishment
10. Business Advancement
11. Social Advancement
12. Increased Enjoyment (from food, drink, entertainment, etc.)

According to the same excellent source, people also want to:

Be good parents
Have influence over others
Be sociable, hospitable
Be gregarious
Express their personalities
Resist domination by others
Satisfy their curiosity
Be up-to-date
Emulate the admirable
Appreciate beauty
Be proud of their possessions
Be creative
Acquire or collect things
Be efficient
Win others' affection

* Victor O. Schwab, *How to Write a Good Advertisement* (New York: Schwab & Beatty, Inc., 1945).

Be "first" in things
Improve themselves mentally
Be recognized as authorities

And people also want to save money, time, work, discomfort, worry, doubts, risks, embarrassment, offense to others, boredom, personal self-respect and prestige.

Use the following as examples to help you write more effective sales letters:

Dear Sir:

How would you like to be one of the most interesting and best-informed men in your community?

How would you like to be in a position to discuss the important social, economic, political, national and international affairs of the day—not by reading more, but *by reading less!*

You can, so easily, just by reading WORLD NEWS MAGAZINE! This fascinating digest of world events brings you all the vital and significant news stories of the week. It tells you about people, places, things— everything that's going on—in condensed, quick-reading form.

You cannot really grasp the shape of our times unless you get the story *whole*—unless you know everything that's happening, here and abroad. You should not only know what statesmen, scientists, world leaders in all fields are doing, saying and planning to help shape the world's future. You should also know what *plain people* everywhere in the world are doing, saying and thinking.

And that's what WORLD NEWS brings you: *all* the news, about *all* people, *all* over the world! Issue after issue brings you the news of treaties, agreements, international meetings, conferences, discoveries, inventions . . . news as sharp and clear and true as experienced on-the-spot reporters and journalists can make it.

But side by side with these big stories of the week, WORLD NEWS brings you the little *human* stories that never break into the headlines. WORLD NEWS brings you stories of people in every part of the world working, fighting, dreaming, laughing, loving—people at work and people at play—intimate, dramatic stories to enrich your knowledge of humanity and make you a more brilliant, well-informed conversationalist.

WORLD NEWS is the favorite magazine of doctors, bankers, lawyers, architects, engineers, business executives. It's the favorite magazine of nearly *two million* alert, intelligent families like yours from coast to coast!

We know it will be *your* favorite magazine, too— once you start reading it. We know you'll wait for it eagerly, week after week, read it from cover to cover, mark things to remember, clip items to save. . . .

Try WORLD NEWS at the Special Introductory Rate that brings you a whole year's subscription for only $5. That's a real saving—$2.80 less than the 52 copies would cost you on the newsstand!

Remember: *Even if you don't read anything else all week,* WORLD NEWS *will make you one of the most interesting and best-informed persons in your community!*

The special saving is available for a limited time only. So please sign the enclosed postage-paid card and *air mail it back to us today!*

Sincerely yours,

Dear Sir:

Are you the sort of person who makes snap judgments? Are you the sort of person who takes important steps in the dark?

It's my guess you are not! It's my guess you are neither rash nor impulsive . . . that you feel your way carefully . . . that you get all the facts and data you can before taking action.

How do I know? That's easy! You were once a subscriber to Kellogg's National Letters. That means you wanted *the best information available from Washington to fortify your own judgments and help you make important decisions.*

What puzzles me is why you are not getting the Letters now. I think that you, particularly, should be interested in resubscribing—and *at once!* For what happens in Washington during the next few months is likely to affect your business profoundly.

Naturally you can't *go* ahead unless you can *see* ahead. And to see ahead, you must have a clear picture of what's happening and what's likely to happen —how world news is affecting home affairs—how labor, industry and finance are reacting. You must know what's going on in the nation's capital, and how unexpected shifts and trends can affect even your most carefully and intelligently thought-out plans.

It isn't enough to read the papers, listen to radio and television, talk things over with your friends. You must *know.* You must have facts and forecasts—you must have advance information, soundly interpreted.

I'm sure you'll agree from your own previous experience that there's no more regular, authoritative, *dependable* source of such information than the Kellogg National Letters!

The Kellogg staff is made up—not of ordinary reporters—but of *experts,* each a specialist in his own field. Their opinions are based on fact; their appraisals are shrewd; their forecasts are accurate and helpful.

The list of clients who subscribe to Kellogg's National Letters reads like an impressive Who's Who in American business. Many have been subscribers for *more than 25 years!*

You, too, need the Letters to give you important advance information—to point out the trends that are developing—to help you *see ahead* and chart a wise, safe course of action! You need these vital reports from Washington more urgently than ever before; for much is happening, and *will* happen, in the months ahead.

So may we put your name back on our list, and start sending you the Letters again? The fee is still only $20 a year, a tiny investment when you realize that a single item in any one Letter might save you thousands of dollars!

Just fill in and mail the enclosed card today—but *hurry!* We'll bill you later. If you mail the card right now, you'll receive next week's Letter . . . and it happens to be an especially important one.

Sincerely yours,

Dear Madam:

Can you tell a lark from a starling? Can you tell a robin from a wren? Do you know what birds are helpful to your garden, and how you can attract them year after year?

Now you can become an expert, in almost no time at all! The GARDEN LOVERS' BIRD GUIDE is the most complete, authoritative, practical and *beautiful* book of its kind ever published! It identifies every bird in North America, tells you everything you want to know about it, gives you a wealth of interesting and practical information about bird life.

If you are the least bit interested in birds, we can promise you this: *You'll love the* BIRD GUIDE! It's far more than a handy reference and guide. It's a book that offers many, many hours of fascinating reading!

The text tells the whole life story of each bird, briefly but completely—and in a most readable style. It describes:

 —the songs and calls of each bird
 —its nests and eggs
 —its color, size and plumage
 —its food and behavior

—its associates
—its nature and range of flight
—its habits of migration
—its habits of courtship and breeding

Every bird is illustrated in full color, making this a truly magnificent book for your own library or for a gift. Imagine! There are over 500 full-color illustrations of birds, beautifully reproduced from paintings made especially for the book. Delighted gardeners and bird lovers tell us this collection of color plates alone is well worth the price of the book—and *more!*

Richard G. Cleve of the scientific staff of the National Bird Society says: "By every standard, the GARDEN LOVERS' BIRD GUIDE is a superlative achievement. It's the best book of its kind I have ever seen. It should delight the heart of any nature lover."

The BIRD GUIDE is published in handy size for carrying into the woods or fields (4½ x 7¼ inches). It is bound in handsome, flexible, *water-resistant* binding, stamped in gold. It is arranged and indexed for quick, easy reference . . . and it even contains maps to show where the various species of birds are to be found!

Wouldn't you like to have a *first edition* of this superb book? It has just been published, and if you act promptly you can secure one of the prized first copies. Don't send any money now. We'll be glad to send the BIRD GUIDE on approval. You have the privilege of returning it in a week, or sending *only $3.00 plus a few cents postage in full payment!*

Hurry! Get your order in today. We enclose a special order form and stamped envelope for your convenience.

Sincerely yours,

Dear Madam:

You may not know this, but as a charge customer you are a *privileged character!* We have a warm spot in our hearts for regular customers like you. . . .

Among other things, we like to take you into our confidence. We like to tell you what's happening here in the store even before it happens—tip you off about important sales and things.

For example, right now we're planning a wonderful sale of imported English doeskin gloves. They are beautiful, butter-soft gloves—exactingly made of the very finest skins—in the classic 4-button length. They come in chamois and white; and they're not only lovely and luxurious to wear, but *practical,* too. For you can wash them over and over again, as easily as a pair of cotton gloves.

We haven't had imported doeskin gloves like these in years. And as they'll be amazingly low priced at only $3.98 a pair when they go on sale next week, you can be sure they'll go *fast.* That's why we're letting you know about it ahead of time. If you send in your order now, we'll reserve as many pairs as you want. Otherwise you may rush in the day of the sale, and not be able to get the sizes and colors you want.

We don't want that to happen to you! So use the special order blank we are enclosing *for charge customers* only. Let us put aside two, three—or even half a dozen pairs of these marvelous doeskin gloves, earmarked especially for you.

But don't delay, as your order may get to us too late. Fill in the color and sizes you want and *mail today.*

Sincerely yours,

Dear Madam:

Wouldn't you like to be able to enjoy a cup of hot, steaming, delicious coffee—whenever and wherever you want it—with no more trouble than heating a little water?

Well, you *can!* For now there's something new—something marvelous—a real time and trouble saver! Now there's coffee you can make *right in the cup,* quickly and easily, in just the time it takes to heat the water!

It's JIF, the new Instant Coffee, and people every-where say they never tasted coffee more *completely satisfying*. They say it's coffee at its best—rich and full-bodied—wonderful in flavor and aroma.

Yet JIF is made in a jiffy, right in the cup, with-out coffee pot or percolator! It requires practically no preparation whatever. You just put a teaspoon of JIF in a cup, add hot water—and stir. That's all there is to it! Your coffee is ready almost before you can say "In-stantaneous!"

Think of the time JIF will save in the morning, when you're busy with breakfast! Think what a con-venience it will be in midafternoon or evening—*any* time you want or need a cup of coffee—how much easier and quicker than preparing it the old-fashioned way!

JIF Instant Coffee saves money, too. There's no waste. You make exactly as many cups as you want —no more, no less—and every cup *delicious!* You'll say, "Why didn't somebody think of this before!"

JIF is now available at grocery stores in 25¢ and 50¢ jars. To introduce this amazing new Instant Coffee, we are making a special offer—*good until October 1 only*. Take the enclosed Complimentary Card to your grocer and he'll give you the regular, full-sized 25¢ jar for only 10¢.

Don't miss this opportunity to try JIF Instant Cof-fee at a saving—a *big* saving of more than half! Take the Complimentary Card to your dealer *today!*

Sincerely yours,

Dear Madam:

Would you buy a new Easter bonnet with your eyes closed? Of course not! You'd want to try it on, see how it looks on you, decide whether it's flattering.

Then why buy *face powder* without trying it on? How do you know the shade you select is the right shade for you . . . the most *youthful* . . . the most *exciting*?

Now at last you don't need to guess or gamble— now you can *know!* For you can *try on* the season's most popular shades of powder without cost! You can try them one after another, right on your own skin, before your own mirror—and find the one that does the most for your appearance!

Just send your name and address on the enclosed card, and you'll receive the GYPSY QUEEN SAMPLER, entirely without cost. It contains samples of the five newest, most fascinating shades of Gypsy Queen Face Powder. It's fun to try them on . . . to see the effect of each shade on your skin . . . to find the one that's best for you, that makes your whole face look more exciting and glamorous.

Send for the GYPSY QUEEN SAMPLER today! Remember—it contains samples of the *five* newest and most popular powder shades of the season. Here's your chance to try them all!

When you find the shade of Gypsy Queen Face Powder that's best for you, buy the full-sized box at your favorite drug or cosmetic counter—only $1 for a generously sized, attractive boudoir box.

Don't forget! Fill in the card and mail it *right now* for your free GYPSY QUEEN SAMPLER.

Sincerely yours,

Dear Sir:

Remember the scramble it was last year to get all your Christmas cards out in time?

This year *be good to yourself!* Order your Christmas cards early, while there's still a good selection. And address them at your leisure to avoid that hectic last-minute rush.

We have an unusual collection of cards to show you this year. We know you'll enjoy seeing them. Many are reproductions of paintings by famous artists, and are —in our opinion—the most *beautiful* cards we have ever been in a position to offer. The prices are amazingly low for cards of such quality and distinction.

Come early, and allow plenty of time for personalizing the cards you select. You can take the envelopes with you and address them while the cards are being printed or engraved.

Don't put it off! Remember—the earlier you come, the better the selection. And remember, too, sending out Christmas cards is lots more fun when you do it *leisurely.*

We'll be looking forward to seeing you and showing you our selection of cards sometime in the next few days.

Sincerely yours,

Dear Madam:

Thank you for your inquiry about Fidex Dog Food. We are sending you the booklet you requested; and also another little book we thought you might like to have on *The Intelligent Care and Training of Dogs.* We hope you will find these books interesting and helpful.

If you love your dog and want him to be well, *be careful of the food you give him.* Occasional table scraps may do no harm; but a steady diet of any-old-kind of scraps is bound to ruin his digestion and seriously affect his health and well-being.

Fidex is an improved dog food, scientifically balanced to provide the nutrition a healthy dog needs. It's a delicious, top-quality product—as clean and wholesome as any food prepared for human consumption.

A can of Fidex is a *complete meal* for your dog—

appetizing, nutritious and *economical*. Keep a supply on hand to keep your dog happy and well.

Ask your dealer *today* for Fidex Dog Food!

Sincerely yours,

Dear Madam:

If you have ever wished you had extra sleeping space in your house—a cozy place to put up an overnight guest—here's your answer!

Here's a charming and graceful piece of furniture, decorative and compact—yet it opens up to a *full-size double bed!*

It's the new Shelton Chaise-Bed—fascinating to look at, practical to use, and a wonderful convenience when someone must be put up overnight.

The Shelton Chaise-Bed has an unusual new patented mechanism for opening—made of Duraluminum, which is 35 pounds lighter than steel. This makes an amazing "finger-tip control"—so easy to manage, a child can open or close the bed in half a minute!

The luxurious innerspring mattress is full length, 48 inches wide, and supremely comfortable. No breaks, bumps, lumps or ridges . . . this chaise-bed is designed for *good, sound, restful sleep!*

We enclose illustrations to show you how attractive the Shelton Chaise-Bed is. You can have it in your choice of dozens of beautiful upholstery fabrics.

Come in and see it. A demonstrator will show you how easily it works. We know you'll agree it's the most convenient and practical piece of furniture you have seen in a long, long time!

How about stopping in tomorrow? We'll be delighted to show you the Shelton Chaise-Bed—with no obligation to you, of course. Make it *today*, if you can!

Sincerely yours,

Dear Sir:

There's a chill in the air. . . . Have you noticed it? And that chill spells *danger* to your car!

Don't wait for signs of trouble. Come in and give your car the cold weather servicing it needs—*right now!*

Servicing at this time of the year keeps your car in sound, smooth-running condition . . . protects its trade-in value. But even more important, expert servicing now means safer driving all winter for you and your family.

We'd like you to know we have improved service facilities, skilled mechanics, up-to-date equipment, time-saving tools, genuine parts—everything for making your car perform at its best.

So drive in some time during the next day or two, and let us look over your car. We'll see if it has any dangerous symptoms of neglect. We'll tell you what it needs in the way of a winter pick-up or tonic. *Be smart!* A check-up and servicing now may save you a lot of time and money later when the real cold weather comes around!

Drive in today or tomorrow. . . . Hand the enclosed card of introduction to one of our attendants, and he'll see that you get special, personal attention.

Don't put it off—*you may be sorry!* It pays in every way to *act now* and beat the cold!

                                        Sincerely yours,

Dear Madam:

I was driving by your house the other day, and I noticed what a fine garden you have. It must give you great pride to have one of the most attractive gardens in the neighborhood.

It would give *me* great pride to protect your lovely garden from the beetles, bugs and scores of destructive pests that attack in force about the first of August. I hope you won't let them damage your garden this year!

You see, I have a weekly spraying service that protects gardens like yours. I'd like to drop in and tell you about it, if I may. I didn't want to ring your bell, and perhaps disturb you when you're busy—that's why I'm writing.

I use my own patented spray (sorry, I can't tell you what it is—*that's* a secret!). But my customers tell me it's very effective. They say it keeps the old bugs and beetles away, without injury to trees, plants or grass. It can't harm children or pets, either; I *know*, because I had it tested and approved.

I hope you'll let me come and tell you more about my garden-spraying service. My rates are very reasonable. And you can be sure I'll do a thorough and conscientious job, because I hate to see a lovely garden attacked and damaged by pests.

A post card with your name and address will bring me to your door. Or call NE. 6-2100 and tell me when to come. Thank you.

Yours very truly,

Dear Sir:

If you ever bought a suit or coat that was "nearly right"—you know what a disappointment it turned out to be. Clothes must fit perfectly—they must feel right and look right—otherwise you aren't happy in them.

"Nearly right" isn't good enough for home insulation, either. It must be *exactly right,* otherwise you'll be disappointed . . . you'll be sorry. . . .

Remember! You can't change insulation the way you can change a suit or coat. You insulate your house only once, so *the job must be done right the first time.* And you can't *see* the difference between good and

poor work in insulation. Therefore your choice of a
contractor is extremely important.

The U.S. Bureau of Mines says: "Insulation is no
better than the man who installs it."

You take no risk when "the man who installs it"
is an approved Mitchell Home Insulation Contractor!
He's trained, experienced, competent and *reliable*. He
knows his job and does it well. He applies Mitchell
Rock Wool scientifically, in full measure and to the
right density, to prevent voids or "empty pockets"
that let the heat leak out. He does it . . . not "nearly
right" . . . but *100% right* down to the last detail!

We'll be glad to send an authorized Mitchell Home
Insulation Contractor to see you and talk things over.
He'll tell you how you can save up to 35% in fuel year
after year, and keep your house up to 15% cooler in
summer.

There is no obligation. Just fill in the enclosed card
and mail it back to us today.

                                    Sincerely yours,

Dear Subscriber:

"Parting is such sweet sorrow. . . ." according to
Shakespeare.

But is it? Perhaps there was some sweetness in
Juliet's sorrow as she stood whispering good-by to her
beloved. But there's no sweetness in *our* parting! We're
filled with sadness at the thought of losing you as a
subscriber.

And lose you we must, unless you renew your subscription *at once* to MODERN HOME MAGAZINE! As
much as we hate to part with you, we must remove
your name from our lists . . . unless you say: "Wait!
Stop! I'm staying to enjoy all the good things you are
planning for the coming year!"

So we are writing you *just this once more* in the hope
you will change your mind. We are writing to say,

"Please don't go! Stay on with us. . . . Renew your subscription for another year. . . ."

A renewal form and return envelope are enclosed. Decide right now there'll be no parting for good old friends like us! Fill in the renewal form and rush it back to us *today*.

Sincerely yours,

LETTERS THAT SELL GOOD WILL

Strictly speaking, the letters in this section are not sales letters. They are written to establish or strengthen friendly relations, and to build good will.

Dear Doctor:

Here's another handy timesaver for you! It's designed to fill a real need in the practice of a busy doctor.

This pad of leaflets contains 50 copies of *The Hygiene of Pregnancy*. You'll find it very convenient to keep on your desk, pulling off one leaflet at a time as you need it.

The leaflet answers the most frequently asked questions of an expectant mother concerning personal hygiene during the prenatal period. You can save time by giving her one of these leaflets instead of answering all her routine questions in the routine way.

The leaflet has been carefully checked and approved by well-known obstetricians. The instructions are *general*, containing nothing to take the place of diagnosis. There is space at the bottom of each leaflet for any special instructions you may wish to add.

Initial and return the enclosed card for your pad of leaflets today. They will be sent to you with the compliments and good wishes of Blank Baby Soap.

Sincerely yours,

Dear Mr. Thompson:

This is to tell you how very much I appreciate the cordial reception you gave me on my first visit to Dallas.

As a new salesman in your territory, it was especially gratifying to me to be received so well—and treated so kindly.

Thank you very much, not only for the order but for your friendly interest. I appreciate more than I can say your helpful advice about local conditions and problems.

I shall do my best to repay you by any "extras" of service that are within my power to provide.

I look forward with great pleasure to seeing you again in April.

Cordially yours,

Dear Mr. Gibbs:

It was just one year ago today that I called on you for the first time. You were most gracious to me on that occasion, and I have not forgotten it.

In fact, the purpose of this note is to express my deep appreciation for the friendship and confidence you have shown me during the past year. I only hope that the service I have been able to give you has in some small measure repaid the many kindnesses you have shown me.

I have thoroughly enjoyed our association, and hope it shall continue for many years to come.

Cordially yours,

Dear Mrs. Harkness:

We were flattered and pleased by your choice of Bingham Inn for your vacation.

We sincerely hope you enjoyed your three weeks here, and that the Inn lived up to your expectations in every way.

We look forward to greeting you again some day, and to the pleasure of extending once more the full hospitality of Bingham Inn.

Sincerely yours,

Dear Mr. Ballard:

Most letters between agent and client are written for a specific business purpose. But this letter is written only to say we *like* you. . . . We're happy to serve you . . . and we hope we can continue serving you for many years to come!

You may think there's some other more selfish motive behind this letter—something we want, or hope to gain. But we assure you there isn't!

We just want to say "Thank you" for believing in us, and for working with us in such a friendly spirit of understanding and co-operation.

Cordially yours,

Dear Mr. Sawyer:

About the time this letter reaches you, clocks all over the country will be ticking out the last hours of the year. . . .

It has been a *good* year for us, here at Smith and Turner. And as we pause to look back, we are especially grateful for the friendship and confidence you have shown us.

We hope you know how happy and proud we are to count you among our clients. We send affectionate greetings from the entire organization . . . and sincere wishes for your happiness, health and continued prosperity throughout the New Year.

Cordially yours,

Dear Mr. Borden:

No one knows better than I the part you have played in making this one of our most successful years.

At this holiday season, I'd like to express my deep appreciation for your friendship and good will.

I wish you and yours happiness at Christmas time, and the best of everything in the New Year.

Cordially yours,

5

Letters of Application

"We are all salesmen, every day of our lives," said the late Charles M. Schwab. "We are selling our ideas, our plans, our energies, our enthusiasm to those with whom we come in contact."

The purpose of a letter of application is to help you *sell yourself*. It should state clearly the job you want, and should tell what your abilities are and what you have to offer. It should give a quick, clear picture of your qualifications, your accomplishments and your aims. It should present you to possible employers in the best light.

A well-written letter of application does not necessarily guarantee a position; but it does insure *consideration* and a better chance of an interview. You cannot hope to get your whole story into a letter, but you should cover enough ground to intrigue the prospective employer and make him want to see you, speak to you and find out more about you. It takes more than a good letter to land a good job; it takes ability, specific experience and good character. But the letter *opens the door for you* and gives you the chance to sell yourself.

Your letter of application should be simple, human, personal —and brief without omitting any essential or pertinent facts. It should be as carefully prepared as an advertisement, since, like an advertisement, it is intended to attract attention, create interest, impel action.

Try not to write a dull, stereotyped letter of application.

Make it *interesting*. A letter can reveal character and personality in many unexpected ways. It's not easy to write a good letter of application, but it's worth all the effort you put into it. For a good letter almost always receives careful consideration from a prospective employer. *Good letters are rare.*

The appearance of your letter is extremely important. Remember that the purpose of a letter of application is to *impress* the prospective employer, to win his interest and confidence. You cannot hope to do a good job of selling yourself with a letter that is sloppy, untidy, poorly written, hard to read, or full of finger marks, erasures or blots.

A letter of application is usually discarded at once if it's written:

> —in pencil, crayon or red ink
> —on wrinkled or dirty paper
> —on hotel stationery
> —on stationery with a business letter-
> head that has been crossed out
> —on odd-sized or odd-shaped stationery
> —on perfumed stationery
> —on brightly colored stationery
> —on a post card

Type your letter of application if possible, for a typed letter is easier to read than a handwritten one. Use standard business-size stationery of good quality, plain white and unlined. If you are applying for a job in an executive capacity, it's helpful to have your own personal letterheads. Otherwise, type your address in the upper right corner above the date.

If you can neither type your letter nor have it typed by some-one, write it out very neatly and legibly. No busy employer is going to waste his time and his eyesight trying to decipher what you have written. Use letter-size stationery of good quality, plain white or very pale buff or gray and *black ink only*. Never send out a letter that discredits you by its appearance.

When writing a letter of application, use simple, familiar words that express your meaning clearly. Watch your spelling;

be sure your punctuation and grammar are correct; avoid the misuse of words; avoid long, involved, confusing sentences.

There may be some excuse for lack of training and education, or even for lack of originality in your letter; but there can be no excuse for grammatical errors, misspelled words, trite phrases or poor punctuation. In these respects at least, let your letter be perfect. One sure way to mark your letter for the wastebasket is to misspell the name of the firm or the name of the individual to whom your letter is addressed.

The opening paragraph of your letter is perhaps the most important part of it. For if the first few sentences fail to win the reader's attention, the rest of the letter may not be read at all. Try to key your opening remarks to the needs or interests of the prospective employer—not to your own needs or desires. *Offer* something instead of asking for something. Right at the start, in the very first sentence if you can, make it clear that you have a *giving* attitude rather than a *getting* attitude. Put yourself in the reader's place; try to imagine the questions he would ask if he were seated across the table from you; try to capture his attention by showing a knowledge of, or a special interest in, his particular business.

For example, instead of opening your letter with some such trite, worn-out statement as, "I saw your advertisement in today's paper," plan your first sentence to arouse interest at once. You might say, "I have made a careful study of your advertising during the past six months," or, "I have made a survey in my neighborhood to find out how many housewives use your product and why they like it."

If there is nothing interesting or different in the first sentence or two of your letter, there is no incentive for a busy employer to read on. But if you can capture his attention at the beginning of your letter, hold it through your list of qualifications and experience, and close with specific information that makes it easy for him to get in touch with you for an interview . . . your letter has at least done a workmanlike job.

A very long letter that rambles on and on—long-winded and disorganized—makes no hit with busy executives. So try to keep your letter as brief and concise as you can. However be sure you tell everything about yourself that you think is necessary for getting the job. To avoid any essential facts concerning experience, training or education is to create a feeling of *evasion,* which, of course, does you more harm than good. Look upon your letter as an "interview on paper" in which you anticipate all likely questions and answer them clearly, to the point.

In writing a letter of application, bear in mind that the things a prospective employer is most likely to want to know about you are:

> Your age
> Your education
> Your domestic status (married or single)
> Your personality (how you get along with others)
> Your training
> Your experience
> Your abilities (what can you do?)
> Your record (what have you done?)
> Your work habits
> Your character
> Your aims or ambition

Some of the things you can be sure no prospective employer wants to read about in a letter of application—and which only annoy and offend him—are long, irrelevant accounts of:

> Your family troubles
> Your bad luck
> Your unfortunate childhood
> Your lack of advantages
> Your "tough breaks"
> Your prejudices
> Your complexes
> Your personal interests and hobbies (unless
>   they have direct bearing on the job)

Try to avoid generalities in your letter of application. *Be specific.* Tell exactly which college you graduated from; give the names of the firms you worked for; be precise about kinds of jobs you have held. Above all, *be specific about the kind of job for which you are now applying.* Do not make the mistake of saying, "I'll do anything!" That's a sure way to rule yourself out. Ask for the *exact* job you want, and give the reasons why you feel you have something of special interest and value to bring to such a job.

If possible, avoid any mention of salary in your letter—unless the employer has requested it in his advertisement or in previous communication with you. It's always best not to give a specific figure, as the difference of a small amount may keep you from making a good connection. Rather than avoid the subject entirely, you might say: "As to salary, may we talk it over?" or "I'll be glad to discuss salary in a personal interview."

College graduates looking for their first positions often ask, "What can I offer in a letter? Employers want experience—which, naturally, no beginner has."

The answer is that *everything you've ever done is experience.* Were you ever on a debating team? Have you ever taken part in amateur theatricals? Did you ever sell subscriptions to magazines? Sift out all your experiences, whatever their nature, and see exactly what you have of value to offer the business world. If you have been president of your school literary club, won a prize for domestic science, edited the school paper, or even been voted first in a popularity contest, say so. A good mixer is an asset in any organization. So is the ability to write good English. So is a knowledge of foods, a knack for selling or a talent for acting or directing. Any evidence of initiative, dependability, originality, perseverance or skill is well worth mentioning in your letter of application if you have no previous business experience to offer. Refuse to be discouraged or dismayed by that lack; *dramatize what you have.*

It's important to write a good strong closing for your letter. Avoid such colorless phrases as "awaiting a favorable reply" or "hoping to hear from you soon." Make a specific request for an interview, such as, "May I telephone you on Thursday morning to arrange for an interview?" Or give the prospective employer something definite to do or expect, such as, "I'll telephone tomorrow at ten o'clock to arrange for an interview" or, "If your secretary will telephone me at Jamiston 4-6700, I'll be happy to arrange for an interview any time to suit your convenience."

An excellent idea is to enclose a stamped, self-addressed envelope with your letter of application. That makes it easier and more convenient for a prospective employer to get in touch with you . . . and at the same time shows that you have initiative and confidence in yourself. Another good idea is to enclose a post card addressed to yourself and asking you to call for an interview—leaving a blank space for the date and hour to be filled in by the employer. It may be just some such simple device that turns the tide in your favor when a busy employer is going over scores of letters and does not know which to choose.

Be *different* in your letter of application. Be original. But be careful not to make yourself appear eccentric or bizarre. Stunt or "trick" letters attract attention—and sometimes compel the interest of the reader where a more familiar or commonplace approach might fail to do so. But such devices should be used only when applying for a job where promotional, imaginative, creative or dramatic abilities are required. In general, freakish or stunt letters are received with skepticism and distaste in the average business office.

Always sign your name very carefully. We suggest that you type or print out your name under the written signature so that the prospective employer won't have to study it to make out the proper spelling. Many an excellent job opportunity has been lost because of an illegible signature.

If you send a photograph with your application, be sure it's not too informal. For example, do not send a picture of yourself in a bathing suit on the beach, or romping with your dog or posing in front of the family car. The picture should be of *you* and nothing else. Don't send a passport photograph that makes you look like an ex-convict. Don't send a group picture with a circle drawn around yourself. Such pictures lack dignity and do not help your cause. A small full-face photograph showing your general appearance is best.

Here are a few "don'ts" that may be helpful to you in preparing your letter of application:

Don't give details of your childhood and early schooling.

Don't relate your experiences in the war unless they have some direct bearing on the job for which you are applying.

Don't brag or boast; if you have some outstanding ability, simply state the facts and let the employer draw his own conclusions.

Don't be a bore; when you've said what you have to say, close the letter. Don't add postscripts.

Don't refer to yourself as "the writer." It is not the best form to say, "The writer has had five years' experience." Say, "I have had five years' experience."

Don't ask for a job because you need it . . . because your father died . . . or your sister is an invalid. *Never base your appeal for work on sympathy*, but only on ability and what you have to offer.

Don't offer to work for very little "to get experience." It's unwise to sell yourself as a bargain. People take you at your own estimate of yourself; and if you don't think you are worth much, no one else will.

Don't say you are not interested in salary; that makes it sound as though you *are*.

Don't discuss "secret" ambitions or pet peeves. Concentrate on selling your abilities and qualifications.

Don't use the vague and ambiguous *"etc."* For example, don't say "I can typewrite, operate a switchboard, etc." Enumerate *all* your capabilities.

Don't complain about, or criticize, a former employer. That hurts your chances more than it helps them.

Don't apply for a job for which you are unsuited, or for which you have inadequate qualifications. Go after the kind of job *you know you can do well*.

Don't use bookish, unfamiliar words in an effort to make an impression. Business men like terse, to-the-point language.

Don't waste space on unrelated subjects. If a man is looking for a copy writer, he is not interested in the fact that you were a marbles champion or won a waltz contest. He might, however, be very much interested in the fact that you won a prize for a short story.

Don't make demands. Don't write in an aggrieved tone, as though the world owes you a job and you are determined to get it. Employers are quick to perceive and to resent such an attitude.

Don't emphasize *your* needs, *your* hopes, *your* plans . . . what *you* expect or want from the job. Keep the employer's interests foremost. . . . Tell him what *he* will get and how *he* will benefit.

Don't be satisfied until you have written a letter you feel is original, interesting and forceful enough to stand apart from others, attract attention, *win you a hearing*.

Every year millions of letters are sent out by people looking for jobs. An appalling percentage of these letters are sheer waste, for they receive little or no attention. Why? Because there is a deadly sameness to them! They look alike; they read alike; they *are* alike. They show no evidence of original thought or constructive reasoning. They have no freshness or personality. Therefore a really *good* letter instantly stands out and wins over competition.

It pays to take pains with your letter of application, to write and *rewrite* it until you are sure it shows you to best advantage.

The following examples should help you prepare an effective, well-integrated letter. But use these examples as guides only, not as exact forms to follow. Use your own ideas and express your own personality—even though it may mean violating one or two of the points listed above. You needn't accept these points as absolute "musts"—though, in general, it's best to be guided by them, and by the examples that follow, unless you have good reasons to the contrary.

Dear Sir:

According to this morning's *Times,* you want an experienced, efficient secretary.

During the past 12 years I have served in that capacity to three prominent executives, all three of whom will vouch for my efficiency and dependability. They are:

Mr. Matthew Borden, Hollins-Borden Company, Trenton, N.J. (Hospital supplies) 19—-19—.

Mr. Curtis Thompson, Worden Associates, New York. (Manufacturers of surgical instruments) 19—-19—.

Mr. John Peterson, Billings, Holt & Company, New York. (Advertising agency) 19—-19—.

Following the recent reorganization of Billings, Holt & Company, Mr. Peterson was transferred to Chicago—which is the reason I am now looking for another connection.

I am 29 years of age, a high school graduate, unmarried, living at home with my family. I am in excellent health, and am told that I make an especially good appearance for a secretary.

My former associates will tell you I am neat, accurate and painstaking in my work; that I am tactful and courteous; resourceful; loyal to the job; and of pleasing personality.

I am well-trained and experienced in all the many duties and responsibilities of a good secretary; and I should like the opportunity of coming in and talking with you personally. May I?

The self-addressed card is for your convenience. Just write on it when you would like me to come for an interview.

Sincerely yours,

Dear Sir:

It seemed, as I read your advertisement in this morning's *Herald,* that it must have been written for me and me alone! For my training, experience and qualifications fit your requirements *exactly.*

You want a stenographer who has had some experience in the publishing business: *All* my experience—9 years of it—has been with publishing firms.

You want a speedy, competent stenographer: I take 160 to 175 words a minute, and I type 90 words a minute neatly, without mistakes.

You want an intelligent, well-educated young woman, interested in books: I am 30 years old, a graduate of Smith College, and so deeply interested in books that I have never accepted a job that wasn't in some way connected with them. I am considered by those who know me to be alert, intelligent and well-informed.

The personal side is best told by others. I'm sure the firms for which I have worked will tell you I have an agreeable personality, good appearance, desirable work habits—that I am an accurate and dependable stenographer. I refer you to:

Mr. Ellis Hartley, Brandt & Co. New York, publishers of medical books.

Mr. James Whitney, Garden City Publishing Company, New York.

Mr. Myron L. Boardman, Prentice-Hall, Inc.,
New York.

I'll be very happy to come for an interview any time
you say. My telephone number is HA. 4-6300.

Sincerely yours,

Dear Sir:

I am a typist, but not an ordinary one! I *like* typing.
I thoroughly *enjoy* it. I take pride in turning out clean,
attractive, well-spaced copy.

Your advertisement in this morning's *Transcript*
appeals to me because I know I'd especially enjoy
typing radio scripts. I offer my qualifications in the
hope you will consider me for the job.

I am 24 years of age, a high school graduate and a
graduate of the National Business Institute where I
studied stenography as well as typing. I can take dicta-
tion when required, and I can operate a teletype machine; but I specialize in typing.

For two years I typed manuscripts for Mr. Charles
Weston, writer of mystery stories.

When Mr. Weston went to Hollywood, I joined the
typing staff of Fred Olcott Associates, where I typed
play scripts, synopses and reports. I was there for three
years, then accepted the job I now hold with Lehn
and Fisher, attorneys, where I am required to do the
most exacting kind of legal typing.

It would be fascinating to type scripts again after
a year of nothing but dull legal documents. I'd bring
more than speed and efficiency to the job. I would
bring a delighted new interest and enthusiasm—and
that, of course, would mean more and better work for
you.

Please check my former employers, including Lehn
and Fisher who know about this letter. They will tell
you I am conscientious, that I have an agreeable per-

sonality and appearance and that I get along well with everyone.

My telephone number is Lincoln 2046. I can start at once, if you like, as my present employers have known for some time that I plan to make a change.

Sincerely yours,

Dear Sir:

Your advertisement offers a most tempting job to a young man just out of college. I can't think of any job I'd like better than consumer research for a famous organization like yours. I look upon it as a wonderful opportunity, and here is what I can offer you in return:

I am 22 years of age, make a good appearance and get along exceedingly well with people.

I have an inquisitive and analytical mind—I enjoy finding out about things—I have tact and good humor —and the ability to draw people out.

Perhaps you will agree that these qualities—plus enthusiasm, persistence, and the willingness to work hard and long—make me acceptable for the job you offer as a beginner on your research staff.

I specialized in advertising and merchandising at New York University, from which I graduated in June—and I have unusual letters of recommendation from my instructors in these subjects. I should like the opportunity of showing them to you.

Although I have had no actual experience in consumer research, I am familiar with the procedure, and fully understand its significance in charting buying habits and trends.

I enclose a card addressed to myself, in the hope you will use it to tell me when to come for an interview. Or if you prefer calling, my telephone number is Plaza 6-3454.

Sincerely yours,

Dear Mr. Bolton:

I understand from Mr. James Harris that there is an opening for a reporter on the staff of the New York *Times*.

Four years' experience on the Middletown *Star*—writing a daily sports column as well as covering a regular news beat—gives me the confidence to apply for this desirable post.

I decided five years ago, when I graduated from Princeton, that reporting the news was my love—and my life's work. My first job was a sort of combination copy boy and rewrite man on the Middletown Press, where I learned the ropes . . . and got the idea for my somewhat unusual sports column. On the strength of this idea, I got a job on the regular staff of the *Star*, where I have been ever since.

I like my job. It has been a lot of fun. And Mr. Philip Jennings, the managing editor, will tell you I've been more than moderately successful; I've proved myself a good reporter and an alert, dependable newspaper man.

The reason for wanting to make a change at this time is an exciting reason to any young and ambitious reporter: *there's an opening on the New York Times!* That's opportunity knocking with both fists. What intelligent newspaper man wouldn't welcome the broader opportunities of a big metropolitan daily like the *Times*.

So I'm putting in my bid for the job, Mr. Bolton. I'm 26 years old, of good appearance and personality, married and have a year-old son. I like hard work, and I don't care how long my hours are. I'm told that I have a flair for quick and easy writing, a sense of the dramatic—and the well-known "nose for news."

I'll be in New York next Thursday, and will take the liberty of telephoning your secretary at 10 o'clock for an appointment sometime during the day. In the meantime, I enclose clippings of my column and a few of my news stories to give you an idea of the kind of writing I can do.

I look forward to the pleasure of a personal interview.

Sincerely yours,

Dear Mr. Winslow:

The Lowen Placement Agency informs me there will soon be an opening in your organization for an art director . . . and I ask you to consider my qualifications.

I am 43 years old, a graduate of Columbia University and the New York School of Fine and Applied Arts, and I have 20 years of successful experience behind me.

My first job was in the Bureau of Engravings, where I got a good basic training.

After a year I moved on to Frederick's Department Store where I was in full charge of all layouts and art work for newspaper advertising, booklets, mailing pieces and catalogs.

Two years later, having learned all I could from this job, I accepted an offer from Benton-Curt & Co. as art director on food accounts. Here I received the best training and experience of all, learning to know and practice all art and layout forms and techniques, how to organize an efficient staff, how to work constructively and well with others. Here I learned to be a good advertising executive as well as a good art director.

From Benton-Curt I went on to the Preston Agency, where I am now employed. I am director of the entire art department here; but as the emphasis is on radio and television rather than printed word, the scope of my job is somewhat limited. That is my reason for wanting to make a change.

I have always admired your organization and should welcome the opportunity of becoming associated with it. My previous employers will tell you I am thoroughly competent and dependable, and that I have no undesirable traits of character or personality.

I enclose a card addressed to myself. Please fill in the day and hour you would like me to come, and I'll bring along some examples of my own art work, as well as proofs of the many varied types of campaigns I have supervised and directed.

Sincerely yours,

Dear Mr. Chase:

You once gave a talk at the Advertising Club, and I was in the audience. You said, "In a big advertising agency nothing is ever done in the dark. Everything is carefully tested, checked and *double-checked*, until there is very little margin for error."

I wrote that down, Mr. Chase . . . and many other of the interesting and important things you said that night. And now that I'm looking for a job as research director of an advertising agency, I turn to you before anyone else. For I think as *you* do about tested appeals in advertising; and I have developed a method of copytesting which I think will be of interest to you . . . and of value to your clients.

For the past three years I have been associated with Pratt & Reynolds as assistant to the account executive on Lanol Soap. In that capacity I was able to try out and check my method of copytesting against those in general use today. I should like an opportunity to tell you what I found out. I know you will be very much interested in the results, and how they were applied toward greatly increasing the sales of Lanol Soap.

I am a graduate of Amherst College, class of 19—. The first year after college, I was with Smith, Cross & Co., in the production department. The next two years I was with the Cary Advertising Agency as a junior copy writer, learning what makes people stop, look and read advertising . . . and dig down in their pockets to buy. Then I joined Pratt & Reynolds, first as a copywriter, but quickly moving up to the job of assistant account executive.

I am still with Pratt & Reynolds. I like my job, and I'm keen about the people with whom I'm associated. . . .

But all my education, training and experience have been in one direction only: *to prepare me for the job of research director of a big agency like yours.* That's the job I want—the job for which I am ready, and to which I can make a useful and impressive contribution.

I know you are looking for a research director. I know I can fill that job, efficiently and well . . . bringing to it the plus of my own copytesting method. I have the reputation of being thorough and accurate; I believe in working hard and seeing a job through; I get along well with others; and I feel certain you will find my appearance and personality beyond reproach.

May I come for an interview? I'd like to show you what I've done for Pratt & Reynolds, and tell you some of the things I'd *like* to do as director of research for your agency.

Your secretary can reach me any morning at Pe. 6-4100 to make an appointment.

Sincerely yours,

Letters of Reference

Dear Mr. Jones:

I am very glad of this opportunity to give Miss Helen Fraser a reference.

She was my secretary at the New York office of the Kenyon, Day Company; and I was certainly sorry to lose her when I was transferred to the Chicago office.

Miss Fraser is an excellent secretary. She is efficient and conscientious, always pleasant to everyone, tactful and intelligent.

I recommend her without reservation, as I know you will find her a most helpful and responsible secretary.

Sincerely yours,

Dear Mr. Cranston:

It is with great pleasure that I recommend Mr. John Haley for the position of copy chief in your organization.

I consider Mr. Haley one of the best advertising writers I have ever known. He is original and imaginative, full of ideas, clever and forward-thinking. His ideas are sound and practical, and many of them have been outstandingly successful.

Here at Cramer and Lathrop, Mr. Haley was one of our most important copy writers for a period of nearly 8 years. During the last two years he was, in effect, a copy chief . . . for he was head of the food and drug group and was responsible for all copy turned out by writers in that group. He was well liked by his own staff, by the account executives and clients, and by all with whom he came in contact.

Perhaps the one quality to commend him most is his unfailing enthusiasm for the job at hand—an enthusiasm that naturally transmits itself to those who work with him.

I am happy to give Mr. Haley my wholehearted endorsement. In my opinion, he'd make a wonderful copy chief for any advertising agency.

Sincerely yours,

Dear Mr. Burke:

I find it rather awkward to answer your letter about Mr. Alan Roberts. I like him personally, but I cannot in all fairness recommend him to you.

Roberts is unquestionably a talented young man, with a flair for the dramatic and a real sense of showmanship. He was program director of two of our daytime shows for about a year; and he certainly knows his business and can do a good job if he wants to.

But that's just the trouble: *he doesn't always want to.* Sometimes he wants to drink instead, and then you can't depend on him. He'll walk out on the job for a couple of days and let somebody else take over. . . . That's why he isn't here any more.

I'm sorry to have to tell you this, because Roberts has great talent and ability, and he could probably become the best program director in television if he didn't drink.

Perhaps if you talked the situation over with him, and gave him the job on the understanding that he'd be fired the first time he took a drink, it might make a difference. I think it would be well worth trying, because he has so much to offer.

Sincerely yours,

Letters of Introduction and Reference

Dear Mr. Thompson:

This will introduce Miss Marilyn Hagen, who has asked me to write a letter of reference for her.

I do so with pleasure, for Miss Hagen has been by far the best secretary I have ever had. It is only because of reorganization here, and my own retirement on March 1, that she is looking for a new connection.

Miss Hagen was my secretary for more than six years. It would be difficult to put into words all she did for me during that time—the many details and responsibilities she took over—and the intelligent efficiency with which she always handled her job.

I recommend her to you without qualification . . . as an excellent, completely reliable secretary.

Sincerely yours,

Dear Mr. Mannerly:

The young lady who hands you this letter is Miss Joyce Miller, whose father we both knew well. He was Kenneth Miller . . . and I remember you used to say he was the best script writer in the business.

Ken was killed in an automobile accident a couple of years ago, as you probably recall. His daughter has just graduated from the Interstate Business School, and she is looking for a job as typist—preferably with an advertising agency. She tells me she intends to follow in her father's footsteps and become a first-rate script writer like he was. I think she will, too.

Perhaps you can help her on the way by giving her a job on your typing staff. According to the letters she will show you from her school, she is a very competent typist—speedy and accurate.

I know you'll do whatever you can for her.

Sincerely yours,

Dear Mr. Brown:

The bearer of this letter, Richard Collins, was my son's roommate at Exeter, and is a recent graduate of Harvard Law School. He is looking for a job in a law office where he can get sound basic training and experience, and he has asked me to give him a letter to you.

I have known young Collins for more than 10 years, and I can truthfully say I have never met a more likable, intelligent and ambitious young man. I only wish he had studied architecture instead of law—I'd take him on as an assistant without thinking twice about it!

I hope you can find room for Collins in your office, and start him on the way to the brilliant career I feel certain is ahead of him. If not, I know he'll appreciate just meeting and talking with you, as he has always had the greatest admiration for you and your work.

I'll be glad to return the compliment any time you want to send an ambitious young architect to see me!

Cordially yours,

Letters Requesting Information from References

Dear Sir:

Mr. James Merrill has given us your name as reference. He tells us he was credit manager of your store for three years, and that he left of his own accord to make another connection.

We should like to know whether you think Mr. Merrill is capable of handling the credit department of a large organization like ours. We shall appreciate any information you can give us about his personality, reliability, judgment . . . and especially his ability to work well with others.

We will, of course, keep your reply strictly confidential.

Very truly yours,

Dear Mr. Countway:

Miss Mary Hall is being considered by us for the position of office manager. She has given your name as reference, and says she was employed by your firm in that capacity from June, 19—, to October, 19—.

Will you let us know in confidence whether you recommend Miss Hall, and what you think of her personality and ability to get along with people. Do you consider her a person of tact and good judgment, with a sense of responsibility toward her job?

We shall wait to hear from you before making a decision; and we shall, of course, be very grateful for your co-operation.

Sincerely yours,

Gentlemen:

We are considering the application of Mr. John H. Payne for the position of accountant.

We understand that Mr. Payne was employed by you in that capacity from 19— to 19—.

It would be very helpful to us to have a statement from you as to his character, personality and ability. Can you tell us why he left your employ? He seems somewhat vague on that point.

Thank you very much for your help. You can be sure that any information you give us will be kept confidential.

Sincerely yours,

"Thank You" Letters for Help in Getting a Job

Dear Mr. Butler:

I am now credit manager of Lambert, Strauss and Company—and very happy about it!

I know that the fine letter about me which you sent Mr. Strauss had a lot to do with getting me the job. I'm deeply grateful to you, not only for this particular reference but for the help and encouragement you have always given me.

I shall certainly make every effort to do an outstanding job here and justify your faith in me.

Sincerely yours,

Dear Mr. Countway:

I understand you gave me a wonderful reference, and that largely on the strength of it I am now the office manager of Ewald & Blaine, Inc.

I had my heart set on this job, and I don't know how to thank you for helping me get it!

The least I can do is live up to all the fine things you said about me in your letter, and *that* I intend to do! You can be sure you'll never have reason to regret recommending me so highly.

Thank you, Mr. Countway.

Sincerely yours,

Dear Mr. Peterson:

Thanks to your help, I have just the job I've always wanted!

It was good of you to write such a complimentary letter about me, and I'm more grateful than I can say.

I'll do my best to live up to the good things you said about me; and I certainly hope I shall have the pleasure of thanking you personally some day.

Cordially yours,

6

Your Club Correspondence

In your club correspondence, simply follow the same general rules as business correspondence. Keep in mind the *reason why* the letter is being written, and say what you have to say briefly, to the point—without rambling or writing of other things.

A great deal of club correspondence is about membership and dues. The following letters are offered as helpful suggestions.

Dear Mrs. Kellogg:

I wish to propose Miss Martha Jenkins for membership in the Women's Club. She has recently moved to Chicago from Middletown, Connecticut, where she was president of the Women's Club for three years.

I am sure Miss Jenkins would be a real addition to our club, not only because of her charming personality, but because of her ability as a writer and speaker. She is a well-known authority on New England.

Miss Jenkins is to be my guest at our next meeting when I hope you will permit me to present her to you.

Yours sincerely,

Dear Mrs. Richmond:

I would like to present Mrs. Thomas Young for membership in the Century Club.

Mrs. Young has recently moved to Concord from New York. She has long been interested in civic improvement, and through her lectures has encouraged many clubs to undertake important projects for town and city betterment.

I am sure Mrs. Young would be a real addition to our membership.

Yours sincerely,

Dear Mrs. Carelton:

The Monmouth Garden Club takes great pleasure in inviting you to become a member.

We have sent you a folder containing all the information about our club. As you have already visited us several times, you know how charming the clubhouse and grounds are; and we know you will find the members interesting and congenial.

Our annual autumn flower show is scheduled for September 25, and is to be followed by a dinner and dance at the clubhouse. We hope you will be a member by that time and we look forward to having you with us.

Please let us know this week, if possible, whether you accept our invitation and will share our club activities.

Sincerely yours,

Dear Mr. Clark:

You have been suggested to me as a man who might like to take part in the very important work we are doing here at the Civic Center.

I am sure you are familiar with the work of this organization. I am enclosing booklets which tell about our aims and purposes, and some of our accomplishments. I am also enclosing our current program of events in the hope that you will find time to attend some of them—and see for yourself the work we are doing and its great value to the community.

I should like the privilege of proposing your name for membership. Will you be my guest at the next regular meeting, October 3rd, at eight o'clock? I'd like to meet you personally and answer any questions you may have about the organization.

                                            Cordially yours,

Dear Mrs. Williams:

I am delighted to inform you that you have been elected a member of the Community Forum.

The next meeting will be at my home on Thursday, June 21, at three o'clock. Mrs. Philip Thorne is the guest speaker, and the subject is: "China Today."

I look forward to seeing you at the meeting and welcoming you as a new member of our club.

                                            Sincerely yours,

Dear Mr. Esmond:

I am pleased to report that at the meeting of the Stamp Society, held on January 10th, you were elected to membership.

There will be a meeting at the home of Mr. Peter Crane, 46 Lake Drive, on Tuesday, January 28th, at eight o'clock.

We hope you will be with us at that time, and we look forward to greeting you as a member.

                                            Sincerely yours,

Dear Mrs. Harkins:

It gives me great pleasure to accept your invitation to join the Ladies' Club.

I have long been interested in the programs and activities of the Club, and am delighted to become a member.

                                            Sincerely yours,

Dear Mrs. Collins:

Please thank the Women's Civic Association for inviting me to become a member.

I am very glad to accept and shall be present at the next regular meeting on Thursday, November 10th.

                              Sincerely yours,

Dear Mrs. Parsons:

Ever since we moved to Middletown last August, my husband and I have been eager to join the Choral Group.

We are delighted to accept your gracious invitation, and shall be at your home on Friday when the next meeting is held.

Thank you so much for proposing us!

                              Sincerely yours,

Dear Mr. Pratt:

I appreciate the honor and courtesy of being nominated for membership in the Oakdale Council.

I am sorry I am unable to accept, but I am leaving for Manila at the end of this month to open a branch office of the Telecast Company—and I'll probably be gone for a year or more.

Please express my sincere thanks to the Nominating Committee. I hope I shall again be given the opportunity to join on my return from Manila.

                              Sincerely yours,

Dear Miss Evans:

Thank you for your most gracious letter!

I'm delighted to become a member of the Music Club, and wish to thank the membership committee for inviting me.

I look forward to the meetings with great pleasure.

                              Sincerely yours,

Dear Mr. Manton:

In totaling and closing the Club's books for the year, I find that your dues have not been paid.

I'm sure this is just an oversight on your part, and that you will take care of the matter at once.

As soon as I receive your dues, I shall be able to close the books for the year and prepare my annual financial report.

Sincerely yours,

Dear Mrs. Thompson:

This is to remind you that your dues for the year have not been paid. I wrote you about it a few weeks ago but apparently my letter went astray.

Will you please send your check just as soon as you conveniently can?

Sincerely yours,

Dear Mr. Burke:

We're sorry we must write again to remind you about your dues.

As you know, a welfare organization like ours cannot function without the support of its members. If dues are not paid regularly by every member, the program of welfare and charitable work laid out for the year cannot be carried through.

We know your great interest in the organization, and we know you want to do your part. So won't you please send a check for your back dues, *right away?*

Sincerely yours,

Notification of Election
to Office

Dear Mr. Crosby:

The Executive Committee of the Camden Sky Club has instructed me to notify you that you have been unanimously elected president for the coming year.

Your election is a great source of satisfaction to the members of the club. We look forward to a happy and successful year under your leadership and guidance.

Sincerely yours,

Dear Miss Williams:

As secretary of the Community League, I have the pleasure of informing you that you have been elected president for a term of two years.

We are delighted by the choice, and feel sure the League will be greatly enriched by your administration.

Sincerely yours,

Dear Mrs. Nesbit:

At a meeting of the Executive Committee on Tuesday, April 4th, you were re-elected president of the Mothers' Club.

Members of the Committee know how busy you are, and how much of your time and effort are cheerfully given to the Club. While they do not wish you to continue at the cost of hardship or inconvenience to yourself, they feel there is no one who can carry forward the many projects now under way as brilliantly and well as you can.

We take this opportunity to thank you for your unselfish devotion and inspired leadership of the past; and we earnestly hope you will retain the presidency for another year.

Sincerely yours,

Dear Mr. Harrison:

Thank you for your letter confirming my election as president of the Historical Society.

I am happy and proud to receive this great honor, and shall do everything I can to make my term of office a pleasant and successful one for the Society.

Sincerely yours,

Dear Mrs. Phillips:

Please thank the members of the Executive Committee for electing me president of the Garden Club.

I am honored to accept, and shall devote myself wholeheartedly to the duties of my new office.

Sincerely yours,

Letters of Resignation

Dear Mr. Simms:

I sincerely regret that I must resign my membership from the Tennis Club.

In a few weeks I am leaving New York to settle permanently in St. Paul where my firm has opened a branch office.

Please express my appreciation to the Executive Committee for the many courtesies shown me and my family. I'm certainly sorry to leave the Club and the many fine acquaintances I made there.

Sincerely yours,

Dear Mrs. Leslie:

Illness and unexpected duties at home make it impossible for me to continue my Club interests and activities. I am compelled to offer my resignation, effective at once.

I am sure you must know I do this with regret, for I have always enjoyed the Club and my association with the fine group of women who make up its membership.

I send my very best wishes for the continued success of the Club.

Sincerely yours,

Dear Mrs. Worth:

I am extremely sorry, but I find that I must retire from the Dramatic Club.

Since the twins were born, I have very little time for anything but taking care of them. I'm sure you understand.

I know I'll miss the Club and my many friends there; but perhaps when the twins are older, I shall be able to rejoin.

Cordially yours,

Dear Mr. Carroll:

Please accept my resignation from the Community Club.

I'm sorry, but I cannot agree with the views of the president and therefore I do not wish to remain a member.

I'm sure you know that my high personal regard for you and most of the members remains unchanged.

Sincerely yours,

Dear Mrs. Blanding:

Your letter of resignation was read at a meeting of the Ladies Club yesterday.

We are all sorry to hear you are moving to another part of the country and that you will no longer be with us. We accept your resignation only because we must.

We hope that you and your family will be happy and successful in California.

Cordially yours,

Requests to Speak or Entertain at a Club

Dear Mrs. Johnson:

I wonder if you would be willing to give your lecture on "India" before the Middletown Social Club on the afternoon of October 6th at three o'clock.

There will be an audience of approximately two hundred women.

We do hope you are able to accept this engagement, as we are all anxious to meet you and to hear what we have been told is a most fascinating lecture.

Sincerely yours,

Dear Mr. Adams:

Could you give your talk on "Child Psychology" before the Mothers' Club on the evening of June 10th at eight o'clock?

If so, will you please let me know what your terms are, and also what equipment you would require for showing the pictures.

We hope your many engagements will not prevent you from accepting this invitation.

Sincerely yours,

Dear Mrs. Hubbard:

The members of the Music League enjoyed your concert at the Town Hall so much last week that they are eager to have you give it this winter at one of our club meetings.

Will you let me know whether you would consider playing for us, and if so, what your terms are?

We would like you to give your concert here at the clubhouse on the evening of January 3rd, 10th or 17th —whichever is most convenient for you.

Sincerely yours,

Dear Mr. Stratford:

The Yacht Club is entertaining Mr. Robert Yorke at dinner on July 23rd.

As you know, Mr. Yorke is a world-famous yachtsman who has won many prizes here and abroad.

We should like to have you act as toastmaster at this dinner, as we know your witty remarks would add much to the success and enjoyment of the occasion.

May we hear from you soon—and *favorably?* I speak for all the members of the club when I say it would give us all great pleasure to have you act as official toastmaster of the evening.

Cordially yours,

Dear Mr. Grasslands:

The members of the Artists' Club are most interested in your lecture on "Modern American Painting."

Would it be possible for you to give this lecture on Tuesday, May 12th, at eight o'clock? We meet in the Art Exhibits Building, 92 Center Street, in Auditorium B. There are always at least 125 members at each meeting; and we usually pay $100 for feature lectures like yours.

We hope to have the pleasure of welcoming you on the twelfth and hearing your lecture.

Sincerely yours,

Dear Miss Chadwicke:

Will you come to Forest Hills on April 4th, at eight o'clock, to sing before the Choral Club?

You are an outstanding favorite among the members of this Club, and it would give us great pleasure to hear you in a program of your own selection.

We know how busy you are, and we shall therefore be doubly grateful for your acceptance of this invitation.

Sincerely yours,

Dear Mr. Crile:

Bob Lanson has told me of your recent visit to Russia, and of the fascinating collection of color slides you brought back with you.

At the next regular meeting of our Town Forum, on September 20th, we plan to discuss Russia; and it would certainly be interesting and helpful if someone who was actually there could tell us about it.

Would you be willing to come to this meeting as our guest of honor to tell us what you saw in Russia and show us some of your pictures. It would be of tremendous interest to the members, and I'm sure they would greatly appreciate your courtesy and kindness.

We can supply a slide projector and screen unless you prefer using your own.

Sincerely yours,

Answers to Invitations
from Clubs

Dear Mrs. Colwell:

I shall be delighted to speak on "Modern Homemaking" before your Mothers' Group on Wednesday, August 6th.

No, I don't require any props or equipment. I'll bring along everything I need for the lecture.

I understand I am to speak from 8:30 to 9:30 P.M., and then answer questions for about half an hour. I plan to get there about eight so that I can meet you and talk with you for a few minutes before the lecture.

Sincerely yours,

Dear Mr. Hilton:

It gives me great pleasure to accept your invitation to speak before the Hawthorne Club on April 5th.

My lecture takes approximately fifty minutes. All I need is a small table on which to place my illustrated easel; a bridge table serves the purpose very nicely.

Thank you for your very complimentary remarks. I shall be delighted to make your acquaintance, and to meet the members of the celebrated Hawthorne Club.

Sincerely yours,

Dear Mrs. Brown:

I am happy to accept your invitation to play before the Music League on Tuesday evening, January 10th.

In addition to the Beethoven and Tchaikovsky selections you heard at my Town Hall concert, I'd like to play Brahms' *Rhapsodie* and Schumann's *Carnival*. I shall arrange the numbers and send you a complete program in a few days.

My fee is $200 for a two-hour recital.

Thank you for your interest, and for your most gracious invitation.

Sincerely yours,

Dear Mrs. Richards:

You can count on me for Monday evening, June 15th, at eight o'clock—for a brief talk on "Juvenile Delinquency."

I have a number of interesting photographs which I like to project on a screen during my talk. I'll bring my own projector with me, but will you please see that I am provided with a screen?

I look forward to the pleasure of meeting you on the fifteenth.

Cordially yours,

Dear Mrs. Melton:

I wish I could accept your invitation to address the Women's Guild on February 5th. But unfortunately I already have an engagement for that evening, to address the Lowell Club in Boston.

Thank you for asking me. I'm certainly sorry I can't say "Yes."

Sincerely yours,

Dear Mr. Pearce:

Your invitation to address the Community Club comes at a most inopportune time. I am leaving Bangor on March 5th for a survey of housing conditions in New England, and shall be gone for at least six weeks

—possibly longer. Under the circumstances, I am unable to accept any speaking engagements for March or April.

I'm sorry to miss this opportunity of meeting you and addressing the Forum, but perhaps you'll ask me again some time.

Sincerely yours,

Dear Mrs. King:

I'd love to come and sing for the Choral Club on April 4th, but I'll be in Washington on that day.

From Washington I go to Philadelphia, and then to New York, for a series of concerts. I won't be back here until May 30th, and therefore cannot make any engagements until after that date.

Please tell the members of the Club how sorry I am, and how deeply I appreciate the honor of their invitation. I hope they'll ask me again some day—and that the next time I'll be able to accept.

Sincerely yours,

Dear Mr. Martin:

I'm sorry I cannot accept your invitation to talk before the Kiwanis Club on July 12. It would be a real pleasure to see you again, and to meet your fellow members.

However, I'll be in Memphis on July 12—so I must ask you to count me out.

Perhaps there will be another occasion soon; and if so, I certainly hope I shall be in a position to accept.

Sincerely yours,

Letters of Thanks for Speaking or Entertaining at a Club

When an invited guest speaks before a club or an organization —or sings, plays or otherwise entertains the members—a letter of appreciation should be written. This may be either a formal note of thanks in the name of the club secretary; or it may be a friendly, informal note written by the person who was responsible for the invitation.

Here is the way a formal note of thanks is generally expressed:

Dear Mr. Perkins:

The Program Committee of the Mothers' Club wishes to thank you for your lecture on March 10th.

We appreciate your interest in the Club, and your fine spirit of co-operation.

We'd like you to know that the members were unanimous in their praise of your most interesting and helpful talk.

Sincerely yours,

Informal notes are on a more friendly basis, expressing not only the thanks of the club but the personal appreciation of the member who issued the invitation. Frequently a gift accompanies the letter of thanks.

Dear Mrs. Emmett:

It was gracious of you to come all the way to Middletown to sing at the luncheon of the Professional Women's Club. I hope you know how much we appreciate it!

I speak for the entire membership when I thank you for giving so generously of your time and talent. We owe you a real debt of gratitude for one of the most delightful and enjoyable meetings of the year.

We hope you like the little gift we are sending with this letter to say, "Thank you for a wonderful concert!"

Cordially yours,

Dear Mr. Wade:

As Program Chairman of the Literary Club, I want to thank you for giving us one of the most fascinating talks we have had in a long time. In fact, no program we have had in *years* has inspired so many delighted and enthusiastic comments!

Everyone who heard your talk thoroughly enjoyed it. But I'm sure no one enjoyed it more than I—for I took personal pride in presenting such a fine speaker.

Thank you for the Club, and for myself!

Cordially yours,

Dear Mr. Jones:

Your talk before the Kiwanis Club yesterday was so exceptional, I feel I must write and tell you so.

In the twenty years I have been a member of the Club, I have never heard anyone pack so much information and entertainment into a half-hour talk!

It was a privilege and a delight to have you as our guest speaker; and I thank you for the Club and for myself.

Sincerely yours,

If the secretary of an organization writes to thank you for making an address or giving a concert, no acknowledgment is necessary. But a personal and complimentary note, telling you how well you spoke or played—and how much everyone enjoyed it—deserves a brief note of acknowledgment. For example:

Dear Mr. Leslie:

Thanks for the fine letter about my talk in Washington last week. I'm glad to know you liked it.

It was a most enjoyable experience addressing the members of your organization; and if my message contributed to the success of the meeting, I'm mighty happy about it.

Sincerely yours,

Dear Mrs. Mason:

How nice of you to write me such a flattering letter!

I thoroughly enjoyed singing at the Community Club, and I'm glad the members liked me. I liked *them*, too! It's always gratifying to have such an attentive and appreciative audience.

It was a real pleasure to meet you and Mr. Mason, and I hope our paths will cross again.

Sincerely yours,*

* For additional information on CLUB CORRESPONDENCE, see pages 659 to 664.

Book V

Children's Correspondence

I

The Letters All Children
Must Learn to Write

The ability to express oneself easily and well on paper is an important asset, of ever-increasing usefulness throughout life . . . and children cannot be trained too early to acquire it. One way is to encourage them, from a very early age, to write their own letters.

This does not mean composing letters for children to copy in their own sprawling, uncertain handwriting—dictating word for word what they should say. While that may help give the child a sense of responsibility toward letter writing, it won't do much to help develop the ability of self-expression.

Youngsters should be permitted to compose their own little social notes, their own personal letters to members of the family, as soon as they are able to guide a pen across paper and express themselves in understandable language. Grownups may make tactful suggestions, if they like; but they should not dictate. And they should not be too critical of a child's first efforts; for praise does far more than criticism toward encouraging a better effort next time.

So let the child express himself in his own words, however quaintly misused those words may be. A letter that clearly conveys the personality of the child and expresses his own thoughts and ideas, has far greater charm and appeal than any precisely expressed letter in a child's handwriting but a grownup's words.

Children may hate to write letters, and may bitterly resent any obligation which makes letter writing necessary. Nevertheless there are certain letters every well-bred child *must* write. These include letters of thanks for gifts, favors and hospitality

. . . letters of congratulation to young relatives and friends
. . . letters of invitation and acknowledgment. And most important of all, perhaps—because they are the most eagerly awaited—are the letters children away at school or camp are expected to write to their doting parents back home.

Even very young children should be taught to recognize their responsibilities and write the letters expected of them *without waiting to be told*. They should grow up with an awareness of their obligation to those who are kind to them, who give them presents or entertain them in their homes. They should not be permitted to take such kindnesses or courtesies for granted, to let them go unnoticed. They should be taught that it's bad manners not to write the letters expected of them, and *especially* letters of thanks. Surely the aunt, uncle, grandparent or friend who sends a gift deserves a note of appreciation. And the more enthusiastic the note is, the more natural and spontaneous—and characteristic of the child's own personality—the more pleasure it is bound to give.

CHILDREN'S THANK-YOU NOTES
FOR GIFTS

Children should be trained to write their notes of thanks while the glow is still with them—while they are excited and happy about the gift. They should get their gratitude down on paper while it's still gurgling inside them, not wait until it's worn off. A delighted, "Auntie, you darling! I *love* the skates—they're just what I wanted!" is more gratifying than a calm and sensible, "Dear Aunt Mary: Thank you very much for the skates."

Here are some examples of letters of thanks to guide the young beginner. The first few are presumably the letters of very young tots, just learning how to express themselves; the others are those of somewhat older children:

Dear Aunt Lillian:

I love my new doll. She is very pretty. I call her Judy. Thank you for sending Judy on my birthday.

She is the most beautiful doll in the whole world. Are you coming soon to see Judy and me?

With love,
Barbara

Dear Uncle Jim:

I always wanted a train. Thank you for sending me a train for Christmas. It is wonderful. It lights up and whistles like a real train.

I got a drum and a wagon, too. But I like my train best of all. I like to make it go through the tunnel.

I hope you will come and see us soon.

With love,
Peter

Dear Aunt Beth and Uncle Joe:

I was excited when the scooter came. I had to go right out and try it. How did you know I wanted a scooter?

Thank you very much. I can't wait to go out and ride my scooter again. I am glad it is red. Alan has a green scooter. He lives next door.

I had a birthday party and it was fun. We played a lot of games.

Mother says you are coming on Sunday. I'm glad. I'll show you how fast I can go on my scooter. I'm happy and I love you.

Jerry

Dear Aunt Jean:

That's a wonderful dollhouse you sent me. It's so big and beautiful. Thank you very, very much. All my friends say I am lucky to have such a nice aunt.

When you come to see me, I'll show you how I fixed up the house with furniture. I make believe it's a real house. Mother is making curtains for the windows.

I didn't have a party this year because Ginny was sick. But she is better now. This morning she got out of bed to see my dollhouse.

I almost forgot to tell you—Dad gave me a little black kitten for my birthday. He's the cutest thing! He has white feet, and his name is Jinx. You must come and see him.

Thanks again for the beautiful dollhouse.

With love,
Patsy

Dear Grandma:

The dress you sent me is lovely, and it fits just right. I wore it at my birthday party yesterday, and everybody said how pretty it looked.

I love it, Grandma. You were sweet to send me such a beautiful present all the way from New York!

I miss you very much. I hope you will come and stay with us again this summer. Mother said you might come, and Peter and I are very happy about it.

Mother and Dad gave me a desk for my birthday. I like it very much. Now I have a good place to do my homework.

I hope you are well, Grandma, and that you will write to me soon.

With love,
Arlene

Dear Aunt Susan:

The baby alligator came this morning. I was so excited I couldn't eat any breakfast. Mother bought me a tank to keep him in, and I fixed it just like you said in your letter—with gravel at one end and water on the other. I'm going to take very good care of him.

Thanks very much, Aunt Susan. I love the cute little alligator, and I know I'll have a lot of fun watching him grow.

I hope you are having a good time in Florida. I hope the weather is better than it is here. It rained a lot last week, and now it is very cold and windy.

Mother and Dad said to send you their love. I'll write again soon and tell you how the alligator is getting along.

Love,
Timmy

Dear Cousin Martha:

Thank you for the bed jacket. It is lovely. I always wanted one because I like to read in bed. Mother says it's the prettiest one she ever saw, and I think so, too.

I wish you didn't live so far away so we could see you more often. Are you coming to Oakdale this summer? I hope so. We always have such fun when you visit us.

Mother just wrapped a box of cookies for me to take to the post office when I go to mail this letter. She baked them for you this morning. I hope they don't get there all broken.

Please come and see us soon, if you can. We all miss you since you moved to Chicago.

With love to you and Cousin Bert,

Affectionately,
Alice

Dear Peggy:

I'm sorry you couldn't come to my party. I hope your cold is better now.

Thank you for the books. I'm reading *Heidi* now, and I love it.

Can you come and see me when you are better? I have a new game I'd like to play with you. It's lots of fun.

Guess what? My dad promised me a puppy! We're going to pick it out on Saturday. I'm so excited about it I can hardly wait.

Thanks again for the books, Peggy—and hurry and get well!

>   Your friend,
>   Anita

Dear Aunt Rose:

I want to thank you again for the beautiful belt you gave me. I like it a lot. I can wear it with so many of my skirts and dresses.

We had a wonderful time in Philadelphia. I always enjoy going to your house. The dinner was delicious. And I enjoyed going to the aquarium in the afternoon.

I hope you will soon come to see us in New York. Love to Uncle Henry and the boys,

>   Your niece,
>   Evelyn

Dear Mrs. Cranston:

I was so surprised to receive your gift. It was sweet of you to remember me at Christmas.

I like the scrap book very, very much. I think it's beautiful. I'm going to save it just for very special clippings, and keep it always.

Thank you, Mrs. Cranston—and I hope you and Mr. Cranston have a very happy New Year.

>   Affectionately,
>   Rosalind

Dear Aunt Ruth:

I just can't think of *anything* I'd have liked more than "The Treasury of Stephen Foster"! I love the songs and I'll enjoy playing them. The pictures are so beautiful, too. It's a simply wonderful graduation gift, and I'm delighted with it.

Thank you so much, Aunt Ruth! I hope you'll come and see us soon so that I can play some of the songs for you and hear you sing them. I wish I had a voice like yours!

The graduation exercises were very nice. I'm sorry you couldn't come. I got the silver Music Medal and two honor certificates.

Mother and Dad send their love. Thanks again. . . .

Affectionately,
Janice

Dear Aunt Kate and Uncle Joe:

Thank you very much for the beautiful pen. It writes very smoothly as you can see.

It is too bad you cannot attend my graduation. I should have liked to see you there. But I know it's much too far for you to come.

Thanks again for the gift and for your good wishes.

With love,
Harold

Dear Mrs. Thomas:

Your flowers and lovely note came just as I was leaving for school. They made me feel so happy! Thank you very much.

The graduation was wonderful. I'll never forget it. But I'm sorry I won't be going to P.S. 69 any more.

Many thanks for the flowers, Mrs. Thomas. Mother and I hope to see you soon.

Affectionately,
Claire

Dear Grandma:

I am sorry you were too ill to come to my confirmation. Everybody was disappointed not to see you there. I hope you are all better now.

Thanks for the brief case. I like it a lot. I'll have good use of it in high school.

Dad gave me a watch just like Jerry's. It's shock-proof and waterproof. I like the watch and your brief case best of all the gifts I received.

Hurry and get well, Grandma. We don't like you to be ill. Love from all of us,

Dick

Dear Dr. and Mrs. Brown:

The key chain is a honey! It's one of the nicest gifts I received. Thank you both very much.

I was glad to see you at my confirmation, as I thought you might not be able to come. But it's too bad you couldn't stay for the party afterward.

Thanks again for the swell gift, and for the wonderful letter of congratulations that came with it.

Sincerely yours,
Larry Walters

CHILDREN'S THANK-YOU NOTES
FOR HOSPITALITY

When a child is entertained as a house or week-end guest at the home of a friend, a note of thanks should be written to the young host or hostess. The mother also should be thanked, either in the same letter or in a separate one. How gratifying, for example, to receive a note like the following from a young week-end guest!

Dear Mrs. Watson:

I want to thank you for the lovely time I had at your house. It was one of the best times I ever had. I enjoyed the movies so much; and I just loved the buffet supper in the garden.

I hope you will let Anita come and spend a week end with us soon.

Mother and Dad send best regards.

Sincerely yours,
Patsy

A note like that, in a child's round scrawl, certainly makes one want to invite her again! And even though an occasional word is misspelled, one doesn't mind; for it shows that the note was written by the little girl herself, without grown-up help.

Here are some examples of thank-you notes from children to young friends who entertained them:

Dear Fred:

I had a wonderful time at your house. It was lots of fun to go ice skating on the pond. I wish we had a pond like that near *our* house!

Please tell your mother I enjoyed the barbecue very much. I think it was swell of her to go to so much trouble for me.

Don't forget! You promised to come here for a week end real soon. Mother says she'll get tickets for the Music Hall as soon as she knows when you are coming.

Thanks for everything.

Your pal,
Eddie

Dear Betsy:

That was a wonderful week end I had at your house! I can't tell what I enjoyed most—the movies your father showed Saturday night, the pillow fight with Joey, or the picnic on Sunday afternoon. It was *all* such fun!

Thanks for a grand time, Betsy—and please give my thanks to your mother, too.

I hope you can come and spend a week end with me soon. I'll try and give you as good a time as I had.

With love, your friend

Dinah

Dear Sandra:

Thank you for the lovely time I had at your house.

I've just been telling Mother what fun I had. You always dream up the most unusual ideas! I think I enjoyed the Treasure Hunt most of all—especially the nice prize I won.

Be sure and thank your mother for me. That was a wonderful dinner party she gave us on Saturday; and the beach picnic was simply *super*. Wasn't Claire funny in the charades? I still giggle every time I think of her trying to act out *The Egg and I!*

Remember—we expect you here on July 15th. Let us know what train you are taking and we'll meet you at the station. I'm not as clever as you are, but I promise you a good time anyway!

> Your loving friend,
> Lenore

CHILDREN'S PERSONAL CORRESPONDENCE

There is essentially little difference between the personal correspondence of children and that of adults . . . except, of course, that children's phraseology is simpler, and usually more natural and spontaneous. In that very simplicity and spontaneity of expression lies the great charm of children's letters.

In their correspondence with family and friends, youngsters should be encouraged to write as they speak, without self-consciousness or constraint. This is more easily accomplished by *suggestion* than by scolding or faultfinding.

For example, a child going away to school or camp is generally warned to "write as soon as you get there!" He is reminded half a dozen times "now don't you forget!" As a result, his letters home are usually brief and hurried . . . and sadly inadequate. They sound something like this:

Dear Mom:

I am fine. How are you? Please send me some cookies.

> Love,
> Johnny

Then, perhaps, the disappointed parent writes back . . . and scolds . . . "Why don't you write me a nice long letter? You know how I miss you!"

But instead of warning or scolding, the youngster should be encouraged by *helpful suggestion.* He should be told what is expected of him in a letter home—what he should write about. Not "Why don't you write me a nice long letter"—but this:

> I met Charlie's mother today and she says he has learned how to swim. Imagine! Only two weeks at camp and he can swim. How about you, Johnny? Can you swim yet? What else have you learned to do at camp? Be sure and write me all about it in your next letter so I can tell Charlie's mother what *you* can do.

Don't expect too much of a very young child away from home for the first time. The newness and excitement of strange surroundings often make it difficult for a child to write. Just give the youngster some stamped, addressed stationery (to make it as easy as possible) and suggest that you would be interested to know:

> —how he enjoyed the trip to camp or school
> —how he likes his new surroundings
> —how he likes his new young friends
> —what he did the first day or two
> —what he likes most about school or camp
> —whether there's anything he wants or needs

Remember: Don't scold, criticize or find fault—*make suggestions* instead. Children can be encouraged and drawn out in their letters the same as in conversation. The following examples, read to children before they go away to school or camp, may prove helpful. They start with the uncertain letters of a seven-year-old, away for the first time—and progress through various stages of childish development to the confident letters of a teen-ager.

Dear Mother:

I like it very much at camp. It is fun. We play games and go swimming. I am learning how to swim. On the train I sat with Peter, and he let me look at his comic books.

Peter is in my bunk. His bed is next to mine. There is another boy whose name is Tommy. I like him.

Are you coming to see me soon? Mothers can come on Sunday.

Love,
Tommy

Dear Mother:

I love it at camp. I don't ever want to leave. Jane and Peggy are in my bunk and we have fun. Today we had a swimming lesson. The big girls had a canoe race. Tomorrow we are going on a nature walk. I will write you about it.

I send a big kiss to you and daddy. Come and see me soon.

Marilyn

Dear Mother:

It is nice here. The lake is right near my bunk. There is a little house with rabbits, snakes and turtles. There are some ducks, too. The nature teacher takes care of them, but he lets us watch when they eat dinner.

I like shop best of all. We make things in shop. I am going to make a tray for you.

We had chicken for lunch today. It was very good. We had ice cream for dessert. After lunch we all marched out singing camp songs.

I must say good-by now. We are going swimming. Don't forget to come and see me.

With love,
Dick

Dear Mother:

Everything is just wonderful here! I'm in the same bunk with Patsy and Jeanette. We have a very nice counselor. Her name is Ellen.

Yesterday I started to take the canoeing test. I have to finish it today. If I pass the test, I will be able to take canoes out when we go boating.

Tomorrow we are going on a hike to Waterbury Creek. It is four miles each way. We are going to take our lunch along and eat it at the Creek. I need a water canteen for when I go on hikes. Will you please send me one?

Some of the girls are going on a canoe trip to Silver Beach tomorrow. That's lots of fun. When I pass the canoe test I will be allowed to go on canoe trips, too.

How is Billy? Do you think he misses me, or is he too little? Maybe you can bring him along when you and Dad come to see me.

Thanks for the package. The candy was delicious.

> With love,
> Sue

Dear Dad:

Jasper Camp is swell. I like it a lot. The lake is even bigger than Pinecrest; and the fellows say there is good fishing.

All the boys in my bunk have been here before. They know one another from last year. But I made friends with them right away, like you said I should . . . and we get along fine.

We have two teams—the yellow and the green. The teams have tournaments and swimming meets. The good swimmers are allowed to go out in canoes for the boat races. At the end of the year the team that wins gets a prize. I am on the yellow team.

Do you know what? I forgot to take my flashlight along. Will you tell mother to send it, please? I need it at night when we walk back from the Recreation Hall. That's where they show the movies. We are going to see *Meeting at Midnight* tomorrow after dinner.

It's raining today, so we can't go swimming. Isn't that a shame? I guess I like swimming best of all, dad. I'm going to learn how to dive this summer.

How is Mother? I hope everything at home is all right. I miss you both very much.

With love,
Peter

Dear Mother and Dad:

It's fun being back at camp. Stonybrook is just as lovely as ever! The lake looks wonderful, and this year there's a beautiful new float. We go in the water twice a day, and there's a new swimming instructor who is going to teach us fancy diving.

I like the girls in my bunk very much. I know most of them from last year, but there are two new girls— Margaret Ellis and Peggy Lane. Peggy's father is Alan Lane, the famous band leader.

Our counselor is very sweet. Her name is Annette, and she teaches dancing in the Winter. She promised to teach the six of us how to dance if we keep our bunk nice and neat.

I practice every afternoon the way I promised. The piano was tuned and it's much better this year. I was asked to play at the Camp Festival in August, and I said I would. I'll need a party dress, so will you bring my pink one when you come up?

How is everything at home? I miss you both. But don't worry about me because I'm very happy at camp and having lots of fun. Just don't forget to come and see me soon!

Love and kisses,
Marjory

Dear Mother:

Here I am at the Academy, all unpacked and settled and ready for work.

I have the room right next to the one I had last year. It's a little larger, and it has two windows. I like it a lot.

Well, classes start tomorrow at nine. I'm going to study real hard this year and try to get good marks. I'm out to make the Varsity Football Team, and I *can't* make it unless I get an 85 average or better.

By the way, tell Dad I have Mr. Corey for Latin again. He met Mr. Corey when he was up here last year. He's a swell guy!

Thanks a lot for the cookies. I found them when I unpacked the trunk. And I found your note, too. Don't worry. . . . I'll get good marks this year. I want that camera Dad promised me!

I signed up for the same laundry service I had last year. Is that okay? I'll need a check of $25 to give them before October 1st, so please send it in your next letter.

That's all for now, but I'll write you and Dad sometime in the next few days to tell you about my classes.

Love to all the family,

Bill

Dear Mom and Dad:

Well, another week is over and the days are speeding by. Soon I'll be coming home for Christmas. I can hardly wait. It seems *ages* since I saw you!

Everything here is fine. The tests weren't too hard, and I'm sure I passed with high marks. I expect honors in history and math—and maybe in Spanish, too.

I saw the perfect Christmas gift for Judy in a little shop here. I'm not going to tell you what it is because she may see this letter. How is Judy-braids getting along? Is she still having so much trouble with her spelling? I wouldn't know, of course, because she never writes to me. I guess big sisters just don't count with the pigtail crowd!

I got a box of cookies from Aunt Alice last week. They were delicious. Barbara and I had a real picnic in our room. I wrote to Aunt Alice and told her how good they were and how much I enjoyed them. She's so sweet—she's always sending me things. I must get her a real nice Christmas gift this year.

By the way, I went to the Exeter game last Thursday. Exeter beat Andover 17 to 6. It was awfully cold but I wore my beaver coat and my stadium boots and I felt nice and snug. We all had hot chocolates before we went back to school.

I hope you are well and that everything at home is fine. Don't forget to send me my plane ticket. I'd like to take the two-o'clock plane from Boston; there's a train out of here at 11:15 and that would get me to Boston in plenty of time.

My, it's exciting to be going home! I'm counting the days, darlings. Love to you both—and to that little imp, Judy.

> Your devoted
> Suzanne

Dear Aunt Alice:

I received your letter and the box of cookies. Thank you very much. You are sweet to keep thinking of me all the time! My roommate is jealous—she says she wishes *she* had a wonderful aunt like you!

The cookies were simply delicious. I can't remember when I tasted anything so good. Barbara and I had a real picnic!

I'm doing very well in school. We had our tests last week and I know I passed them all. I'll have my marks by the time I come home for Christmas.

Just think, Aunt Alice! In less than two weeks I'll be on my way home. I'm so happy! I can hardly wait to see mother, dad, Judy, you and all my relatives and friends again. I'll have eighteen days at home—isn't that *super?*

Thanks again for the cookies, and for your nice letter. I always enjoy your letters—they're so full of news of home.

I'll be seeing you soon, Aunt Alice. And until then, love and kisses to the sweetest, most thoughtful aunt in the world!

Suzanne

Dear Grandma:

I was sorry to hear you have not been well. I certainly hope you're all better by now.

Mother says you may go to Florida for a few weeks. That's a good idea. You ought to get away from the bleak New England climate—I hear it's been awful this past month. I'm sure the warm sunshine would do you a lot of good.

I've been fine this winter. I haven't had one cold. I'm doing well in my studies, too—much better than last year. Even dad is pleased because I passed Latin with an 80 and got honors in math.

I'm on the football team now, Grandma. I hope you'll feel well enough to come and see me play some time.

But the most important thing is to take care of yourself and *get well*. I can't be having my precious grandmother feeling low. So hurry and write me that you're feeling fit as a fiddle again, and on your way to Florida!

With love,
Bob

Dear Uncle Alfred:

I received the hockey stick yesterday. Thanks a lot. I hope you can get up to see some of our games. Gosh,

I'm crazy about hockey! I like it even better now than football or basketball.

Say, that's good news about your book. I'm glad to hear it. I hope you sell a million copies! I must read it when it comes out—I love mystery stories.

Mother and Dad are coming for Thanksgiving. I only get one day off, and that isn't enough to travel all the way home and back again. So they're coming here, and we'll have dinner together at the Inn. I'm looking forward to it.

I'm doing much better in my school work this year. I *have* to get good marks if I want to stay on the team —so believe me, I'm studying! I'd be the saddest fellow in school if I couldn't play hockey.

Well, Uncle Al—congratulations on the book. I'll be looking for it in the best-seller lists. And thanks again for the swell hockey stick. I know I could never get one like it around here.

Give my love to Aunt Debbie, and write again soon.

Affectionately,
Richard

2

Children's Invitations and Acknowledgments

Children's party invitations are usually in the form of gaily decorated cards with blank spaces for filling in the date, place, hour, occasion and so on. Even very young children should be permitted to fill in and address their own party invitations, as it gives them a sense of social responsibility. But it's wise to check on the time, date and other essential data to make sure it's entirely correct. Otherwise youngsters may arrive on the wrong day or at the wrong hour.

When printed cards of invitation are not used, notes are written—either by the child or by his mother. Naturally a child of three or four needs to have his invitations written for him. Here is an example:

Dear Mrs. Davis:

Jimmy will be four years old on Saturday, June 10th, and I'm having a little birthday party for him.

I know he won't be happy unless his pal, Ronnie, is at the party; so I hope you will let him come.

If you bring Ronnie about three, he'll be just in time for the fun. I'd like you to stay and have tea with the other mothers at five. But if you can't stay, I'll see that Ronnie is safely delivered to your door no later than six o'clock.

Sincerely yours,
Ethel B. Hubbard

Ronnie's mother promptly writes a friendly note of acceptance or regret. If her little boy cannot attend the party, she explains why in her letter.

Dear Mrs. Hubbard:

Ronnie is thrilled and excited about Jimmy's birthday party. Of course he'll be there—with his best party manners, I hope!

I'll bring him at three and call for him about six, so you won't need to bother about getting him home.

I'd like very much to stay and have tea with the other mothers, but I have a previous appointment for the afternoon and I can't very well get out of it. Thanks for asking me.

Sincerely yours,
Martha P. Davis

Dear Mrs. Hubbard:

I haven't told Ronnie about the birthday party because I know how disappointed he would be not to go. But he is scheduled to take a series of allergy tests on June 10th and unfortunately the date cannot be changed.

I am sure you understand, and that you and Jimmy will forgive Ronnie for not being there.

Thank you for Ronnie and myself for your gracious invitation. And many happy returns of the day!

Sincerely yours,
Martha P. Davis

As soon as a child is old enough to write his own invitations, he should be permitted to do so. Don't tell him the *exact words* to write; just make whatever helpful suggestions you think are necessary. Let the invitation be natural and childish.

Dear Marian:

Next Sunday is my birthday. I will be eight years old. I am going to have a cake with eight candles. Can you come to my party? It starts at two o'clock. Good-by, but don't forget to come.

Judy

Dear Richard:

Please come to my birthday party on March 6 from two to five o'clock. I'll be nine years old so I am inviting nine boys. My dad is going to show movies. I hope you can come to my party.

Your pal,
Joseph Hale

Dear Betty:

Mother said I can have a party for my birthday. It's next Friday. Can you come at four o'clock and stay for dinner? My dad is going to drive all the girls home around eight. I hope you can come.

Anita

Dear Bert:

I'm having a birthday party on Saturday afternoon, June 12th, and I'd like you to come. It's from two o'clock to six. It won't be fun without you, so please come! Jerry and Donald will be here, and my twin cousins. Don't be late—we have a lot of games to play!

Eddie Wagner

Dear Peter:

Guess what? I'm having a Hallowe'en Party! It's on Saturday, October 29th. Come at one o'clock, and don't eat anything because you are having lunch here. We'll duck for apples and play "Find the Ghost" in the afternoon.

Now don't forget, Pete! Be here at one. Jim and Fred are coming, and Alan Foster, and some other fellows you don't know. We'll have a lot of fun.

Your friend,
Tommy Ford

Dear Peggy:

Will you come to my house on Wednesday, February 12th, at one o'clock? It's Lincoln's birthday, and there's no school.

Mother's letting me have a real grown-up luncheon party. So come at one, and bring your appetite along! We'll play games in the afternoon, and there's a special surprise . . . but I'm not going to tell you what it is.

I hope you can come. You know most of the girls I've invited and I'm sure you'll have a good time.

Love,
Annette

NOTES OF ACCEPTANCE

Children's party invitations are not, as a rule, as conscientiously acknowledged as adult invitations. They don't need to be. Sometimes the mother telephones to say the young guest will be there. Sometimes the child's presence on the day of the party is the only acknowledgment. It's always more gracious, of course, to write a note of acceptance . . . and youngsters should be encouraged to do so. But there's no question about the need for acknowledgment when a child *cannot* attend. In that case a note of regret must be sent at once, explaining why the invitation cannot be accepted.

Following are specimen letters of acceptance and regret to guide the young beginner in his social duties:

Dear Judy:

Yes, I can come to your birthday party. My mother will bring me on Sunday at two o'clock. I love parties and I am glad you are having one.

Marian

Dear Joseph:

Thank you for inviting me to your party. I am very glad to come. The movies sound wonderful. I'll see you on Saturday.

Your pal,
Richard

Dear Anita:

Your party sounds like lots of fun! I'll be there on Friday at four o'clock, and mother says I can stay until eight as long as someone takes me home. I am looking forward to it.

Your loving friend,
Betty

Dear Eddie:

I'll be glad to come to your party on Saturday, June 12.

It will be nice meeting your twin cousins. I've heard so much about them.

I learned a new game to play at parties. It's fun. I'll tell you about it on Saturday.

Your friend,
Bert

Dear Mrs. Collins:

I want to thank you for inviting me to spend the week end with Joan. I'll be glad to come, and I know I'll have a wonderful time. I always do with Joan!

Dad will drive me to Hawthorne Saturday morning and call for me Sunday evening—but thanks very much for offering to call for me.

I'm looking forward to seeing you this week end.

Sincerely yours,
Phyllis

Notes of Regret

Dear Mary:

I'm sorry I cannot come to your party on Sunday. My grandma is coming and I haven't seen her in a long time. Thank you for asking me. Happy birthday.

Your friend,
Gladys

Dear Tom:

Mother says to tell you I can't come on Friday because my dad's coming back from England, and she wants me to be here.

I hate to miss your party. But I'm sure excited about seeing my dad!

Happy birthday, Tom—and thanks a lot for inviting me.

                                                            Larry

Dear Ruth:

I'm just getting over a sore throat, and mother doesn't think I'll be well enough to go to your party on Friday.

I'm awfully sorry. I know I'll miss a very good time.

Love and congratulations on your thirteenth birthday.

                                                            Jane

Dear Annette:

I wish I could come to your luncheon on Lincoln's birthday. But that's the day we're going to Manhasset to visit my sister and see the new baby.

Mother says that if we get home early enough she'll drop me at your house for an hour or so in the afternoon. I'd like to find out what the "big surprise" is, even though I can't get there in time for luncheon!

I hate to miss any of your parties, they're always such fun. Thanks a lot for inviting me.

                                                    With love,
                                                        Peggy

Book VI

Travel Correspondence

THE CORRESPONDENCE MOST GENERALLY ASSOCIATED WITH travel involves letters requesting information about passports, visas, customs duties, and so on; letters to travel agents and tourist bureaus; letters of reservation and cancellation.* These are strictly business letters, and should be handled as such. They should be brief and to the point, giving all necessary information and clearly stating the purpose or request. The busy agent or representative at the other end doesn't care whether this is your first trip abroad or your tenth. All he is interested in is what specific information or service you need and want. So keep this in mind when you are writing. Don't be tempted to get chatty, to include interesting but unnecessary information which may obscure the real purpose of your letter.

Use business stationery for correspondence in this category, if you have it. Otherwise use plain white stationery of standard size and shape, not small cards or social notes which are not only unsuitable but may be lost or misplaced on a crowded desk.

REQUESTING INFORMATION
FROM A TRAVEL AGENCY

Even experienced travelers find it useful and convenient to make arrangements through a travel agency. A good travel agent can make interesting and helpful suggestions; and as a rule make better transportation and hotel reservations than the traveler can by himself.

It is not necessary to enclose a stamped, self-addressed envelope with a request for information from a travel agency. Answering inquiries is part of the agency's business expense, and profits result from bookings which come from such inquiries.

---

* For the letters of *vacationing*, the personal greetings and reports sent to family and friends back home, see pages 368 to 371, and 398 to 402.

(*To a Travel Agency*)

I am planning a two-week vacation around the Christmas and New Year holidays, and I am interested in taking a Caribbean cruise.

Please send me any literature you have available on cruises scheduled for that time; and your suggestions as to which of such cruises would be most desirable for a young woman traveling alone. Thank you.

I am interested in arranging a trip for my wife and myself of approximately four weeks' duration, beginning July 16th. I would like to include in our itinerary Yellowstone National Park and Glacier National Park in the United States; and Banff, Lake Louise and Jasper in Canada.

Will you prepare a suggested itinerary for me which will include these areas, and any other places of interest that could be combined with them.

REQUESTING INFORMATION FROM
TOURIST BUREAU OF FOREIGN COUNTRY

The tourist bureaus of foreign countries often have literature available which is of value to the traveler. An inquiry directed to the bureau, the address of which can usually be found in the telephone directories of major cities, will bring the information desired. For example:

Spanish Tourist Office,
485 Madison Avenue,
New York, 22, N.Y.

Gentlemen:

I am planning a visit to Spain next April. My itinerary includes Madrid, Seville, Toledo and Málaga.

I would appreciate receiving information concerning these cities, and the areas surrounding them. Literature about climatic conditions, clothing required, customs of the area, and any fiestas or celebrations scheduled for that time of the year would be of interest and value to me.

I would also like to know about customs regulations, as my wife and I plan to do some shopping in Toledo and Madrid.

Very truly yours,

TRANSPORTATION INQUIRIES

(To a Railroad)

Please send me a timetable and schedule of rates for your service from New York to Miami, Florida, during the month of February.

How far in advance of departure may bookings be made?

———————

(To an Airline)

I would like to have a timetable and schedule of rates for your flights to London during the month of May.

I will be traveling with an infant and would like to know what provisions, if any, are made for infant care en route.

———————

(To a Steamship Company)

Please send me your schedule of sailings for the Queen Mary and Queen Elizabeth during the period from April 15 to Sept. 15. I would also appreciate copies of the ships' plans, and rate data. Thank you.

HOTEL INQUIRIES AND RESERVATIONS

Hotel reservations may be made by a wife for "my husband and myself"—or by a husband for "my wife and myself." On arrival at the hotel, however, it is always the husband who registers; and the correct form is "Mr. and Mrs. Thomas Preston." If a young son or daughter accompanies the parents, the form to use in registering is "Mr. and Mrs. Thomas Preston and son" (or daughter). A grown son or daughter registers separately, beneath the name of the parents.

In making hotel reservations by letter, clearly specify the type of accommodations required, the date (and, if possible, the approximate time) of arrival, the date of departure, and any special requirements you may have. Requests for reservations at popular resort hotels should be made well in advance to avoid disappointment.

> The Greenbrier,
> White Sulphur Springs,
> West Virginia.

Gentlemen:

I would like to reserve a double room, with twin beds and bath, for my wife and myself for two weeks beginning August 17th. We plan to arrive in the early afternoon of the 17th, and leave after breakfast on August 31st.

Please confirm this reservation; or, if desirable accommodations are not available for the period specified, let me know the earliest date you can take care of us.

Sincerely yours,

> Reservations Desk,
> The Homestead,
> Hot Springs, Virginia.

Gentlemen:

My husband and I are thinking of spending several weeks at The Homestead this summer. We would like to have a copy of the floor plans, showing the accommodations you can let us have for about three weeks in August. We would require a large, airy room with twin beds and bath. Please include a schedule of rates with the plans; and any literature about the facilities and activities at The Homestead which you think we would find interesting. Thank you.

Very truly yours,

The Manager,
Pine Grove Inn,
Asheville, N.C.

Dear Sir:

Please let me know as soon as possible if you can accommodate my husband and myself, and our teen-age daughter, for the month of July. We would like a twin-bedded double room with bath for ourselves; and, if possible, a connecting single room for our daughter. Otherwise a separate single room for her, on the same floor, would be satisfactory.

If you can provide comfortable accommodations for us, we plan to drive to Asheville from Chicago, leaving on the morning of June 28th and arriving sometime in the early afternoon of July 1st. We would leave after breakfast on July 30th.

Will you also let us know if garage space would be available during that time for our car.

Sincerely yours,

Mr. John Willston, Manager,
Grove Pines,
Pineville, S.C.

Dear Mr. Willston:

Please cancel the reservation for Mrs. Parker and myself for June 14th to 30th. I sincerely regret that unforseen circumstances make it impossible for us to be away at that time.

We hope to have the pleasure of visiting Grove Pines at some future date.

Cordially yours,

The first requirement for travel in a foreign country is a passport. To obtain it, you must apply in person at a passport agency of the United States Government Department of State. There are passport agencies in Washington, D.C., New York, Boston, Chicago, New Orleans, Los Angeles and San Francisco. Elsewhere, application may be made at the passport department of the nearest Federal or State Court.

When planning a trip abroad, be sure to apply for your passport, and whatever visas are required, as far in advance of departure as possible. It takes time to process a passport; you cannot depend on getting it in a week or two. It may take as much as a month or more, especially during peak periods of travel. To obtain a passport you need: (1) proof of citizenship (birth certificate or naturalization papers); (2) two full-face, passport-size photographs; (3) $10 to pay the passport fee.* If you are applying for the first time, you also need an identifying witness who has known you for two or more years (any relative or friend who is over twenty-one, but not a husband or wife).

You can generally secure whatever passport information you need from your travel agent; and if he is making the arrangements and reservations for your trip, he can also usually secure whatever visas you will require. However, if you are not using an agent, and the information you require is not otherwise available, you can write to the U.S. passport agency nearest your home. Or write to Passport Agency, U.S. Dept. of State, 1717 H. Street, N.W., Washington, 25, D.C. Sample letters of request:

> Please send me the booklet containing passport information and requirements for United States citizens traveling to Europe. Thank you.

---

* A United States passport is good for two years, but can be extended for an additional two years for $5. After four years it expires and one must reapply.

Is any special type of passport required for a writer who plans to live for a year or more in a foreign country, in connection with a book he is writing about that country?

Please send me any information I may need when applying for a passport, and any special regulations with which I should be familiar.

LETTERS ABOUT VISAS FOR TRAVEL
IN FOREIGN COUNTRIES

The word *visa* is of French derivation and means "to see" or "to inspect." A visa is simply an official stamp of endorsement showing that the passport has been inspected and that the bearer is permitted to proceed. Some visas are free; for others there is a small charge. Some countries do not require visas; others will not permit entry even for a day without one.

Visas are issued by the consulates of the various countries. If bookings are made through a travel agency, the agency normally arranges for the necessary visas as part of its service. It is therefore not necessary, as a rule, for the prospective traveler to communicate with the consulates of the countries he plans to visit.

However if the traveler purchases his transportation directly from airlines or steamship lines, without the services of an agent, it may be necessary for him to obtain the visas himself. In this case, he must communicate with the consul at the nearest consulate office of each country requiring a visa. A list of countries requiring visas can be obtained from the Passport Office, Department of State, Washington, D.C., or from any passport agency. Consular representatives of most foreign countries are located in principal cities throughout the United States. The addresses of foreign consular offices can be obtained by consulting the Congressional Directory, available in most libraries.

Some countries require a personal interview at the office of the consulate; but many will provide visas by mail or messenger when all required forms, and the passport, are submitted for examination. As this takes time, and as you may need several visas for your trip, it is advisable to make your inquiries and arrangements well in advance. To avoid delay, be sure to give all essential data, such as: duration of visit to the country for which visa is requested, number of persons in the party, type of visa required (tourist, transit or business).

What you enclose with your application depends on the requirements of the particular country. You may be asked to include a police card, vaccination and health certificates, a round-trip ticket, or other evidence that you will not be stranded in the country you are visiting. So the first thing to do, if a travel agent is not doing it for you, is to find out what the requirements are.

Consulate General of Peru,
10 Rockefeller Plaza,
New York, 20, N.Y.

Dear Sir:

My sister and I are planning to visit Peru on a pleasure trip next February. We would appreciate receiving information concerning the requirements for a visa for American citizens.

We will be traveling by ourselves, and would like to remain in Peru 10 days to 2 weeks.

Very truly yours,

Consulate General of Paraguay,
32 Broadway,
New York, 4, N.Y.

Dear Sir:

I am enclosing the completed application form, my U.S. passport, and check for $2.50, in accordance with instructions received from your office.

I would appreciate the prompt return of my passport with your visa, as I have several other visas to obtain before I leave on October 10th. Thank you very much for your cooperation.

Sincerely yours,

LETTERS SUSPENDING DELIVERIES
DURING ABSENCE

It generally takes a few weeks to put a "suspend subscription" order into effect, so make your request well in advance. To avoid the possibility of error (with newspapers and magazines piling up at your front door!) make certain you give your name and address exactly as imprinted on the publication when you receive it. A good idea is to cut this mailing imprint from a copy of the publication and attach it to your letter.

(To a Newspaper)

Please suspend delivery of The Wall Street Journal to me from July 16th to Sept. 4th, as I will be abroad during that time. I would like to have delivery resumed with the Sept. 5th issue. Thank you.

(To a Magazine)

I wish to suspend my subscription to Time Magazine for the summer as I will not be at home to receive it. I will be traveling most of the time and therefore cannot give a summer address.

Please suspend the subscription beginning with the first week in July, and resume the second week in September.

CORRESPONDENCE CONCERNING
FOREIGN PURCHASES

It is never wise to get angry or abusive in a letter, regardless of the circumstances. You only antagonize your correspondent; and more often than not you accomplish less than you would by writing a patient, courteous letter.

(To a Jeweler in India)

On October 14th, while I was in Calcutta, I purchased a star ruby from you which you were to set in a white gold mounting I selected. It was under-stood that this ring was to be delivered to me in New York in time to be used as a Christmas gift for my wife. You promised delivery to me by December 15th at the latest.

As it is now more than two weeks since the prom-ised delivery date and I have not received the ring; I am concerned about it and wonder if it may not have been lost in transit. Naturally I am disappointed not to have had it in time for Christmas.

If you have already forwarded the ring and you think it should have reached me by this time, please put a tracer on it through your shipping agency. If it has not been sent out as yet, or was sent out too recently to have reached me, please let me know when I can expect to receive it.

(*To a Merchant in Greece*)

Your shipment to me of 8 items which I purchased from you on September 21 when I was in Athens reached me today. Unfortunately the two vases in the shipment arrived broken. The four ashtrays and two candy dishes arrived without damage.

As a charge for insured shipping was included in the cost of the purchase, I presume that you will be able to arrange for the insuring agent to replace the broken articles. I trust that you can send these promptly as they were intended as homecoming gifts for friends.

The vases were black, 6 inches tall, and shaped like classic Grecian urns. They were about $6 each in American money.

LETTER PROTESTING
CUSTOMS CHARGE

Collector of Customs, Port of New York,
Protest Section,
Customs House,
Bowling Green, New York.

Dear Sir:

I received a parcel today from Great Britain, sent by International Parcel Post, on which a customs duty charge of $12.77 was collected by the postman.

I declared this item as "unaccompanied baggage to follow" on my customs declaration when I returned to the United States at the port of New York on Pan American Airways, Flight 15, Dec. 12, 1959. As the total value of the goods brought into the country by me was $192, well below my $500 exemption, I wish to request a refund of the charges of $12.77 collected by the postman. The customs duty charge slip for this item was #246242.

If there is any further information required concerning this matter, I will be glad to furnish it.

Very truly yours,

LETTERS OF INTRODUCTION, AND
OF THANKS FOR HOSPITALITY

A letter of introduction, when given to a traveler to present in person, is always left unsealed—with only the name of the friend to whom it is to be presented written on the envelope. The address is given separately to the traveler. The words "Courtesy of Mrs. Harris" (the person presenting the letter) are written in the lower left corner of the envelope.

Dear Laura:

This will introduce one of my very dear friends, Margery Harris, who is visiting France for the first

time. You have much in common, both of you being
writers of children's books; and I know you will
thoroughly enjoy meeting each other. In fact, I insisted that whatever else Margery may do in Paris, she
must meet you and spend some time with you.

I understand that Margery has only a week in Paris.
Perhaps you can tell her what to do and see, and how
to spend that week to best advantage. You can be sure
I will greatly appreciate any courtesy you show her.

Fondly,

A letter of introduction may be mailed, but it is considered
a courtesy to send a copy of the letter to the person being introduced. The following is from the president of a company to a
field manager distantly located, introducing a stockholder who
is going through his area, asking that he be met on arrival and
that courtesies be extended to him and his wife. This is a type of
letter which must frequently be written nowadays, for business
associates and for friends.

Mr. Frederick G. Knowles,
American and International Products Co.,
Avenida Corrientes No 357,
Buenos Aires, Argentina.

Dear Fred:

Mr. Thomas B. Judson is a substantial stockholder
in American and International Products Co., and has
always taken a constructive interest in the affairs of
the company.

He and his wife are leaving the United States on
February 10th for a trip to Latin America, and expect to arrive in Buenos Aires, from Montevideo, via
PAA flight 216 at 5:50 P.M., to spend about a week
there. They will stay at the Plaza Hotel.

Mr. Judson would like to visit some of our branch
offices in Latin America, and I told him you would

take care of him in Buenos Aires. Please have one of
your associates meet him and Mrs. Judson when they
arrive, and extend to them any courtesies which they
may desire. I know they will appreciate it; and you
can be sure I will, too.

Claire joins me in best regards to you and Julia.

Cordially,

Mr. Thomas B. Judson,
277 Park Avenue,
New York, 17, N.Y.

Dear Mr. Judson:

I am enclosing copies of letters I have sent to our
field managers in the various countries which you
will be visiting on your forthcoming trip to South
America. We have operations in all the countries included in your itinerary except Ecuador and Bolivia.

I hope you will have the opportunity to meet some
of our field people and spend a little time with them.
I am sure they will be happy to make your visit as
enjoyable as possible.

My best wishes to you and Mrs. Judson for an interesting and pleasant trip.

Sincerely,

Hospitality or special courtesies received while traveling should
be acknowledged promptly and graciously, and with as much
enthusiasm as the circumstances warrant. Anyone who has
generously entertained a stranger at the request of a mutual
friend deserves an especially warm and appreciative letter.

Dear Mrs. Bowen:

Our visit to Lisbon was the highlight of our trip,
thanks to you and your charming family. You were
all so generous with your time, and so patient with us
and our endless questions!

Bill and I want you to know how very much we appreciate all you did to make our stay in Lisbon interesting and enjoyable. We'll never forget that day we all got up at dawn to watch the fishing boats come in. Bill is still talking about those colorful fishing boats, and the women carrying those huge baskets of fish on their heads. He says he's sure he got some very good pictures for his collection.

We hope that when you return to the United States next spring you will plan on visiting us in Boston. We may not be able to show you sights you haven't already seen, but we'd welcome the opportunity to return your hospitality.

You can be sure the Claytons will hear all about how wonderful you and Mr. Bowen were to us, and what gay, lovely girls your Pat and Jill are. It was a real joy to meet them, and to explore Lisbon in their company.

Thanks to all of you, for a truly unforgettable interlude in Lisbon!

Cordially and gratefully,

Dear Alice:

I'm sure I don't have to tell you how much your kindness meant to George and me during our recent visit to London. Your hospitality quite overwhelmed us! I can only hope that someday you will visit us in California and give us the pleasure of reciprocating.

Surely few visitors have had the opportunity of seeing London for the first time as you showed it to us. It was *your* London we saw, rich in beauty and tradition—not the London of the tourists. We'll never forget the wonderful sights and experiences you made possible.

"Thank you" seems so inadequate for all your many kindnesses and your generosity. But thank you both, for everything! George and I count ourselves fortunate indeed to have had your company in London, and to have seen that historic city through your eyes.

Affectionately,

Book VII

*The Social and Personal
Letters of Business*

LETTERS TO BUSINESS ASSOCIATES, TO EMPLOYERS, TO THE WIVES or families of employees, concerned with the courtesies and amenities rather than the commercial aspects of business life, are grouped here under the general classification of the *social* and *personal* letters of business.

These are the letters motivated by courtesy, kindness and goodwill. The letter of appreciation for the help or advice of a business associate, the note of congratulation upon the achievement or promotion of a colleague, the expression of sympathy to an employer who has suffered an injury or loss—these are the personal and social letters of business. Too often they are postponed or neglected, either in the stress of business affairs or because such letters are frequently difficult to write. But surely they should not be neglected, for such letters can do much to strengthen and enrich business relationships.

Either business or social stationery may be used for the social letters of business, depending on the nature of the communication. For example, a letter of congratulation to a business associate on a promotion, or on some special honor or distinction he has received, may be written quite properly on business stationery. But a letter of congratulation to a business associate on some significant personal occasion, such as his engagement or marriage, or on the birth of a child, should be written on social stationery; and it should follow the spacing and general format of the social letter.

In content, the social letters of business should be brief but not abrupt, cordial but not intimate or chatty. One should always bear in mind that wordy, effusive letters generally sound insincere. Following are various specimen letters which, it is hoped, will be helpful in drafting your own social and personal letters of business.

LETTERS OF THANKS AND APPRECIATION

For a Message of Congratulations

Dear Mr. Ferris:

I'd like you to know how very much I appreciate your note of congratulation on my recent engagement.

Thank you, for my fiancée and myself, for your good wishes for our happiness. I value your kind thoughts more than I can say.

Sincerely yours,

I was happy to receive your message of congratulations on my marriage, and greatly appreciate your good wishes for our happiness.

Thank you, for my wife and myself, for your very kind and gracious letter.

How very nice of you to write! I just can't tell you how pleased I was to receive your charming note of congratulations, and your good wishes on the birth of our baby.

Hearing from you made me a bit nostalgic for the busy, happy days at Barnes & Co., but only for a moment! I find that being a wife and mother is now career enough for me.

My husband joins me in thanking you for your good wishes.

Your note of June 10th has given me much pleasure. Thank you very much indeed for your congratulations on my new book, and for taking the time and trouble to write me so kindly about it. I greatly appreciate your good wishes for its success.

How thoughtful of you to send congratulations on

my son's lecture in Boston last week. I am sending your letter on to him as I know he will enjoy it.

I am, of course, very proud of Ralph's accomplishments, and happy to know that so many of my good friends and business associates share in my pleasure. Thank you so much for writing!

I appreciate your very kind letter of Sept. 14th, on my recent series of lectures before the Kiwanis Club. The subject, as you know, is one in which I have a very great interest; and it has been most gratifying to find that so many of my fellow townsmen share that interest.

Letters like yours make all the time and preparation put into this project well worth the effort. Thank you sincerely!

This is to thank you, on behalf of the firm and myself, for your congratulations and good wishes on the happy occasion of our 30th Anniversary. It was good of you to write, and all of us here at Brand & Sons sincerely appreciate your good wishes.

Our two firms have enjoyed an unusually fine and pleasant relationship through the years, and we highly treasure your friendship and good will.

For Good Wishes

Dear Arthur:

It was most thoughtful of you to drop me your pleasant note of August 2nd.

It is always nice to hear from one's friends and former associates; and I hope that perhaps our new venture in publishing ultimately will result in our being able to work once more together.

Thank you for your good wishes; and do come in and see our offices when you are in the vicinity.

Cordially yours,

You have no idea what a pleasure it was for me to get your friendly note of the tenth. I need all the kind words and encouragement anyone wants to give me at this time!

It is a rather large undertaking for me; and as you know, an entirely new departure. There is much to learn. But I welcome the challenge, and hope to justify the confidence in me which you have so kindly expressed.

Please remember me to all my good friends and former associates at Hadley, Prince & Co. My warm appreciation to you for the thought that prompted your note.

Thank you for your letter. I sincerely appreciate your good wishes.

I have long looked forward to retirement, not for the doubtful pleasure of being lazy but because, as you know, I have always wanted to write. Now I'll have the leisure for it; and now at last I'll find out if I really *can* write.

Yes, I'm sure I'll miss Madison Avenue; but I'll be too busy to mope about it. My very best to you, always.

It was kind of you to write, and I treasure your thoughts very much.

I have had a lot of fun in this business, and it isn't easy for me to retire from it. But you well know, having been in it yourself for so many years, what its enormous pressures and tensions are. I must admit I am looking forward to relaxing for a few months; and after that—well, we'll see! I expect to turn to other interests which I hope will be as much fun, but not quite so demanding.

Let me say again what a pleasure it was to hear

from you, and how very much I appreciate your good wishes.

For Message of Sympathy, Condolence

Dear Mr. Elkins:

Your message of sympathy is much appreciated by my father and all of the family. We wish to thank you for your inquiry and for your good wishes.

My father has improved a great deal in the past week, and he may soon be able to leave the hospital. However the doctors say it will be at least a month before he can return to the office.

Thank you again for your kind letter.

Sincerely yours,

Now that I can sit up and write, I want to thank you for your cheerful and encouraging letter, which I received just after I entered the hospital. It certainly helped my morale and gave me a lift when I needed it most.

It is good to know that the operation is now behind me and that I'll soon be well enough to leave the hospital. I have missed my work and all my friends at the office; and I hope it won't be too long before I can get back to my job and in the swing of things.

I appreciate your thoughtfulness in writing. Please remember me to everyone at the office.

Thank you for your message of sympathy and for your good wishes. It was thoughtful of you to write.

I am told that I am making a very good recovery and should be well enough to leave the hospital in about a week. I am hoping to be able to return to the office by the first of October.

This is the first day I have been permitted to sit up and write letters. Though I feel wobbly (and I am sure my writing shows it!) I must let you know without further delay how very much I appreciate all the cheerful notes I received from you here at the hospital. It was wonderful of you to write so often, and to send me all the news of the office. Your letters gave me a real lift, and I'm sure they played no small part in my recovery.

I hope to be leaving here in about a week; and I may be able to return to the office by March 10th. I certainly hope so! Thanks again for all your kindness.

I am writing this letter for my mother. She would like you to know how very much she appreciates your message of sympathy, and your desire to help us in our grief and anxiety.

The kindness and generosity of my father's business associates have been a great source of strength and comfort to us. But there is nothing anyone can do now except to hope and pray. My father was very critically injured in the accident, as you know; but at least we now have been given some hope for his recovery.

We are all grateful to you for your very kind letter.

Thank you for your thoughtful letter, which I was unable to acknowledge before this.

I am feeling much better now. Except for a fractured ankle and several deep cuts in my forehead, the injuries were not too serious. The accident could have been much worse, and I am grateful it wasn't.

I'm sorry to be away from the office at this busy time; and I would like you to know that I sincerely appreciate your kindness and consideration.

The preceding letters of thanks are for messages of sympathy during illness or after an accident. Those which follow are for messages of condolence on the death of a business associate or a member of the family.

Dear Miss Porter:

My family and I acknowledge your kind letter, and wish to thank you for your expression of sympathy. We appreciate your thoughtfulness.

Sincerely yours,

Please convey my appreciation, and that of my family, to the members of your department for their splendid tribute to Mrs. Blair.

I am deeply grateful to all of you for your sympathy and kindness.

Your letter was a great comfort to my mother. She has asked me to write and thank you for it.

We are grateful to you for all your many kindnesses to my father during his illness, and for your thoughtful message of sympathy to us now. Please accept our sincere appreciation.

On behalf of the family, I wish to thank you for your kind message of sympathy.

My father's sudden death was a great shock to us; but we try to find consolation in the fact that he went quickly and did not suffer. The kindness of his many friends and business associates has been a comfort to us.

Thank you for your message of sympathy, and for your fine tribute to my brother. Your letter has been a great comfort to the family; and we shall all long remember your kindness with gratitude.

The officers and the personnel of Anderson & Company wish to thank you for your expression of sympathy on the death of our President, Mr. Harold Parker.

We have sustained a great loss in the death of Mr. Parker. All of us here feel that the greatest tribute we can pay his memory is to hold to the ideals and high standards he represented.

Please accept the sincere appreciation of the members of this organization for your kind message of sympathy on the death of our Treasurer, Mr. Charles Bolton. His abilities and his exceptional personal qualities have meant much to this firm through the years. He will be missed greatly by all of us.

For Hospitality Received

Dear Mr. Perkins:

I have just returned to the office from my eastern trip.

I would like you to know that the day I spent with you in New York was by far the most pleasant in all the three busy weeks of my schedule. The leisurely, relaxed luncheon at the University Club was just what I needed after all the hectic hopping around of the previous week. And attending the theatre with you provided one of the most enjoyable evenings I have had in a very long time.

I am indebted to you for your kindness and hospitality, and look forward to the opportunity of reciprocating when you come this way.

Cordially,

You were most generous and hospitable to me in Boston last week, and I'd like you to know how very much I appreciate it.

Lunching at your club and meeting so many of your friends was an unexpected pleasure. And that was certainly an interesting old restaurant you took me to for dinner! The food was superb; I can't remember when I enjoyed a meal more.

Thank you for everything, Paul—but mostly for being so very cordial and giving me so much of your valuable time.

I must tell you how very pleasant it was to see you last week, and how much I enjoyed visiting your home and meeting your delightful family.

I hope it will not be too long before you have occasion to come to Washington, as it would give me great pleasure to entertain you as graciously as you entertained me in Toledo.

My sincere thanks to you and Mrs. Beardsley for your kindness and hospitality.

For a Personal Favor or Some Special Help

Dear Miss Hewitt:

Your help in assembling data and writing letters for me during the preparation of my "Anthology of American Humor" was most helpful, and far over and above the call of duty. I am most appreciative.

Surely a routine "Thank you" is inadequate for the valuable assistance you gave me thoughout this project. So please add this little book-charm to your bracelet, as a reminder that you had a very big part in my book's preparation.

Sincerely and gratefully,

I have had a most satisfactory interview with Mr. Lawrence, and he has given me every reason to believe there will be an interesting opening for me in his organization before the first of the year.

I know it was only because of your personal request that I was able to secure an interview with Mr. Lawrence; and that the fine letter of recommendation you wrote helped me convince him of my ability to write and direct television scripts. If the job materializes, and I am reasonably certain that it will, I can thank you for it. But whether it does or not, I am grateful to you for your kindness; and especially for your confidence in me.

I will let you know of further developments. In the meantime, please accept my sincere appreciation.

It was good of you to send me so much interesting material on the history and development of cosmetics. It is exactly what I have been searching for, and will help me enormously in the preparation of my report.

I can't thank you enough for your courtesy and cooperation!

This is to thank you again for all the kindness and consideration you showed me on my recent visit to the Ardsley plant.

It was most interesting to see Ardsley cosmetics in the process of manufacture; and I was certainly impressed by the precision and immaculate care which go into the handling of your products.

The visit was not only interesting but highly informative, and will be of great help to me in the preparation of my manuscript. I want to thank you especially for the fascinating old prints, and for your permission to use them in my report on the history and development of cosmetics. I am delighted to have them.

My sincere thanks to you for the useful and interesting material you sent in connection with our display at the drug convention in Buffalo next month. Your suggestions are excellent, and I am delighted to have them. They will help us in developing an effective display.

You were kind to cooperate so generously, and I appreciate it very much indeed.

You did it again! Everybody's talking about the wonderful lecture you gave at the Advertising Club on Wednesday. I know you consented to this assignment only as a favor to me, and I appreciate it more than I can say.

Your talk was interesting and timely; and well-organized, as usual. It was a splendid contribution to the series. My sincere thanks, Bert, for the committee and for myself.

I have been reading the galley proofs of my new book, and I can't help realizing how indebted I am to you for the sound medical background you provided. Without it the plot would have had little substance or credibility.

I just had to write and tell you this; and thank you once again for all your fine help and advice—so generously and so courteously given.

For Favorable Mention or Review

Dear Mr. Houghton:

That was a most flattering notice you gave me in your column last night, and I am very grateful for it. I am so pleased to know that you liked my performance, as there is no one whose opinion I value more.

Please accept my sincere thanks.

Cordially yours,

I have read with great pleasure your fine review of the opening of "April Evening" at the *Embassy* last night.

On behalf of the producer, director and cast, I wish to thank you for your generous and enthusiastic comments. We are all very happy to have your approval.

I am delighted with your favorable review of my book, "One Was Saved" in the current issue of *The Observer*. It makes me happy and proud to have your approval.

Thank you very much indeed for your kind remarks about the book.

Thank you for the excellent review of my book, "Mood for Murder" in this morning's *Times*. It was good of you to give it such favorable notice; and *very* good of you indeed not to give away the surprise ending! I am most appreciative.

I must write and tell you how very grateful I am for your glowing account of my recital at Town Hall last night. I can't think of anyone whose opinion and approval I value more highly.

I hope this brief note expresses my deep appreciation.

I am happy to know that you approved of my talk before the County Medical Society last week. It was a pleasure to read your fine report of it in the *Bulletin*; and I wish to thank you for your very complimentary remarks.

Thanks to an Immediate Superior or an Employer

Dear Mr. Bigly:

This is to acknowledge your very kind letter, and your congratulations on my recent engagement. I sincerely appreciate your good wishes.

Very truly yours,

Thank you so much for the check you sent me as a wedding gift, and for the wonderful letter which accompanied it. I appreciate your thoughtfulness.

Both my husband and I are grateful for the good wishes you have expressed for our future happiness.

I was happy to receive your note of congratulation on the birth of my son. Thank you very much for your thoughtfulness, and for your good wishes to my wife and myself.

I would like to express my appreciation for the unexpected and generous increase in salary which you have put into effect for me.

The increase is welcome, of course; but it is of secondary importance. What I value most is this evidence of your confidence in me; and I assure you that I shall continue to give my very best to the company and to the job.

I feel I must tell you again, formally and in writing, how pleased and appreciative I am about my promotion to junior executive on the Benton Baby Food account. This is the opportunity I had hoped for and had been working toward, but I did not expect it so soon.

Thank you for making it possible; and please be assured that I shall make every effort to justify your faith in me.

I am pleased and happy to have been named office manager, and wish to thank you for the unexpected promotion. I value this evidence of confidence in me very much indeed, and will make every effort to prove worthy of it.

I wish to thank you for including me in the dinner party for Mr. Thomas Manning at the Athletic Club last night. It was a most interesting and enjoyable occasion, and I was delighted to be there.

I would just like to say that I think this year's Christmas party was the best ever! I have been to them all since 1943, and I can't remember when there was so much good fun, good spirits, and good fellowship. Surely this must reflect the great loyalty and affection we old-timers have developed through the years for you and for the Winston Company.

Thank you, and a very happy New Year.

I feel I must let you know how very pleased I was, as a recent newcomer, to be invited to the company's annual Christmas party. Thank you for asking me. It was a wonderful party and I was delighted to be there.

May I add that I am happy and proud to be associated with such a warm and friendly organization.

A gift from an employer to an employee is acknowledged to the employer at the business address. A gift from an employer and his wife to an employee is acknowledged to them jointly, at their home address. A gift from an employer's wife to one of her husband's employees for some special favor, service or courtesy, is acknowledged to the wife at her home address. A gift from an employer and his wife to an employee and his wife (or husband)—as, for example, a wedding or baby gift—is generally acknowledged by the wife for herself and her husband; and is addressed to the employer and his wife at their home. However if the employee has never met the employer's wife, he or she may prefer to send the acknowledgment to the employer at his business address, thanking both him and his wife in the letter. Either form of address is permissible; the important thing is that a gift received from husband and wife must be acknowledged to *both*, regardless of how the letter is addressed. Following is a variety of specimen letters thanking an employer or immediate superior for a gift.

Dear Mr. Smith:

I sincerely appreciate your generous Christmas check, and the good wishes which accompanied it. Thank you for both; and please accept my own good wishes for a very happy New Year.

Very truly yours,

It was thoughtful of you to remember me at Christmas, and I appreciate it very much. Thank you for the beautiful pin; I will wear it with pleasure and pride.

My best wishes to you for the New Year.

It was a pleasure to work with you on the anthology. I do not feel I did any more than should have been expected of me as your secretary; but I am glad to know I was of help.

Your thanks, so sincerely given, are always adequate. But I must admit I am thrilled with the little book-charm, and shall add it proudly and with pleasure to my bracelet.

Thank you for your thoughtfulness. And good luck with the anthology—I hope it becomes the best-seller it deserves to be!

It is with mixed feelings that I write this note of thanks.

I am delighted with the lovely pin, and so very happy to have it. But at the same time I am concerned that you should have rewarded me so lavishly for the little extra help I was able to give you with your research on the history of cosmetics. Surely it was no more than should have been expected of me as your secretary.

Thank you very much for your generous gift. But please believe me when I say your appreciation so warmly expressed, was more than enough for me.

What a pleasant surprise to receive a gift from you on your return from France! The little figurine is charming and unusual, and I am delighted with it.

Thank you very much for your thoughtful remembrance.

―――――

I am always happy to type your letters and assist you any way I can in your charitable activities.

As the work was done here in the office, on Mr. Foster's time, surely there was no need to send me a gift. But I'm truly delighted with the perfume—it's my favorite kind!—and I appreciate your thoughtfulness very much indeed.

Thank you especially for your gracious letter. I am happy to have been of some small help in such a worthy cause.

―――――

I just can't tell you how thrilled and delighted I am with the coffee service! It is one of the most beautiful gifts I have received.

Please express my appreciation, and that of my fiancé, to Mrs. Harper. We send you both our sincere thanks for your generous gift and your good wishes.

―――――

I would like to say again how thrilled I was that you remembered yesterday was my 10th anniversary with the Dakar Company. It is wonderful of you to take such an interest in your employees.

Thank you for the flowers, and especially for your very kind letter. I value your good opinion of me very highly indeed.

LETTERS OF CONGRATULATION, GOOD WISHES
On a New Venture or Connection

Dear Mr. Heller:

I have just read about your interesting new venture in the advertising column of the New York *Times*.

Please count me among those who wish you every success and happiness.

Sincerely yours,

As a former associate who has always regarded you as one of the truly great of the legal profession, may I offer my best wishes for the future? I am sure that the interesting venture on which you are now embarking will add new distinction to your already illustrious name.

Congratulations, and every good wish for your continued success and happiness.

I read in this morning's paper that you have just joined Compton Press as editorial chief. I'm delighted by the news, as are all your many friends and former associates here at the Blaine Company. The consensus of opinion seems to be that Compton just couldn't have made a better choice!

I hasten to add my congratulations to the many you must be receiving today; and to wish you great success and satisfaction in your new position.

On a Promotion or Advancement

Dear Mr. Richards:

I was happy to see in this morning's paper that you have been made a vice president of the Wharton Agency. It's an advancement you have well earned through your record of past achievements; and I am so pleased that it has come to you.

My hearty congratulations, and every good wish for success in your new capacity.

Sincerely,

Congratulations! I have just heard that you have been made Sales Manager of your firm, and nobody could be more pleased about it than I am. It's a promotion that has long been due you, as I don't know anyone who has been so consistently hard-working and devoted to his job as you have been all the years I've known you.

It's a wonderful opportunity, Tom; and I know you will make a success of it and go on to further achievement. I send you my very best wishes for continued success and happiness ahead.

I have just received the exciting announcement that Harris, Blaine & Co. is now Harris, Blaine and Wright. May I add my congratulations to the many you must be receiving today on becoming a member of the firm you have served so ably for so many years. I cannot think of anyone who deserves this honor more.

My best wishes to you for ever-increasing success and happiness in the years ahead.

All of us here at Rand & Company are pleased to hear that you have become a partner in the firm of Mitchell, Barnes, Inc. Please accept our congratulations.

We have thoroughly enjoyed our relationship with you in the past, and look forward to a continuation of it in your new capacity.

On An Honor or Distinction

Dear Jim:

My warmest congratulations to you on your election as President of the Pennsylvania Bar Association. It is a great honor, and one you richly deserve. Congratulations are due the Association also for making such a brilliant choice.

Claire joins me in sending every best wish to you for a happy and successful administration.

Cordially,

This is just to tell you that all your friends and former associates here at Wayne & Cross are delighted to learn that you have been named "Man of the Year." Congratulations! We can't think of anyone who deserves the honor more.

It was a real pleasure to read in this morning's *Wall Street Journal* that you have received an honorary degree from Harvard University, in recognition of the important technological developments achieved by your company. Congratulations on this well-deserved and most fitting tribute!

On a Speech, Article, Book

Dear Mr. Curtis:

Congratulations on the splendid address you gave at the Science Club yesterday. I'm so glad I was there to hear it! In my opinion it was the most interesting and provocative talk we have had at the club in years; and I'm sure everyone else who was there feels as I do. We are indebted to you for an outstanding and truly memorable evening.

Sincerely yours,

I read your article in yesterday's *Beacon* with great interest. You have certainly made an exhaustive study of consumer reactions to television advertising; and I think you have come up with some very significant conclusions.

Congratulations! You have made a real contribution. I'm sure that all of us who write television commercials will profit from your findings.

Congratulations on your fine article, "What It Takes to Be an Executive," which I have just read in *Mid-Week Magazine*. It is one of the most interesting articles I have ever read on the subject, full of ideas and helpful advice. It should be required reading for anyone who aspires to executive status.

I know how busy you are, so please don't feel you must acknowledge this note. But *do* call me when you have time for a leisurely lunch at the club. It has been much too long since we have seen each other.

The announcement of your book in this morning's *Times* came as an exciting surprise. I knew you were interested in the history of the theatre, but I didn't know you were writing a book about it. That was certainly a fine review it got in Bud Chadwick's column! You can be sure I won't lose any time getting myself a copy.

Congratulations, Jim! I hope your "History of the Theatre" is a big success, and that there will be other books to follow.

I saw the announcement of your new mystery, "Mood for Murder" in this morning's *Tribune*. It's a mystery to me how you turn them out so fast!

My hearty congratulations on this new one, **Paul.** I hope it is an even bigger success than the last.

On Accomplishment of Son or Daughter

Dear Ray:

Bill Frenchon sent me clippings of the first reviews of "Early Autumn," and it looks as though a new hit is in the making. I am sure you must be very proud of your son's first venture as a playwright.

My congratulations to him, and to you. I hope "Early Autumn" enjoys a long run; and that it will be the first of many successful plays by young Mark.

Cordially yours,

I would like you to know how thrilled I was by your daughter's recital at Town Hall last night. It was magnificent, and I'm so happy to have been there.

My sincere congratulations to both of you; and my very best wishes to Miss Frazer at the beginning of what I am sure will be a brilliant and successful career.

I was delighted to read in last night's *Bulletin* that your son has won the Eastern tennis championship. You must be very proud of him. I have no doubt that he will be national champion some day.

Please give him my congratulations, and best wishes for continued success.

On a Business Anniversary

Dear Charles:

I take great pleasure in sending you congratulations and good wishes on the Twenty-Fifth Anniversary of the Kimball Company.

You can indeed be proud of the growth and progress of your company through the years, and the high esteem in which it is held. Such success is no accident. It is clearly the result of your own exceptional qualities, a tribute to your vision, judgment and leadership— and especially to the integrity and high ethical standards for which you are so widely known and so well respected.

I am glad that the occasion of your anniversary gives me the opportunity to say these things, and to wish you continued success and happiness in the years ahead.

Most cordially,

Please add our greetings and congratulations to those of your many friends on the occasion of your Fortieth Business Anniversary.

Yours has been an enviable record of growth and achievement through the years; and you have earned the respect and confidence of all who have been associated with you.

May Hastings & Co. continue to enjoy progress and success for many years to come!

I hope you will not consider it presumptuous for a comparative newcomer to offer congratulations and good wishes on the firm's Fiftieth Anniversary.

In the two years I have been here, I have come to understand and appreciate the high standards and ideals, and the inspired leadership, for which the organization is so well known.

I could not resist the opportunity to tell you this, and to wish you continued happiness and success in the years ahead.

On An Important Personal Occasion

I understand you are leaving at the end of the month to be married. Although I am sincerely sorry to see you go, I am pleased to learn of your approaching marriage; and I wish you every happiness in the future.

Sincerely,

I have just been informed of your engagement and approaching marriage. That's fine news!

My hearty congratulations to you, and every good wish to you and your fiancée.

Please accept this check with my congratulations and best wishes on your marriage.

I hope you and your bride will have many years of joy and happiness together.

This is to congratulate you and Mrs. Johnson on the safe arrival of your son. I know how pleased and happy you both must be, and it is a pleasure to share that happiness.

A long life and a happy one to the young fellow; and to you and Mrs. Johnson my good wishes for a lifetime of joy and happiness in your new son.

I have just learned with great pleasure that you have become a grandfather. I know from experience what a wonderful feeling that is, as I have two grandchildren of my own.

This note is just to say how delighted I am, and to wish you and Mrs. Simpson every happiness with your grandson. Please convey my congratulations and best wishes to your daughter and her husband on their baby's safe arrival.

This is to express my warm congratulations to you and Mrs. Hayden on your 25th wedding anniversary. I know it's a proud and significant milestone for you; and I cannot let the occasion go by without wishing you both many, many more years of abundant happiness together.

On Retirement

Dear Tom:

I have heard of your approaching retirement, and would like to add my good wishes to those of your many friends and admirers.

I know that retirement for you, with all your varied interests, will mean that you will be as busy and active as ever—but doing the things you never had time for before. I envy you that! I am looking forward to my own retirement in a few years, and the leisure at last to travel and to paint. I know those are two of your special interests, also.

All of which is by way of saying, "Congratulations!" It's great to retire, and I'm all for it. My best wishes to you for increased happiness ahead.

Sincerely,

I would like to express my best wishes to you on your approaching retirement, and congratulate you on your forty successful and productive years with the organization. I am deeply appreciative of the many innovations you brought into your department which have been of such significant value to us.

I'm sure it isn't necessary to tell you how very much you will be missed here at Clark & Holmes. It won't seem the same without you. But we know that retirement will give you the leisure you so richly deserve, and time at last for your many personal interests and hobbies—especially the White Marsh Community Forum which you helped organize and in which you have been so active these last few years.

Good luck to you; and much happiness and contentment in the years ahead.

LETTERS OF CONDOLENCE, SYMPATHY

Dear Mr. Hennessy:

On returning to the office this morning, I learned of your sad loss. I was so very sorry to hear of it, and would like you to know how deeply I sympathize with you in your bereavement.

Sincerely yours,

It was with profound regret that I learned this morning of Mrs. Walker's death, and I send you my sincere sympathy.

If there is anything I can do for you here at the office during your absence, or any way at all I can be of help, please have someone let me know.

I was shocked to hear of the tragic death of your son. I know there is nothing anyone can say to comfort you at a time like this. But I would like to express my heartfelt sympathy to you and Mrs. Clinton; and to offer any help that is within my power to give.

I was heartsick when I heard the sad news this morning. I wish there were something I could do or say to help you. My deepest sympathy to you and Grace in your bereavement.

Words cannot express my grief and sorrow at the sudden passing of your husband.

John Harmon was a man of rare qualities, admired and respected by everyone who knew him. All of us here feel his loss keenly, none more than I who was so closely associated with him through the years. I could not feel a deeper sense of sorrow if I had lost a member of my own family.

I speak for myself and for the organization in expressing heartfelt sympathy on your great loss.

It is with a heavy heart that I write to express deep sympathy to you and your family on the death of your daughter.

All of us here at Vickers, Holt & Co. share your loss, for Helen Meyers was long a well-loved and highly-respected member of our organization. She will be greatly missed.

I know that words can do little to ease your burden of sorrow. But perhaps the affection and cherished memories of Helen's many friends here may give you some small measure of comfort. That is what we are all hoping.

I have just learned of your accident, and hasten to add my regrets to those of your many friends and associates here at the office. All of us are saddened by the news, and hope you will make a quick and complete recovery.

It was a shock to hear about your accident when I returned to the office today. I was much relieved, how-

ever, to learn that your injuries are not critical and
that you are expected to be as good as new again before
too long.

I called the hospital but was told to wait a few more
days before visiting you. In the meantime, I would like
you to know how very sorry I am you were hurt. If
there is anything I can take care of in your absence,
please have Mrs. Ellis call me. I'll be glad to help in
any way I can. Best wishes for your swift recovery.

I read in this morning's paper of the accident in
which your daughter was seriously injured. I would
like to express my sincere sympathy, and the hope that
she will quickly recover from her injuries.

Your many former associates here at the Norris Co.
join me in sending sympathy to you and your family,
and best wishes for your daughter's recovery.

All of us are glad to know that the operation is now
safely behind you, and that you are making good
progress toward recovery.

We miss you; and we'll be very glad to see you when
you are well enough to return. But don't rush it! Take
plenty of time to get well and strong again. Your
work is being taken care of in your absence, so don't
even think of coming back until you have completely
recovered.

Everyone sends greetings, and best wishes for a
quick and comfortable convalescence.

I was sorry to hear from Jim Adler that you have
been seriously ill, and were still in the hospital re-
cuperating. I sincerely hope that you are making good
progress toward recovery, and will soon be completely
well again.

Jim says your biggest complaint is that the days are
long and time goes so slowly for you at the hospital. I

can well understand how boring that would be for someone as busy and active as you have always been.

I know you like mysteries, so I am sending you several which I think are especially good. They may help the time pass a bit more pleasantly for you.

My wife joins me in sending best wishes for your quick return to health.

A WIFE'S SOCIAL LETTERS TO HER HUSBAND'S BUSINESS ASSOCIATES

Occasionally a wife is required to write a social note, or a letter of courtesy, to her husband's employer or one of his business associates. For example, an invitation may need to be acknowledged. A letter of thanks may be required for hospitality received, or perhaps for some special favor. Such letters can be difficult, especially if the wife does not know the person to whom she is writing.

In general, a letter written by a wife to one of her husband's business associates, or to his employer, should be brief, natural and friendly in tone; and above all, to the point. The letter that goes cordially but concisely to the heart of the matter is always a welcome letter to a busy person.

A friendly letter, by the way, does not mean an effusive, gushy letter. The warmth of your message depends not on how much you say, but how you say it. Any letter concerned with the social amenities, and especially a letter to someone you do not know well, should sound to the recipient as though you enjoyed writing it—not as though it were a burdensome duty. Try to write as you would speak to someone you especially like and admire. Use your own familiar vocabulary. Be on guard against any striving for effect, or perhaps the unwary impulse to make an impression on your husband's business superior. The more naturally you write, the more friendly and sincere your letter will sound.

When a gift, courtesy or kindness requires acknowledgment, it should be attended to promptly. The longer it is put off, the more difficult it becomes to write it; and the less appreciative it is likely to sound. An invitation particularly should be acknowledged without delay, and in kind. If given verbally to the husband and relayed to the wife, the acceptance or regret may be given verbally by the husband for himself and his wife; or a note may be written by the wife, if that is preferred. However if a written invitation is received, a written acknowledgment is required. The wife writes a note of acceptance or regret for her husband and herself, and sends it either to the business associate at his office, or to his wife at their home address—depending on the circumstances. For example, an invitation to attend a company social event such as a Christmas party would be acknowledged to the employer at his business address. But an invitation to a social function at his home would be acknowledged to his wife (or to both) at their home address.

In accepting an invitation, always do so with a show of pleasure; and when the occasion warrants it, with enthusiasm. An indifferent, half-hearted acceptance is an affront to the person who has offered hospitality. Your note should emphasize your pleasure and appreciation, but without being frothy about it. It is advisable to name the function specifically in your acceptance, and to repeat essential details such as date and time to avoid the possibility of error.

A letter of regret is, of course, more difficult than an acceptance, especially when the invitation is from the wife of your husband's employer or one of his business superiors. Here, too, appreciation should be clearly indicated; and both disappointment and regret should be expressed at not being able to accept. Long explanations are not necessary; and excessive apologies should be avoided. It is not enough, however, just to say that you are sorry you cannot accept. The reason must be given; and it should be a real reason, not some transparent excuse. It is always best in any letter, however awkward the circumstances, to be straightforward and sincere. Just give the facts as tactfully and graciously as you can, say how disappointed you and your husband are, and how very much you appreciate the courtesy and kindness of the invitation. You may wish to add that you hope to be invited again some time when you are in a position to accept.

Acknowledgment of a written invitation should not be made by telephone, except in an emergency. In fact, the telephone should not be used for any of the social amenities of business unless, for some good reason, one is obliged to do so. Social calls are not welcome, as a rule, during the business day; they are always an interruption and often an inconvenience.

Following are examples of various types of letters a wife may be called upon to write, on occasion, to her husband's business associates, his employer, or his employer's wife.

Dear Mr. Gale:

Thank you so much for including me in the luncheon party celebrating the Twentieth Anniversary of the company, on Friday, February 10th. Jim assures me I won't be intruding as a number of other wives will be there.

It was good of you to invite me and I appreciate your kindness. I would like to take this opportunity of congratulating you on your anniversary, and wishing the Gale Company continued progress and success.

Sincerely yours,

I am so delighted to be included in this year's Christmas party! Thank you for inviting me.

Bob and I will be at the Gotham on December 23rd at six o'clock. We are both looking forward to it with great pleasure.

This is just to tell you how very much I enjoyed the company Christmas party on Friday. It was kind of you to include me; and I'd like you to know that both Charles and I appreciate your thoughtfulness.

We send you our very best wishes for the New Year.

My husband and I are delighted to accept your kind invitation for dinner on Tuesday, March 18th, at seven o'clock.

Thank you so much for asking us. We are looking forward to it with great pleasure.

I am acknowledging with pleasure your invitation for Sunday, June 26th, at two o'clock. Mr. Akins and I will be delighted to come to your luncheon, and we appreciate your kindness in asking us.

We have heard about your beautiful rose garden; and it will be a great treat to both of us to see it.

It is with extreme disappointment that I must tell you Mr. Davis and I cannot accept your kind invitation for Saturday evening, December 18th. I regret this more than I can say.

My favorite niece is being married that evening, and our two daughters are to be bridesmaids. As you can well imagine, we have all been looking forward to the wedding for months.

But I am so sorry to miss your Holiday Buffet! I have heard what an accomplished hostess you are, and I know Mr. Davis and I are missing something very special.

We wish to thank you and Mr. Fawcett for asking us. We sincerely appreciate your invitation, and hope that you will give us an opportunity to accept your hospitality some other time.

Reluctantly, and with sincere regret, my husband and I must forego the pleasure of accepting your gracious invitation for Saturday, October 3rd.

My mother is critically ill, and I am with her most of the time. Until she is out of danger, it is impossible for me to accept any invitations or make any plans. I am sure you understand my anxiety and the need to stand by.

Charles and I are grateful to you for thinking of us and including us in your plans for the 3rd. We regret that we cannot be with you, and hope you will invite us again at some happier time.

My husband and I would like you to know how very much we enjoyed our visit to Long Ridge on Sunday. It was a pleasure to see your beautiful home and grounds, and to meet your delightful children.

Our sincere thanks to you and Mr. Craddock for your hospitality. Truly it was a wonderful day, one we shall both long remember!

Arthur tells me that you are celebrating the 30th Anniversary of the Forstman Company this week.

I know this is a proud and significant occasion to you, and I would like to add my congratulations and good wishes to those of your many associates and friends. May the years ahead bring you ever-increasing achievement and happiness.

I was extremely sorry to hear from my husband that you have been ill. I hope that by the time you receive this note you will be feeling very much better; and that you will soon be enjoying perfect health again.

My husband has just told me of your great loss. I would like to say how sorry I am, and express my heartfelt sympathy to you in your bereavement.

I think it was just wonderful of you to send such a generous check for the baby! Jim and I appreciate it more than we can say.

We are starting an educational savings fund with it for Jim, Jr., and some day we'll tell him who started him on his way to college.

Thank you so much for your kindness.

Your letter brought us comfort and strength in a very dark hour. My husband and I were deeply touched by your message, and we will always treasure your kind words.

Tom gave me your letter. It was good of you to write and I appreciate your kind message.

My mother had been critically ill for some time, and we had been given little hope for her recovery. Still it is always a very great sorrow to lose one's mother. Your letter was a comfort to me and I thank you for it.

Mr. Harris tells me that only through your efforts were we able to get immediate plane reservations to Los Angeles. That was kind of you, and we are certainly grateful.

Thanks to you, we were able to reach the hospital before the baby was born, and our daughter was so very happy and relieved to see us. The baby, a little boy, arrived less than three hours after we arrived; so you can see what a great favor it was to get those tickets for us.

Mr. Harris is flying back tomorrow, and will be at the office some time in the afternoon. Thank you so much for your courtesy and help.

It was thoughtful and kind of you to offer my husband as much time as necessary to be with me here in Boston during the ordeal of our son's operation. It is too soon to know the outcome, but we have been given some hope that the sight of at least one eye will be saved.

Mr. Rowland is returning to Chicago tomorrow, and will be at the office on Thursday. I would like you to know that we are both extremely grateful to you for all the kindness and consideration you have shown us during this trying time.

Book VIII

Special, Difficult, and Unusual Letters

IN THIS SECTION IS CONCENTRATED A VARIETY OF SPECIAL AND unusual letters which do not fall into any one broad general classification, and which are often difficult to write. So if you cannot find the specimen letter you want elsewhere in the book, look for it here. The chances are you will find it, or something close to it.

We suggest that you try to avoid writing an especially important or difficult letter when you are tired, angry or depressed. Your mood may carry over into your letter and destroy its effectiveness. It is better to wait a day or two and write when you are in a more relaxed state of mind. If you feel fine when you start but become irritated as you write, stop and put the letter aside. You cannot be sure your letter says what you wish it to say, that it accomplishes wisely and tactfully the purpose for which it is intended, if you are emotionally upset and your judgment is clouded by your feelings. You will find that you can generally express yourself much better on an awkward or difficult matter when you are calm and in control of your thinking. Losing your temper or tact in a letter is worse than in conversation, for the written word remains and can become a source of embarrassment and regret.

Letter of Complaint to a Neighbor

Dear Mrs. Fenton:

On several occasions I have spoken to your son about running across our grounds and disturbing the flower beds. Robert has always been most courteous in explaining that he was just getting his ball; and he promised that he would try not to let it roll in again.

But he still keeps running in after his ball; and today he trampled some of my tulips. I don't like to complain, especially to a good neighbor like you; but I am heartsick about the damage to my tulips. As you have such a beautiful garden yourself, I am sure you understand.

I would appreciate it very much if you would speak to Robert and ask him to please play where his ball can't roll or fall into our place. I will greatly appreciate your cooperation.

Cordially yours,

Neighbor's Letter of Apology

Dear Mrs. Hartley:

I can't tell you how sorry I am about the damage to your tulips. I feel I am to blame; I should have seen to it that Robert did not play so close to your garden.

I have had a long talk with Robert, explaining how tulip bulbs must be planted the year before, and how his carelessness had destroyed in a few seconds what nature had taken so long to produce. He was much impressed, and very sorry for the damage he had caused. He promised me that he will never again invade your garden, and that he will not play ball anywhere near your grounds. You can be sure I'll see to it that he keeps his promise.

Please accept Robert's apology, and mine. I hope you will never have reason to complain again.

Sincerely yours,

Letter of Request to Teacher, School Principal

Dear Miss Baker:

My son John tells me that he finds it very difficult to see the blackboard from his desk in your classroom. As you know, John wears glasses for the correction of a visual impairment; but his doctor says that even with the glasses his vision is still deficient and cannot be further improved.

If John sits further forward in the classroom, he can see what is written on the blackboard much more clearly. I hope you will not think it presumptuous of me to request that you let him sit near the front, where his visual deficiency would be less of a handicap to him. Thank you for your cooperation.

Sincerely yours,

Dear Mr. Curtis:

My daughter, Joan, is now returning for her sophomore year at Sayville High School. During the summer she suffered an accident in a fall from a horse and sustained a fractured pelvis. The injury is healing satisfactorily, but Dr. George Hobalt has advised that she avoid all physical activities other than a moderate amount of walking. Therefore I am requesting that Joan be excused from physical education activities for the present term.

If you require a letter from Dr. Hobart confirming his advice, I'll be glad to have it forwarded to you.

Sincerely yours,

Letter of Complaint to a Manufacturer

Gentlemen:

In June of this year I purchased an Atkin Power Mower on the recommendation of a neighbor who has owned and used one with complete satisfaction for several years.

Apparently the Atkin mower I received was defective, as it broke down after a few weeks of use. I telephoned the dealer from whom I purchased it and was told that he was ill. I called again a few days later and learned he had died of a heart attack. The dealer was Mr. Roy T. Cummins of 97 Judd Place, Toledo, Ohio. His place of business is closed and I do not know when, if ever, it will reopen.

In the meantime I am without a mower just when I need it most. I have tried to have it repaired but nobody can do anything with it. Would it be possible for you to arrange with some other dealer in this area who carries the Atkin Power Mower to exchange the defective one for one in good working order? Or will you make good on the guarantee if I ship the defective mower directly to you, and send you all the sales data? I have a slip signed by Mr. Cummins showing the date of purchase, and the price paid—which was $169.50. I also have a 3-year unconditional guarantee.

I would like to know as soon as possible what you advise me to do.

Very truly yours,

Gentlemen:

We had our living-room floor covered with Gotham Super-Tex carpeting five weeks ago. We find that it sheds such an unusual amount of lint and fluff, it must be vacuumed daily. When we complained about this to the dealer from whom we purchased the carpeting —Scott & Sons in Great Neck, Long Island—we were told that such excessive shedding was normal and nothing could be done about it.

My husband and I do not believe any carpeting should shed as much as our Gotham Super-Tex does, and we are wondering if we haven't been sold defective merchandise. We would like to know how much shedding to expect from new carpeting; how long the condition is likely to last; and if there is any way to control or diminish it.

We would appreciate hearing from you as soon as possible concerning this matter.

Sincerely yours,

Letter of Request to a Manufacturer

Dear Mr. Mansfield:

Once again the Women's Community Club is giving its annual Christmas Party for the children of the North Side Orphanage. We are happy to report that we have received unusually generous donations of toys, books and clothes for these underprivileged youngsters; and they should have a truly wonderful Christmas this year.

But no Christmas party is complete without candy, and that we still need. Last year your company was good enough to donate all the candy we required, and we hope you will be willing to do that again this year. There are 80 children; and you will be playing Santa in a big way if you send enough candy for all of them. But we'll be grateful for whatever you send; and you can be sure your gift will help make the youngsters happy on this one big day of the year to which they all look forward so eagerly.

On behalf of both the Club and the Orphanage, I wish to thank you for your cooperation.

Sincerely yours,

Requesting a Loan; Acknowledging the Request

Dear Bill:

You once said that if I ever needed help, I could count on you. I am now forced to accept that generous offer. I urgently need $2000 to meet bills resulting from Edna's last illness and death. The funeral expenses must be paid by the end of next week, and I just don't know whom I can turn to in this emergency except you.

As you know, I invested heavily in a new venture just before Edna became ill; otherwise I would not need help now. I no longer have any interest in the venture, now that Edna is gone. As soon as my mind is more composed I will sell my interest in it, and you will be the first to be repaid.

Thank you, Bill, for all your kindnesses during Edna's illness. I'll never forget everything you did for her and for me; and I regret more than I can say that I must ask you for help. I wish with all my heart it were not necessary.

As ever,

Dear Aunt Ellen:

Jack and I have an opportunity to buy exactly the kind of house we have always dreamed about. We hadn't thought of looking for a house for another few years, but one of the men in Jack's office is being transferred and he must sell his place in the next month or so.

We went to see it yesterday, and it is just perfect for our needs. There's a wonderful playroom for the children, and a simply beautiful garden and back yard —what a difference that would be after the tiny apartment we've been living in since we were married!

Jack and I would like very much to buy this house if we could manage it. We need $5000 for a down payment, of which we have $3500. If you could lend us $1500, Jack would pay it back out of his salary at the rate of $100 a month.

I feel embarrassed to make this request of you, Aunt Ellen; and Jack, of course, was very much against it. But there is no one else either of us can turn to, and we want this house so badly. We think it's an exceptional value, and a wonderful opportunity for us. Will you drive out on Sunday and let us show it to you? Love from all of us,

Ruth

Dear Fred:

You know I am only too happy to help at this trying time. I am enclosing a check for $2000; you can repay it at your convenience, when you have settled your affairs and everything is in order at home.

Jane and I hope you will come and spend an evening with us whenever you feel you would like company. Don't wait for an invitation; the more often you come, the more pleased we will be.

Cordially,
Bill

Dear Fred:

It would make me very happy to be able to send you the $2000 you need; but unfortunately I just can't do it at this time. The best I can manage is $500, and I am enclosing a check for that amount.

Perhaps someone else can lend you the balance. If not, I'm sure you can get a loan at your bank, putting up your stock as security.

I wish I could do better, Fred. I'm sure you know I would, very gladly, if I were in a position to do so.

Cordially,
Bill

Dear Ruth:

You were right to come to me with your problem, and I am so pleased that you did. I'll be happy to help you and Jack buy the house, since you are both so sure it is exactly what you want and you can get it at a good price.

I would like very much to see it, but I cannot drive out this Sunday. I can make it the Sunday following if that is convenient for you. In the meantime, I am enclosing my check for $1500, so that you can proceed with purchase arrangements if you and Jack wish to do so. It isn't necessary for me to see the house first and give my approval; I have the utmost confidence in both of you, so if you want the house go ahead and buy it before someone else does.

I have thought for some time that you and Jack should have a house. With two active youngsters like Jill and Tony, you have certainly outgrown that tiny apartment. I am glad you have found what you like, and that I can help you get it.

Give my love to Jack and the children. I look forward to seeing you all soon.

> Fondly,
> Aunt Ellen

Dear Ruth:

Your request for financial aid comes at a most inconvenient time for me. I have made some extensive investments in the past few months and have practically no liquid funds. I would have to sell some of my holdings to provide the money you need, and this is a bad time to sell.

I hope you and Jack understand. I would be happy to help if I were in a position to do so; but I can't manage it right now. I do think you and Jack have outgrown your small apartment; and if, as you say, this house is such an exceptional value, I think you should try to take advantage of the opportunity. I am sure Jack could arrange something at his bank; and perhaps I'll be able to help later on.

I'm sorry I cannot come on Sunday, as I am going to Boston for the week-end. But I will come soon; it has been much too long since I've seen you and the children.

> With love,
> Aunt Ellen

Requesting a Contribution

Dear Mr. Dodson:

The Medford Association for Handicapped Children opens its annual drive for funds today, with pride and confidence—and with immense gratitude for what we have been able to accomplish with the help of our friends and supporters.

Founded twenty years ago, this organization has helped thousands of blind, deaf, crippled and otherwise handicapped children adjust successfully to the normal world around them. It has made it possible for these children to secure an education, acquire useful skills, and become self-supporting, self-respecting young men and women. For us it has been a rewarding experience. For them it has been the difference between despair and hope, between dependence on others and a life of their own.

If this important work is to continue, funds are urgently required for the coming year. There are hundreds of children on our waiting list who need and must have special help and attention. We ask you, on behalf of these unfortunate children, to contribute as generously as you can.

Every dollar contributed to the Association is put to work for the benefit of the children. No part of the fund is used for administrative expenses, not even for postage, which is paid for by committee members out of their own pockets. The services of doctors, nurses, therapists, teachers and psychiatrists are donated; the project could not continue without their devoted, unselfish participation. However food, clothing, medicines, textbooks must be purchased. Facilities must be improved and expanded. Braces, wheel chairs, hearing aids and other expensive equipment must be provided. It is for these vital purposes that your dollars will be used.

Can we count on you to help the helpless of our community? Will you join us in making it possible for them to become useful, happy citizens? We enclose an addressed envelope and urge you to return it promptly with your check. We hope you will be generous, as the need is very great this year.

Very sincerely yours,

Dear Mr. Bostwick:

In the past you have given generously to the Children's Fund of the Women's League; and I'd like you to know that we have always been proud of your support and very grateful for it.

As our drive opens for the current year, I am writing to ask that you again pledge your aid in the work our group is doing. I am sure you are familiar with most of our projects. We provide facilities and care for minor children while their mothers are at work; play areas to keep youngsters off the streets, professional teen-age counseling; and special help for needy, underprivileged children.

In the year ahead we hope to expand our activities to include a clubhouse for teen-agers, to help combat the alarming increase in juvenile mischief in and around the community. We believe, and we hope you agree with us, that providing a clubhouse to keep our young people off street corners and highways will do much to correct and control teen-age problems.

It is in connection with this project that we particularly need your cooperation. I am enclosing a pledge for $500, which we urgently ask you to contribute to the Clubhouse Fund. But please be assured that regardless of the amount you send, it will be very much appreciated.

Cordially yours,

Refusing Request for a Contribution

Dear Mrs. Edwards:

I sincerely regret that I cannot contribute to the Association for Handicapped Children at this time.

I am interested in a number of charitable organizations to which I donate regularly, among them a free clinic for crippled children. I am fully committed for the year; and although I admire the work you are doing and would like to help, I cannot make any further contributions just now.

With best wishes for continued success in your fine project,

Sincerely yours,

Dear Mrs. Harris:

I cannot agree with you that providing a clubhouse for teen-agers will solve the problem of juvenile delinquency here or anywhere. In my opinion it is far too serious a problem for such a simple solution.

I do not believe that a clubhouse will keep unruly teen-age gangs off the streets, or reckless teen-age drivers off the highways. The young people who would go to your clubhouse for social interests and activities would be the ones who never get into trouble anyway.

I may be wrong, of course; but that is the way I feel about it. I can see no real value to a teen-age clubhouse, and therefore I cannot support the idea. However I do commend you and your organization for your interest in this growing problem, and your desire to do something about it. I hope you will be successful in your efforts.

Most sincerely,

Dear Mrs. Morton:

I regret that I am unable to make a contribution to the Community Garden Fund this year.

I have become interested in a number of charitable organizations to which my husband and I have contributed very generously; and we do not feel we can make any further commitments at this time.

We admire the splendid work you are doing in the community and wish you success with your Garden Club activities.

Cordially yours,

Refusing Use of Name for Fund Raising

Dear Mrs. Carleton:

I am sorry I cannot comply with your request for the use of my name as a sponsor of the Community Youth Forum. It has been my policy not to sponsor any organization that I am not associated with personally and do not know about fully and completely.

At this time I am associated with several charitable drives and community groups with which I work closely. These activities take up as much of my time as I can spare for such purposes. I must therefore regretfully refuse your invitation to join the sponsoring committee of the Community Youth Forum. But thank you for asking me; and my best wishes for the success of your project.

Sincerely yours,

Dear Mr. Hayden:

It is with regret that I must decline your request for the use of my name as a sponsor of International Charities, Inc.

I understand the motives behind your organization, and I sincerely admire what you are trying to accomplish. But first things come first; and I feel that there are too many worthy charities right here at home which are not receiving adequate support. I prefer lending my name to such domestic charities, rather than international ones about which I know nothing.

Though I cannot sponsor it, I heartily wish you success with International Charities.

Cordially,

Inviting Participation in a Project or Activity

Dear Mrs. Young:

As you know, I have long been interested in the blind and their problems, and have been active in various projects to improve and enrich their daily lives.

My latest long-term project, and one in which I am especially interested, is the development of a rental library for the blind, consisting of books in Braille which may be rented for a small fee. I'm sure I don't need to tell you what such a library can mean to the approximately 900 blind men, women and children of our city.

This letter is to inform you of the proposed plan, and invite you to become a member of the book-selection and general advisory committee which is now being organized. We urgently need your help, and hope you will find it convenient to join us in this important project. I will be glad to discuss the details of the Braille book rental plan with you any time you suggest.

Sincerely yours,

Refusing to Participate in a Project or Activity

Dear Mrs. Taylor:

Your work in behalf of the blind is well known to me; and I sincerely admire you for what you are do-

ing. I have often thought I would like to participate
in this fine project, and I would be only too happy to
become a member of your committee if I were in a
position to do so. But unfortunately that is not possible at the present time.

You may or may not know that my major interest
is in underprivileged children, and I am active in numerous projects connected with their aid and welfare.
I feel that in justice to them, and to myself, I cannot
undertake any additional responsibilities.

However, to assure you of my interest in your work
and my admiration for what you are doing, I am enclosing a check for $50 to go into the Braille book
fund. My best wishes to you for the success of your
splendid project.

Sincerely yours,

Dear Mrs. Fleming:

It is difficult for me to say "No" to your invitation
to join the Women's League and to take an active part
in its affairs. But the fact is that it would be quite
impossible for me to undertake any outside interests
at this time. I have just completed a project on which
I have been working for nearly two years; and now I
have another important assignment which must be
completed by next February.

Therefore much as I regret it, I must forego the
pleasure of working with you on civic and community
affairs, at least for the time being. Let us not consider
the matter closed, but merely deferred until a more
convenient time. In the meantime, to assure you of
my interest and my desire to help, please accept the
enclosed check as a donation to the Women's League,
to be used any way you see fit.

Most cordially yours,

Dear Mrs. Frank:

You are certainly to be commended for the devoted and unselfish work you are doing in behalf of needy children. I admire and respect you for it.

You can be sure I would join you in this worthy activity if my program allowed. However I am already involved in several community projects and am serving on a number of committees, some of which I think you know about. Whatever time remains is taken up with personal projects, which are often sadly neglected in the stress of community affairs.

Under the circumstances I must reluctantly decline to serve on the board of your charity drive. I am sure you understand.

Cordially yours,

Suggesting an Idea to Editor, Producer

Dear Mr. Goelet:

I would like very much to have the opportunity of discussing with you an idea I have for a television program.

I have made a lifetime study of the origins of customs, and have written many articles on this subject for national magazines. The program I have in mind dramatizes the simple, everyday customs of life in an unusual and interesting way, tracing them back to their primitive source.

In preparing a sample script for discussion, I have worked out an idea for linking the cultural and educational background of the program with audience participation in the form of a quiz session. I think you will find that the unusual combination of these two appeals makes for an interesting and provocative program.

Please let me know when I may have an appointment to show you the sample script and discuss it with you.

Sincerely yours,

Dear Mr. Hartman:

Would you be interested in a series of articles for *Inspiration Magazine* telling the dramatic, human stories behind famous quotations?

I have spent considerable time doing research and collecting material in this field, and have a large and fascinating file of stories I would like to use in an inspirational series. I have written one and am sending it with this letter to show you how I think the articles could be done.

I think *Inspiration Magazine* is the ideal medium for this type of material and that your readers would enjoy the series. I am hoping you will think so, too.

Cordially yours,

Suggesting Product or Idea to a Manufacturer

Gentlemen:

I have often wondered why it is impossible to find large square tablecloths, and why some enterprising manufacturer does not put such cloths on the market.

My dining-room table is 68 x 68, and requires a cloth at least 92 x 92; but I have never been able to find a cloth of that size in the stores. An oblong cloth does not provide adequate hang-over on the two shorter sides; therefore I must always have my important dinner cloths custom made.

I realize, of course, that round and oblong cloths are most in demand; but surely there must be others besides myself who have square tables. I hope that as one of the largest manufacturers of table linens in the country, you will give this matter some thought; and if you ever put large square cloths on the market, let me know where I can buy them!

Very truly yours,

Gentlemen:

I would like to suggest an idea for a basic new design in shoe construction in which I think you may be interested.

As you know, in an ordinary high-heeled shoe the foot tends to slide forward, crowding the toes and often distorting them. My idea is to prevent this sliding forward of the foot by means of a depression in the heel part of the shoe, shaped to cup, or cradle, the heel of the foot. This "Cradle Heel" construction keeps the foot in a level position and comfortably in place. The wearer walks *flat* instead of on *tiptoe,* and enjoys the kind of day-long walking comfort formerly provided only by so-called sensible shoes with low heels or wedge soles.

I am enclosing a sketch which shows the details of the "Cradle Heel." As you can see, it does not affect the styling of the shoe in any way, but certainly makes a big difference in comfort to the wearer. To summarize its advantages: (1) It keeps the foot from sliding forward in the shoe. (2) It gives comfort without sacrificing appearance. (3) It makes closed-toe shoes more comfortable by eliminating pressure on the big toe. (4) It keeps open-toe shoes from quickly losing shape and fit. (5) It keeps comfortable shoes from becoming uncomfortable with wear. (6) It makes it easier, more pleasing to be fitted.

If you are interested in trying out the "Cradle Heel" in one of your lines of shoes, I'll be very happy to come in and discuss it with you in detail.

Sincerely yours,

Requesting Information, Data

Dear Mr. Beardsley:

I believe that your company made a study of television commercials last year, and published a report on the findings. I would like very much to obtain a copy of this report, in connection with a talk I am giving on the subject at the Advertising Club next month.

If you still have a copy of the report and can send it to me, I'll be most grateful for the courtesy. If not, please let me know the title and the date of publication, and I'll try to find it at the library.

Sincerely yours,

U.S. Government Printing Office,
Washington, D.C.

Gentlemen:

It is my understanding that Government publications are available giving useful data about travel in foreign countries. I am wondering if there is a list of such publications available; and if so, how I go about securing a copy.

I am interested in information about the habits, customs and traditions of the people in various foreign countries; and especially any official information I can secure about how Americans should conduct themselves abroad to avoid giving offence and making a bad impression.

I will greatly appreciate any help you can give me.

Very truly yours,

Requesting Permission to Use Published Material

Dear Miss Faulkner:

I am writing to request permission to use an excerpt from your book, "The World's Great Hymns" in our church paper.

The item I would like to use is on page 83, and tells the story of how "Lead, Kindly Light" came to be written. I am sure the readers of our church paper would find this interesting and inspiring; and I would sincerely appreciate your permission to use it.

Cordially yours,

Dear Mr. Udall:

I am preparing a history of advertising in the United States, and would like to include examples of early soap and dentifrice advertising—among them several prepared by your agency. Photostats of these are enclosed; and I hope I can secure permission to use them.

The purpose of the book is to dramatize the impact of advertising on our habits and customs; and to show how the promotion of new products and new ideas improved our standards of living. The advertisements I am selecting are for the purpose of illustrating milestones of progress along the way. I will sincerely appreciate your cooperation.

Most cordially,

Requesting Opportunity to Appear on Program

If you wish to apply for the opportunity to appear as a contestant on a radio or television show, here is a composite of helpful information from several producers of such shows: Your letter should be brief, concise, to the point. Use no more words than necessary to give all the interesting and pertinent facts about yourself. The longer and more detailed your letter, the less attention it will get; for producers are busy people, and their offices are usually inundated with mail. Don't try to be witty, literary, clever. Don't make a play for sympathy, emphasizing how much you need the opportunity. Flattery will get you nowhere. Neither will hinting about important "connections." Neither will boasting about your many triumphs and achievements. State your purpose at once, in the first paragraph. Follow up with your background, qualifications, availability.

Though it is not always required, it is helpful to include a small, clear photograph of yourself—one that does not need to be returned.

Basically your letter should follow the simple format which follows. If you add anything, be sure it makes you more interesting and desirable as a contestant—and say it in as few words as possible.

Gentlemen:

I would like to appear as a contestant on (NAME OF SHOW).

I am (OCCUPATION) and have a wide knowledge of (SUBJECT OR SUBJECTS, with brief mention of background and how knowledge of subject was obtained.)

I can visit your offices (DAY) between —— and ——.

Sincerely,
NAME
ADDRESS
TELEPHONE NUMBER

It is recommended that you do not apply to more than one program at a time. Every producer prefers contestants who have not appeared on other programs; and should the producer to whom you are applying learn that you have made similar applications elsewhere, he will not consider you for his show. So wait for a rejection from one program before you apply to another.

Following are some sample letters of application which you may find helpful:

Dear Sir:

This letter is to request the opportunity to appear as a contestant on your "Knowledge Is Power" program.

I am a medical consultant for a pharmaceutical company. I have made a lifetime study of medical history, and know the life stories of every important medical pioneer. I believe I could make a good showing on your program in this category.

I expect to be in New York on November 10th, and can come to your office for an interview any day and any time during the week of November 10th to 17th.

Cordially yours,

Gentlemen:

I would like to appear on your Musical Quiz program.

I am a graduate of the Julliard School; a concert pianist; and can play several other instruments including the harp. I was editor of *Music World* from 1956 to 1958; and during that time I wrote biographical sketches of many of the greats of music and the theater.

I am available for an interview any Wednesday afternoon from 2 to 5.

Sincerely yours,

Letter of Resignation

A letter of resignation is usually preceded by an informal discussion with one's immediate superior, or with the head of the firm. The action is subsequently confirmed by letter to make the resignation official.

Dear Mr. Brooks:

It is with great reluctance that I am submitting my resignation, to take effect on September 30th.

My association with the J. P. Hardy Corporation has been a most pleasant one; and as I explained to you when we discussed this matter last week, had it not been for the extremely attractive offer I have received in the field in which I have always been interested, I would not have considered making this change. But in all fairness to the interests of my family and myself, the increased opportunities and financial rewards associated with this change cannot be ignored.

Thank you for your friendly and understanding attitude in this severance of our long and pleasant business association.

Sincerely yours,

Letter to a Public Official

The Honorable John Blank,
United States Senate,
Washington, D.C.

Dear Sir:

I know you like to hear from your constituents as to their views on pending legislation.

I am writing you at this time about the proposed extension of the reciprocal trade agreements now being discussed in the Senate. I have always felt that these agreements have been in the interest of our country, and particularly the people of our state. If we refuse to accept exports from other countries it has a two-fold influence, both of which are detrimental. Products from abroad frequently permit lower pricing so that a larger number of people can enjoy their benefits, and at the same time providing a competitive stimulus to our domestic producers.

We in our state must have export markets for the tremendous quantities of the dairy products which we produce. As it is impossible for our domestic economy to absorb all of our production, it is important for us that foreign countries be in a position to purchase our surplus. Only by providing them with dollar purchasing power through the importation of their goods will they be able to reciprocate by buying ours.

I urge you to use your influence toward the renewal of these trade agreements which are currently expiring.

Sincerely yours,

Letter of Request to a Doctor

Dear Dr. Forest:

As you know I have moved to Ridgewood, New Jersey; and because it would be extremely difficult for me to continue to avail myself of your services, I have placed myself in the hands of Dr. John Newcomb of Ridgewood. He has suggested that I ask you to forward to him a résumé of your findings and treatment in my case.

I am sorry to find it necessary to break off a relationship with you of many years' standing. I have always been pleased in every way with the care you have given me, and which I sincerely believe on one occasion actually saved my life. I will always be grateful to you.

Thank you very much for taking care of this request, and for your many past kindnesses.

Cordially yours,

Letter to Income Tax Bureau

Income tax matters are usually too complicated to handle by correspondence. It is suggested that you either secure professional help, or go to your local income tax bureau in person. Only a comparatively simple question should be handled by correspondence. For example:

District Director of Internal Revenue,
210 Livingston Street,
Brooklyn, 1, New York.

Dear Sir:

I am the owner of 10 Government of Bolivia 6% External Bonds of 1955. For the last 22 years no interest payments were made by the government of Bolivia. Recently a settlement was effected with a bond holders' protective committee which extended the maturity to 1975 and set the rate of interest at 1½ per cent.

The first interest payment of $75 was made on the basis of this settlement one month ago. Is this sum to be entered in my current year's tax return as "interest received" or should it be considered a return of capital?

In appreciation of your help,

Sincerely yours,

Letters Concerning Social Security

Social Security Administrator,
42 Broadway,
New York, 4, N.Y.

Dear Sir:

I have lost my social security card and I wish to have a duplicate of it. I do not remember the number, and am currently unemployed. My former employer is now out of business.

I trust you will be able to duplicate the card from my name and address. Thank you.

Very truly yours,

Dear Sir:

I have recently changed jobs, and because of what appeared to be lax bookkeeping methods in my previous place of employment, I am not certain that the report of my social security deductions were properly reported.

I was employed by the H. G. Wilkins Co., 126 Juniper Street, from August 2, 1958 to November 15, 1958, at a salary of $82.50 per week.

Would it be possible for you to check my account and let me know if it is in order? Thank you very much.

Sincerely yours,

Dear Sir:

I will be 65 years old on August 6th, and plan to retire at that time. I would like to know what social security benefits I will be entitled to.

My wife is now 64 years of age and will be 65 on November 14. My children are past the age of 18.

Very truly yours,

Dear Sir:

I am a widow, and will be 62 in a few months. I understand that I am entitled to social security based on my husband's earnings. Am I also entitled to social security based on my own earnings? I have not been employed for over 10 years, but was regularly employed as a typist up to that time.

My social security number is 074-56-830.

Sincerely yours,

Some Special Club Correspondence

Clubs which are owned by members do not have open membership arrangements. New members must be proposed by existing members when an ownership participation is available. For example:

Mr. Frank Knox,
Chairman, Membership Committee,
Beech Park Country Club,
Beech Park, Conn.

Dear Frank:

I am proposing Mr. George Burke for the membership relinquished by Jim Watt when he moved to California.

I have known George Burke and his family for over 20 years and I think they are wonderful people. George has a high executive position with Arthur Duryea & Co., an advertising agency. I am sure we could all get along very well with him, with his wife Grace, and with their two sons—one of whom is at Harvard, the other at Tufts University School of Medicine.

George is very desirous of joining our club as he knows a number of members other than myself. I shall be happy to make myself available to your committee for any further details.

Cordially,

There is a growing number of clubs which are not owned by the members, but where membership is on an annual or seasonal fee basis. A prospective member writes his own letter to the membership committee, indicating his interest in joining the club. For example:

Membership Committee,
Pinecrest Golf Club,
Narbryn, Pennsylvania.

Gentlemen:

I am interested in membership in the Pinecrest Golf Club for my wife and myself.

I would like to receive information concerning membership requirements and dues.

Very truly yours,

As a rule, a club member who wishes to put up an out-of-town guest or business associate at his club for a day or two merely calls up the manager and makes a reservation for him. A card is generally provided. However some clubs require that all requests for overnight guest accommodations be referred to the house committee for approval. In such cases, the following type of letter would be in order:

Mr. William Graves,
Chairman, House Committee,
University Club,
Newark, N.J.

Dear Bill:

Mr. John Harris of Providence is coming to see me on a business matter on June 12th. He plans to stay in Newark for three days, and I would like to put him up at the club during that time.

John Harris is a fine man and I can personally vouch for his character and decorum.

Please let me know your decision on this request as soon as possible so that I can notify him of what arrangements I have made.

Sincerely yours,

Mr. Robert Wilmot,
Chairman, Entertainment Committee,
Far Harbor Beach and Country Club,
Newbury, Rhode Island.

Dear Bob:

I would like to suggest that during the coming summer season we plan two or three evening beach parties at which barbecued food would be served. Several years ago we had one such evening which was a great success, and I don't know why we have never had another.

I was talking with Tom Potter yesterday, and he too remembers that evening most pleasantly and suggests that we have another one.

I wish you would take up this suggestion with your committee; and I hope you will see fit to incorporate the idea in our club entertainment program.

Sincerely,

Mr. Frederick Baxter,
Chairman, House Committee,
Beech Park Country Club,
Beech Park, Conn.

Dear Fred:

I am reluctant to bring a matter of this sort to your attention, but for the good of the club I feel that someone should.

Several times this past month the Harwoods have had two young nephews as guests. They seem to be about 8 and 10 years of age, which is well below the 12-year age limitation which all the rest of us observe.

Neither I nor the other members would have minded that they were below our age requirement, except that they were noisy and unruly at the pool and were a source of annoyance to members. Children of that age are expected to be noisy and difficult to control, which of course is the reason for the club's age limitation.

I am sure you will agree with me that the Harwoods should be officially notified not to bring underage guests in the future.

                                        Sincerely yours,

Mr. Clifford Jackson,
House Committee,
Pinecrest Golf Club,
Narbryn, Pennsylvania.

Dear Clifford:

During the recent hot spell, many of us have been extremely uncomfortable in the dressing area of the women's locker room. Especially when it's crowded, the entire locker room is almost unbearable, and the dressing alcoves are particularly bad.

It seems to me that air-conditioning would be very desirable, and the cost would not be excessive in rela-

tionship to the degree of comfort that would be provided. Please make this proposal to the members of
your committee, and I certainly hope they look favorably on this suggestion.

Yours very truly,

Dear Member:

Your entertainment committee has planned a gala
formal evening for Saturday, August 3rd. This will
be our big event of the summer season and we have
gone all out to make it a memorable affair.

We have been fortunate in obtaining Tex Springer
and his talented band. We have also signed Patty
Smith as vocalist. Those of you who had the pleasure
of hearing Patty Smith last year will certainly want
to hear her again.

Guests are permitted; but because of the expected
attendance we must strictly limit the number of guests
to two per member. Please make your reservations
early for the convenience of your committee.

Very truly yours,

Chairman,
Entertainment Committee

Dear Member:

The finance committee has completed its annual
accounting for the fiscal year ending Sept. 30th. Op-
erating costs exceeded income by $895. This amount
has been withdrawn from the reserve fund, leaving a
balance of $1208.

Anticipated costs of operation for the next fiscal
year are estimated at 8% above last year's costs. In
addition we have budgeted a capital expenditure of
$4600 to modernize the kitchen which is urgently in
need of improvement.

These items, plus an amount which will bring the
reserve back to at least $2000, which your committee

feels is the minimum that should be maintained, will result in an increase in dues. This has been calculated to amount to $360 per member, as against last year's figure of $320. We feel that this amount is the minimum to permit satisfactory operation of our club.

This proposed budget and annual dues figure will be presented to the membership at the annual meeting next month, and we hope that you will approve the work of the committee by voting for its adoption.

Yours very truly,

Chairman,
Finance Committee

Appendix

Forms of Address

Appendix

FORMS OF ADDRESS

There are many alternate forms of address and salutation permissible, especially in informal correspondence. But all these many variations of local usage can not be included. The chart following gives the forms in customary usage, and is as complete as possible for a book of this size and scope. For additional information, see *Webster's New International Dictionary*, "Forms of Address," beginning page 3012.

Forms of salutation beginning with *"My dear"* are not included in the chart. In all cases, *"My dear"* may be used instead of *"Dear"* for greater formality. (This applies to the United States only, as in Great Britain the reverse is true.)

The words *"honor"* and *"honorable"* are spelled according to the residence of the person addressed. In the United States, *"honor"* and *"honorable"* are preferred; in Great Britain *"honour"* and *"honourable"* are the preferred forms.

Social invitations to a married man of title or rank are addressed to the man *and* his wife. For example:

> Senator and Mrs. James Blank
> The President and Mrs. Blank
> Lord and Lady Blank
> Their Excellencies, The French Ambassador and
> Mrs. Blank

When the wife is the person of title or rank, the husband's name is still written first on the envelope and inside address. For example:

> Mr. John and the Honorable Mary Smith
> Mr. Frank and Dr. Margaret Symonds
> Mr. George and Lady Mary Blakely

The use of the word *to*—as in "To his Grace, the Duke of York"—is optional. There is no hard and fast rule about it; you may use it or not, as you prefer. Our own choice is for the simpler form: "His Grace, the Duke of York."

In addressing an envelope, the phrase "His Excellency" may be abbreviated to "H.E."—and "Their Excellencies" may be abbreviated to "T.E." But in general, abbreviations should be avoided—and especially in the salutation or beginning of a letter.

Old feudal phrases of courtesy like "My Lord" and "Your Lordship" are not used in the United States. But they should be used by an American writing to dignitaries of foreign countries entitled by tradition to such forms of address.

Rank or Title   Abbot

Address the Envelope   Begin the Letter

The Lord Abbot of Fieldston   Dear Father Abbot:
        or   My Lord Abbot:
The Right Reverend Abbot Blank

Air Force Officers

Like Army and Naval Officers

Alderman

Alderman John Smith   Dear Sir:
                                          Dear Mr. Smith:

Ambassador (American)

His Excellency the American Ambas-   Sir:
    sador to Great Britain   Your Excellency:
American Embassy   Dear Mr. Ambassador:
London, England
        or

Rank or Title   Ambassador (American)

Address the Envelope   Begin the Letter

The* Honorable John D. Smith
American Ambassador to Great Brit-
ain
American Embassy
London, England

Ambassador (British)†

His Excellency the Ambassador of   Sir:
   Great Britain   Excellency:
British Embassy   Your Excellency:
Washington, D.C.   Dear Mr. Ambassador:
       or
His Excellency John Farbish
Ambassador of Great Britain
British Embassy
Washington, D.C.

Archbishop (Anglican)

His Grace the Lord Archbishop of   My Lord Archbishop:
   London   Your Grace:

Archbishop (Catholic)

The Most Reverend John Smith   Most Reverend Sir:
Archbishop of St. Louis   Most Reverend Arch-
       or   bishop:
The Most Reverend Archbishop   (In England:)
   Smith   Your Grace:
(Followed by postal address)   My Lord:
                            My Lord Archbishop:

* "Honorable" or "The Honorable" may be used; both are correct.
† The same general form is used in addressing the ambassadors of other foreign
countries.

Rank or Title   Archdeacon:

Address the Envelope   Begin the Letter

The Venerable John Falten   Venerable Sir:
Archdeacon of New Orleans

Army Officers:

Always address letters to army officers   Sir: (formal)
in accordance with their exact rank.   Dear General Fiske:
(In the salutation, however, you   Dear Colonel Pryor:
drop the qualifying adjective—such   Dear Sgt. Blank:
as the "Lieutenant" in "Lieutenant   Dear Corporal Smith:
Colonel." In other words, letters to
both "Lieutenant Colonel Phillips"
and "Colonel Pryor" would begin
"Dear Colonel ——") A retired
army officer is addressed by his title,
with "U.S.A., Ret." following his
name. A doctor, dentist or clergyman may be addressed either by his
professional degree or his army
rank, unless he is in an administrative capacity—in which case the
army rank is always used.

Lieutenant General John Fiske
Commanding Officer
Army of the United States
3rd Corps Area
(Followed by postal address)

Major General John Crane, U.S.A.
Commanding Officer, 2nd Tank
    Corps

Colonel Arthur Pryor
Medical Corps, U.S.A.

Rank or Title

Army Officers:

Address the Envelope   Begin the Letter

Major Thomas Quinn, U.S.A., Ret.
(Postal address only)

Captain James T. Ballard
Field Artillery, U.S.A.

Lieutenant Peter Adams
Coast Artillery, U.S.A.
        or
Peter Adams
Lieutenant, Coast Artillery, U.S.A.

Corporal Henry T. Smith
5th Quartermaster Corps, U.S.A.
        or
Henry T. Smith
Corporal, 5th Quartermaster Corps,
    U.S.A.

Assemblyman

The Honorable John B. Rogers   Sir:
Member of Assembly   Dear Sir:
Albany, New York   Dear Mr. Rogers:
        or
Assemblyman John B. Rogers
The State Capitol
Albany, New York

Assistant Secretary (Assistant to a cabinet officer)

The Assistant Secretary of Commerce   Sir:
Washington, D.C.   Dear Sir:
        or   Dear Mr. Hansen:

Rank or Title

    Assistant Secretary (Assistant to a cabinet officer)

        Address the Envelope   Begin the Letter

Honorable John B. Hansen
Assistant Secretary of Commerce
Washington, D.C.

          Associate Judge of a Court of Appeals

The Honorable John Clearly   Sir:
Associate Judge of the Court of Ap- Dear Sir:
  peals   Your Honor:
Albany, New York   Dear Mr. Justice:

       Associate Justice of a State Supreme Court

The Honorable Frank Parsons   Sir:
Associate Justice of the Supreme   Dear Sir:
  Court   Your Honor:
Albany, New York   Dear Mr. Justice:

   Associate Justice of the Supreme Court of the United States

The Honorable Edward Brent   Dear Sir:
Associate Justice of the Supreme   Dear Mr. Justice:
  Court   Dear Justice Brent:
Washington, D.C.
      or
The Honorable Edward Brent
Justice, Supreme Court of the United
  States
Washington, D.C.
      or
Mr. Justice Brent
Supreme Court of the United States
Washington, D.C.

Rank or Title   Attorney General

Address the Envelope   Begin the Letter

The Honorable   Sir:
The Attorney General of the United   Dear Sir:
    States   Dear Mr. Attorney Gen-
Washington, D.C.   eral:
      or
The Honorable John Lane
Attorney General of the United States
Washington, D.C.

Baron

The Right Honourable Lord Blakely   My Lord:
    or
The Lord Blakely

Baroness

The Right Honourable the Baroness   Madam:
    Cleve
    or
The Lady Cleve

Baronet

Sir John Holt, Bt. (or Bart.)   Sir:

Bishop (Anglican)

The Right Reverend the Lord Bishop   My Lord Bishop:
    of Sussex   My Lord:
      or
The Lord Bishop of Sussex

Rank or Title   Bishop (Catholic)

Address the Envelope   Begin the Letter

The Most Reverend Thomas Hall   Your Excellency:
Bishop of Chicago   Dear Bishop Hall:
          or
The Right Reverend Bishop Hall

Bishop (Methodist)

The Reverend Bishop John Smith   Dear Bishop Smith:

Bishop (Protestant)

The Right Reverend Michael Vale   Right Reverend **and**
Bishop of Cleveland   Dear Sir:
                                         Dear Bishop Vale:

Cardinal

His Eminence John, Cardinal Blank   Your Eminence:

Chief Judge of a Court of Appeals

The Chief Judge of the Court of Ap-   Sir:
    peals   Dear Sir:
Albany, New York   Dear Judge Brown:
          or
The Honorable Myron F. Brown
Chief Judge of the Court of Appeals
Albany, New York

Rank or Title—Chief Justice of a State Supreme Court

Address the Envelope	Begin the Letter
The Chief Justice Supreme Court of the State of New York Albany, New York *or* Honorable Patrick Gilmore Chief Justice of the Supreme Court Albany, New York	Sir: Dear Sir: Dear Mr. Chief Justice: Dear Mr. Justice Gilmore:

Chief Justice of the United States

The Chief Justice of the United States Washington, D.C. *or* The Honorable John Blank Chief Justice of the Supreme Court of the United States Washington, D.C. *or* The Chief Justice Washington, D.C.	Sir: Dear Sir: Dear Mr. Chief Justice: Dear Mr. Justice Blank:

Clergyman

The Reverend Frank Hall *or* Reverend and Mrs. Frank Hall *or* (if a doctor of divinity) Reverend Dr. Frank Hall	Dear Sir: Reverend Sir: Dear Mr. and Mrs. Hall: Dear Dr. Hall:

Rank or Title—Commissioner of a Government Bureau

Address the Envelope   Begin the Letter

The Commissioner of the Bureau of   Sir:
   Education   Dear Sir:
Department of the Interior   Dear Mr. Commissioner:
Washington, D.C.   Dear Mr. Kelley:
          or
The Honorable Dwight Kelley
Commissioner of the Bureau of Edu-
   cation
Department of the Interior
Washington, D.C.

Congressman

See Representative in Congress

Consul

The American Consul at London   Sir:
London, England   Dear Sir:
          or   Dear Mr. Smith:
Mr. John Smith
American Consul at London
London, England

Countess

The Right Honourable the Countess   Madam:
   of Blank   Dear Lady Greystone:
          or
The Countess Greystone

Rank or Title   Deacon

Address the Envelope   Begin the Letter
The Reverend Deacon Black   Reverend Sir:

Dean (Ecclesiastic)

The Very Reverend the Dean of   Very Reverend Sir:
  Barth   Sir:

Dean of a College or University

Dean Albert S. Frank   Dear Sir:
School of Business   Dear Dean Frank:
Columbia University   Dear Dr. Frank:
New York, N.Y.   Dear Mr. Frank: (if he
  or   does not hold a doc-
Albert S. Frank, Ph.D.   tor's degree)
Dean of the School of Business
Columbia University
New York, N.Y.
  or
Dr. Albert S. Frank
Dean of the School of Business
Columbia University
New York, N.Y.

Delegate (Member of the House of Delegates
of a State Legislature)

The Honorable John F. Weylin   Sir:
The House of Delegates   Dear Sir:
Charleston, West Virginia   Dear Mr. Weylin

Rank or Title   Duchess

Address the Envelope   Begin the Letter

Her Grace, the Duchess of Blank   Madam:
                                       Your Grace:

Duchess of the Royal Blood

Her Royal Highness the Duchess of   Madam:
   Kent   May it please your Royal
                                        Highness:

Duke

His Grace, the Duke of Blank   My Lord Duke:
                                      Your Grace:

Duke of the Royal Blood

His Royal Highness the Duke of Kent   Sir:
                                      May it please your Royal
                                        Highness:

Earl

The Right Honourable the Earl of   My Lord:
   Blank   Sir:
          or   Dear Lord Grayson:
The Earl of Blank

Earl's Wife

See "Countess" above

Rank or Title   Governor of a State

Address the Envelope   Begin the Letter

The Honorable the Governor of   Sir:
  Michigan   Dear Sir:
Lansing, Michigan   Your Excellency:
    or   Dear Governor Tarr:
His Excellency
The Governor of Michigan
Lansing, Michigan
    or
His Excellency, John E. Tarr
Governor of Michigan
Lansing, Michigan
    or
The Honorable John E. Tarr
Governor of Michigan
Lansing, Michigan

Head of a State Department

The Secretary of State*   Sir:
The State Capitol   Dear Sir:
Topeka, Kansas   Dear Mr. Blank:
    or
The Secretary of State
State of Kansas
Topeka, Kansas
    or
The Honorable John C. Blank
Secretary of State
The State Capitol
Topeka, Kansas

* Some states (like Pennsylvania and Massachusetts) use the term "Commonwealth" instead of "State." The first line in that case would read: "The Secretary of the Commonwealth."

Rank or Title—Instructor in a College or University

Address the Envelope	Begin the Letter
John T. Rice, Ph.D.	Dear Sir:
Department of Economics*	Dear Dr. Rice:
Harvard University	Dear Mr. Rice: (if he
Cambridge, Massachusetts	holds no doctor's de-
or	gree)
Dr. John T. Rice	
Department of Economics	
Harvard University	
Cambridge, Massachusetts	

> *or*
> (if the instructor does not hold a doctor's degree)

Mr. John T. Rice
Department of Economics
Harvard University
Cambridge, Massachusetts

Judge of a Federal District Court

The Honorable Frank Preston	Sir:
United States District Judge	Dear Sir:
Eastern District of New York	Dear Judge Preston:
Brooklyn, New York	

Justice of the Supreme Court

See Associate Justice of the Supreme
Court of the United States

---

* If the word "Instructor" is substituted for "Department" the word "in" is used instead of "of." For example: "Instructor in Economics" (but "Department *of* Economics").

Rank or Title   King

Address the Envelope   Begin the Letter

The King's Most Excellent Majesty   Sir:
or   May it please your Maj-
His Most Gracious Majesty, King   esty:
George

Lady

The title "Lady" is held by all peer-   Madam:
esses under the rank of Duchess.   My Lady:
It is also held by all daughters of   Your Ladyship:
dukes, marquises and earls—and by
the wives of baronets, knights and
lords of session.
The envelope is addressed:
  Lady Florence Heath
    or
  Lady Heath
    or
  The Honourable Lady Florence

Legislator

The Honorable Arthur James   Sir:
The State Legislature   Dear Sir:
Albany, New York   Dear Mr. James:
    or
The Honorable Arthur James
Member of Legislature
The State Capitol
Albany, New York

Rank or Title   Lieutenant Governor of a State

Address the Envelope	Begin the Letter
The Lieutenant Governor	Sir:
State of Wisconsin	Dear Sir:
Madison, Wisconsin	Dear Mr. Doyle:
or	
The Honourable Edward Doyle	
Lieutenant Governor of Wisconsin	
Madison, Wisconsin	

Lord of Session

Honourable Lord Overton   My Lord:

Marchioness

The Most Honourable the Marchi-   Madam:
oness of Blankton

Marine Officers

Like Army and Naval Officers. The appropriate designation—U.S.M.C. (United States Marine Corps)— should follow the branch of the service in which the person addressed is engaged. For example:

> Colonel Roy Tait
> Medical Corps, U.S.M.C.

Marquis

The Most Honourable the Marquis of   My Lord Blank:
Blank
        or
The Marquis of Blank

Rank or Title   Mayor of a City

Address the Envelope	Begin the Letter
The Mayor of the City of Chicago City Hall Chicago, Illinois *or* The Honorable John F. Blank Mayor of the City of Chicago City Hall Chicago, Illinois	Sir: Dear Sir: Dear Mayor Blank: Dear Mr. Mayor:

Minister (Diplomatic) *American*

His Excellency The American Minister Stockholm, Sweden *or* His Excellency Carl Hawks American Minister Stockholm, Sweden *or* The Honorable Carl Hawks American Minister Stockholm, Sweden	Sir: Your Excellency: Dear Mr. Minister: Dear Sir:

Minister (Diplomatic) *Foreign*

His Excellency The Swedish Minister The Swedish Legation Washington, D.C. *or* The Honorable James Fount Minister of Sweden The Swedish Legation Washington, D.C.	Sir: Your Excellency: Dear Mr. Minister: Dear Sir:

Rank or Title   Minister of Religion

    Address the Envelope   Begin the Letter

See clergyman, priest, rabbi

Monsignor

The Right Reverend Monsignor   Right Reverend Sir:
  Blank   Dear Monsignor:

Mother Superior of a Sisterhood

Reverend Mother Superior   Reverend Mother:
           or   Dear Reverend Mother:
Reverend Mother Mary (followed by
  initials designating the order)
           or
Reverend Mother Superior Mary
  (without the initials designating
  the order)
           or
Mother Mary, Superior
Convent of the Blessed Virgin

Naval Officers:

Always address letters to naval offi-   Sir: (formal)
cers in accordance with their exact   Dear Admiral Bailey:
rank. (In the salutation, however,   Dear Captain Blank:
you drop the qualifying adjective   Dear Cadet Holt:
—such as the "Rear" in "Rear Ad-
miral." In other words, letters to
both "Admiral Bailey" and "Rear
Admiral Shannon" would begin
"Dear Admiral ——") A doctor,

Rank or Title   Naval Officers:

    Address the Envelope   Begin the Letter

dentist or clergyman may be addressed either by his professional
degree or his naval rank, unless he
is in an administrative capacity—
in which case the rank is always
used.

Admiral James K. Bailey
Chief of Naval Operations
Navy Department
Washington, D.C.

Rear Admiral Thomas Shannon
New London Submarine Base
New London, Connecticut

Captain John Blank, U.S.N.
U.S.S. Missouri
Pensacola, Florida

Lieutenant Commander John Wagner
Medical Corps, U.S.N.
Philadelphia Navy Yard
Philadelphia, Pennsylvania

Nun

See Sister of a Religious Order

Pope

His Holiness the Pope   Your Holiness:
His Holiness, Pope Pius XII   Most Holy Father:

Rank or Title   Postmaster General:

Address the Envelope   Begin the Letter

The Honorable the Postmaster Gen-   Sir:
  eral   Dear Sir:
Washington, D.C.   Dear Mr. Postmaster
        or   General:
The Honorable William Kane   Dear Mr. Kane:
The Postmaster General
Washington, D.C.

President of a College or University

John Smith, LL.D. (or Lit.D., D.Sc.,   Dear Sir:
  etc.)   Dear President Smith:
President of Dartmouth College
Hanover, New Hampshire
        or
Dr. John Smith
President of Dartmouth College
Hanover, New Hampshire
  or (if he holds no doctor's degree)
President John Smith
Dartmouth College
Hanover, New Hampshire

President of a Theological Seminary

The Reverend President John K.   Dear Sir:
  Hancock   Dear President Han-
Western Theological Seminary   cock:
Austin, Texas

Rank or Title   President of State Senate

Address the Envelope   Begin the Letter

The Honorable Richard Daly   Sir:
President of the State Senate of Kan-
sas
The State Capitol
Topeka, Kansas

President of the Senate of the United States

The Honorable   Sir:
The President of the Senate of the
United States
Washington, D.C.
or
The Honorable Thomas Fenton
President of the Senate
Washington, D.C.

President of the United States

The President   Sir:
The White House   Dear Mr. President:
Washington, D.C.
or
The President of the United States
The White House
Washington, D.C.
or
The President
Washington, D.C.
or
President John Blank
Washington, D.C.
or
His Excellency
The President of the United States
Washington, D.C.

Rank or Title   President's Wife

Address the Envelope   Begin the Letter

Mrs. John Blank   Dear Mrs. Blank:
The White House
Washington, D.C.

Priest

Reverend James E. Murphy   Dear Father:
          or   Reverend Father:
Reverend Father Murphy   Dear Father Murphy:

Prince of the Royal Blood

His Royal Highness Prince Charles   Sir:

Princess of the Royal Blood

Her Royal Highness the Princess   Madam:
      Mary

Professor in a College or University

Professor John Smith   Dear Sir:
Department of Mathematics   Dear Professor Smith:
Northwestern University   Dear Dr. Smith:
Evanston, Illinois
          or
John Smith, Ph.D.
Professor of Mathematics
Northwestern University
Evanston, Illinois
          or
Dr. John Smith
Department of Mathematics
Northwestern University
Evanston, Illinois

Rank or Title   Queen   ᵇᵎ

Address the Envelope	Begin the Letter
The Queen's Most Excellent Majesty *or* Her Gracious Majesty, the Queen	Madam: May it please your Majesty:

Rabbi

Rabbi Kenneth Bogen Temple Emanu-el Fifth Avenue New York, N.Y. *or* Reverend Kenneth Bogen *or* Reverend Kenneth Bogen, D.D. *or* Dr. Kenneth Bogen	Reverend Sir: Dear Sir: Dear Rabbi Bogen: Dear Dr. Bogen: (if he holds a doctor's degree)

Representative in Congress

The Honorable John Smith The House of Representatives Washington, D.C. *or* Representative John Smith The House of Representatives Washington, D.C. *or* (if sent to his home) The Honorable John Smith Representative in Congress (Followed by postal address)	Sir: Dear Sir: Dear Congressman Smith: Dear Representative Smith: Dear Mr. Smith:

Rank or Title   Secretary of Agriculture

Address the Envelope   Begin the Letter

The Honorable   Sir:
The Secretary of Agriculture   Dear Sir:
Washington, D.C.   Dear Mr. Secretary:
            or
The Honorable John Smith
Secretary of Agriculture
Washington, D.C.

Secretary of Commerce

The Honorable   Sir:
The Secretary of Commerce   Dear Sir:
Washington, D.C.   Dear Mr. Secretary:
            or
The Honorable Thomas Crane
Secretary of Commerce
Washington, D.C.

Secretary of Labor

The Honorable   Sir:
The Secretary of Labor   Dear Sir:
Washington, D.C.   Dear Mr. Secretary:
            or
The Honorable Philip Dale
The Secretary of Labor
Washington, D.C.

Secretary of State

The Honorable   Sir:
The Secretary of State   Dear Sir:
Washington, D.C.   Dear Mr. Secretary:
            or

Rank or Title   Secretary of State

Address the Envelope   Begin the Letter

The Honorable Lee Thompson
Secretary of State
Washington, D.C.

Secretary of the Interior

The Honorable   Sir:
The Secretary of the Interior   Dear Sir:
Washington, D.C.   Dear Mr. Secretary:
or
The Honorable Frank Dash
Secretary of the Interior
Washington, D.C.

Secretary of the Navy

The Honorable   Sir:
The Secretary of the Navy   Dear Sir:
Washington, D.C.   Dear Mr. Secretary:
or
The Honorable Thomas Cary
Secretary of the Navy
Washington, D.C.

Secretary of the Treasury

The Honorable   Sir:
The Secretary of the Treasury   Dear Sir:
Washington, D.C.   Dear Mr. Secretary:
or
The Honorable Williard Ball
Secretary of the Treasury
Washington, D.C.

Rank or Title   Secretary of War

Address the Envelope   Begin the Letter

The Honorable   Sir:
The Secretary of War   Dear Sir:
Washington, D.C.   Dear Mr. Secretary:
or
The Honorable Philip Jenks
Secretary of War
Washington, D.C.

Senator

The Honorable John Blank   Sir:
United States Senate   Dear Sir:
Washington, D.C.   Dear Senator Blank:
or
Senator John Blank
The United States Senate
Washington, D.C.
   or (if sent to a home address)
The Honorable John Blank
United States Senator
(Followed by home address)

Sister of a Religious Order

Sister Mary Angela   Dear Sister Angela:
or   Dear Sister:
The Reverend Sister Angela

Speaker of the House of Representatives

The Honorable   Sir:
The Speaker of the House of Repre-   Dear Sir:
   sentatives   Dear Mr. Speaker:
Washington, D.C.
              or

Rank or Title   Speaker of the House of Representatives

Address the Envelope	Begin the Letter
The Speaker of the House of Representatives Washington, D.C. *or* The Honorable Frederick Knight Speaker of the House of Representatives Washington, D.C.	

State Representative

The Honorable Peter Blank The House of Representatives The State Capitol Jefferson City, Missouri	Sir: Dear Sir: Dear Mr. Blank:

State Senator

The Honorable John Smith The State Senate Trenton, New Jersey *or* Senator John Smith The State Capitol Trenton, New Jersey	Sir: Dear Sir: Dear Senator Smith:

Undersecretary of State

The Undersecretary of State Washington, D.C. *or* The Honorable Robert Corey Undersecretary of State Washington, D.C.	Sir: Dear Sir: Dear Mr. Corey:

Rank or Title—Vice President of the United States

Address the Envelope	Begin the Letter
The Honorable	Sir:
The Vice President of the United	Dear Sir:
States	Dear Mr. Vice President:
Washington, D.C.	

or

The Vice President
Washington, D.C.

or

The Honorable Michael Brent
Vice President of the United States
Washington, D.C.

COMMISSIONED RANKS IN THE ARMY AND NAVY

THE ARMY

2nd Lieutenant
Lieutenant
Captain
Major
Lieutenant Colonel
Colonel
Brigadier General
Major General
Lieutenant General
General
General of the Army

THE NAVY

Ensign
Lieutenant Junior Grade
Lieutenant
Lieutenant Commander

COMMISSIONED RANKS IN THE ARMY AND NAVY *(Continued)*

THE NAVY *(Continued)*

Commander
Captain
Commodore
Rear Admiral
Vice Admiral
Admiral
Admiral of the Fleet

Index